Python Challenges

100 Proven Programming Tasks
Designed to Prepare You for Anything

Michael Inden

Apress®

Python Challenges: 100 Proven Programming Tasks Designed to Prepare You for Anything

Michael Inden
Zurich, Switzerland

ISBN-13 (pbk): 978-1-4842-7397-5
https://doi.org/10.1007/978-1-4842-7398-2

ISBN-13 (electronic): 978-1-4842-7398-2

Managing Director, Apress Media LLC: Welmoed Spahr
Acquisitions Editor: Steve Anglin
Development Editor: James Markham
Coordinating Editor: Mark Powers
Copyeditor: Mary Behr

Cover designed by eStudioCalamar

Cover image by Michael Inden

Distributed to the book trade worldwide by Apress Media, LLC, 1 New York Plaza, New York, NY 10004, U.S.A. Phone 1-800-SPRINGER, fax (201) 348-4505, e-mail orders-ny@springer-sbm.com, or visit www.springeronline.com. Apress Media, LLC is a California LLC and the sole member (owner) is Springer Science + Business Media Finance Inc (SSBM Finance Inc). SSBM Finance Inc is a **Delaware** corporation.

For information on translations, please e-mail booktranslations@springernature.com; for reprint, paperback, or audio rights, please e-mail bookpermissions@springernature.com.

Apress titles may be purchased in bulk for academic, corporate, or promotional use. eBook versions and licenses are also available for most titles. For more information, reference our Print and eBook Bulk Sales web page at www.apress.com/bulk-sales.

Any source code or other supplementary material referenced by the author in this book is available to readers on GitHub (github.com/apress). For more detailed information, please visit www.apress.com/source-code.

Printed on acid-free paper

For our lovely princess Sophie Jelena

Table of Contents

About the Author

 **Michael Inden** is an Oracle-certified Java developer with over 20 years of professional experience designing complex software systems for international companies, where he has worked in various roles such as SW developer, SW architect, consultant, team leader, CTO, head of academy, and trainer. After being a freelancer for more than a year, he is currently working as a Head of Development.

His special interests are creating high-quality applications with ergonomic GUIs, developing and solving programming puzzles, and coaching. He likes to pass on his knowledge and has led various courses and talks, both internally and externally, as well as at conferences such as JAX/W-JAX, JAX London, and Oracle Code One.

He is also an author of technical books. His German books *Der Weg zum Java-Profi*, *Java Challenge*, and *Python Challenge* are all published by dpunkt.verlag.

About the Technical Reviewers

Aravind Medamoni is an experienced software developer. He works as a freelance mobile application developer. He has proficiency in Java, Kotlin, Flutter, Dart, PHP, JavaScript, Nodejs, MongoDB, and SQL. He worked as Tech Lead at OpenStackDC for one year as a backend and Android developer. Aravind has trained many students to start their career in the software domain. He has won a national level Hackathon.

Charles Bell conducts research in emerging technologies. He is a member of the Oracle MySQL development team and is a principal developer for the MySQL cloud services team. He lives in a small town in rural Virginia with his loving wife. He received his Doctor of Philosophy in Engineering from Virginia Commonwealth University in 2005. Dr. Bell is an expert in the database field and has extensive knowledge and experience in software development and systems engineering. His research interests include 3D printers, microcontrollers, three-dimensional printing, database systems, software engineering, and sensor networks. He spends his limited free time as a practicing maker focusing on microcontroller projects and refinement of three-dimensional printers.

Preface

First of all, thank you for choosing this book. In it you will find a wide range of practice exercises on a broad mix of topics that will help you improve your Python coding skills in an enjoyable manner.

Practice Makes Perfect

We all know the saying *practice makes perfect*. In crafts and other areas of real life, there is a lot of practice, but the serious case is rare, such as in sports, music, and other fields. Oddly enough, this is often significantly different for us software developers. We actually spend almost all of our time implementing and tend to rarely spend time practicing and learning—sometimes not at all. Why is that?

Presumably, this is due to the time pressure that usually dominates our professional lives, and the fact that there isn't much suitable exercise material available, even if there are textbooks on algorithms and coding. Those tend to be either too theoretical or too source code-focused and contain too little explanation of the solutions. This book aims to change that.

Why This Book?

So how did I come to tackle this book project? There are several reasons. On the one hand, I was asked again and again by mail or personally by participants of my workshops for a tutorial book as a supplement to my book *Der Weg zum Java-Profi* [Ind20]. That's how the first idea came about.

What really triggered the whole thing was that a recruiter from Google approached me quite by surprise with an employment opportunity. As preparation for the upcoming interviews and to refresh my knowledge, I started to search for suitable material. Additionally, I developed some exercises for myself. In the process, I discovered the great, but also partly quite challenging book *Cracking the Coding Interview* by Gayle Laakmann McDowell [McD16], which inspired me further.

As a result, I initially set out on a Java-focused book project called *Java Challenges* in German and later in English. In the meantime, the idea came up to implement something similar for Python, first as a German version and later as an English version. So this Python edition is based on the Java version, but the whole book was revised and "Pythonified." For this purpose, I added, slightly modified, or partially removed things in some places. In particular, I show (if appropriate) how to use Python features like List Comprehensions and so on to make solutions more concise.

Who Is This Book Aimed At?

This book is explicitly not intended for programming novices. It is aimed at readers who already have basic or even good knowledge of Python and want to deepen it with exercises. By solving small programming exercises, you will expand your knowledge about Python, algorithms, and sound OO design in an entertaining way.

The following target groups are addresses in particular:

- **High school and college students**: First of all, this book is meant for pupils with an interest in computer science as well as for students of computer science who already know Python quite well as a language and now want to deepen their knowledge by tackling some exercises.

- **Teachers and lecturers**: Of course, teachers and lecturers may also benefit from this book and its large number of exercises of varying difficulty, either as a stimulus for their own teaching or as a template for exercises or exams.

- **Hobby programmers and young professionals**: In addition, the book is aimed at dedicated hobby programmers and also young professionals who like to program with Python and want to develop themselves further. Furthermore, solving the exercises will help them to be well prepared for potential questions in job interviews.

- **Experienced software developers and architects**: Finally, the book is intended for experienced software developers and architects who want to supplement or refresh their knowledge to be able to assist their junior colleagues more effectively and are looking for some inspiration and fresh ideas to do so. In addition, various exercises can also be used in job interviews, with the convenience of having the sample solutions directly at hand for comparison. Also, for the old hands there should be one or two "aha" experiences while finding solutions and rethinking about algorithms and data structures.

What Does This Book Teach?

This book provides a widespread mix of exercises on different topics. Some puzzles may not be of direct, practical importance, but indirectly they help improve your creativity and your ability to find solutions.

In addition to exercises and documented solutions, each topic covered in the book starts with a short introduction. You can use the introductions to get up to speed with the exercises to about the level of difficulty. In each subject area, there are always a few easier exercises to get you started. With a little practice, you should also be able to tackle more difficult problems. Occasionally there are some really challenging exercises, which experts can try their hand at (or those who want to become experts).

Practical Tips and Advice

This book is packed with various practical tips. They include interesting background information as well as pitfalls to avoid.

HINT: TIP FROM THE TRENCHES

In boxes formatted like this you will find some tips worth knowing and additional hints to the actual text later in the book.

Difficulty Level at a Glance

A well-balanced, appealing exercise book needs a large number of tasks of different levels of difficulty, which offer you as a reader the possibility to improve your knowledge step by step. Although I assume a good understanding of Python, the solutions never require deep knowledge of a specific topic or special language features.

To keep the level of difficulty obvious and straightforward, I use the star categorization known from other areas, whose meaning in this context is explained in more detail in Table 0-1.

Table 0-1.Levels of Diffiulty

Stars (meaning)	Estimation	Duration
★☆☆☆☆ (very easy)	These tasks should be solvable in a few minutes with simple Python knowledge.	< 15 min
★★☆☆☆ (easy)	The tasks require a little bit of thinking, but then they are directly solvable.	< 30 min
★★★☆☆ (medium)	The tasks are not overly challenging, but need some thinking, a little bit of strategy and sometimes a look at different constraints.	~ 30 – 45 min
★★★★☆ (difficult)	Proven problem-solving strategies, good knowledge of data structures, and Python knowledge are required for the solution.	~ 45 – 90 min
★★★★★ (very difficult)	The tasks are really tricky and difficult to solve. These exercises should only be tried once you're able to solve the book's easier exercises without difficulty.	> 60 min

These ratings are only estimations from my side and are rather rough classifications. Please keep in mind that the difficulty perceived by each individual also depends very much on their background and level of knowledge. I have seen colleagues have a hard time with tasks that I considered quite easy. But I also know the opposite: While others seem to solve a task easily, you are in despair yourself because the penny just won't drop. Sometimes a break with a coffee or a short walk helps. Do not get demotivated! Everyone struggles with some task at some time or another.

NOTE: POSSIBLE ALTERNATIVES TO THE SAMPLE SOLUTIONS

Please note that for some problems there are almost always some variants, which might be even be more catchy for you. Therefore I will present interesting alternatives to the (sample) solution from time to time as food for thought.

Structure of This Book

Now that you have a rough picture of the contents of this book, I will introduce the topics of each chapter briefly. As indicated, the exercises are grouped thematically. In this context, the six chapters after the introduction build the basis and the subsequent three chapters deal with more advanced topics.

Chapter 1: This chapter describes the basic structure of the following chapters with an introduction, exercises, and solutions. Additionally, it provides a framework for the unit tests that are often used to prove that the solutions are working. Finally, I give some hints for trying out the examples and solutions.

Chapter 2: The second chapter is dedicated to mathematical operations as well as tasks about prime numbers and the Roman numeral system. Besides, I present a few ideas for number games.

Chapter 3: Recursion is an important basic building block concerning the definition of algorithms. This chapter provides a short introduction, and the various exercises should help you to understand recursion.

Chapter 4: Strings are known to be sequences of characters that offer a variety of methods. A solid understanding is important since almost no program can operate without strings. Therefore you will get to know the processing of strings through various exercises.

Chapter 5: Python offers lists, sets, and dictionaries by default. For everyday programming, a proficient use of all three containers is of great advantage, and you'll get training through the exercises.

Chapter 6: Arrays form basic building blocks in many programming languages. In Python, lists are more common. Regarding performance and memory consumption, arrays have advantages, which is reason enough to take a closer look at the whole thing in this chapter.

Chapter 7: Chapter 3 covered the topic of recursion in an introductory manner. This chapter reveals more advanced aspects of recursion. You start with the optimization technique called memoization. After that, you look at backtracking as a problem-solving strategy, which is based on trial and error. Just trying out possible solutions may help keep various algorithms fairly understandable and elegant.

Chapter 8: Tree structures play an important role in computer science theory and practice. In many application contexts, trees can be used profitably. This is the case, for example, for the administration of a file system, the representation of a project with subprojects and tasks, or a book with chapters, subchapters, and sections.

Chapter 9: Searching and sorting are two elementary topics in computer science in the area of algorithms and data structures. The Python standard library implements both of them and thus does the work for you. However, it is also worth looking behind the scenes, for example, at different sorting methods and their specific strengths and weaknesses.

Chapter 10: In this chapter, I summarize the book and give an outlook on supplementary literature. To expand your skills, besides the training in programming, it is recommended to study further books. A selection of helpful titles closes the main part of this book.

Appendix A: Unit tests have proven to be useful for testing smaller modules. Many of the solutions created in this book are tested with unit tests using pytest. This appendix provides an introduction to the topic.

Appendix B: This appendix describes decorators. They allow elegant realizations of cross-cutting functionality to be done transparently (i. e., without extensions in the implementation of a function itself). For example, decorators can be used for parameter checks and for memoization, an advanced recursion topic.

Appendix C: In this book, I sometimes estimate the running time behavior and classify the complexity of algorithms. This appendix presents essentials about it.

Appendix D: This appendix presents some of the enhancements coming with the current Python 3.10 that may be relevant to you.

Conventions and Executable Programs
Fonts Used

Throughout the text, the following conventions are applied concerning fonts:

- Normal text appears in the present font.

- Important text passages are marked *italic* or ***italic and bold***.

- Sourcecode listings are written in `this font` to clarify that this text is a part of a Python program. Also, classes, methods, function, and parameters are displayed in this font.

Abbreviations Used

In the book, I use the abbreviations shown in Table 0-2. Other abbreviations are listed in parentheses in the running text after their first definition and subsequently used as needed.

Table 0-2. Abbreviations

Abbreviation	Meaning
API	Application programming interface
ASCII	American Standard Code for Information Interchange
(G)UI	(Graphical) user interface
IDE	Integrated development environment

Python Version Used

This book was initially developed and tested with Python 3.9.6 but rechecked with the new Python 3.10, which was released in October 2021 and is briefly covered in Appendix D. Many of the solutions should also run in Python 2.7 with minimal adjustments. However, I have only randomly checked this. In general, it makes sense to use the more modern Python 3 for new projects.

Download, Source Code, and Executables

The source code of the examples is available at `www.apress.com/python-challenges`.

There is a PyCharm project[1] integrated. Because this is a hands-on book, many of the programs are executable—it is possible to run them in the IDE or as a unit test.

However, many code snippets are great to try out in the Python command line interpreter. To ensure this, functions that have already been developed are shown again at suitable places.

---

[1] PyCharm is a highly recommended IDE and is a Python-oriented variant of IntelliJ IDEA which is available for free at `www.jetbrains.com/de-de/pycharm/`.

Some examples use special libraries that must be installed up front, like numpy, pytest, and others, as follows:[2]

```
pip install pytest
pip install numpy
```

Please consult the installation instructions provided on the download site for further information.

Acknowledgments (English Book)

First of all, I am very grateful to all the people mentioned below in the acknowledgments section for the German version of this book. Making this English version more than a dream and realizing it was possible due to the effort of Steve Anglin of APress. He organized a lot to finalize the contract and all the nitty-gritty details around publishing rights. Additionally, Mark Powers was a great help by offering information on the process and many other things around finalizing the manuscript. Guys, my warm thanks go to you.

Acknowledgments (German Book)

Writing a technical book is a beautiful but laborious and tedious task. You can hardly do it on your own. Therefore, I would like to thank those who have directly or indirectly contributed to the book's emergence. In particular, I benefited from a strong team of proofreaders during the preparation of the manuscript. It is helpful to learn from different perspectives and experiences.

Many thanks to Martin Stypinski for various valuable hints and suggestions. Also, I want to thank Jean-Claude Brantschen for his practical proposals. You have Pythonified me even more :-) Multiple comments by Rainer Grimm and Tobias Overkamp around Python and elegant solutions have further improved the book. Finally, as with many of my books, Michael Kulla critically reviewed this Python version. Many thanks to all of them!

---

[2] Please remember to install pytest using the pip tool: `pip install pytest` (on Mac, use `pip3` instead of `pip`).

Since this book was written based on the Java version, the acknowledgments in *Java Challenge* are repeated below:

First of all, I would like to thank Michael Kulla, who is well known as a trainer for Java SE and Java EE, for his multiple, thorough reviews of many chapters, the well-founded comments, and great effort. I am also very grateful to Prof. Dr. Dominik Gruntz for a multitude of suggestions for improvements. Besides, I received one or the other helpful suggestions from Jean-Claude Brantschen, Prof. Dr. Carsten Kern, and Christian Heitzmann. Once again, Ralph Willenborg read it very carefully and found several typing errors. Many thanks for that!

Thanks also go to the team at dpunkt.verlag (Dr. Michael Barabas, Anja Weimer, and Veronika Schnabel) for great cooperation. Also, I would like to thank Torsten Horn for his sound professional review and Ursula Zimpfer for her eagle eyes in copy editing.

Finally, I would like to thank my wife, Lilija, for her understanding and support, especially for several nudges to get on the bike and go for a ride instead of just working on the book.

Suggestions and Criticism

Although great care has been taken and the text was proofread several times, misunderstandable formulations or even errors can unfortunately not be completely excluded. If any of these should be noticeable to you, please do not hesitate to let me know. I am also happy to receive suggestions or ideas for improvement. Please contact me by mail at `michael_inden@hotmail.com`.

Zurich, April 2022
Michael Inden

## CHAPTER 1

Introduction

Welcome to this workbook! Before you get started, I want to briefly outline what you can expect when reading it.

This book covers a broad range of practice-relevant topics, represented by exercises of different levels of difficulty. The exercises are (for the most part) independent of each other and can be solved in any order, depending on your mood or interest.

Besides the exercises, you will find the corresponding answers, including a short description of the algorithm used for the solution and the actual source code, which is commented on at essential points.

1.1 Structure of the Chapters

Each chapter shares the same structure, so you will quickly find your way around.

1.1.1 Introduction

Each chapter begins with an introduction to the topic to get you familiar with the subject area or get you in the right mood for the tasks that follow.

1.1.2 Exercises

The introduction is succeeded by a bunch of exercises and the following structure:

Task Each exercise first will have an assignment. In it, the desired functionality to be realized is described in a few sentences. Often a function signature is already included as a clue to the solution.

Examples Supplementary examples are almost always given for clarification with inputs and expected results. For some quite simple tasks, which mainly serve to get to know an API, examples are sometimes omitted.

© Michael Inden 2022
M. Inden, *Python Challenges*, https://doi.org/10.1007/978-1-4842-7398-2_1

Often, different value assignments of input parameter(s), as well as the expected result, are shown in a table.

Input A	Input B	Result
[1, 2, 4, 7, 8]	[2, 3, 7, 9]	[2, 7]

The following notation styles apply to the specifications:

- "AB" represents textual specifications.

- True/False stands for Boolean values.

- 123 represent numeric values.

- [value1, value2, ...] represents collections like sets or lists, but also arrays.

- { key1 : value1, key2 : value2, ... } describes dictionaries.

1.1.3 Solutions

The part of solutions follows the structure described below.

Task definition and examples First, you find the task description again so that you don't have to constantly flip back and forth between tasks and solutions. Instead, the description of solutions is self-contained.

Algorithm A description of the chosen algorithm follows. For didactics, I sometime present an erroneous way or a not-very-optimal solution to then uncover pitfalls and iteratively come to an improvement. In fact, one or the other brute force solution is sometimes even usable but offers optimization potentials. I then present corresponding, sometimes astonishingly simple, but often very effective improvements.

Python shortcut Sometimes the task explicitly excludes certain Python standard functionality for realizing the solution in order to penetrate a problem algorithmically. In practice, however, you should use the defaults. In the separate short section named "Python shortcut" I show how to make the solution shorter and more concise.

Examination Some of the tasks are quite easy or only serve to get used to syntax or API functionality. For this, it often seems sufficient to execute a few calls directly in the Python command line interpreter. That's why I don't use unit tests for this. The same applies for a graphical presentation of a solution, such as displaying a Sudoku board and if the corresponding unit test would probably be more difficult to understand.

However, the more complicated the algorithms become, the more sources of errors exist, such as wrong index values, an accidental or omitted negation, or an overlooked edge case. For this reason, it makes sense to check functionality with the help of unit tests. In this book, for reasons of space, this is only accomplished for important inputs. The companion resources contain over 80 unit tests with roughly 600 test cases, a pretty good start. Nevertheless, in practice, the amount of unit tests and test cases should be even more voluminous if possible.

1.2 Basic Structure of the PyCharm Project

The included PyCharm project closely follows the structure of the book. It offers a separate folder for each relevant chapter (those with exercises), such as ch02_math or ch08_recursion_advanced.

Some of the source code snippets from the respective introductions are located in the subfolder intro. The provided (sample) solutions are collected in their own subfolder named solutions and the modules are named according to the task as follows: ex<no>_<taskdescription>.py.

Sources Figure 1-1 shows an outline for Chapter 2.

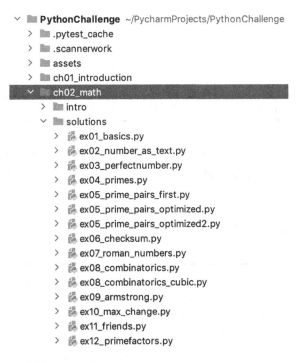

Figure 1-1. *Outline of Chapter 2 sources*

Utility modules All the useful utility functions developed in the respective chapters are included in the provided PyCharm project in the form of utility modules. They are combined into a module xyz_utils, which resides in its own subdirectory util—for the chapter about mathematical tasks in the subdirectory ch02_math.util. The same applies to the other chapters and topics.

Test classes Figure 1-2 shows some associated tests.

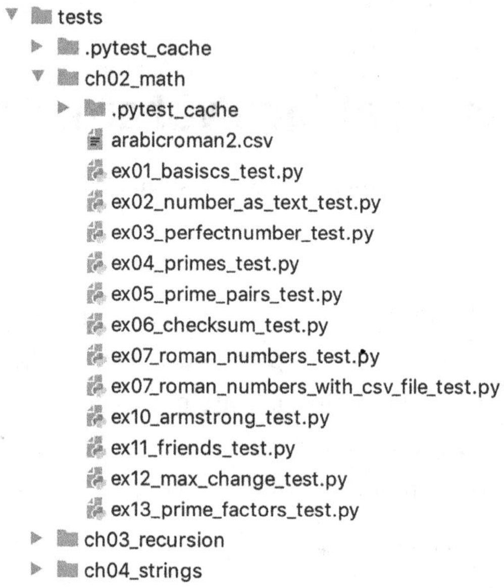

```
▼ ██ tests
    ▶ ██ .pytest_cache
    ▼ ██ ch02_math
        ▶ ██ .pytest_cache
          ▣ arabicroman2.csv
          ▧ ex01_basiscs_test.py
          ▧ ex02_number_as_text_test.py
          ▧ ex03_perfectnumber_test.py
          ▧ ex04_primes_test.py
          ▧ ex05_prime_pairs_test.py
          ▧ ex06_checksum_test.py
          ▧ ex07_roman_numbers_test.py
          ▧ ex07_roman_numbers_with_csv_file_test.py
          ▧ ex10_armstrong_test.py
          ▧ ex11_friends_test.py
          ▧ ex12_max_change_test.py
          ▧ ex13_prime_factors_test.py
    ▶ ██ ch03_recursion
    ▶ ██ ch04_strings
```

Figure 1-2. *Tests*

HINT: INSTALLATION OF EXTERNAL LIBRARIES OR FRAMEWORKS

Some examples use special libraries that must be installed up front, like numpy, pytest, and others, using the pip tool (on Mac use pip3 instead of pip) as follows:

```
pip install pytest
pip install parameterized
pip install numpy
```

1.3 Basic Framework for Unit Tests with Pytest

To not exceed the scope of the book, the illustrated unit tests only show the test methods but not the test module and the imports. To provide you with a basic framework into which you can insert the test functions and as a starting point for your own experiments, a typical test module is as follows:

```python
import pytest

from ch02_math.solutions.ex01_basics import calc, \
    calc_sum_and_count_all_numbers_div_by_2_or_7_v2

@pytest.mark.parametrize("m, n, expected",
                         [(6, 7, 0), (3, 4, 6), (5, 5, 5)])
def test_calc(m, n, expected):
    assert calc(m, n) == expected

@pytest.mark.parametrize("n, expected",
                         [(3, {"sum": 2, "count": 1}),
                          (8, {"sum": 19, "count": 4}),
                          (15, {"sum": 63, "count": 8})])
def test_calc_sum_and_count_all_numbers_div_by_2_or_7(n, expected):
    assert calc_sum_and_count_all_numbers_div_by_2_or_7_v2(n) == expected
```

In addition to the import needed, this example shows parameterized tests that are extensively used since they allow testing multiple combinations of values in a simple way. For details, please see Appendix A.

1.4 Note on Programming Style

During discussions while writing this book the question came up if certain things should be made more compact. This is why I would like to mention in advance something about the programming style used in this book.

1.4.1 Thoughts on Source Code Compactness

The most important things for me when programming and especially for the implementations in this book are easy comprehensibility and a clear structure. This leads to simplified maintainability and changeability. Therefore, the shown implementations are programmed as understandable as possible. I like to favor this aspect in this book. In practice, it is often easier to live with a bit more verbosity than with bad maintainability but more compact programming.

1.4.2 Example 1

Let's have a look at a small example for clarification. First, let's examine the readable, easy-to-understand variant for inverting the contents of a string, which also shows very nicely the two important elements of recursive termination and descent:

```python
def reverse_string(text):
    # recursive termination
    if len(text) <= 1:
        return text

    first_char = text[0]
    remaining = text[1:]

    # recursive descent
    return reverse_string(remaining) + first_char
```

The following much more compact variant does not offer these advantages:

```python
def reverse_string_short(text):
    return text if len(text) <= 1 else \
        reverse_string_short(text[1:]) + text[0]
```

Think briefly about in which of the two methods you feel safe making subsequent changes. And what if you want to add unit tests? How do you find suitable value sets?

1.4.3 Example 2

Let's bring in another example to illustrate my point. It concerns the following function count_substrings() which is modeled after the standard count() function. The later counts the number of occurrences of one string in another, and for the two inputs "hellohe" and "he," it returns the result 2.

First, we implement this reasonably straightforwardly as follows:

```python
def count_substrings(text, value_to_find):
    # recursive termination
    if len(text) < len(value_to_find):
        return 0

    count = 0
    remaining = ""

    # does the text start with the search string?
    if text.startswith(value_to_find):
        # match: continue the search for the found
        # term after the location where it was found
        remaining = text[len(value_to_find):]
        count = 1
    else:
        # remove first character and search again
        remaining = text[1:]

    # recursive descent
    return count_substrings(remaining, value_to_find) + count
```

Let's try to realize this compactly:

```python
def count_substrings_short(text, value_to_find):
    return 0 if len(text) < len(value_to_find) else \
        (1 if text.startswith(value_to_find) else 0) + \
        count_substrings_short(text[1:], value_to_find)
```

Would you prefer to change this function or the one shown before?

By the way, the lower one still contains a subtle functional deviation! For the inputs of "XXXX" and "XX" the first variant always *consumes* the characters and finds two occurrences. The lower, however, moves only one character at a time and thus finds three occurrences.

Further, integrating the previously realized functionality of advancing by the whole search string into the second variant will lead to more obscure source code. On the other hand, you can easily shift by only one character by simply adjusting the upper `text[len(value_to_find):]` call and then even pull this functionality out of the `if`.

1.4.4 Decorators and Sanity Checks at the Beginning of Functions

To ensure stable programs, it is often a good idea to check the parameters of central functions for validity. These checks are adequate in the form of simple `if` statements. In Python, however, this can often be accomplished more elegantly with the help of decorators. To get started, please have a look at Appendix B.

1.4.5 Block Comments in Listings

Please note that there are various block comments in listings, which serve as orientation and for better understanding. It's advisable to use such comments with caution, and it's preferable to extract individual source code sections to methods or functions in practice. For the book's examples, these comments serve as reference points because the introduced or presented facts are probably still new and unfamiliar to you as a reader.

```python
# does the text start with the search string?
if text.startswith(value_to_find):
    # match: continue the search for the found
    # term after the location where it was found
    remaining = text[len(value_to_find):]
    count = 1
else:
    # remove first character and search again
    remaining = text[1:]
```

1.4.6 PEP 8 and the Zen of Python

Besides my already presented thoughts about the programming style, I would like to mention two things explicitly:

- PEP 8 Coding Standard (PEP = Python Enhancement Proposal)

- The Zen of Python—thoughts about Python

PEP 8 Coding Standard

The official coding standard is available online at www.python.org/dev/peps/pep-0008/ as PEP 8. This is intended to help write clean, consistent, and understandable Python code. There is a tendency in the Python community to put more emphasis on pretty source code than in other languages. In general, *make it work somehow* is not a sustainable strategy, as I have also motivated.

However, there are a few things about which opinions may differ, for example the limitation of the line length to 79 characters. With today's HiDPI monitors and resolutions beyond Full-HD, longer lines of around 120 characters are certainly possible. But a line should also not be too long—especially if you want to compare two versions of a file with each other; this can otherwise be annoying.

I may violate indentation hints for split lines to favor readability when optically appropriate. Additionally, I occasionally name lambdas, which usually encapsulate only a tiny piece of functionality and thus should not be named, for a better insight into how things work or express more clearly what was intended. The latter is reported as E731 do not assign a lambda expression, use a def. Please find more info in a moment.

The Zen of Python

Interestingly, the Python command line interpreter (indicated by >>>) includes a built-in output of style guides, also known as the Zen of Python. This is obtained by a call to

```
>>> import this
```

The following output occurs:

```
The Zen of Python, by Tim Peters
Beautiful is better than ugly.
Explicit is better than implicit.
```

Simple is better than complex.
Complex is better than complicated.
Flat is better than nested.
Sparse is better than dense.
Readability counts.
Special cases aren't special enough to break the rules.
Although practicality beats purity.
Errors should never pass silently.
Unless explicitly silenced.
In the face of ambiguity, refuse the temptation to guess.
There should be one-- and preferably only one --obvious way to do it.
Although that way may not be obvious at first unless you're Dutch.
Now is better than never.
Although never is often better than *right* now.
If the implementation is hard to explain, it's a bad idea.
If the implementation is easy to explain, it may be a good idea.
Namespaces are one honking great idea -- let's do more of those!

Tooling As mentioned, PyCharm offers itself as IDE and provides various hints for style and improvement possibilities directly in the editor. A configuration is possible under Preferences > Editor > Code Style > Python as well as Preferences > Editor > Inspections > Python. In particular, the latter gives you the option to enable PEP8 coding style violation.

Alternatively or complementary, you can install the tool flake8 as follows—here, and in the following text I always use $ to indicate input on the console (i.e., the Windows command prompt and the terminal on MacOS). Please remember to use pip3 on Mac insted of pip.

```
$ pip install flake8
```

This helps to uncover various potential problems and violations against PEP 8 if you call it as follows:

```
$ flake8 <mypythonmodule>.py mydirwithmodules ...
```

Sample run for the project sources Please find an example run that excludes the virtual environment of Python and ignores some potential problems, just showing the lambdas assignments mentioned before:

```
$ flake8 --exclude=venv --ignore=E501,F811,E126,E127,W504
./tests/ch02_math/ex09_armstrong_test.py:13:5: E731 do not assign a lambda
expression, use a def
./ch03_recursion/intro/intro.py:137:5: E731 do not assign a lambda
expression, use a def
./ch03_recursion/intro/intro.py:138:5: E731 do not assign a lambda
expression, use a def
./ch03_recursion/solutions/ex01_fibonacci.py:56:5: E731 do not assign a
lambda expression, use a def
./ch05_datastructures/intro/basics.py:41:1: E731 do not assign a lambda
expression, use a def
./ch06_arrays/solutions/ex06_erase_and_fall_down.py:146:5: F841 local
variable 'book_example' is assigned to but never used
./ch07_recursion_advanced/solutions/ex01_towers_of_hanoi.py:39:5: E731 do
not assign a lambda expression, use a def
```

Just for your info, these checks are excluded:

- `E501 line too long (80 > 79 characters`: As already stated, 79 characters per line are pretty few these days.

- `F811 redefinition of unused` '...' `from line ...`: Samples sometimes redefine variables and functions.

- `E126 continuation line over-indented for hanging indent`: Minor deviations from the standard to achieve a nicer layout.

- `E127 continuation line over-indented for visual indent`: Minor deviations from the standard to achieve a nicer layout.

- `W504 line break after binary operator`: Minor deviations from the standard to achieve a nicer layout.

HINT: SONAR AS AN ALTERNATIVE

There are other tools for checking your sources. Although somewhat more complex, for larger projects it is recommended to perform a static source code analysis using Sonar. For this, you must install Sonar and a Sonar Runner. In return, though, you get a nice overview as well as a history so that you can quickly recognize both positive and negative trends and take countermeasures if necessary.

1.4.7 More Information

For more information on how to write clean Python, see the following books:

- *Python Tricks: A Buffet of Awesome Python Features* by Dan Bader [Bad17]

- *Mastering Python* by Rick van Hattern [vH16]

1.5 Note on the Exercises

When solving the tasks, the goal is to deal with the appropriate algorithms and data structures. Python offers an extensive collection of functionalities, for example for calculating sums and minimums of lists or even more complex things like computing permutations.

Some of the tasks can be solved with the ready-made standard functionalities in a few lines. However, this is not the goal within this book, because the exercises serve the algorithmic understanding and the extension of your problem-solving strategies. By exploring and solving this yourself, you learn a lot in the process. Developing things yourself is only for training, not for practical use: please keep in mind that in real projects the standard functionality of Python should always be preferred and you should not dream of inventing something yourself for which there is already a ready-made solution. That's why I often point out in a separate short section named "Python shortcut" a solution that uses standard Python functionality.

1.6 Trying Out the Examples and Solutions

Basically, I prefer to use as comprehensible constructs as possible instead of fancy syntax or API features of special Python versions. In many cases, you can simply copy the source code snippets shown into the Python command line interpreter and execute them. Alternatively, all relevant sources are provided in the PyCharm project that comes with the book. There, the programs may be launched by a `main()` function or checked by corresponding unit tests that are often available.

1.7 Let's Go: Discovering the Python Challenge

So, enough of the preface! You are probably already excited about the first challenges through the exercises. I hope you will enjoy this book and gain some new insights while solving the exercises and experimenting with the algorithms.

   If you need a refresher on pytest, decorators, or O-notation, you might want to take a look at the appendices first.

PART I

Fundamentals

CHAPTER 2

Mathematical Problems

In this chapter, you start learning some basics about a few mathematical operations, including prime numbers and the Roman numeral system. Additionally, I present a couple of ideas for number games. The chapter is rounded off by a short introduction to lambdas. With all this knowledge, you should be well prepared for the exercises.

2.1 Introduction

2.1.1 Short Introduction to Division and Modulo

Besides multiplication and division, the modulo operation (%) is also used quite frequently. It is intended to determine the remainder of a division. Let's illustrate this as follows for integers where division remainders fall under the table:

$$(\mathbf{5} * 7 + 3) \: // \: 7 = 38 \: // \: 7 = 5$$
$$(5 * 7 + \mathbf{3}) \: \% \: 7 = 38 \: \% \: 7 = 3$$

Even with these few operations, you can solve various tasks. Please recall the following things for actions on (integer) numbers:

- n / 10: Obviously divides by the value 10. Since Python 3, this returns a floating point number as result. If you need an integer, you can use a type conversion with int(), such as int(value / 10).

- n // 10: Also divides by the value 10. Because the // operator performs an integer division without a remainder, it is possible to truncate the last digit with it.

- n % 10: Determines the remainder of a division by 10 and thus the last digit.

© Michael Inden 2022
M. Inden, *Python Challenges*, https://doi.org/10.1007/978-1-4842-7398-2_2

Extraction of digits To extract the digits of a number, combine modulo and division as long as the remaining value is greater than 0.

```python
def extract_digits(number):
    remaining_value = number
    while remaining_value > 0:
        digit = remaining_value % 10
        remaining_value = remaining_value // 10
        print(digit, end=' ')
    print()
```

In Python, there is another special feature with the built-in function divmod(), which returns both the divisor and the remainder as a result—as a shortcut for the operators that are often called in combination. In addition, you can exploit tuple unpacking in the following, whereby the result is assigned to the respective variable:

```python
def extract_digits(number):
    remaining_value = number
    while remaining_value > 0:
        remaining_value, digit = divmod(remaining_value, 10)
        print(digit, end=' ')
    print()
```

Let's call this method once to understand its way of working—please note that the digits are output in reverse order.

```python
>>> extract_digits(123)
3 2 1
```

Determine number of digits Instead of extracting individual digits, you can also use a repeated division to determine the number of digits in a decimal number by simply dividing by 10 until there is no remainder left:

```python
def count_digits(number):
    count = 0
    remaining_value = number
    while remaining_value > 0:
        remaining_value = remaining_value // 10
        count += 1
    return count
```

2.1.2 Short Introduction to Divider

In the following, you examine how to determine all real divisors of a number (i. e., those without the number itself). The algorithm is quite simple. Initially, the result contains the number 1, as this is always a valid divider. Then you go through all numbers starting by 2 up to half of the value (all higher values cannot be integer divisors if 2 is already a divisor) and check if they divide the given number without a remainder. If this is the case, then this number is a divisor and is included in a result list. You implement the whole thing as follows:

```python
def find_proper_divisors(value):
    divisors = [1]
    for i in range(2, value // 2 + 1):
        if value % i == 0:
            divisors.append(i)
    return divisors
```

One more small note about naming: For loop variables, short names like i are common, but current_number would also be a readable alternative.

Using list comprehension[1] you can write the calculation more concisely:

```python
def find_proper_divisors(value):
    return [i for i in range(1, value // 2 + 1) if value % i == 0]
```

Let's call this method once to understand its operation and confirm it to be working well based on the output conforming to expectations:

```python
>>> find_proper_divisors(6)
[1, 2, 3]
>>> find_proper_divisors(24)
[1, 2, 3, 4, 6, 8, 12]
```

---

[1] List comprehension is the term used to describe an expression that generates a new result list based on a sequence of values and a calculation rule (see subsection 5.1.2).

2.1.3 Short Introduction to Prime Numbers

A prime number is a natural number that is greater than 1 and exclusively divisible by itself and by 1. There are two quite understandable algorithms for checking whether a given number is prime or for calculating primes up to a given maximum value.

Brute force algorithm for prime numbers Whether a number is a prime number or not can be determined as follows. You look for the number to be checked starting from 2 up to at most half of the number, whether the current number is a divisor of the original number.[2] In that case, it's not a prime. Otherwise, it needs to be checked further. In Python, this can be written as follows:

```python
def is_prime(potentially_prime):
    for i in range(2, potentially_prime // 2 + 1):
        if potentially_prime % i == 0:
            return False
    return True
```

To try it out, run the function in a loop and determine all prime numbers up to the value 25. The program output demonstrates that the functionality works correctly.

```python
>>> primes = []
>>> for number in range(2, 25):
...     if is_prime(number):
...         primes.append(number)
... print(primes)
```

Using list comprehension, you can write this more concisely:

```python
>>> primes = [number for number in range(2, 25) if is_prime(number)]
... print(primes)
```

In both cases, you get the prime numbers less than 25 as the correct result:

```python
[2, 3, 4, 5, 7, 11, 13, 17, 19, 23]
```

---

[2] As an optimization, you actually only have to calculate up to the root. I briefly discuss this in the following practical tip "Possible optimizations."

Optimization: Sieve of Eratosthenes Another algorithm for determining prime numbers up to a given maximum value is called the *Sieve of Eratosthenes*. It dates back to the Greek mathematician with the same name.

The whole thing works as follows. Initially, all numbers starting at the value 2 up to the given maximum value are written down, for example

$$2, 3, 4, 5, 6, 7, 8, 9, 10, 11, 12, 13, 14, 15$$

All numbers are initially considered as potential candidates for prime numbers. Now the numbers that cannot be prime numbers are eliminated step by step. The smallest unmarked number is taken, in this case, the number 2, which corresponds to the first prime number. Now all multiples of it are eliminated, in the example 4, 6, 8, 10, 12, 14:

$$2, 3, \not{4}, 5, \not{6}, 7, \not{8}, 9, \not{10}, 11, \not{12}, 13, \not{14}, 15$$

You continue with the number 3, which is the second prime number. Again, the multiples are eliminated. These are the numbers 6, 9, 12, 15:

$$2, 3, \not{4}, 5, \not{6}, 7, \not{8}, \not{9}, \not{10}, 11, \not{12}, 13, \not{14}, \not{15}$$

The next unmarked number and thus a prime number is 5. The procedure is repeated as long as there are still unmarked numbers after the current prime number:

$$2, 3, \not{4}, 5, \not{6}, 7, \not{8}, \not{9}, \not{10}, 11, \not{12}, 13, \not{14}, \not{15}$$

This leads to the following result for all prime numbers smaller than 15:

$$2, 3, 5, 7, 11, 13$$

In exercise 4, you are supposed to implement the Sieve of Eratosthenes by yourself. Then you may use the following values to test your algorithm in addition to the above:

Limit	Result
25	[2, 3, 5, 7, 11, 13, 17, 19, 23]
50	[2, 3, 5, 7, 11, 13, 17, 19, 23, 29, 31, 37, 41, 43, 47]

HINT: POSSIBLE OPTIMIZATIONS

As you can see, numbers are often crossed out several times. If you are mathematically a little more experienced, you can prove that at least one prime factor of a composite number must always be smaller equal to the root of the number itself. The reason is that if x is a divisor greater than $sqrt(n)$, then it holds that $p = n/x$ is smaller than $sqrt(n)$ and thus this value has already been tried. Thus you can optimize the multiples' elimination. Firstly, you start the elimination with the square of the prime number since all smaller multiples are already eliminated. Secondly, the calculation has to be done only up to the root of the upper limit. More details are supplied under `https://en.wikipedia.org/wiki/Sieve_of_Eratosthenes`.

2.1.4 Roman Numbers

The Roman numeral system works with special letters and combinations of them to represent numbers. The following basic mapping is applicable:[3]

Roman number	I	V	X	L	C	D	M
Value	1	5	10	50	100	500	1000

The corresponding value is usually calculated by adding the values of the individual digits from left to right. Normally (see the following rules), the largest number is on the left and the smallest number is on the right, for example, XVI for the value 16.

Rules

Roman numerals are composed according to certain rules:

1. **Addition rule**: The same digits next to each other are added, for example XXX = 30. Likewise, this applies to smaller digits after larger ones, so XII = 12.

---

[3] Interestingly the value 0 does not exist in Roman numerals.

2. **Repetition rule**: No more than three identical digits may follow
    each other. According to rule 1, you could write the number 4 as
    IIII, which this rule 2 forbids. This is where the subtraction rule
    comes into play.

3. **Subtraction rule**: If a smaller number symbol appears in front of a
    larger one, the corresponding value is subtracted. Let's look again
    at 4. It can be represented as subtraction 5 – 1. This is expressed
    as IV in the Roman numeral system. The following rules apply to
    the subtraction:

    •   I precedes only V and X.

    •   X precedes only L and C.

    •   C precedes only D and M.

Examples

For better understanding and clarification of the above rules, let's look at some notations
of Roman numerals and their corresponding values:

VII	$= 5 + 1 + 1$	$= 7$
MDCLXVI	$= 1000 + 500 + 100 + 50 + 10 + 5 + 1$	$= 1666$
MMXVIII	$= 1000 + 1000 + 10 + 5 + 1 + 1 + 1$	$= 2018$
MMXIX	$= 1000 + 1000 + 10 - 1 + 10$	$= 2019$

Noteworthy

The Arabic numerals common in our modern world rely on the decimal system. The
digits' position determines their value: thus, 7 can be the number itself, but it can also
represent 70 or 700. However, in the Roman numeral system, the V always stands for a 5,
regardless of the position.

Because of this particular structure of Roman numerals, many math operations are
complex; even a simple addition may cause a bigger or sometimes even a complete change
of the number. This becomes very obvious for the numbers 2018 and 2019 or for the
addition III + II = V. Even worse, significantly more complex is a multiplication or division—
there are speculations that this was one of the factors why the Roman Empire collapsed.

NOTE: LARGER NUMBERS

There are special notations for representing larger Roman numerals (in the range of ten thousand and above) because no four or more Ms are allowed to follow each other. This has no relevance for the tasks of this book. If interested, you may consult the Internet or other sources.

2.1.5 Number Games

In this section, you'll look at a few special number constellations:

- Perfect numbers

- Armstrong numbers

- Checksums

In many of the algorithms used below, you subdivide numbers into their digits to be able to perform corresponding number games.

Perfect Numbers

By definition, a number is called a ***perfect number*** if its value is equal to the sum of its real divisors (i. e., excluding itself). This may sound a bit strange, but it is quite simple. Let's consider the number 6 as an example. It possesses as real divisors the numbers 1, 2, and 3. Interestingly, it now holds

$$1 + 2 + 3 = 6$$

Let's look at another counterpart: the number 20, which has the real divisors 1, 2, 4, 5, and 10, but their sum is 22 and not 20.

$$1 + 2 + 4 + 5 + 10 = 22$$

Armstrong Numbers

In this section you examine Armstrong numbers. These are numbers whose individual digits are first exponentiated by the number of digits in the number and then added together. If this sum then corresponds to the original number's value, it is called an Armstrong number. To keep things a little simpler, let's look at the special case of three-digit numbers. To be an Armstrong number, the following equation must be satisfied with this number:

$$x * 100 + y * 10 + z = x^3 + y^3 + z^3$$

The digits of the number are modeled as *x*, *y*, and *z* and are all in the range from 0 to 9.

The formula $x * 100 + y * 10 + z$ results from the position of the digits and a textual representation of "xyz", so

$$1*100+5*10+3 = "153"$$
$$3*100+7*10+1 = "371"$$

Let's consider two examples for which this formula is satisfied:

$$153 = 1*100+5*10+3 = 1^3 + 5^3 + 3^3 = 1 + 125 + 27 = 153$$
$$371 = 3*100+7*10+1 = 3^3 + 7^3 + 1^3 = 27 + 343 + 1 = 371$$

Variation As a modification, it is also quite interesting for which digits or numbers of the following equation are fulfilled:

$$x * 100 + y * 10 + z = x^1 + y^2 + z^3$$

or

$$x * 100 + y * 10 + z = x^3 + y^2 + z^1$$

For the first equation, there are the following solutions:

[135, 175, 518, 598]

For the second equation, there is no solution for *x*, *y*, and *z* in the range up to 100. If you like, you can verify this yourself when implementing the bonus part of exercise 9—or look at the solutions.

Algorithm for a Simple Checksum

A checksum is coded into various numbers so that it is easy to prove validity. This applies, for example, to credit card numbers and to data transfers via special protocols.

Let's assume that a checksum has to be calculated for a number with four digits (hereafter modeled as *a* to *d*). Then you can perform the following calculation based on the position:

$$abcd \Rightarrow (a*1+b*2+c*3+d*4)\%10$$

Once again, let's illustrate the calculation with examples:

Input	Position calculation	Value	Checksum
1111	1 * 1 + 1 * 2 + 1 * 3 + 1 * 4	1 + 2 + 3 + 4 = 10	10 % 10 = 0
1234	1 * 1 + 2 * 2 + 3 * 3 + 4 * 4	1 + 4 + 9 + 16 = 30	30 % 10 = 0
4321	4 * 1 + 3 * 2 + 2 * 3 + 1 * 4	4 + 6 + 6 + 4 = 20	20 % 10 = 0
7271	7 * 1 + 2 * 2 + 7 * 3 + 1 * 4	7 + 4 + 21 + 4 = 36	36 % 10 = 6
0815	0 * 1 + 8 * 2 + 1 * 3 + 5 * 4	0 + 16 + 3 + 20 = 39	39 % 10 = 9
5180	5 * 1 + 1 * 2 + 8 * 3 + 0 * 4	5 + 2 + 24 + 0 = 31	31 % 10 = 1

2.1.6 Getting Started with Lambdas

This subsection briefly introduces lambda expressions (***lambdas*** for short). The language construct lambda comes from ***functional programming***. Lambdas reflect the mathematical concept of functions with input, processing, and output, for example a squaring $f(x) = x * x$. This can also be implemented using functions in Python, but lambdas offer an even shorter notation. Simply speaking, a ***lambda*** is a container for some source code or an anonymous function, such as one without a function name. Although lambdas are useful in many ways, sometimes readability and comprehensibility suffer. Therefore the Python style guide (PEP 8) is not necessarily in favor of lambdas.

Lambda Syntax

Lambdas, unlike functions, have no name, no `return`, and do not need to be introduced with `def`. This results in an even shorter notation, reduced to the essentials, with the following syntax where only expressions are allowed, but not statements:

`lambda` parameter(s): expression

A few simple examples of lambdas are the addition of two numbers, the multiplication by a factor of 2 or two numbers, and the calculation of power. These actions can be written as lambdas as follows:

```
>>> add_one = lambda x: x + 1
>>> double_it = lambda x: x * 2
>>> mult = lambda a, b : a * b
>>> power_of = lambda x, y: x ** y
```

Please note that the PEP 8 style guide states to not assign a lambda expression and to use a def instead. Occasionally, as in the above case, I name lambdas for a better insight into how things work or to express more clearly what was intended even though they usually encapsulate only a tiny piece of functionality and thus should not be named.

As an example, to perform doubling as well as exponentiation:

```
>>> double_it = lambda x: x * 2
>>> power_of = lambda x, y: x ** y
>>> print(double_it(7))
14
>>> print(power_of(2,8))
256
```

In fact, these lambdas look pretty unspectacular, and in particular, it becomes clear that a lambda is just a small piece of executable source code. Let's take another look at the corresponding function definitions for the first two examples to differentiate them:

```
def add_one(x):
    return x + 1

def double_it(x)
    return x * 2
```

Lambdas in Action with sort( )

For lists Python offers a method named sort() to sort the elements. To get started, let's look at a list of numbers. First, you sort them according to their natural order:

```
>>> numbers = [11, 2, 30, 333, 14, 4444, 100, 2222]
>>> numbers.sort()
```

```
>>> print(numbers)
[2, 11, 14, 30, 100, 333, 2222, 4444]
```

When calling sort() you can use the named parameter key to control sorting. Now you want to sort the numbers by length. Therefore, you use a lambda to convert the numbers to strings using str() and sort them by their length with len()—within the same length the ordering is not defined.

```
>>> numbers = [11, 2, 30, 333, 14, 4444, 100, 2222]
>>> numbers.sort(key=lambda x: len(str(x)))
>>> print(numbers)
[2, 11, 30, 14, 333, 100, 4444, 2222]
```

A second sort criterion can easily be added using the following tuple:

```
>>> numbers.sort(key=lambda x: (len(str(x)), x))
>>> print(numbers)
[2, 11, 14, 30, 100, 333, 2222, 4444]
```

2.2 Exercises

2.2.1 Exercise 1: Basic Arithmetic (★☆☆☆☆)

Exercise 1a: Basic Arithmetic Operations (★☆☆☆☆)

Write function calc(m, n) that multiplies two variables m and n of type int, then divides the product by two, and outputs the remainder with respect to division by 7.

Examples

m	n	m * n	m * n // 2	Result ((n * m // 2) % 7)
6	7	42	21	0
5	5	25	12	5

A short reminder: With an integer division, the remainder is truncated. Therefore 25//2 results in the value 12.

Exercise 1b: Statistics (★★☆☆☆)

Count as well as sum up the natural numbers that are divisible by 2 or 7 up to a given maximum value (exclusive) and output it to the console. Write function calc_sum_and_count_all_numbers_div_by_2_or_7(max_exclusive). Extend it so that it returns the two values instead of performing the console output.

Examples

Maximum	Divisible by 2	Divisible by 7	Result Count	Sum
3	2	-/-	1	2
8	2, 4, 6	7	4	19
15	2, 4, 6, 8, 10, 12, 14	7, 14	8	63

Exercise 1c: Even or Odd Number (★☆☆☆☆)

Create the functions is_even(n) and is_odd(n) that will check if the passed integer is even or odd, respectively.

2.2.2 Exercise 2: Number as Text (★★☆☆☆)

Write function number_as_text(n) which, for a given positive number, converts the respective digits into corresponding text.

Start with the following fragment for the last digit of a number:

```python
def number_as_text(n):
    remainder = n % 10
    value_to_text = ""

    if remainder == 0:
        value_to_text = "ZERO"
    if remainder == 1:
        value_to_text = "ONE"

    # ...

    return value_to_text
```

Examples

Input	Result
7	"SEVEN"
42	"FOUR TWO"
24680	"TWO FOUR SIX EIGHT ZERO"
13579	"ONE THREE FIVE SEVEN NINE"

2.2.3 Exercise 3: Perfect Numbers (★★☆☆☆)

By definition, a natural number is called a perfect number if its value is equal to the sum of its real divisors. This is true, for example, for the numbers 6 and 28:

$$1 + 2 + 3 = 6$$

$$1 + 2 + 4 + 7 + 14 = 28$$

Write function calc_perfect_numbers(max_exclusive) that calculates the perfect numbers up to a maximum value, say 10,000.

Examples

Input	Result
1000	[6, 28, 496]
10000	[6, 28, 496, 8128]

2.2.4 Exercise 4: Prime Numbers (★★☆☆☆)

Write function calc_primes_up_to(max_value) to compute all prime numbers up to a given value. As a reminder, a prime number is a natural number greater than 1 and exclusively divisible by itself and by 1. To compute a prime number, the Sieve of Eratosthenes was described before.

Examples

Check your algorithm with the following values:

Input	Result
15	[2, 3, 5, 7, 11, 13]
25	[2, 3, 5, 7, 11, 13, 17, 19, 23]
50	[2, 3, 5, 7, 11, 13, 17, 19, 23, 29, 31, 37, 41, 43, 47]

2.2.5 Exercise 5: Prime Number Pairs (★★☆☆☆)

Compute all pairs of prime numbers with a distance of 2 (twin), 4 (cousin), and 6 (sexy) up to an upper bound for n. For twins then the following is true:

$$is\_Prime(n)\,\&\,\&is\_Prime(n+2)$$

Examples

The following results are expected for limit 50:

Type	Result
twin	{3: 5, 5: 7, 11: 13, 17: 19, 29: 31, 41: 43}
cousin	{3: 7, 7: 11, 13: 17, 19: 23, 37: 41, 43: 47}
sexy	{5: 11, 7: 13, 11: 17, 13: 19, 17: 23, 23: 29, 31: 37, 37: 43, 41: 47, 47: 53}

2.2.6 Exercise 6: Checksum (★★☆☆☆)

Create function `calc_checksum(digits)` that performs the following position-based calculation for the checksum of a number of any length given as a string, with the n digits modeled as z_1 to z_n:

$$z_1 z_2 z_3 \ldots z_n \Rightarrow (1*z_1 + 2*z_2 + 3*z_3 + \ldots + n*z_n)\%10$$

Examples

Input	Sum	Result
"11111"	1 + 2 + 3 + 4 + 5 = 15	15 % 10 = 5
"87654321"	8 + 14 + 18 + 20 + 20 + 18 + 14 + 8 = 120	120 % 10 = 0

2.2.7 Exercise 7: Roman Numbers (★★★★☆)

Exercise 7a: Roman Numbers ➤ Decimal Numbers (★★★☆☆)

Write function from_roman_number(roman_number) that computes the corresponding decimal number from a textually valid Roman number.[4]

Exercise 7b: Decimal Numbers ➤ Roman Numbers (★★★★☆)

Write function to_roman_number(value) that converts a decimal number to a (valid) Roman number.

Examples

Arabic	Roman
17	"XVII"
444	"CDXLIV"
1971	"MCMLXXI"
2020	"MMXX"

---

[4] For syntactically invalid Roman numbers, such as IXD, an incorrect result, here 489, can be computed by applying subtraction rule twice in a row: 0 − 1 − 10 + 500.

2.2.8 Exercise 8: Combinatorics (★★☆☆☆)

Exercise 8a: Computation of $a^2 + b^2 = c^2$

Compute all combinations of the values a, b, and c (each starting from 1 and less than 100) for which the following formula holds:

$$a^2 + b^2 = c^2$$

Bonus (★★★☆☆) Reduce the running time of $O(n^3)$ to $O(n^2)$. If needed, consult Appendix C for an introduction to O-notation.

Exercise 8b: Computation of $a^2 + b^2 = c^2 + d^2$

Compute all combinations of the values a, b, c, and d (each starting from 1 and less than 100) for which the following formula holds:

$$a^2 + b^2 = c^2 + d^2$$

Bonus (★★★☆☆) Reduce the running time of $O(n^4)$ to $O(n^3)$.

2.2.9 Exercise 9: Armstrong Numbers (★★☆☆☆)

This exercise deals with three-digit Armstrong numbers. By definition, these are numbers for whose digits x, y, and z from 1 to 9 satisfy the following equation:

$$x*100 + y*10 + z = x^3 + y^3 + z^3$$

Write function `calc_armstrong_numbers()` to compute all Armstrong numbers for x, y, and z (each < 10).

Examples

$$153 = 1*100 + 5*10 + 3 = 1^3 + 5^3 + 3^3 = 1 + 125 + 27 = 153$$
$$371 = 3*100 + 7*10 + 1 = 3^3 + 7^3 + 1^3 = 27 + 343 + 1 = 371$$

Bonus Find a generic version with functions or lambdas and then try the following three formulas:

$$x*100 + y*10 + z = x^3 + y^3 + z^3$$
$$x*100 + y*10 + z = x^1 + y^2 + z^3$$
$$x*100 + y*10 + z = x^3 + y^2 + z^1$$

2.2.10 Exercise 10: Max Change Calculator (★★★★☆)

Suppose you have a collection of coins or numbers of different values. Write function `calc_max_possible_change(values)` that determines, for positive integers, what amounts can be *seamlessly* generated with it starting from the value 1. The maximum value should be returned as a result.

Examples

Input	Possible values	Maximum
1	1	1
1, 1	1, 2	2
1, 5	1	1
1, 2, 4	1, 2, 3, 4, 5, 6, 7	7
1, 2, 3, 7	1, 2, 3, 4, 5, 6, 7, 8, 9, 10, 11, 12, 13	13
1, 1, 1, 1, 5, 10, 20, 50	1, 2, 3, 4, 5, 6, ... 30, ... 39	39

2.2.11 Exercise 11: Related Numbers (★★☆☆☆)

Two numbers n_1 and n_2 are called friends (or related) if the sum of their divisors is equal to the other number:

$$sum(divisors(n_1)) = n_2$$
$$sum(divisors(n_2)) = n_1$$

Write function `calc_friends(max_exclusive)` to compute all friends numbers up to a passed maximum value.

Examples

Input	Divisors
$\sum(divisors(220)) = 284$	div(220) = 1, 2, 4, 5, 10, 11, 20, 22, 44, 55, 110
$\sum(divisors(284)) = 220$	div(284) = 1, 2, 4, 71, 142
$\sum(divisors(1184)) = 1210$	div(1184) = 1, 2, 4, 8, 16, 32, 37, 74, 148, 296, 592
$\sum(divisors(1210)) = 1184$	div(1210) = 1, 2, 5, 10, 11, 22, 55, 110, 121, 242, 605

2.2.12 Exercise 12: Prime Factorization (★★★☆☆)

Any natural number greater than 1 can be represented as a multiplication of primes. Remember the fact that 2 is also a prime. Write function `calc_prime_factors(value)` that returns a list of prime numbers whose multiplication yields the desired number.

Examples

Input	Prime factors	Result
8	2 * 2 * 2	[2, 2, 2]
14	2 * 7	[2, 7]
42	2 * 3 * 7	[2, 3, 7]
1155	3 * 5 * 7 * 11	[3, 5, 7, 11]
2222	2 * 11 * 101	[2, 11, 101]

2.3 Solutions

2.3.1 Solution 1: Basic Arithmetic (★☆☆☆☆)

Solution 1a: Basic Arithmetic Operations (★☆☆☆☆)

Write function `calc(m, n)` that multiplies two variables *m* and *n* of type int, then divides the product by two, and outputs the remainder with respect to division by 7.

Examples

m	n	m * n	m * n // 2	Result ((n * m // 2) % 7)
6	7	42	21	0
5	5	25	12	5

A reminder: With an integer division, the remainder is truncated. Therefore 25//2 results in the value 12.

Algorithm The implementation directly follows the mathematical operations:

```
def calc(m, n):
    return m * n // 2 % 7
```

Instead of the particular operator //, you can also perform a conversion of the result of the simple division into an integer by calling int():

```
def calc_v2(m, n):
    return int(m * n / 2) % 7
```

Solution 1b: Statistics (★★☆☆☆)

Count as well as sum up the natural numbers that are divisible by 2 or 7 up to a given maximum value (exclusive) and output it to the console. Write function calc_sum_and_count_all_numbers_div_by_2_or_7(max_exclusive). Extend it so that it returns the two values instead of performing the console output.

Examples

Maximum	Divisible by 2	Divisible by 7	Result Count	Sum
3	2	-/-	1	2
8	2, 4, 6	7	4	19
15	2, 4, 6, 8, 10, 12, 14	7, 14	8	63

Algorithm The implementation is a tiny bit more complex than before. It uses two variables for count and sum as well as a loop. The modulo operator helps to check whether divisibility is given.

```python
def calc_sum_and_count_all_numbers_div_by_2_or_7(max_exclusive):
    count = 0
    sum = 0

    for i in range(1, max_exclusive):
        if i % 2 == 0 or i % 7 == 0:
            count += 1
            sum += i

    print("count:", count)
    print("sum:", sum)
```

What remains is the desire to return the two values. With Python, this is an easy task since tuples are applicable for this, for example, with return (sum, count) or the even shorter return sum, count.

It is even clearer to use a dictionary. This makes the unit test very readable in the end:

```python
def calc_sum_and_count_all_numbers_div_by_2_or_7_v2(max_exclusive):
    count = 0
    sum = 0

    for i in range(1, max_exclusive):
        if i % 2 == 0 or i % 7 == 0:
            count += 1
            sum += i

    return {"sum": sum, "count": count}
```

NOTE: SHADOWING OF BUILT-INS IN SMALL SCOPES

Please note that there is a minor inconvenience in the two code samples: the shadowing of the built-in function sum() by the local variable named sum. Of course, it is easily possible to use sum_ as a variable name. But due to the small scope, I prefer to stick to the more readable but shadowing name sum. This should never cause a real problem.

If your functions grow and get more complex, please avoid shadowing to prevent bugs.

NOTE: STRUCTURING WITH BLANK LINES

Blank lines sometimes cause problems when processed in the Python command line interpreter. In IDEs like PyCharm, on the other hand, this is possible without problems. I will use empty lines for the examples if this means clearer source code.

Solution 1c: Even or Odd Number (★ ☆ ☆ ☆ ☆)

Create functions is_even(n) and is_odd(n) that will check if the passed integer is even or odd, respectively.

Algorithm The implementation uses the modulo operator in each case. A number is even if a division by 2 has no remainder; otherwise, it is odd.

```python
def is_even(n):
    return n % 2 == 0

def is_odd(n):
    return n % 2 != 0
```

Verification

For the test of exercise 1a, use a parameterized test and a comma-separated enumeration for the specification of the input values for m and n and the result. To refresh your knowledge of pytest, look at Appendix A.

```python
@pytest.mark.parametrize("m, n, expected",
                         [(6, 7, 0), (3, 4, 6), (5, 5, 5)])
def test_calc(m, n, expected):
    assert calc(m, n) == expected
```

To verify the exercise part 1b, use the Python command line:

```python
>>> calc_sum_and_count_all_numbers_div_by_2_or_7(8)
count: 4
sum: 19
```

For professional programming, it is generally advisable to create unit tests. In other languages, even a combined return value would be a first hurdle. With Python and tuples in combination with dictionaries, this is very easy:

```
@pytest.mark.parametrize("n, expected",
                         [(3, {"sum": 2, "count": 1}),
                          (8, {"sum": 19, "count": 4}),
                          (15, {"sum": 63, "count": 8})])
def test_calc_sum_and_count_all_numbers_div_by_2_or_7_v2(n, expected):
    assert calc_sum_and_count_all_numbers_div_by_2_or_7_v2(n) == expected
```

Testing exercise 1c for even or odd is so simple that I'll just limit the output to two exemplary calls in the Python command line:

```
>>> is_even(2)
True
>>> is_odd(7)
True
```

2.3.2 Solution 2: Number as Text (★★☆☆☆)

Write function number_as_text(n) which, for a given positive number, converts the respective digits into corresponding text.

Examples

Input	Result
7	"SEVEN"
42	"FOUR TWO"
24680	"TWO FOUR SIX EIGHT ZERO"
13579	"ONE THREE FIVE SEVEN NINE"

Algorithm Always compute the remainder (i. e., the last digit), print it out, and then divide by ten. Repeat this until no remainder exists anymore. Note that the digit's representation must be appended to the text's front since the last digit is always extracted. Otherwise, the digits would appear in the wrong order.

```
def number_as_text(n):
    value = ""
    remaining_value = n
    while remaining_value > 0:
```

```
        remainder_as_text = digit_as_text(remaining_value % 10)
        remaining_value = int(remaining_value / 10)
        value = remainder_as_text + " " + value

    return value.strip()
```

Implement the mapping from digit to text with a dictionary as follows:

```
value_to_text_mapping = {
    0: "ZERO", 1: "ONE", 2: "TWO", 3: "THREE", 4: "FOUR",
    5: "FIVE", 6: "SIX", 7: "SEVEN", 8: "EIGHT", 9: "NINE"
}

def digit_as_text(n):
    return value_to_text_mapping[n % 10]
```

Python shortcut As mentioned in the introduction, the built-in Python function divmod() is often useful for division and modulo. Therewith the process changes only minimally:

```
def number_as_text(n):
    value = ""
    remaining_value = n
    while remaining_value > 0:
        remaining_value, remainder = divmod(remaining_value, 10)
        value = digit_as_text(remainder) + " " + value

    return value.strip()
```

There is another variant that iterates character by character through the number. It is first converted into a string. To access the dictionary, you reconvert it into a number.

```
def number_as_text_shorter(n):
    value = ""
    for ch in str(n):
        value += digit_as_text(int(ch)) + " "

    return value.strip()
```

Verification

For testing, use a parameterized test that can be formulated elegantly using pytest:

```python
@pytest.mark.parametrize("n, expected",
                         [(7, "SEVEN"),
                          (42, "FOUR TWO"),
                          (7271, "SEVEN TWO SEVEN ONE"),
                          (24680, "TWO FOUR SIX EIGHT ZERO"),
                          (13579, "ONE THREE FIVE SEVEN NINE")])
def test_number_as_text(n, expected):
    assert number_as_text(n) == expected
```

2.3.3 Solution 3: Perfect Numbers (★★☆☆☆)

By definition, a natural number is called a perfect number if its value is equal to the sum of its real divisors. This is true, for example, for the numbers 6 and 28:

$$1 + 2 + 3 = 6$$
$$1 + 2 + 4 + 7 + 14 = 28$$

Write function calc_perfect_numbers(max_exclusive) that calculates the perfect numbers up to a maximum value, say 10,000.

Examples

Input	Result
1000	[6, 28, 496]
10000	[6, 28, 496, 8128]

Algorithm The simplest variant is to check all numbers from 2 to half of the desired maximum value to see if they represent the original number's divisor. In that case, the sum of the divisors is increased by exactly that value. The sum starts with the value 1 because this is invariably a valid divisor. Finally, you only have to compare the determined sum with the initial number.

```
def is_perfect_number_simple(number):
    # always divisible by 1
    sum_of_multipliers = 1

    for i in range(2, int(number / 2) + 1):
        if number % i == 0:
            sum_of_multipliers += i

    return sum_of_multipliers == number
```

Based on this, the actual function is straightforward to implement:

```
def calc_perfect_numbers(max_exclusive):
    results = []
    for i in range(2, max_exclusive):
        if is_perfect_number_simple(i):
            results.append(i)

    return results
```

Python shortcut Using list comprehensions, this can be written a little shorter and more elegantly:

```
def calc_perfect_numbers_comprehension(max_exclusive):
    return [i for i in range(2, max_exclusive) if is_perfect_number_simple(i)]
```

Verification

For testing, use the following inputs, which show the correct operation for dedicated numbers:

```
@pytest.mark.parametrize("n, expected",
                        [(6, True), (28, True),
                         (496, True), (8128, True)])
def test_is_perfect_number_simple(n, expected):
    assert is_perfect_number_simple(n) == expected
```

Now you have tested the basic building block of the examination. However, you should still make sure that no other values than perfect numbers are supplied—in fact, only these—for the testing, thus the first four perfect numbers are namely the numbers 6, 28, 496, and 8128:

```
@pytest.mark.parametrize("n, expected", [(50, [6, 28]),
                                         (1000, [6, 28, 496]),
                                         (10000, [6, 28, 496, 8128])])
def test_calc_perfect_numbers(n, expected):
    assert calc_perfect_numbers(n) == expected
```

Implementation Optimization

Based on the function find_proper_divisors(n) presented in the introductory section of this chapter that finds all true divisors, you can simplify the check as follows:

```
def is_perfect_number_based_on_proper_divisors(number):
    divisors = find_proper_divisors(number)

    return sum(divisors) == number
```

Conveniently, there is a built-in functionality in Python that sums the elements of a list. This is the function sum(), which you use here.

2.3.4 Solution 4: Prime Numbers (★★☆☆☆)

Write function calc_primes_up_to(max_value) to compute all prime numbers up to a given value. As a reminder, a prime number is a natural number greater than 1 and exclusively divisible by itself and by 1. To compute a prime number, the so-called Sieve of Eratosthenes was described before.

Examples

Check your algorithm with the following values:

Input	Result
15	[2, 3, 5, 7, 11, 13]
25	[2, 3, 5, 7, 11, 13, 17, 19, 23]
50	[2, 3, 5, 7, 11, 13, 17, 19, 23, 29, 31, 37, 41, 43, 47]

Algorithm The algorithm follows the Sieve of Eratosthenes. At first, a list of `booleans` is created and initialized with `True` since all numbers are considered potential prime numbers. Mentally, this is analogous to initially writing down the numbers 2, 3, 4, ... up to a given maximum value:

$$2, 3, 4, 5, 6, 7, 8, 9, 10, 11, 12, 13, 14, 15$$

Now, starting at the value 2, the "sieving" is started. Because the number 2 is not crossed out, it is included in the list of prime numbers. Afterwards every multiple of it is crossed out, because they can't be prime numbers:

$$2, 3, \not{4}, 5, \not{6}, 7, \not{8}, 9, \not{10}, 11, \not{12}, 13, \not{14}, 15$$

Iteratively you look for the next not-eliminated number. In this case, it is 3, which is the second prime number. Once again, all multiples of this number are eliminated:

$$2, 3, \not{4}, 5, \not{6}, 7, \not{8}, \not{9}, \not{10}, 11, \not{12}, 13, \not{14}, \not{15}$$

This procedure is repeated until half of the maximum value is reached. This prime number calculation is implemented in Python as follows:

```python
def calc_primes_up_to(max_value):
    # initially mark all values as potential prime number
    is_potentially_prime = [True for _ in range(1, max_value + 2)]

    # run through all numbers starting at 2, optimization only up to half
    for number in range(2, max_value // 2 + 1):
        if is_potentially_prime[number]:
            erase_multiples_of_current(is_potentially_prime, number)

    return build_primes_list(is_potentially_prime)
```

The crossing out or erasing the multiples is extracted to the helper function `erase_multiples_of_current()`. As a trick, use on the one hand the step size of i and on the other hand that the first multiple is determined by adding the start value. For first attempts, the commented console output can be helpful.

```python
def erase_multiples_of_current(values, number):
    for n in range(number + number, len(values), number):
        values[n] = False
        # print("Eliminating:", n)
```

Finally, you need to reconstruct a list of numbers from the list of booleans. It is essential that you start from the value 2 because the two values below this value are not set to False (by mistake, but here without negative effect):

```python
def build_primes_list(is_potentially_prime):
    primes = []
    for number in range(2, len(is_potentially_prime)):
        if is_potentially_prime[number]:
            primes.append(number)

    return primes
```

Python shortcut With the help of list comprehensions, this can be written a little shorter and more elegantly in Python:

```python
def build_primes_list(is_potentially_prime):
    return [number for number in range(2, len(is_potentially_prime))
            if is_potentially_prime[number]]
```

Python shortcut I would like to show another variant based on compress() from the module itertools. This allows you to get a new sequence from a sequence of data and a sequence of selectors in the form of Boolean values with only the values for which the selector has the value True or 1:

```python
>>> import itertools
>>> print(list(itertools.compress("ABCDEF", [1, 0, 1, 0, 1, 0])))
['A', 'C', 'E']
```

For the prime number calculation, you use this as follows:

```python
import itertools

def calc_primes_up_to_v2(max_value):
    is_potentially_prime = [True for _ in range(1, max_value + 2)]

    for number in range(2, int(max_value / 2) + 1):
```

```
    if is_potentially_prime[number]:
        erase_multiples_of_current(is_potentially_prime, number)

# mark values 0 and 1 as no prime number
is_potentially_prime[0:2] = False, False

# merging / selection of values
return list(itertools.compress(range(len(is_potentially_prime)),
                               is_potentially_prime))
```

Verification

For testing, use the following inputs that show the correct operation:

```
def input_and_expected():
    return [(2, [2]),
            (3, [2, 3]),
            (10, [2, 3, 5, 7]),
            (15, [2, 3, 5, 7, 11, 13]),
            (20, [2, 3, 5, 7, 11, 13, 17, 19]),
            (25, [2, 3, 5, 7, 11, 13, 17, 19, 23]),
            (50, [2, 3, 5, 7, 11, 13, 17, 19, 23, 29, 31, 37, 41, 43, 47])]

@pytest.mark.parametrize("n, expected",
                         input_and_expected())
def test_calc_primes_up_to(n, expected):
    assert calc_primes_up_to(n) == expected

@pytest.mark.parametrize("n, expected",
                         input_and_expected())
def test_calc_primes_up_to_v2(n, expected):
    assert calc_primes_up_to_v2(n) == expected
```

2.3.5 Solution 5: Prime Number Pairs (★★☆☆☆)

Compute all pairs of prime numbers with a distance of 2 (twin), 4 (cousin), and 6 (sexy) up to an upper bound for n. For twins then the following is true:

$$Is\_Prime(n) \&\& is\_Prime(n + 2)$$

Examples

The following results are expected for limit 50:

Type	Result
Twin	{3: 5, 5: 7, 11: 13, 17: 19, 29: 31, 41: 43}
Cousin	{3: 7, 7: 11, 13: 17, 19: 23, 37: 41, 43: 47}
Sexy	{5: 11, 7: 13, 11: 17, 13: 19, 17: 23, 23: 29, 31: 37, 37: 43, 41: 47, 47: 53}

Algorithm As a first step, you need to define the conditions for pairs. This can be done explicitly via if statements or more elegantly by the definition of suitable predicates. For all numbers starting at 2 up to a desired upper limit, you must check whether the number itself and the corresponding other number added by 2, 4, or 6 are prime numbers. For this purpose, you can call function is_prime(n), which in turn uses the previously written function for determining the prime numbers. For twins, I still use the rather non-Pythonic for loop with if check here. For the other two, dict comprehensions come into play. For more details on prime twins, see https://en.wikipedia.org/wiki/Twin_prime.

```python
def main():
    def is_twin_pair(n):
        return is_prime(n) and is_prime(n + 2)

    def is_cousin_pair(n):
        return is_prime(n) and is_prime(n + 4)

    def is_sexy_pair(n):
        return is_prime(n) and is_prime(n + 6)

    # manual update
    twin_pairs = {}
    for i in range(1, 50):
        if is_twin_pair(i):
            twin_pairs.update({i: i + 2})

    # dict comprehensions
    cousin_pairs = {i: i + 4 for i in range(1, 50) if is_cousin_pair(i)}
    sexy_pairs = {i : i + 6 for i in range(1, 50) if is_sexy_pair(i)}
```

```
    print("Twins:", twin_pairs)
    print("Cousins:", cousin_pairs)
    print("Sexy:", sexy_pairs)

def is_prime(n):
    primes = calc_primes_up_to(n + 1)
    return n in primes
```

The realization shown here uses already implemented functionality, which is preferable in principle, but has two drawbacks in this case:

1.   Every time all prime numbers are computed again up to the given maximum value. This can be optimized by performing the computation only once and caching the results appropriately.

2.   At the moment, the checks are still all interwoven. It is clearer to use a validation function that checks only one condition and returns only one result.

Optimization of the Implementation

Vulnerability 1: Repeated calls First, you should compute the primes up to the maximum value only once. In this case, you need to raise the limit by 7 so that you can map all pairs correctly.

```
def calc_prime_pairs(max_value):
    primes = calc_primes_up_to(max_value + 7)

    def is_twin_pair(n):
        return is_prime(primes, n) and is_prime(primes, n + 2)

    def is_cousin_pair(n):
        return is_prime(primes, n) and is_prime(primes, n + 4)

    def is_sexy_pair(n):
        return is_prime(primes, n) and is_prime(primes, n + 6)

    # manual update
    twin_pairs = {}
    for i in range(1, max_value):
        if is_twin_pair(i):
```

```
            twin_pairs.update({i: i + 2})
```

```
    # dict comprehensions
    cousin_pairs = {i: i + 4 for i in range(1, max_value) if is_cousin_pair(i)}
    sexy_pairs = {i: i + 6 for i in range(1, max_value) if is_sexy_pair(i)}

    print("Twins: ", twin_pairs)
    print("Cousins: ", cousin_pairs)
    print("Sexy: ", sexy_pairs)
```

Computing the prime numbers is performed once at the beginning of the function. Thus you achieve a significant performance improvement.

Finally, you move the check for a prime number to the following function:

```
def is_prime(primes, n):
    return n in primes
```

Vulnerability 2: Unclear program structure Your goal is to write more general-purpose functions. You have already created the basic building blocks. However, the determination of the pairs should be moved to function calc_pairs(). This way, you can write it more clearly and understandably as follows:

```
def calc_prime_pairs_improved(max_value):
    twin_pairs = calc_pairs(max_value, 2)
    cousin_pairs = calc_pairs(max_value, 4)
    sexy_pairs = calc_pairs(max_value, 6)

    print("Twins:", twin_pairs)
    print("Cousins:", cousin_pairs)
    print("Sexy:", sexy_pairs)

def calc_pairs(max_value, distance):
    primes = calc_primes_up_to(max_value + distance)

    return {number: number + distance for number in range(1, max_value)
            if is_prime(primes, number) and is_prime(primes, number +
            distance)}
```

This conversion also lays the foundation to be able to test the whole thing with unit tests.

Verification

If you call the method with the maximum value of 50, you get this result:

```
Twins: {3: 5, 5: 7, 11: 13, 17: 19, 29: 31, 41: 43}
Cousins: {3: 7, 7: 11, 13: 17, 19: 23, 37: 41, 43: 47}
Sexy: {5: 11, 7: 13, 11: 17, 13: 19, 17: 23, 23: 29, 31: 37, 37: 43, 41:
47, 47: 53}
```

Now let's create another unit test with one test function per special case:

```
@pytest.mark.parametrize("n, expected",
                          [(2, {3: 5, 5: 7, 11: 13, 17: 19, 29: 31,
                            41: 43}),
                           (4, {3: 7, 7: 11, 13: 17, 19: 23, 37: 41,
                            43: 47}),
                           (6, {5: 11, 7: 13, 11: 17, 13: 19, 17: 23, 23:
                            29, 31: 37, 37: 43, 41: 47, 47: 53})])
def test_calc_pairs(n, expected):
    max_value = 50

    assert calc_pairs(max_value, n) == expected
```

2.3.6 Solution 6: Checksum (★★☆☆☆)

Create function `calc_checksum(digits)` that performs the following position-based calculation for the checksum of a number of any length given as a string, with the n digits modeled as z_1 to z_n:

$$z_1 z_2 z_3 \ldots z_n \Rightarrow (1 * z_1 + 2 * z_2 + 3 * z_3 + \ldots + n * z_n)\%10$$

Examples

Digits	Sum	Result
"11111"	$1 + 2 + 3 + 4 + 5 = 15$	$15 \% 10 = 5$
"87654321"	$8 + 14 + 18 + 20 + 20 + 18 + 14 + 8 = 120$	$120 \% 10 = 0$

Algorithm Traverse all digits from the front to the last position, extract the digit at the given position, and multiply its numerical value by the current position. Add this to the sum. Finally, the modulo operation maps the sum to a digit.

```python
def calc_checksum(digits):
    if not digits.isdigit():
        raise ValueError("illegal chars: not only digits")

    crc = 0

    for i, current_char in enumerate(digits):
        value = (int(current_char)) * (i + 1)
        crc += value

    return int(crc % 10)
```

Verification

For testing, use the following inputs, which show the correct operation for valid inputs and check the handling of errors for wrong inputs:

```python
@pytest.mark.parametrize("n, expected",
                         [("11111", 5),
                          ("22222", 0),
                          ("111111", 1),
                          ("12345678", 4),
                          ("87654321", 0)])
def test_calc_checksum(n, expected):
    assert calc_checksum(n) == expected
def test_calc_checksum_with_letters_as_wrong_input():
    with pytest.raises(ValueError) as excinfo:
        calc_checksum("ABC")

    assert "illegal chars" in str(excinfo.value)
```

2.3.7 Solution 7: Roman Numbers (★★★★☆)

Solution 7a: Roman Numbers ➤ Decimal Numbers (★★★☆☆)

Write function from_roman_number(roman_number) that computes the corresponding decimal number from a textually valid Roman number.[5]

Examples

Arabic	Roman
17	"XVII"
444	"CDXLIV"
1971	"MCMLXXI"
2020	"MMXX"

Algorithm You must pay particular attention to the addition rule described in section 2.1.1: The relevant value is normally obtained by adding the individual digits' values from left to right whenever a larger character precedes a smaller one. However, if a smaller number character precedes a larger one, the corresponding value is subtracted.

With this knowledge, you traverse the characters from right to left and look up the relevant value in a dictionary. To decide between addition or subtraction, remember the last relevant character.

```python
def from_roman_number(roman_number):
    value = 0
    last_digit_value = 0

    # for i in range(len(roman_number) - 1, -1, -1):
    #     roman_digit = roman_number[i]
    for roman_digit in reversed(roman_number):
        digit_value = value_map[roman_digit]

        add_mode = digit_value >= last_digit_value
        if add_mode:
```

---

[5] For syntactically invalid Roman numbers, such as IXD, an incorrect result, here 489, can be computed by applying subtraction rule twice in a row: 0 − 1 − 10 + 500.

```
            value += digit_value
            last_digit_value = digit_value
        else:
            value -= digit_value

    return value

value_map = {"I": 1, "V": 5, "X": 10, "L": 50,
             "C": 100, "D": 500, "M": 1000}
```

In the code, I use a nicer variant of the traversal. Using the standard functionality `reversed()`, you get an iterator that traverses the data in the opposite direction and provides access to the respective element. Shown in the comment is index-based processing, which is a little less Python-like (Pythonic).

Solution 7b: Decimal Numbers ➤ Roman Numbers (★★★★☆)

Write function `to_roman_number(value)` that converts a decimal number to a (valid) Roman number.

Algorithm When converting a decimal number to a Roman numeral, you again use a dictionary. You sort this in descending order so that the largest value (1000) is at the beginning. The current number value is divided by this factor. This yields the number of required repetitions of this value. Now the remainder is determined by modulo. The procedure is repeated until all values are checked and the remainder is greater than 0. In the following, the procedure is shown for the number 7:

```
7 =>  7 / 1000 => 0 => 0 x 'M'
         ...
         7 / 5 = 1 => 1 x 'V'
         7 % 5 = 2
         2 / 1 = 2 => 2 x 'I'
         2 % 1 = 0
    => 'VII'
```

The procedure is implemented in Python as follows (please note that a little pitfall is included):

```
def to_roman_number(value):
    result = ""
```

```
    remainder = value

    # descending order => start with largest value
    for i in sorted(int_to_roman_digit_map.keys(), reverse=True):
        if remainder > 0:
            multiplier = i
            roman_digit = int_to_roman_digit_map[i]

            times = remainder // multiplier
            remainder = remainder % multiplier
            result += roman_digit * times

    return result

int_to_roman_digit_map = {1: "I", 5: "V", 10: "X", 50: "L",
                          100: "C", 500: "D", 1000: "M"}
```

Here again the function divmod() is a good choice. Then the invocation

```
times = remainder // multiplier
remainder = remainder % multiplier
```

results in the following one-liner:

```
times, remainder = divmod(remainder, multiplier)
```

However, the conversion shown above is not yet 100 % correct because it does not respect the rule of three and also repeats digits four times. Try it yourself using 147 as input, resulting in CXXXXVII. To fix this problem, you may think about implementing special treatments that are only hinted at below:

```
multiplier = i
roman_digit = int_to_roman_digit_map[i]

if remainder >= 900 and roman_digit == 'D':
    result += "CM"
    remainder -= 900}
# ...
elif remainder >= 4 and roman_digit == 'I':
    result += "IV"
    remainder -= 4
```

```
else:
    times = remainder / multiplier
    remainder = remainder % multiplier

    result += roman_digit * times
```

However, this quickly becomes confusing.

More elegant is the insertion of other lookup values for the exceptional cases:

```
int_to_roman_digit_map = {1: "I", 4: "IV", 5: "V", 9: "IX", 10: "X",
                        40: "XL", 50: "L", 90: "XC", 100: "C",
                        400: "CD", 500: "D", 900: "CM", 1000: "M"}
```

Using this enhanced lookup dictionary solves the problem and you get correct answers.

Verification

Let's start the unit test with different values that show the correct conversion, especially including the four values 17, 444, 1971, and 2020 from the example:

```
def arabic_to_roman_number_map():
    return [(1, "I"), (2, "II"), (3, "III"), (4, "IV"),
            (5, "V"), (7, "VII"), (9, "IX"), (17, "XVII"),
            (40, "XL"), (90, "XC"), (400, "CD"), (444, "CDXLIV"),
            (500, "D"), (900, "CM"), (1000, "M"), (1666, "MDCLXVI"),
            (1971, "MCMLXXI"), (2018, "MMXVIII"), (2019, "MMXIX"),
            (2020, "MMXX"), (3000, "MMM")]
```

```
# attention different order, so you do not have to define it twice
@pytest.mark.parametrize("expected, roman_number",
                        arabic_to_roman_number_map())
def test_from_roman_number(roman_number, expected):
    assert from_roman_number(roman_number) == expected
```

Now let's take a look at how the testing of the reverse direction is accomplished. Here you already benefit from the previously defined function arabic_to_roman_number_map() to provide the test results.

```python
@pytest.mark.parametrize("roman_number, expected",
                              arabic_to_roman_number_map())
def test_to_roman_number(roman_number, expected):
    assert to_roman_number(roman_number) == expected
```

Without the extraction of the values into a list of tuples, there would have been a duplication of the specifications. Only when specifying expected and roman_number, you have to be a bit careful because this is a bidirectional mapping.

Providing data in a CSV file To avoid duplication, you could also read the values from a file. With the help of the csv module, reading from a CSV file is implemented as follows:

```python
def arabic_to_roman_number_map():
    result = []
    with open('arabicroman2.csv','rt') as file:
        data = csv.reader(file)

        skip_first = True
        for row in data:
            if not skip_first:
                result.append((int(row[0].strip()), row[1].strip()))
            skip_first = False

    return result
```

Assume that the content has the correct structure, as shown below. Furthermore, the CSV file looks like the following:

```
arabic,roman
1, I
2, II
3, III
4, IV
5, V
7, VII
...
```

2.3.8 Solution 8: Combinatorics (★★☆☆☆)

Solution 8a: Computation of $a^2 + b^2 = c^2$

Compute all combinations of the values a, b, and c (each starting from 1 and less than 100) for which the following formula holds:

$$a^2 + b^2 = c^2$$

Algorithm The brute force solution uses three nested loops and then checks if the above formula is satisfied.

```python
# brute force, three nested loops
def solve_quadratic_simple():
    for a in range(1, 100):
        for b in range(1, 100):
            for c in range(1, 100):
                # if a ** 2 + b ** 2 == c ** 2:
                # if pow(a, 2) + pow(b, 2) == pow(c, 2):
                if a * a + b * b == c * c:
                    print("a =", a, "/ b =", b, "/ c =", c)
```

For squaring, simple multiplication provides better readability than the use of pow() or of the operator ** implied in the comment.

Python shortcut By using list comprehension, you can have all tuples generated. However, such construction is already a bit stylistically dubious.

```python
def solve_quadratic_shorter():
    return [(a,b,c) for a in range(1, 100) for b in range(1, 100)
                    for c in range(1, 100) if a * a + b * b == c * c]
```

Bonus: Reduce the Running Time of $O(n^3)$ to $O(n^2)$ (★★★☆☆)

You see three nested loops in the upper solution, resulting in a running time of $O(n^3)$. Now let's reduce this to $O(n^2)$. To achieve this, apply the following transformation (resolving to c):

$$c = \sqrt{a*a + b*b}$$

Based on this transformation or resolution of the equation to *c*, the square root is calculated and then the formula is verified:

```python
import math

def solve_quadratic():
    for a in range(1, 100):
        for b in range(1, 100):
            c = int(math.sqrt(a * a + b * b))
            if a * a + b * b == c * c:
                print("a =", a, "/ b =", b, "/ c =", c)
```

This solution still contains a small flaw. Now *c* can also be greater than 100! Therefore, you must ensure that *c* is below 100. To this end, you supplement the check as follows:

```python
def solve_quadratic():
    for a in range(1, 100):
        for b in range(1, 100):
            c = int(math.sqrt(a * a + b * b))
            if c < 100 and a * a + b * b == c * c:
                print("a =", a, "/ b =", b, "/ c =", c)
```

Verification

For testing, call the function `solve_quadratic()` and perform the computation for some values:

```python
>>> solve_quadratic()
a = 3 / b = 4 / c = 5
a = 4 / b = 3 / c = 5
a = 5 / b = 12 / c = 13
a = 6 / b = 8 / c = 10
...
```

NOTE: WHY DOES THE COMPUTATION WORK AT ALL?

Looking only briefly at the conversion, you might wonder why the computation does not yield a successful comparison for all values. In fact, this would be the case purely mathematically, since you are deriving c from a and b. However, you also use a cast to an int.

```
c = int(math.sqrt(a * a + b * b))
if a * a + b * b == c * c:
    print("a =", a, "/ b =", b, "/ c =", c)
```

As a result, the decimal digits are truncated. This, in turn, leads to the comparison being successful only for certain values.

Solution 8b: Computation of $a^2 + b^2 = c^2 + d^2$

Compute all combinations of the values a, b, c, and d (each starting from 1 and less than 100) for which the following formula holds:

$$a^2 + b^2 = c^2 + d^2$$

Algorithm Analogous to the previous part of the exercise, the brute force solution consists of four nested loops. Therein a check whether the above formula is satisfied is performed. In this particular case, the simple multiplication offers, to my taste, slightly better readability than the use of the operator **.

```
# brute force, four nested loops
def solve_cubic_simple():
    for a in range(1, 100):
        for b in range(1, 100):
            for c in range(1, 100):
                for d in range(1, 100):
                    if a * a + b * b == c * c + d * d:
                        print("a =", a, " / b =", b, " / c =", c,
                        " / d =", d)
```

Python shortcut By using list comprehension, you can have all tuples generated, although such a structure is already stylistically a bit questionable, since it is slightly too complex:

```python
def solve_cubic_shorter():
    return [(a, b, c, d)
            for a in range(1, 100) for b in range(1, 100)
            for c in range(1, 100) for d in range(1, 100)
            if a * a + b * b == c * c + d * d]
```

Please note that both variants are not optimal in respect to performance. The next task is to improve this.

Bonus: Reduce the Running Time of $O(n^4)$ to $O(n^3)$ (★★★☆☆)

As can easily be seen, the solution uses four nested loops, resulting in a running time of $O(n^4)$. Now you want to reduce this to $O(n^3)$. For that purpose, use transformations. First, you separate to d and then you resolve to d:

$$d*d = a*a + b*b - c*c \Rightarrow d = \sqrt{a*a + b*b - c*c}$$

Based on this transformation or resolution of the equation to d, you can compute the square root and then validate the formula. Additionally, you must ensure that the value is not negative and the resulting d is below 100.

```python
import math

def solve_cubic():
    for a in range(1, 100):
        for b in range(1, 100):
            for c in range(1, 100):
                value = a * a + b * b - c * c
                if value > 0:
                    d = int(math.sqrt(value))
                    if d < 100 and a * a + b * b == c * c + d * d:
                        print("a =", a, " / b =", b, " / c =", c,
                        " / d =", d)
```

Verification

For testing, use a function call and check some of the values:

```
>>> solve_cubic()
a = 1 / b = 1 / c = 1 / d = 1
a = 1 / b = 2 / c = 1 / d = 2
a = 1 / b = 2 / c = 2 / d = 1
a = 1 / b = 3 / c = 1 / d = 3
a = 1 / b = 3 / c = 3 / d = 1
...
```

2.3.9 Solution 9: Armstrong Numbers (★★☆☆☆)

This exercise deals with three-digit Armstrong numbers. By definition, these are numbers for whose digits x, y, and z from 1 to 9 satisfy the following equation:

$$x*100+y*10+z = x^3 + y^3 + z^3$$

Write function `calc_armstrong_numbers()` to compute all Armstrong numbers for x, y, and z (each < 10).

Examples

$$153 = 1*100+5*10+3 = 1^3 + 5^3 + 3^3 = 1+125+27 = 153$$
$$371 = 3*100+7*10+1 = 3^3 + 7^3 + 1^3 = 27+343+1 = 371$$

Algorithm Iterate through all combinations of three-digit numbers using three nested loops. The numeric value is calculated based on the position using the formula $x*100+ y*10 + z$. Also, compute the third power for each digit, sum them, and check if the sum matches the number.

```python
def calc_armstrong_numbers():
    results = []

    for x in range(1, 10):
        for y in range(1, 10):
            for z in range(1, 10):
                numeric_value = x * 100 + y * 10 + z
```

```
        cubic_value = int(pow(x, 3) + pow(y, 3) + pow(z, 3))

        if numeric_value == cubic_value:
            results.append(numeric_value)

return results
```

NOTE: WHY DON'T THE LOOPS START AT 0?

Although you could also use the value 0, this is unusual. In the first place, a value assignment with $x = 0$ and $y = 0$ would correspond to the value z. However, there is another reason not to start with 0. A leading 0 is used to mark octal numbers, so we will not use it here. By the way, since Python 3.8, octal numbers start with the prefix 0o.

Verification

To test, call the above method and examine whether the two combinations of values given as examples are included in the result list:

```
def test_calc_armstrong_numbers():
    assert calc_armstrong_numbers() == [153, 371]
```

Bonus (★★★☆☆)

Find a generic version with functions or lambdas and then try the following three formulas:

$$x*100 + y*10 + z = x^3 + y^3 + z^3$$
$$x*100 + y*10 + z = x^1 + y^2 + z^3$$
$$x*100 + y*10 + z = x^3 + y^2 + z^1$$

Algorithm Instead of the concrete calculation, you invoke a matching cubic_function:

```
def calc_numbers(cubic_function):
    results = []
    for x in range(1, 10):
        for y in range(1, 10):
            for z in range(1, 10):
                numeric_value = x * 100 + y * 10 + z
```

```
            cubic_value = int(cubic_function(x, y, z))
            if numeric_value == cubic_value:
                results.append(numeric_value)
    return results
```

Thus, the computation can be expressed as a function or a lambda. Please note that lambdas usually encapsulate only a tiny piece of functionality and thus you should not name them and assign them to a variable. In this book, I sometimes break this PEP-8 rule for a better insight into how things work or express more clearly what was intended.

```
def special(x,y,z):
    return int(pow(x, 3) + pow(y, 3) + pow(z, 3))

special_as_lambda = lambda x, y, z: int(pow(x, 3) + pow(y, 3) + pow(z, 3))
```

Based on this more general solution, you can now easily try other variants of computation rules without much effort:

```
def special2(x, y, z):
    return int(pow(x, 1) + pow(y, 2) + pow(z, 3))
```

Likewise, you finally define the following:

```
def special3(x, y, z):
    return int(pow(x, 3) + pow(y, 2) + pow(z, 1))
```

Verification

For testing, you invoke above function with different computation rules and look for that of Armstrong numbers whether the two combinations of values given as examples are included in the result list:

```
>>> def special(x,y,z):
...     return int(pow(x, 3) + pow(y, 3) + pow(z, 3))
...
>>> print(calc_numbers(special))
[153, 371]

>>> def special2(x,y,z):
...     return int(pow(x, 1) + pow(y, 2) + pow(z, 3))
```

```
...
>>> print(calc_numbers(special2))
[135, 175, 518, 598]

>>> special3 = lambda x, y, z: int(pow(x, 3) + pow(y, 2) + pow(z, 1))
>>> print(calc_numbers(special3))
[]
```

2.3.10 Solution 10: Max Change Calculator (★★★★☆)

Suppose you have a collection of coins or numbers of different values. Write function
`calc_max_possible_change(values)` that determines, for positive integers, what
amounts can be *seamlessly* generated with it starting from the value 1. The maximum
value should be returned as a result.

Examples

Input	Possible values	Maximum
1	1	1
1, 1	1, 2	2
1, 5	1	1
1, 2, 4	1, 2, 3, 4, 5, 6, 7	7
1, 2, 3, 7	1, 2, 3, 4, 5, 6, 7, 8, 9, 10, 11, 12, 13	13
1, 1, 1, 1, 5, 10, 20, 50	1, 2, 3, 4, 5, 6, ... , 30, ... , 39	39

Algorithm You could try solving this exercise by computing a mapping to all
permutations of the sum of the numbers, but this gets complex fast. Let's consider
another approach and start sorting the values for ease of use.

Input	Possible values	Maximum
1, 2, 3, 7	1, 2, 3, 4, 5, 6, 7, 8, 9, 10, 11, 12, 13	13
1, 2, 3, 8	1, 2, 3, 4, 5, 6, => _ <= , 8, 9, 10, 11, 12, 13, 14	6

If you take a look at the two examples, you may recognize for the cases 1, 2, 3, 7 and 1, 2, 3, 8 the clue to simplify the calculation decisively. Instead of always calculating all permutations and then checking for a gap in the number line, here indicated by an underscore (_), it is possible to start at the first number, always add the numbers to the previous sum, and repeat this iteratively until *next_number* > *sum* + 1 becomes true.

Let's apply this to Python. First, sort the input values. Start with the assumption that there is nothing to change initially, so *max_possible_change* = 0. Now check the following condition for each value. If *current_value* > *max_possible_change* + *1* holds, then it is impossible to change. Otherwise, add the current value to *max_possible_change*. Repeat this until all values are processed or until the termination condition is met. This leads to the following implementation:

```python
def calc_max_possible_change(values):
    # wrappng / copying necessary so that we do not sort the original
    sorted_numbers = list(values)
    sorted_numbers.sort()

    max_possible_change = 0

    for current_value in sorted_numbers:
        if current_value > max_possible_change + 1:
            break

        max_possible_change += current_value

    return max_possible_change
```

Verification

For testing, use the following inputs, which show the correct operation:

```python
@pytest.mark.parametrize("coins, max_change",
                [([1], 1),
                 ([1, 1], 2),
                 ([1, 5], 1),
                 ([1, 2, 4], 7),
                 ([1, 2, 3, 7], 13),
                 ([1, 2, 3, 8], 6),
```

```
                    ([1, 1, 1, 1, 5, 10, 20, 50], 39)])
def test_calc_max_possible_change(coins, max_change):
    assert calc_max_possible_change(coins) == max_change
```

2.3.11 Solution 11: Related Numbers (★★☆☆☆)

Two numbers n_1 and n_2 are called friends (or related) if the sum of their divisors is equal to the other number:

$$sum(divisors(n1)) = n_2$$

$$sum(divisors(n2)) = n_1$$

Write method function `calc_friends(max_exclusive)` to compute all friends numbers up to a passed maximum value.

Examples

Input	Divisors
$\sum(divisors(220)) = 284$	div(220) = 1, 2, 4, 5, 10, 11, 20, 22, 44, 55, 110
$\sum(divisors(284)) = 220$	div(284) = 1, 2, 4, 71, 142
$\sum(divisors(1184)) = 1210$	div(1184) = 1, 2, 4, 8, 16, 32, 37, 74, 148, 296, 592
$\sum(divisors(1210)) = 1184$	div(1210) = 1, 2, 5, 10, 11, 22, 55, 110, 121, 242, 605

Algorithm It is easy to check whether two numbers are friends by determining for each number its divisors and therefrom its sum. Now the divisors can be determined from this sum and then added together. If this second sum is equal to the original number, then the numbers are friends.

```
def calc_friends(max_exclusive):
    friends = {}

    for i in range(2, max_exclusive):
        divisors1 = find_proper_divisors(i)
        sum_div1 = sum(divisors1)
        divisors2 = find_proper_divisors(sum_div1)
```

```
    sum_div2 = sum(divisors2)

    if i == sum_div2 and sum_div1 != sum_div2:
        friends[i] = sum_div1

return friends
```

For the implementation, you also use the function `find_proper_divisors()` to find all real divisors. This was already presented in the introduction. Once again, it shows the advantage of subdividing software into smaller, self-contained functionalities.

Verification

In this case, you again use a parameterized test, which returns both the maximum value and a dictionary with the two numbers:

```
@pytest.mark.parametrize("max, friends",
                        [(250, {220: 284}),
                         (300, {220: 284, 284: 220}),
                         (2_000, {220: 284, 284: 220,
                                  1_184: 1_210, 1_210: 1_184})])
def test_calc_friends(max, friends):
    assert calc_friends(max) == friends
```

For some numbers I use the notation of separating the digits with an underscore, which is an excellent way to simulate a thousand point. This is especially helpful with larger numbers and serves here only for demonstration.

2.3.12 Solution 12: Prime Factorization (★★★☆☆)

Any natural number greater than 1 can be represented as a multiplication of primes. Remember the fact that 2 is also a prime. Write function `calc_prime_factors(value)` that returns a list of prime numbers whose multiplication yields the desired number.

Examples

Input	Prime factors	Result
8	2 * 2 * 2	[2, 2, 2]
14	2 * 7	[2, 7]
42	2 * 3 * 7	[2, 3, 7]
1155	3 * 5 * 7 * 11	[3, 5, 7, 11]
2222	2 * 11 * 101	[2, 11, 101]

Algorithm Start by dividing the number by 2 as long as the number is even and greater than 2. Then, at some point, you reach an odd number. If it is 1, you are done (see the case for the number 8). Otherwise, you check if the odd number is a prime number and collect it. In this case, you are done (for example, above for the number 14). If not, you have to split the odd number further. Let's take 50 as an example. First, you divide by 2, there 25 remains, which is not a prime number. For these, you check for all prime numbers if they represent a divisor. You continue this procedure until you reach the number 1, which means that all divisors have been collected. For more info, see https://en.wikipedia.org/wiki/Integer_factorization.

```
def calc_prime_factors(value):
    all_primes = calc_primes_up_to(value)

    prime_factors = []
    remaining_value = value

    # as long as even, divide by 2 again and again
    while remaining_value % 2 == 0 and remaining_value >= 2:
        remaining_value = remaining_value // 2
        prime_factors.append(2)

    # check remainder for prime
    if is_prime(all_primes, remaining_value):
        prime_factors.append(remaining_value)
    else:
        # remainder is not a prime number, further check
        while remaining_value > 1:
```

```
        for current_prime in all_primes:
            if remaining_value % current_prime == 0:
                remaining_value = remaining_value // current_prime
                prime_factors.append(current_prime)
                # start again from the beginning, because every divisor
                # may occur more than once
                break

    return prime_factors

def is_prime(all_primes, n):
    return n in all_primes
```

Optimized algorithm If you look at the algorithm just developed, you might be bothered by all the special treatments. With a little thought, you may conclude that you don't need to check number 2 separately since it is also a prime number. Thus, this is covered by the while loop. Instead of the break for repeated checking of the same number, this can be expressed in a more stylistically pleasing way with a while loop. With these preliminary considerations, you arrive at the following implementation:

```
def calc_prime_factors_optimized(value):
    all_primes = calc_primes_up_to(value)

    prime_factors = []

    remaining_value = value
    while remaining_value > 1:
        for current_prime in all_primes:
            while remaining_value % current_prime == 0:
                remaining_value = remaining_value // current_prime
                prime_factors.append(current_prime)

    return prime_factors
```

Verification

For testing, use the following inputs, which show the correct operation:

```python
def value_and_prime_factors():
    return [(8, [2, 2, 2]),
            (14, [2, 7]),
            (42, [2, 3, 7]),
            (1155, [3, 5, 7, 11]),
            (2222, [2, 11, 101])]

@pytest.mark.parametrize("value, primefactors",
                         value_and_prime_factors())
def test_calc_prime_factors(value, primefactors):
    assert calc_prime_factors(value) == primefactors

@pytest.mark.parametrize("value, primefactors",
                         value_and_prime_factors())
def test_calc_prime_factors_optimized(value, primefactors):
    assert calc_prime_factors_optimized(value) == primefactors
```

2.4 Summary: What You Learned

This chapter on basic mathematical knowledge introduces the modulo operator, which is quite essential, for example, for the extraction of digits and in the calculation of checksums. The exercises on combinatorics have shown how small tricks can easily reduce the running time by an order of magnitude. Also, prime numbers offer some interesting facets, such as variants to their calculation. In retrospect, this turns out to be much easier than perhaps first thought. In general, when trying to find a solution for a problem, the algorithm and the approach should be roughly understood because then, for example, even the the decomposition into prime factors loses its possible horror.

Now let's move on to recursion as an important technique to break down a more complex task into several simpler subtasks.

## CHAPTER 3

Recursion

In nature and mathematics, you can find the topic ***self-similarity*** or recurring structures, such as snowflakes, fractals, and Julia sets, which are interesting graphical formations. In this context, one speaks of ***recursion***, meaning that things repeat or resemble each other. Related to methods, this means that they call themselves. Important therefore is a termination condition in the form of special input values, which leads to the end of the self calls.

3.1 Introduction

Various computations can be described as recursive functions. The goal is to break down a more complex task into several simpler subtasks.

3.1.1 Mathematical Examples

Below you will take a look at the computation of the factorial, summation, and Fibonacci numbers, three introductory examples for recursive definitions.

Example 1: Factorial

Mathematically, the ***factorial*** for a positive number n is defined as the product (i. e., the multiplication) of all natural numbers from 1 to n, inclusive. For notation, the exclamation mark is placed after the corresponding number. For example, 5! stands for the factorial of the number 5:

$$5! = 5 * 4 * 3 * 2 * 1 = 120$$

This can be generalized as follows:

$$n! = n * (n-1) * (n-2) * \ldots * 2 * 1$$

© Michael Inden 2022
M. Inden, *Python Challenges*, https://doi.org/10.1007/978-1-4842-7398-2_3

Based on this, the recursive definition is derived:

$$n! = \begin{cases} 1, & n=0, n=1 \\ n.(n-1)!, & \forall n > 1 \end{cases}$$

Here, the inverted »A« ($\forall$) denotes *for all*.

For the first n, you get the following value progression:

n	1	2	3	4	5	6	7	8
n!	1	2	6	24	120	720	5040	40320

Calculation of the factorial in Python Let's take a quick look at how the recursive calculation formula of the factorial can be transferred into a function of the same kind:

```python
def factorial(n):
    if n < 0:
        raise ValueError("n must be >= 0")

    # recursive termination
    if n == 0 or n == 1:
        return 1

    # recursive descent
    return n * factorial(n - 1)
```

Figure 3-1 clarifies what this recursive definition generates in terms of calls.

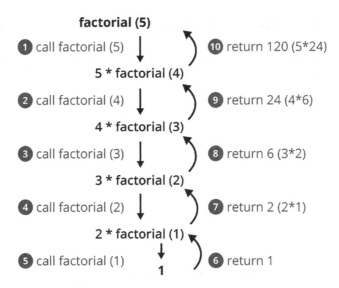

Figure 3-1. *Recursive calls to* factorial(5)

Python shortcut To demonstrate that Python can be used to write compact source code, I will repeatedly show which shortcuts exist in the following sections. In this case, you can write the calculation in the form of a lambda as a one-liner. The brevity often offers some disadvantages: Here there is no handling of wrong inputs and the whole thing is a little bit less readable. All in all, the distinction between recursive termination and descent is more challenging to recognize. In addition, the mathematical formula is not so clearly evident:

```
factorial = lambda n: n if n == 1 else n * factorial(n - 1)
```

Please note that lambdas usually encapsulate only a tiny piece of functionality and thus you should not name them and assign them to a variable. In this book, I sometimes break this PEP-8 rule for a better insight into how things work or to express more clearly what was intended.

There are almost always many ways to Rome and the solution. As a variant, I present the function reduce() from the module functools, which requires an import as shown below. However, no recursion is used and the readability decreases, which can be compensated by a meaningful function name.

```
import functools

def factorial(n):
    return functools.reduce(lambda n_1, n: n_1 * n, range(1, n + 1))
```

Example 2: Calculation of the Sum of Numbers Up to *n*

Mathematically, the **sum** for a number *n* is defined as the addition of all natural numbers from 1 ascending up to and including *n*:

$$\sum_{1}^{n} i = n + n - 1 + n - 2 + \ldots + 2 + 1$$

This can be defined recursively as follows:

$$\sum_{1}^{n} i = \begin{cases} 1, & n = 1 \\ n + \sum_{1}^{n-1} i, & \forall n > 1 \end{cases}$$

For the first *n*, you get the following value progression:

n	1	2	3	4	5	6	7	8
sum_of(n)	1	3	6	10	15	21	28	36

Calculation of the sum in Python Again, you convert the recursive calculation formula of the summation into a recursive function:

```python
def sum_of(n):
    if n <= 0:
        raise ValueError("n must be >= 1")

    # recursive termination
    if n == 1:
        return 1

    # recursive descent
    return n + sum_of(n - 1)
```

Python shortcut For the calculation of sums it is possible to use a lambda, but again without error handling and a bit less readable:

```python
sum_of = lambda n: n if n == 1 else n + sum_of(n - 1)
```

Likewise, the function `reduce()` from the module `functools` can be used, with the disadvantages and possibilities hinted at earlier to compensate:

```python
import functools

def sum_of_with_reduce(n):
    return functools.reduce(lambda n_1, n: n_1 + n, range(1, n + 1))
```

Optimized calculation of the sum Please keep in mind that the algorithms presented here only served to illustrate the recursive nature or the functionalities from the Python standard library. However, because there is a formula for calculating the sum of the numbers from 1 to n that determines the whole thing performance-optimally in $O(1)$, you should not use the previous variants in practice:

$$\sum_1^n i = \frac{(n+1) * n}{2}$$

Example 3: Fibonacci Numbers

Fibonacci numbers are also excellent for recursive definitions, although the formula is already a tiny bit more complex:

$$fib(n) = \begin{cases} 1, & n=1 \\ 1, & n=2 \\ fib(n-1) + fib(n-2), & \forall n > 2 \end{cases}$$

For the first n, you get the following value progression:

n	1	2	3	4	5	6	7	8
fib(n)	1	1	2	3	5	8	13	21

If the calculation formula is visualized graphically, it quickly becomes obvious how wide the tree of self calls potentially spans. For larger n, the call tree would be much more expansive, as indicated by the dashed arrows (see Figure 3-2). Even with this exemplary invocation, it is evident that various calls are made several times, for example for $fib(n-4)$ and $fib(n-2)$, but especially three times for $fib(n-3)$. This very quickly leads to costly and tedious computations. You will learn how to optimize this later in section 7.1.

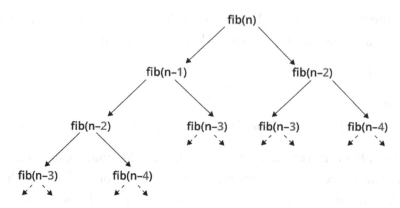

Figure 3-2. *Fibonacci recursive*

HINT: DIFFERENT DEFINITION WITH ZERO AS THE START VALUE

It should furthermore be noted that there is a variation that starts at the value of 0. Then $fib(0)$ = 0 and $fib(1) = 1$ are the base values and afterwards you get $fib(n) = fib(n − 1) + fib(n − 2)$ according to the recursive definition. This produces the same sequence of numbers as the definition above, only with the value for 0 added.

ATTENTION: RESTRICTED CALL DEPTH

Keep in mind that self calls happen again and again for summing up and computing the Fibonacci numbers. That's why you can only pass inputs around 990 here. Larger values will result in a RecursionError: maximum recursion depth exceeded. For other recursive functions, there are similar restrictions on the number of self calls. Other programming languages like Java allow significantly more self calls. In Java, over 10,000 self calls are easily possible.

There are several variants in recursion. An advantageous one is called tail-recursive. This is characterized by the fact that the recursive call is the last action in the calculation. Such functions can be processed without the otherwise usual storing of intermediate results on a stack.

3.1.2 Algorithmic Examples

In the introduction, you looked at mathematical examples. But recursion is also very well suited for algorithmic tasks. For example, it is possible to check for an array or list whether the values stored form a palindrome. A palindrome is a word that reads the same from the front and the back, such as OTTO or ABBA. Here it is meant that the elements match pairwise from the front and the back. This applies, for example, to a list with the following values: { 1, 2, 3, 2, 1 }.

Example 1: Palindrome—Recursive Variant

You can easily test for a palindrome property recursively. Let's look at this as a program after I have briefly described the algorithm.

Algorithm If the array or list has the length 0 or 1, then it is a palindrome by definition. If the length is two and greater, you must check the outer left and outer right elements for a match. After that, a copy of the array or the list is created, shortened by one position at the front and one at the back. Further checking is then performed on the remaining part of the array or the list, as shown in the following code:

```
def is_palindrome_simple_recursive(values):
    # recursive termination
    if len(values) <= 1:
        return True

    left = 0
    right = len(values) - 1

    if values[left] == values[right]:
        # attention: end is exclusive
        remainder = values[left + 1 : right]

        # recursive descent
        return is_palindrome_simple_recursive(remainder)

    return False
```

However, the described and implemented approach leads to many copies and extractions of subarrays or sublists. It is affordable to avoid this effort by keeping the idea but modifying the algorithm minimally by using a trick.

Optimized algorithm Rather than using a copy, you still use the original data structure. You include two position markers left and right, which initially span the entire array or list. Now you check if the left and right values referenced by these positions match. If this is the case, the position markers are moved inward by one position on both sides, and the whole procedure is called recursively. This is repeated until the left position pointer reaches or skips the right one.

The implementation changes as follows:

```python
def is_palindrome_recursive_optimized(values):
    return is_palindrome_recursive_in_range(values, 0, len(values) - 1)

def is_palindrome_recursive_in_range(values, left, right):
    # recursive termination
    if left >= right:
        return True

    if values[left] == values[right]:
        # recursive descent
        return is_palindrome_recursive_in_range(values, left + 1,
        right - 1)

    return False
```

Perhaps you wonder why I don't write the process more compactly and even use less return statements. My main concern in presenting algorithms is comprehensibility. Multiple returns are really only a problem if a function is very long and confusing.

HINT: AUXILIARY FUNCTIONS FOR FACILITATING RECURSION

The idea of position pointers in arrays, lists, or strings is a common tool used in solutions to recursion for optimization and avoidance of, say, array copying. To prevent the whole thing becoming inconvenient for callers, it is a good idea to have a high-level function calling a helper function that has additional parameters. This allows you to include certain information in the recursive descent. In this example, these are the left and right limits, so that potentially costly copying can be eliminated. Many subsequent examples will take advantage of the general idea.

Example 1: Palindrome—Iterative Variant

Although a recursive definition of an algorithm is sometimes quite elegant, the recursive descent produces self calls. This potentially creates quite a bit of overhead. Conveniently, any recursive algorithm can be converted into an iterative one. Let's look at this for the palindrome calculation. You use two position pointers for the iterative conversion—instead of the recursive descent, you use a while loop. This terminates when all elements have been checked or if a mismatch has been detected before.

```python
def is_palindrome_iterative(values):
    left = 0
    right = len(values) - 1

    same_value = True
    while left < right and same_value:
        same_value = values[left] == values[right]
        left += 1
        right -= 1

    return same_value
```

Again, a note on compactness: This function could be written as follows, omitting the auxiliary variable:

```python
def is_palindrome_iterative_compact(values):
    left = 0
    right = len(values) - 1

    while left < right and values[left] == values[right]:
        left += 1
        right -= 1

    # left >= right or values[left] != values[right]
    return left >= right
```

The return value is determined by the condition implied by the comment, if *left* >= *right* holds, then values is not a palindrome. With this variant, however, you have to think much more about the return. Again, I prefer understandability and maintainability over brevity or performance.

Python shortcut Of course, the whole thing can be achieved much more easily by calling the built-in functionality [::-1]. This produces a string or list (or even an array) with the letters or elements in reverse order. I discuss this feature of Python called slicing later in Chapters 4 and 5. Let's return to the exercise of checking the palindrome property of a list, which can be written exceptionally compactly with slicing:

```python
def is_palindrome_shorter(values):
    return values == values[::-1]
```

Also, consider for this variant that in the presumably rare case of enormous amounts of data, an inverse variant of the original list is generated here. Thus, the memory is required twice.

Example 2: Fractal Generation

As mentioned in the beginning, recursion allows you to create graphics as well. In the following, a graphically simple variant is displayed, which is based on the subdivisions of a ruler:

```
-
==
-
===
-
==
-
```

This can be implemented with a two times recursive descent as follows:

```python
def fractal_generator(n):
    if n < 1:
        return
    if n == 1:
        print("-")
    else:
        fractal_generator(n - 1)
        print("=" * n)
        fractal_generator(n - 1)
```

If you use more complex drawing functions instead of ASCII characters, you can use recursion to create exciting and appealing shapes, for example the snowflake in Figure 3-3.

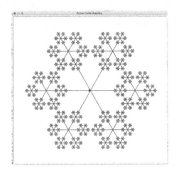

Figure 3-3. *Recursive graphic with draw_snowflake( )*

This stylized representation of a snowflake can be implemented as follows:

```python
import turtle

def draw_snowflake(turtle, length, depth):
    # recursive termination
    if depth == 0:
        return

    for _ in range(6):
        turtle.right(60)
        turtle.forward(length)

        # recursive descent
        draw_snowflake(turtle, length // 3, depth - 1)

        turtle.back(length)

screen = turtle.Screen()
turtle.speed(10)
draw_snowflake(turtle, 240, 5)
screen.exitonclick()
```

3.1.3 Steps When Multiplying the Digits of a Number

To conclude the algorithmic examples, I would like to clarify the individual steps and self calls once more. As an artificial example, use the multiplication of the digits of a number, also called cross product, for example for the value $257 \Rightarrow 2 * 5 * 7 = 10 * 7 = 70$. Using modulo, the extraction of the individual digits and their multiplication can be implemented quite simply as follows:

```
def multiply_all_digits(value):
    remainder = value // 10
    digit_value = value % 10
    print("multiply_all_digits: %-10d | remainder: %d, digit: %d" %
        (value, remainder, digit_value))

    if remainder > 0:
        result = multiply_all_digits(remainder)
        print("-> %d * %d = %d" % (digit_value, result, digit_value *
        result))
        return digit_value * result
    else:
        print("-> " + str(value))
        return value
```

Let's look at the outputs for the two numbers 1234 and 257:

```
>>> multiply_all_digits(1234)
multiply_all_digits: 1234        | remainder: 123, digit: 4
multiply_all_digits: 123         | remainder: 12, digit: 3
multiply_all_digits: 12          | remainder: 1, digit: 2
multiply_all_digits: 1           | remainder: 0, digit: 1
-> 1
-> 2 * 1 = 2
-> 3 * 2 = 6
-> 4 * 6 = 24
24
```

```
>>> multiply_all_digits(257)
multiply_all_digits: 257        | remainder: 25, digit: 7
multiply_all_digits: 25         | remainder: 2, digit: 5
multiply_all_digits: 2          | remainder: 0, digit: 2
-> 2
-> 5 * 2 = 10
-> 7 * 10 = 70
70
```

It is clearly visible how the recursive calls happen with a continuously shorter sequence of numbers. Finally, the result is constructed or calculated based on the last digit in the other direction.

Python shortcut Again, the whole thing can be accomplished much more easily by calling the functionality `reduce()` from module `functools` Still, the point here is to get acquainted with the recursive description of multiplying the digits of a number:

```
import functools

def multiply_all_digits_shorter(value):
    return functools.reduce(lambda x, y: int(x) * int(y), str(value))
```

3.1.4 Typical Problems: Endless Calls and RecursionError

Recursion often allows problems to be expressed and implemented in an understandable way. A detail worth knowing is that the self calls lead to them being stored temporarily on the stack. For each function call, a so-called stack frame containing information about the called function and its parameters is stored on the stack. The stack is, however, limited in its size. Thus only a finite number of nested function calls can take place—usually around 990. This was already discussed briefly in a practical tip.

A huge number of recursive calls can result in a `RecursionError: maximum recursion depth exceeded`. Sometimes the problem occurs because there is no termination condition in the recursion or the condition is formulated incorrectly.

```
# attention: deliberately wrong for demonstration
def infinite_recursion(value):
    infinite_recursion(value)

def factorial_no_abortion(number):
    return number * factorial_no_abortion(number - 1)
```

Sometimes the call is also just wrong, simply because no decreased value is passed:

```
# attention: deliberately wrong for demonstration
def factorial_wrong_call(n):
    if n == 0 or n == 1:
        return 1

    return n * factorial_wrong_call(n)
```

You may still recognize a direct endless self call fairly well. But this becomes more difficult with an increasing number of lines. With some experience and practice in recursion, even the missing termination condition in the function factorial_no_abortion() may still be quite recognizable. But, in the function factorial_wrong_call() this is not that easy to determine. Here you must know more accurately what was intended.

You should take away two things from the examples:

1. **Termination condition**: A recursive function must always include at least one termination condition. But even if defined correctly, it is possible that, for example, the disallowed negative value range is not checked. For factorial(n) a call with a negative value would then lead to a RecursionError.

2. **Complexity reduction**: A recursive function must always subdivide the original problem into one or more smaller subproblems. Sometimes, this is already accomplished by reducing the value of a parameter by 1.

3.2 Exercises

3.2.1 Exercise 1: Fibonacci (★★☆☆☆)

Exercise 1a: Fibonacci Recursive (★☆☆☆☆)

Write function fib_rec(n) that recursively computes Fibonacci numbers based on the following definition:

$$fib(n) = \begin{cases} 1, & n = 1 \\ 1, & n = 2 \\ fib(n-1) + fib(n-2), & \forall n > 2 \end{cases}$$

Example

For example, check the implementation with the following value progression:

Input	1	2	3	4	5	6	7	8
fib(n)	1	1	2	3	5	8	13	21

Exercise 1b: Fibonacci Iterative (★★☆☆☆)

The recursive calculation of Fibonacci numbers is not efficient, and the running time increases enormously from about the fortieth or fiftieth Fibonacci number. Write an iterative version for the calculation.

3.2.2 Exercise 2: Process Digits (★★☆☆☆)

Exercise 2a: Count Digits (★★☆☆☆)

Write recursive function count_digits(value) that finds the number of digits in a positive natural number. We already discussed how to extract digits in the previous chapter in section 2.1.

Exercise 2b: Cross Sum (★★☆☆☆)

Calculate the sum of the digits of a number recursively. Write recursive function calc_sum_of_digits(value) for this purpose.

Examples

Input	Number of digits	Cross sum
1234	4	$1 + 2 + 3 + 4 = 10$
1234567	7	$1 + 2 + 3 + 4 + 5 + 6 + 7 = 28$

3.2.3 Exercise 3: GCD (★★☆☆☆)

Exercise 3a: GCD Recursive (★☆☆☆☆)

Write function gcd(a, b) that computes the greatest common divisor (GCD)[1]. GCD can be expressed mathematically recursively as follows for two natural numbers a and b:

$$\gcd(a,b) = \begin{cases} a, & b=0 \\ \gcd(b,a\%b), & b \neq 0 \end{cases}$$

Examples

Input 1	Input 2	Result
42	7	7
42	28	14
42	14	14

Exercise 3b: GCD Iterative (★★☆☆☆)

Create an iterative version for the GCD calculation.

Exercise 3c: LCM (★☆☆☆☆)

Write function lcm(a, b) that computes the least common multiplier (LCM). For two natural numbers a and b, you can calculate this based on the GCD using the following formula:

$$lcm(a,b) = a*b / gcd(a,b);$$

---

[1] Colloquially, this is the largest natural number by which two integers can be divided without a remainder.

Examples

Input 1	Input 2	Result
2	7	14
7	14	14
42	14	42

3.2.4 Exercise 4: Reverse String (★★☆☆☆)

Write recursive function reverse_string(text) that flips the letters of the text passed in.

Examples

Input	Result
"A"	"A"
"ABC"	"CBA"
"abcdefghi"	"ihgfedcba"

3.2.5 Exercise 5: List Sum (★★☆☆☆)

Write function sum_rec(values) that recursively computes the sum of the values of the given list. No call to the built-in functionality sum() is allowed.

Examples

Input	Result
[1, 2, 3]	6
[1, 2, 3, -7]	-1

3.2.6 Exercise 6: List Min (★★☆☆☆)

Write function min_rec(values) that uses recursion to find the minimum value of the passed list. For an empty list, the value sys.maxsize should be returned. In the implementation, no call to the built-in functionality min() is allowed.

Examples

Input	Result
[7, 2, 1, 9, 7, 1]	1
[11, 2, 33, 44, 55, 6, 7]	2
[1, 2, 3, -7]	-7

3.2.7 Exercise 7: Conversions (★★☆☆☆)

Exercise 7a: Binary (★★☆☆☆)

Write function to_binary(n) that recursively converts the given positive integer into a textual binary representation. No call to int(x, base) may be used.

Examples

Input	Result
5	"101"
7	"111"
22	"10110"
42	"101010"
256	"100000000"

Exercise 7b: Octal and Hexadecimal Numbers (★★☆☆☆)

Write conversions to octal and hexadecimal numbers by implementing the corresponding functions to_octal(n) and to_hex(n). Again, no call to int(x, base) may be used.

Examples

Input	Method	Result
7	octal	"7"
8	octal	"10"
42	octal	"52"
15	hexadecimal	"F"
77	hexadecimal	"4D"

3.2.8 Exercise 8: Exponential Function (★★☆☆☆)

Exercise 8a: Power of Two (★★☆☆☆)

Write recursive function is_power_of_2(n) that evaluates the given positive integer to see if it is a power of two.

Examples

Input	Result
2	True
10	False
16	True

Exercise 8b: Exponentiation Recursive (★★☆☆☆)

Write recursive function power_of(value, exponent) that exponentiates the given positive integer with the positive number specified as second parameter. For example, the call power_of(4, 2) should return the square of 4, so compute $4^2 = 16$. You may not use the built-in functionality pow() or the operator **.

Exercise 8c: Exponentiation Iterative (★★☆☆☆)

Write an iterative version of this exponentiation functionality.

Examples

Input base	Input exponent	Result
2	2	4
2	8	256
4	4	256

3.2.9 Exercise 9: Pascal's Triangle (★★☆☆☆)

Write function print_pascal(n) that prints Pascal's triangle. For the value 5, the following output should be generated:

```
[1]
[1, 1]
[1, 2, 1]
[1, 3, 3, 1]
[1, 4, 6, 4, 1]
```

Starting with the third line, each subsequent line is calculated based on the previous one with the help of an addition, as shown in the last line of the following definition. For each line, these values are flanked by a 1 at the front and at the back. Since this is a two-dimensional structure, the recursive definition is a little more complex.

$$
pascal(row,\ col) = \begin{cases} 1, & row = 1 \text{ and } col = 1 \text{ (top)} \\ 1, & \forall row \in \{1,\ n\} \text{ and } col = 1 \\ 1, & \forall row \in \{1,\ n\} \text{ and } col = row \\ pascal(row - 1,\ col) + \\ pascal(row - 1,\ col - 1), & \text{otherwise (based on predecessors)} \end{cases}
$$

Tip   For background information and an in-depth explanation, please consult https://en.wikipedia.org/wiki/Pascal's_triangle.

3.2.10 Exercise 10: Number Palindromes (★★★★☆)

A palindrome is a word that reads the same from the front and the back. You can extend this definition to the digits of a number. Write recursive function is_number_ palindrome(number) but without converting the number into a string and then using string functionalities like [::-1].

Examples

Input	Result
7	True
13	False
171	True
47742	False

3.2.11 Exercise 11: Permutations (★★★☆☆)

Calculate all permutations of a sequence of letters given as a string; this means all possible combinations of these letters. Implement this calculation in function calc_permutations(text). Consider also the case of duplicate letters, but do not use the standard Python functionality from the itertools module.

Examples

Input	Result
"A"	"A"
"AA"	"AA"
"AB"	"AB", "BA"
"ABC"	"ABC, "BAC", "ACB", "CAB", "CBA", "BCA"
"AAC"	"AAC", "ACA", "CAA"

3.2.12 Exercise 12: Count Substrings (★★☆☆☆)

Write function count_substrings(text, value_to_find) that counts all occurrences of the given substring. Thereby, when a pattern is found, it should be *consumed*; in other words, it should not be available for hits again. This is shown n the following table as the last case. Implement the whole thing yourself without resorting to the standard count().

Examples

Input	Search term	Result
"xhixhix"	"x"	3
"xhixhix"	"hi"	2
"mic"	"mic"	1
"haha"	"ho"	0
"xxxxyz"	"xx"	2

3.2.13 Exercise 13: Ruler (★★☆☆☆)

In the introduction, I showed how to draw a simple shape of a ruler as well as a stylized snowflake (see Figure 3-3) using recursion. In this exercise, you want to imitate an English-style ruler. This involves dividing an area of one inch into 1/2 and 1/4 and 1/8. In doing so, the length of the strokes decreases by one each time.

Example

The output should look somewhat like the following:

```
---- 0
-
--
-
---
-
--
-
```

```
---- 1
-
--
-
---
-
--
-
---- 2
```

3.3 Solutions

3.3.1 Solution 1: Fibonacci (★★☆☆☆)

Solution 1a: Fibonacci Recursive (★☆☆☆☆)

Write function `fib_rec(n)` that recursively computes Fibonacci numbers based on the following definition:

$$fib(n) = \begin{cases} 1, & n=1 \\ 1, & n=2 \\ fib(n-1) + fib(n-2), \forall n > 2 \end{cases}$$

Example

For example, check the implementation with the following value progression:

Input	1	2	3	4	5	6	7	8
fib(n)	1	1	2	3	5	8	13	21

Algorithm The implementation in Python is exactly derived from the mathematical definition:

```python
def fib_rec(n):
    if n <= 0:
        raise ValueError("n must be >= 1")
```

```
# recursive termination
if n == 1 or n == 2:
    return 1

# recursive descent
return fib_rec(n - 1) + fib_rec(n - 2)
```

Python shortcut To calculate Fibonacci numbers, you can use a lambda and write the whole thing as a one-liner—but without error handling and somewhat less readable. In addition, the recursive termination and descent are more difficult to recognize.

```
fib = lambda n: n if n < 2 else fib(n - 1) + fib(n - 2)
```

ATTENTION: OPTIMIZATION

Keep in mind that self calls happen again and again when calculating Fibonacci numbers. Even worse, that is the case for values that have already been calculated before. This is suboptimal. In addition to the iterative variant shown in the following, the technique *memoization* discussed in section 7.1 can be used for optimization. In Python, *decorators* are suitable for this purpose, which I briefly introduce in Appendix B.

Solution 1b: Fibonacci Iterative (★★☆☆☆)

The recursive calculation of Fibonacci numbers is not efficient, and the running time increases enormously from about the fortieth to fiftieth Fibonacci number. Write an iterative version for the calculation.

Algorithm Similarly to the recursive version, the iterative implementation checks at first the input for validity and then for the special cases for the invocation with the values 1 or 2. After that, you use two helper variables and a loop that runs from 2 to n. You then calculate the corresponding Fibonacci number from the sum of the two helper variables. After that, the two helper variables are assigned appropriately. This results in the following implementation:

```
def fib_iterative(n):
    if n <= 0:
        raise ValueError("n must be >= 1")
```

```
if n == 1 or n == 2:
    return 1

fib_n_2 = 1
fib_n_1 = 1

for _ in range(2, n):
    fib_n = fib_n_1 + fib_n_2
    # "shift" by one position
    fib_n_2 = fib_n_1
    fib_n_1 = fib_n

return fib_n
```

Verification

For testing, use the following inputs, which show the correct functioning:

```
def input_and_expected():
    return [(1, 1), (2, 1), (3, 2), (4, 3),
            (5, 5), (6, 8), (7, 13), (8, 21)]

@pytest.mark.parametrize("n, expected", input_and_expected())
def test_fib_rec(n, expected):
    assert fib_rec(n) == expected

@pytest.mark.parametrize("n, expected", input_and_expected())
def test_fib_iterative(n, expected):
    assert fib_iterative(n) == expected
```

3.3.2 Solution 2: Process Digits (★★☆☆☆)

Solution 2a: Count Digits (★★☆☆☆)

Write recursive function count_digits(value) that finds the number of digits in a positive natural number. You explored how to extract digits in the previous chapter in section 2.1.

Examples

Input	Number of digits	Cross sum
1234	4	1 + 2 + 3 + 4 = 10
1234567	7	1 + 2 + 3 + 4 + 5 + 6 + 7 = 28

Algorithm If the number is less than 10, then return the value 1 because this corresponds to a digit. Otherwise, calculate the remaining value by dividing the number by 10. This invokes the counting method recursively as follows:

```python
def count_digits(value):
    if value < 0:
        raise ValueError("value must be >= 0")

    # recursive termination
    if value < 10:
        return 1

    # recursive descent
    return count_digits(value // 10) + 1
```

ATTENTION: SANITY CHECKS AT THE BEGINNING OF THE METHOD

To ensure stable programs, it is often a good idea to check the parameters for validity. This can be accomplished in the form of simple `if` statements, as you have done several times before. In Python, however, this can be achieved more elegantly with the help of decorators, which I briefly introduce in Appendix B.

Python shortcut Of course, there are different variants to solve this task non-recursively and in a more performant way. With list comprehension, every digit is converted into a 1. They are summed up using the built-in sum() function. However, this tends to be a fancy, artificial solution. It is much clearer and more understandable to convert the number into a string and then call the built-in function len() to count the digits:

```python
def count_digits_shorter(value):
    return sum([1 for _ in str(value)])

def count_digits_tricky(value):
    return len(str(value))
```

Solution 2b: Cross Sum (★★☆☆☆)

Calculate the sum of the digits of a number recursively. Write recursive function calc_sum_of_digits(value) for this purpose.

Algorithm Based on the solution for the first subtask, you only vary the returned value for the digit as well as the addition and the self call as follows:

```python
def calc_sum_of_digits(value):
    if value < 0:
        raise ValueError("value must be >= 0")

    # recursive termination
    if value < 10:
        return value

    remainder = value // 10
    last_digit = value % 10

    # recursive descent
    return calc_sum_of_digits(remainder) + last_digit
```

Python shortcut The built-in function divmod() is useful here:

```python
def calc_sum_of_digits(value):
    if value < 0:
        raise ValueError("value must be >= 0")

    # recursive termination
    if value < 10:
        return value

    remainder, last_digit = divmod(value, 10)

    # recursive descent
    return calc_sum_of_digits(remainder) + last_digit
```

To sum the digits, you again use list comprehension, which converts each digit into a numerical value. The sum is calculated with the built-in function `sum()`:

```
def calc_sum_of_digits_shorter(value):
    return sum([int(ch) for ch in str(value)])
```

However, this assignment is not about brevity, but about getting to know the recursive description of the calculation of the sum of the digits.

Verification

For testing, use the following inputs, which show the correct operation:

```
@pytest.mark.parametrize("number, expected", [(1234, 4), (1234567, 7)])
def test_count_digits(number, expected):
    assert count_digits(number) == expected
```

```
@pytest.mark.parametrize("number, expected", [(1234, 10), (1234567, 28)])
def test_calc_sum_of_digits(number, expected):
    assert calc_sum_of_digits(number) == expected
```

3.3.3 Solution 3: GCD (★★☆☆☆)

Solution 3a: GCD Recursive (★☆☆☆☆)

Write function `gcd(a, b)` that computes the greatest common divisor (GCD)[2]. GCD can be expressed mathematically recursively as follows for two natural numbers a and b:

$$gcd(a,b) = \begin{cases} a, & b=0 \\ gcd(b,a\%b), & b \neq 0 \end{cases}$$

---

[2] Colloquially, this is the largest natural number by which two integers can be divided without a remainder.

Examples

Input 1	Input 2	Result
42	7	7
42	28	14
42	14	14

Algorithm The calculation of the GCD can be coded in Python fairly directly from the mathematical definition:

```python
def gcd(a, b):
    # recursive termination
    if b == 0:
        return a

    # recursive descent
    return gcd(b, a % b)
```

Python shortcut Of course, this task can be achieved in a much more straightforward way by calling the built-in functionality gcd() from the module math. However, this assignment is about getting to know the recursive calculation of the GCD.

```python
>>> import math
>>> math.gcd(42, 7)
7
>>> math.gcd(42, 14)
14
```

Solution 3b: GCD Iterative (★★☆☆☆)

Create an iterative version for the GCD calculation.

Algorithm The self call is transformed into a loop that is executed until the condition of the recursive termination is met. The trick is to reassign the variables as specified by the recursive definition.

```
def gcd_iterative(a, b):
    while b != 0:
        remainder = a % b
        a = b
        b = remainder

    # here applies b == 0
    return a
```

Verification

For testing, use the following inputs, which show the correct operation:

```
@pytest.mark.parametrize("a, b, expected",
                         [(42, 7, 7), (42, 28, 14), (42, 14, 14)])
def test_gcd(a, b, expected):
    assert gcd(a, b) == expected

@pytest.mark.parametrize("a, b, expected",
                         [(42, 7, 7), (42, 28, 14), (42, 14, 14)])
def test_gcd_iterative(a, b, expected):
    assert gcd_iterative(a, b) == expected
```

Solution 3c: LCM (★☆☆☆☆)

Write function lcm(a, b) that computes the least common multiplier (LCM). For two natural numbers a and b, you can calculate this based on the GCD using the following formula:

$$lcm(a, b) = a * b / gcd(a, b);$$

Examples

Input 1	Input 2	Result
2	7	14
7	14	14
42	14	42

Algorithm The calculation of the LCM can also be directly implemented from the mathematical definition, as long as you have already completed the functionality for the GCD:

```python
def lcm(a, b):
    return a * b // gcd(a, b)
```

Python shortcut Of course, this task can be achieved in a much more straightforward way by calling the built-in functionality `lcm()` from the module `math`:

```python
>>> import math
>>> math.lcm(2, 7)
14
```

Verification

For testing, use the following inputs, which show the correct operation:

```python
@pytest.mark.parametrize("a, b, expected",
                         [(2, 7, 14), (7, 14, 14), (42, 14, 42)])
def test_lcm(a, b, expected):
    assert lcm(a, b) == expected
```

HINT: CALCULATE LCM WITHOUT USING GCD

Without the calculation of the GCD, you proceeds as follows. You determine both the maximum and the minimum of the two numbers. Starting from the larger number, this is increased by itself until the smaller number divides the resulting number perfectly (i.e., without a remainder).

```python
def lcm_iterative(a, b):
    larger = max(a, b)
    smaller = min(a, b)

    value = larger
    while value % smaller != 0:
        value += larger

    return value
```

3.3.4 Solution 4: Reverse String (★★☆☆☆)

Write recursive function `reverse_string(text)` that flips the letters of the text passed in.

Examples

Input	Result
"A"	"A"
"ABC"	"CBA"
"abcdefghi"	"ihgfedcba"

Algorithm Extract the first character until you have a string of length 1 and then concatenate the whole in reverse order:

```python
def reverse_string(text):
    # recursive termination
    if len(text) <= 1:
        return text

    first_char = text[0]
    remaining = text[1:]

    # recursive descent
    return reverse_string(remaining) + first_char
```

Python shortcut This can be achieved much easier by the following calls:

```python
reversed_text = text[::-1]
```

```python
reversed_text = "".join(reversed(text))
```

However, this task is about getting to know recursion.

Verification

For testing, use the following inputs, which show the correct operation:

```
@pytest.mark.parametrize("input, expected",
                         [("A", "A"), ("ABC", "CBA"),
                          ("abcdefghi", "ihgfedcba")])
def test_reverse_string(input, expected):
    assert reverse_string(input) == expected
```

3.3.5 Solution 5: List Sum (★★☆☆☆)

Write function sum_rec(values) that recursively computes the sum of the values of the given list. No call to the built-in functionality sum() is allowed.

Examples

Input	Result
[1, 2, 3]	6
[1, 2, 3, -7]	-1

Algorithm Compute the partial sum with the recursive definition as long as

$$sum(values(0)) = values[0]$$

$$sum(values(0 \ldots n)) \qquad = values[0] + sum(values(1 \ldots n))$$

until only a single element is left. As mentioned in the introduction, a helper function is useful, containing the actual processing and logic. Here the current value in the list is added to the recursively determined result:

```
def sum_rec(values):
    return sum_helper(values, 0)

def sum_helper(values, pos):
    # recursive termination
    if pos >= len(values):
        return 0

    # recursive descent
    return values[pos] + sum_helper(values, pos + 1)
```

Alternative algorithm Alternatively, it is also possible to let the pos counter run from length - 1 to 0, so the recursion reverses to the following:

$$sum(values(0 \ldots n)) = sum(values(0 \ldots n-1)) + values[n]$$

This can be implemented in the form of functions sum_tail(values) and sum_tail_helper(values, pos) as follows:

```python
def sum_tail(values):
    return sum_tail_helper(values, len(values) - 1)

def sum_tail_helper(values, pos):
    # recursive termination
    if pos < 0:
        return 0

    # recursive descent
    return sum_tail_helper(values, pos - 1) + values[pos]
```

Python shortcut Of course, the whole thing can be achieved in a much more straightforward way by calling the built-in functionality sum(). However, this assignment is about getting to know the recursive description of the sum calculation.

```python
result = sum(values)
```

Likewise, the function reduce() from the module functools can be used—but this is less understandable and less readable:

```python
import functools

def sum_lambda(values):
    return functools.reduce(lambda x, y: x + y, values)
```

Verification

The following inputs show the correct operation:

```python
@pytest.mark.parametrize("values, expected",
                         [([1], 1), ( [1, 2, 3], 6), ([1, 2, 3, -7], -1)])
def test_sum_rec(values, expected):
    assert sum_rec(values) == expected
```

```
@pytest.mark.parametrize("values, expected",
                         [([1], 1), ( [1, 2, 3], 6), ([1, 2, 3, -7], -1)])
def test_sum_tail(values, expected):
    assert sum_tail(values) == expected

@pytest.mark.parametrize("values, expected",
                         [([1], 1), ( [1, 2, 3], 6), ([1, 2, 3, -7], -1)])
def test_sum_lambda(values, expected):
    assert sum_lambda(values) == expected
```

3.3.6 Solution 6: List Min (★★☆☆☆)

Write function min_rec(values) that uses recursion to find the minimum value of the passed list. For an empty list, the value sys.maxsize should be returned. In the implementation, no call to the built-in functionality min() is allowed.

Examples

Input	Result
[7, 2, 1, 9, 7, 1]	1
[11, 2, 33, 44, 55, 6, 7]	2
[1, 2, 3, -7]	-7

Algorithm Check the list starting from the first element and compare it with an initial minimum set to sys.maxsize. If the current element is smaller, it becomes the new minimum. Repeat this check for the list shortened by one position until the position has reached the end of the list.

```
def min_rec(values):
    return min_helper(values, 0, sys.maxsize)

def min_helper(values, pos, min_value):
    # recursive termination
    if pos >= len(values):
        return min_value
```

```
    value = values[pos]
    if value < min_value:
        min_value = value

    # recursive descent
    return min_helper(values, pos + 1, min_value)
```

Python shortcut An invocation of the built-in functionality min() would be much simpler. However, this task is about the recursive determination of the minimum.

```
result = min(values)
```

Verification

For testing, use the following inputs, which show the correct functionality:

```
@pytest.mark.parametrize("values, expected",
                    [([7, 2, 1, 9, 7, 1 ], 1), ([1, 2, 3, -7], -7),
                     ([11, 2, 33, 44, 55, 6, 7], 2), ([], sys.maxsize)])
def test_min_rec(values, expected):
    assert min_rec(values) == expected
```

3.3.7 Solution 7: Conversions (★★☆☆☆)

Solution 7a: Binary (★★☆☆☆)

Write function to_binary(n) that recursively converts the given positive integer into a textual binary representation. No call to int(x, base) may be used.

Examples

Input	Result
5	"101"
7	"111"
22	"10110"
42	"101010"
256	"100000000"

Algorithm The conversion is based on the already known extraction of the last digit and the determination of remainder, as was introduced in section 2.1. To convert a decimal number into a binary number, check whether the number passed can be represented by a single digit in the binary system (i. e., whether it is smaller than 2). Otherwise, the last digit is extracted first using the modulo operator and also the remainder. For this, you call the function recursively and then concatenate the string representation of the last digit. This results in the following sequence for the value 22:

Invocation	Process	Result
to_binary(22)	to_binary(22/2) + str(22%2) => to_binary(11) + "0"	"10110"
to_binary(11)	to_binary(11/2) + str(11%2) => to_binary(5) + "1"	"1011"
to_binary(5)	to_binary(5/2) + str(5%2) => to_binary(2) + "1"	"101"
to_binary(2)	to_binary(2/2) + str(2%2) => to_binary(1) + "0"	"10"
to_binary(1)	str(1) => "1"	"1"

Now let's implement the whole thing in Python as follows:

```python
def to_binary(n):
    if n < 0:
        raise ValueError("n must be >= 0")

    # recursive termination: check for digit in binary system
    if n <= 1:
        return str(n)

    remainder, last_digit = divmod(n, 2)

    # recursive descent
    return to_binary(remainder) + str(last_digit)
```

Solution 7b: Octal and Hexadecimal Numbers (★★☆☆☆)

Write conversions to octal and hexadecimal numbers by implementing the corresponding functions to_octal(n) and to_hex(n). Again, no call to int(x, base) may be used.

Examples

Input	Method	Result
7	Octal	"7"
8	Octal	"10"
42	Octal	"52"
15	Hexadecimal	"F"
77	Hexadecimal	"4D"

Algorithm The algorithm remains basically the same. You check whether the number passed can be represented by a single digit of the desired number system, such as smaller than 8 (octal) or 16 (hexadecimal). Otherwise, you first extract the last digit using a modulo operation and also the remainder. For the remainder, this function is called recursively and then the string representation of the last digit is concatenated. In this solution, you use an explicit division and the modulo operator for octal number processing and the built-in function divmod() when checking for hexadecimal numbers:

```python
def to_octal(n):
    if n < 0:
        raise ValueError("n must be >= 0")

    # recursive termination: check for digit in octal system
    if n <= 7:
        return str(n)

    last_digit = n % 8
    remainder = n // 8

    # recursive descent
    return to_octal(remainder) + str(last_digit)

def to_hex(n):
    if n < 0:
        raise ValueError("n must be >= 0")
```

```
# recursive termination: check for digit in hexadecimal system
if n <= 15:
    return as_hex_digit(n)

remainder, last_digit = divmod(n, 16)

# recursive descent
return to_hex(remainder) + as_hex_digit(last_digit)
```

For the sake of completeness there remains the conversion into a hexadecimal digit:

```
# easier handling of hexadecimal conversion
def as_hex_digit(n):
    if 0 <= n < 9:
        return str(n)
    if 10 <= n <= 15:
        # special character arithmetic
        return chr(ord('A') + (n - 10))

    raise ValueError("value not in range 0 - 15, " + "but is: " + n)
```

HINT: POSSIBLE OPTIMIZATION

Although the implementation shown for converting a single hexadecimal digit to a string is pretty straightforward, there is an amazingly elegant variant that is also readable and understandable. It checks in a given character set with indexed access via [n]:

```
def as_hex_digit_optimized(n):
    if 0 <= n <= 15:
        return "0123456789ABCDEF"[n]

    raise ValueError("value not in range 0 - 15, " + "but is: " + n)
```

Verification

For testing, use the following inputs, which show the correct operation:

```
@pytest.mark.parametrize("value, expected",
                         [(5, "101"), (7, "111"), (22, "10110"),
                          (42, "101010"), (256, "100000000")])
def test_to_binary(value, expected):
    assert to_binary(value) == expected

@pytest.mark.parametrize("value, expected",
                         [(42, "52"), (7, "7"), (8, "10")])
def test_to_octal(value, expected):
    assert to_octal(value) == expected

@pytest.mark.parametrize("value, expected",
                         [(77, "4D"), (15, "F"), (16, "10")])
def test_to_hex(value, expected):
    assert to_hex(value) == expected
```

3.3.8 Solution 8: Exponential Function (★★☆☆☆)

Solution 8a: Power of Two (★★☆☆☆)

Write recursive function is_power_of_2(n) that evaluates the given positive integer to see if it is a power of two.

Examples

Input	Result
2	True
10	False
16	True

Algorithm If the given number is smaller than the value 2, only the value 1 corresponds to a power, namely the 0th (i. e., 2^0). Now you have to check if it is an odd number. If this is the case, it is impossible for it to be a multiple and therefore not a power of 2. If the number is even, then check recursively with the number divided by 2.

```python
def is_power_of_2(n):
    # recursive termination
    if n < 2:
        return n == 1

    if n % 2 != 0:
        return False

    # recursive descent
    return is_power_of_2(n // 2)
```

For the initial check, use a little trick with `return n==1`, which has the following effect:

$$n < 0 : \text{False (negative number, so never the value 1)}$$
$$n = 0 : \text{False } (0 \neq 1)$$
$$n = 1 : \text{True } (1 = 1)$$

Let's take a look at a short version of the implementation. To my mind, the upper one is more comprehensible. Moreover, in the first version, the recursive termination and the recursive descent are much clearer.

```python
def is_power_of_2_short(n):
    return n == 1 or n > 0 and n % 2 == 0 and is_power_of_2_short(n // 2)
```

Solution 8b: Exponentiation Recursive (★★☆☆☆)

Write recursive function `power_of(value, exponent)` that exponentiates the given positive integer with the positive number specified as second parameter. For example, the call `power_of(4, 2)` should return the square of 4, so compute $4^2 = 16$. You may not use the built-in functionality `pow()` or the operator `**`.

Algorithm Invoke the method recursively and multiply the number by the result of the self call until the exponent reaches 0 or 1. Furthermore, you have to reduce the exponent by 1 with each call.

```python
def power_of(value, exponent):
    if exponent < 0:
        raise ValueError("exponent must be >= 0")

    # recursive termination
    if exponent == 0:
        return 1
    if exponent == 1:
        return value

    # recursive descent
    return value * power_of(value, exponent - 1)
```

This alternative has a cost of $O(n)$. But it is quite easy to optimize this and reduce it to $O(log(n))$.

Optimized algorithm For optimization, use the trick of squaring the value and thereby halving the exponent. This leaves only the special treatment of an odd exponent, which requires another multiplication.

```python
def power_of_optimized(value, exponent):
    if exponent < 0:
        raise ValueError("exponent must be >= 0")

    # recursive termination
    if exponent == 0:
        return 1
    if exponent == 1:
        return value

    # recursive descent
    result = power_of_optimized(value * value, exponent // 2)
    if exponent % 2 == 1:
        return value * result

    return result
```

Python shortcut Of course, the whole thing can be achieved in a much more straightforward way by calling the built-in functionality pow() or the operator **. But this task is about getting to know the recursive calculation.

```
result = pow(value, exponent)
result = value ** exponent
```

Solution 8c: Exponentiation Iterative (★★☆☆☆)

Write an iterative version of this exponentiation functionality.

Examples

Input base	Input exponent	Result
2	2	4
2	8	256
4	4	256

Algorithm As with the recursive version, you probably start with the two checks. Besides, the self call has to be converted into a loop, and the number has to be multiplied with the previous intermediate result. Furthermore, in each iteration, the exponent has to be reduced. However, a sharp look quickly shows that the two initial checks are already covered by the general case and therefore are no longer included in the listing.

```python
def power_of_iterative(value, exponent):
    result = 1
    while exponent > 0:
        result *= value
        exponent -= 1

    return result
```

Verification

For testing, use the following inputs, which show the correct operation:

```
@pytest.mark.parametrize("value, expected",
                         [(2, True), (3, False), (4, True),
                          (10, False), (16, True)])
def test_is_power_of2(value, expected):
    assert is_power_of_2(value) == expected

def inputs_and_expected():
    return [(2, 2, 4), (4, 2, 16), (16, 2, 256),
            (4, 4, 256), (2, 8, 256)]

@pytest.mark.parametrize("number, exponent, expected",
                         inputs_and_expected())
def test_power_of(number, exponent, expected):
    assert power_of(number, exponent) == expected

@pytest.mark.parametrize("number, exponent, expected",
                         inputs_and_expected())
def test_power_of_iterative(number, exponent, expected):
    assert power_of_iterative(number, exponent) == expected
```

3.3.9 Solution 9: Pascal's Triangle (★★☆☆☆)

Write function `print_pascal(n)` that prints Pascal's triangle. For the value 5, the following output should be generated:

```
[1]
[1, 1]
[1, 2, 1]
[1, 3, 3, 1]
[1, 4, 6, 4, 1]
```

Starting with the third line, each subsequent line is calculated based on the previous one with the help of an addition, as shown in the last line of the following definition. For each line, these values are flanked by a 1 at the front and at the back. Since this is a two-dimensional structure, the recursive definition is a little more complex.

$$pascal(row, col) = \begin{cases} 1, & row = 1 \text{ and } col = 1 \text{ (top)} \\ 1, & \forall row \in \{1, n\} \text{ and } col = 1 \\ 1, & \forall row \in \{1, n\} \text{ and } col = row \\ pascal(row - 1, col) + \\ pascal(row - 1, col - 1), & \text{otherwise (based on predecessors)} \end{cases}$$

Tip   For background information and an in-depth explanation, please consult https://en.wikipedia.org/wiki/Pascal's_triangle.

Algorithm Implement the recursive definition as function as follows:

```
def calc_pascal(row, col):
    # recursive termination: top
    if col == 1 and row == 1:
        return 1

    # recursive termination: border
    if col == 1 or col == row:
        return 1

    # recursive descent
    return calc_pascal(row - 1, col) + calc_pascal(row - 1, col - 1)
```

Actually, there is no need for a separate termination condition for the top. Nevertheless, this is shown here for the sake of better comprehension—but of course, that is a matter of taste.

To calculate Pascal's triangle, the previous method must now be invoked for each position in the triangle using two nested loops covering all rows and columns:

```python
def print_pascal(n):
    for row in range(1, n + 1):
        for col in range(1, row + 1):
            print(calc_pascal(row, col), end=' ')

        print()
```

To try it out, use the Python console:

```
>>> print_pascal(7)
1
1 1
1 2 1
1 3 3 1
1 4 6 4 1
1 5 10 10 5 1
1 6 15 20 15 6 1
```

Optimized algorithm The pure recursive definition results in quite a lot of computations. It becomes more understandable, comprehensible, and performant if you work line by line.

The starting point is the first line, which contains only the value 1. For all other values, you must call the method itself n times and then use the helper function calc_line(previous_line_values) to compute the new line. But to avoid mixing the computation and the console output, you add a parameter that is capable of performing actions, such as logging intermediate steps to the console.

```python
def calc_pascal_with_action(n, action):
    # recursive termination
    if n == 1:
        if action:
            action([1])
        return [1]
    else:
        # recursive descent
        previous_line_values = calc_pascal_with_action(n - 1, action)
```

```
        new_line = __calc_line(previous_line_values)

        if action:
            action(new_line)

        return new_line
```

You can find a bit more complexity in the helper function __calc_line(previous_line) for calculating the values of the new line based on the previous one. It is important to keep in mind that the previous line contains at least two values and that you do not sum up to the last element, but only to the second last element. With the help of list comprehension, however, this can be implemented quite understandably and briefly as follows:

```
def __calc_line(previous_line):
    # value results from the two values of the previous line
    current_line = [previous_line[i] + previous_line[i + 1]
                    for i in range(len(previous_line) - 1)]

    # flanked by a 1 in each case
    return [1] + current_line + [1]
```

Verification

For testing, use the following call, which shows the correct operation:

```
>>> calc_pascal_with_action(5, print)
[1]
[1, 1]
[1, 2, 1]
[1, 3, 3, 1]
[1, 4, 6, 4, 1]
```

You can then check something more formal with a unit test:

```
@pytest.mark.parametrize("n, expected",
                [(1, [1]),
                 (2, [1, 1]),
                 (3, [1, 2, 1]),
                 (4, [1, 3, 3, 1]),
```

```
                              (5, [1, 4, 6, 4, 1]),
                              (6, [1, 5, 10, 10, 5, 1]),
                              (7, [1, 6, 15, 20, 15, 6, 1])])
def test_calc_pascal_with_action(n, expected):
    assert calc_pascal_with_action(n, None) == expected
```

3.3.10 Solution 10: Number Palindromes (★★★★☆)

A palindrome is a word that reads the same from the front and the back. You can extend this definition to the digits of a number. Write recursive function is_number_ palindrome(number) but without converting the number into a string and then using string functionalities like [::-1].

Examples

Input	Result
7	True
13	False
171	True
47742	False

Algorithm Because of the restriction demanded in the exercise, it is not possible to compare character by character. However, the operations modulo and division are suitable, which you have already used for similar tasks. You use both to separate and compare the left and right digits.

Let's approach the solution with examples:

```
#digits       value           calculation
-----------------------------------------------------------------------
1 digit                       => special case, is always palindrome

2 digits        11            divisor = 10
< 100                         1 % 10 = 1
                              11 / 10 = 1     palindrome
```

```
                    13
                            3 % 10 = 3
                            13 / 10 = 1     X

3 digits            171     divisor = 100
< 1000                      1 % 10 = 1
                            171 / 100 =  1
                            remainder:   7 (171 / 10 = 17 % 10 = 7)
                            => check recursively

4 digits            4774    divisor = 1000
<10000                      4 % 10 = 4
                            4774 / 1000 = 4    ok
                            remainder:   77 (4774 / 10 = 477 % 100 = 77)
                            => check recursively
```

The right and left digits of a digit have to be extracted. If they match, the new value is determined by first dividing by 10 (cutting off the last digit) and then using the modulo operator with the appropriately selected amount of digits to determine the remainder (i. e., cutting off the front number). In particular, you have to figure out the length of the number as a power of ten to get the correct divisor.

```python
def is_number_palindrome(number):
    if number < 10:
        return True

    factor = calc_pow_of_ten(number)
    divisor = int(pow(10, factor))

    if number < divisor * 10:
        left_number = number // divisor
        right_number = number % 10

        # cuts away a leading zero ...
        remaining_number = (number // 10) % (divisor // 10)

        return left_number == right_number and \
                is_number_palindrome(remaining_number)

    return False
```

In the following, the calculation of the power of ten, as well as the counting of digits, are shown as helper functions, which resides in the utility module `math_utils`:

```python
def calc_pow_of_ten(number):
    return count_digits(number) - 1

def count_digits(number):
    count = 0

    while number > 0:
        number = number // 10
        count += 1

    return count
```

The solution shown is by no means optimal since the factors have to be determined constantly. Furthermore, the entire procedure is still quite difficult to understand from the source code, even though helper functions have already been extracted.

Optimized algorithm As an optimization, implement the following version. Always separate the last digit, divide by 10, and call the function with the new values. Beforehand, compute the new value from the current value and the last digit by multiplying the current value by 10 and appending the last digit. If it is a palindrome, then the original value corresponds to the calculated value. The recursive termination occurs when either no more digits exist or only one single digit exists. The trick is that you rebuild the number from the back and finally compare it with the original value. In contrast to the other recursive helper functions presented so far, you need two buffers here, one for the current value and one for the remaining value.

```python
def is_number_palindrome_rec(number):
    return __is_number_palindrome_rec_helper(number, 0, number)

def __is_number_palindrome_rec_helper(original_number, current_value,
                                      remaining_value):
    # recursive termination
    if current_value == original_number:
        return True

    # recursive termination
    if (remaining_value < 1):
        return False
```

```
last_digit = remaining_value % 10
new_current = current_value * 10 + last_digit
new_remaining = remaining_value // 10

print("last_digit: %d, new_current: %d, new_remaining: %d" %
        (last_digit, new_current, new_remaining))

return __is_number_palindrome_rec_helper(original_number, new_current,
                                          new_remaining)
```

The calls for the value 121 can be illustrated as follows:

__is_number_palindrome_rec_helper(121, 0, 121) =>
last_digit: 1, new_current: 1, new_remaining: 12
__is_number_palindrome_rec_helper(121, 1, 12) =>
last_digit: 2, new_current: 12, new_remaining: 1
i__s_number_palindrome_rec_helper(121, 12, 1) =>
last_digit: 1, new_current: 121, new_remaining: 0
__is_number_palindrome_rec_helper(121, 121, 0)
True

Certainly it is of interest to see how the entire procedure works for a number that is not a palindrome, for example 123:

__is_number_palindrome_rec_helper(123, 0, 123) =>
last_digit: 3, new_current: 3, new_remaining: 12
__is_number_palindrome_rec_helper(123, 3, 12) =>
last_digit: 2, new_current: 32, new_remaining: 1
__is_number_palindrome_rec_helper(123, 32, 1) =>
last_digit: 1, new_current: 321, new_remaining: 0
__is_number_palindrome_rec_helper(123, 321, 0)
False

Verification

For testing, use the following inputs, which show the correct operation:

```
@pytest.mark.parametrize("number, expected",
                         [(7, True), (13, False), (171, True),
                          (47742, False), (123321, True),
                          (1234554321, True)])
def test_is_number_palindrome(number, expected):
    assert is_number_palindrome(number) == expected
```

3.3.11 Solution 11: Permutations (★★★☆☆)

Calculate all permutations of a sequence of letters given as a string; this means all possible combinations of these letters. Implement this calculation in function `calc_permutations(text)`. Consider also the case of duplicate letters, but do not use the standard Python functionality from the `itertools` module.

Examples

Input	Result
"A	"A"
"AA"	"AA"
"AB"	"AB", "BA"
"ABC"	"ABC, "BAC", "ACB", "CAB", "CBA", "BCA"
"AAC"	"AAC", "ACA", "CAA"

Algorithm The best way to compute all permutations for a given string is to take a look at the recursive definition and then implement it:

$$
\begin{aligned}
A &\Rightarrow perm(A) & &= A \\
AA &\Rightarrow A + perm(A) \cup A + perm(A) & &= AA \cup AA = AA \\
AB &\Rightarrow A + perm(B) \cup B + perm(A) & &= AB \cup BA \\
ABC &\Rightarrow A + perm(BC) \cup B + perm(AC) \cup C + perm(AB) & &= ABC \cup ACB \cup \ldots
\end{aligned}
$$

You recognize that for a single character, the permutations consist of the character itself. For multiple characters, the permutations are computed by finding the permutations of the remaining string without the character and by later combining them back with the character appropriately—more on this later. The original problem is reduced from a string of length n to n problems for strings of length $n - 1$. Thus, for the string ABC, you obtain the solution illustrated in Figure 3-4.

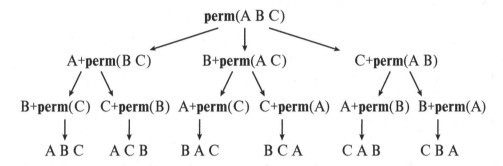

Figure 3-4. *Computation of the permutations of ABC*

With this knowledge in mind, the implementation will become much easier, and you can transform the following steps into Python.

- Select and extract the ith character.

- Build the remaining string and calculate the permutations for it.

- Put the whole thing together again.

This is implemented as follows:

```python
def calc_permutations(text):
    # recursive termination
    if is_blank(text) or len(text) == 1:
        return {text}

    combinations = set()
    # extract i-th character as new first character
    for i, new_first in enumerate(text):
        # recursive descent for rest without i-th character
        permutations = calc_permutations(text[0:i] + text[i + 1:])
```

```
        # adding the extracted character to all partial solutions
        for perm in permutations:
            combinations.add(new_first + perm)

    return combinations

def is_blank(text):
    return not (text and text.strip())
```

This implementation leads to the creation of quite a lot of instances of strings and sets as intermediate buffers. How can this be improved?

Optimized algorithm The drawbacks mentioned above are negligible for a short string. However, the longer the string gets, creating all the temporary objects and performing the string actions become more noticeable. How can this be avoided?

Let's revisit ideas you've seen in other solutions. Instead of assembling the strings, you can cleverly pass them as parameters. One of them defines the remaining string, and the other one the currently already calculated prefix.

```
def calc_permutations_mini_opt(text):
    return __calc_permutations_mini_opt_helper(text, "")

def __calc_permutations_mini_opt_helper(remaining, prefix):
    # recursive termination
    if len(remaining) == 0:
        return {prefix}

    candidates = set()

    for i, current_char in enumerate(remaining):
        new_prefix = prefix + current_char
        new_remaining = remaining[0:i] + remaining[i + 1:]

        # recursive descent
        candidates.update(__calc_permutations_mini_opt_helper(new_
        remaining, new_prefix))

    return candidates
```

Let me comment a bit on the optimization. While calling the method `calc_permutations("abcdefghij")` takes about 7 to 8 seconds with my iMac (i7 4Ghz), `calc_permutations_mini_opt("abcdefghij")` finishes after only about 4 to 5 seconds—this is due to the very large number of calls, for which smaller optimizations may be worthwhile.

However, if you add one additional character to the input, the overhead grows enormously to around 111 seconds and for the optimized version to around 85 seconds. Such increases in running time are, of course, absolutely undesirable. After reading Chapter 7 covering more advanced recursion techniques, you may want to look again at the computation of the permutations to attempt an improvement with the help of memoization. However, this will be at the expense of the required memory.

Python shortcut Interestingly, Python provides ready-made functionality in the `itertools` module. Its result is a bit clumsy because the permutations are represented as a sequence of single characters. For your desired representation of the outcome, you only need to merge the values of the result tuples with `join()`. Again, the performance is better than that of the optimized variant. A call with "abcdefghij" takes about 3 seconds; with one character longer, it takes about 50 seconds.

```python
import itertools

def calc_permutations_built_in(text):
    result_tuples = list(itertools.permutations(text))

    return {"".join(tuple) for tuple in result_tuples}
```

Verification

For testing, use the following inputs, which show the correct operation:

```python
def input_and_expected():
    return [("A", {"A"}),
            ("AA", {"AA"}),
            ("AB", {"AB", "BA"}),
            ("ABC", {"ABC", "BAC", "ACB", "CAB", "CBA", "BCA"}),
            ("AAC", {"AAC", "ACA", "CAA"})]
```

```
@pytest.mark.parametrize("input, expected", input_and_expected())
def test_calc_permutations(input, expected):
    assert calc_permutations(input) == expected

@pytest.mark.parametrize("input, expected", input_and_expected())
def test_calc_permutations_mini_opt(input, expected):
    assert calc_permutations_mini_opt(input) == expected

@pytest.mark.parametrize("input, expected", input_and_expected())
def test_calc_permutations_built_in(input, expected):
    assert calc_permutations_built_in(input) == expected
```

3.3.12 Solution 12: Count Substrings (★★☆☆☆)

Write function count_substrings(text, value_to_find) that counts all occurrences
of the given substring. Thereby, when a pattern is found, it should be *consumed*, so it
should not be available for hits again. This is shown in the following table as the last case.
Implement the whole thing yourself without resorting to the standard count().

Examples

Input	Search term	Result
"xhixhix"	"x"	3
"xhixhix"	"hi"	2
"mic"	"mic"	1
"haha"	"ho"	0
"xxxxyz"	"xx"	2

Algorithm First of all, check whether the first characters from the source text and the
search string match. If this is the case, the number is increased and the search continues.
If there is no match, then the source text is shortened by the first character. The process
is continued recursively as previously described. The termination criterion is that the
length of the given input is smaller than that of the search text. This indicates that no
occurrences can exist.

```python
def count_substrings(text, value_to_find):
    # recursive termination
    if len(text) < len(value_to_find):
        return 0

    count = 0
    remaining = ""

    # does the text start with the search string?
    if text.startswith(value_to_find):
        # hit: continue the search for the found
        # term after the occurrence
        remaining = text[len(value_to_find):]
        count = 1
    else:
        # remove first character and search again
        remaining = text[1:]

    # recursive descent
    return count_substrings(remaining, value_to_find) + count
```

HINT: POSSIBLE VARIATION

You could imagine that a small modification of the requirements would now be to find all potential substrings rather than continuing to search behind them after finding a substring. Interestingly, this simplifies the implementation:

```python
def count_substrings_v2(text, value_to_find):
    # recursive termination
    if len(text) < len(value_to_find):
        return 0

    # does the text starts with the search string?
    count = 1 if text.startswith(value_to_find) else 0

    # remove first character and search again
    remaining = text[1:]

    # recursive descent
    return count_substrings_v2(remaining, value_to_find) + count
```

Optimized algorithm Calls to text[len(value_to_find):] and text[1:] keep generating new strings in the original algorithm. For short input values, this is not so dramatic. But for a very long text, this can be unfavorable.

Well, what might an optimization look like? You still traverse the input from left to right. But instead of shortening the input, it is more feasible to use a position pointer left. This causes the following adjustments:

1. Since the text does not get shorter, you must now subtract the value of left from the original length.

2. You used startswith() to compare for a match. Conveniently there is a variant that allows for providing an offset.

3. If there is a match, you must move the position pointer by the number of characters in the search pattern, otherwise by one position.

This results in the following implementation:

```python
def count_substrings_optimized(text, value_to_find):
    return count_substrings_helper(text, value_to_find, 0)

def count_substrings_helper(text, value_to_find, left):
    if len(text) - left < len(value_to_find):
        return 0

    count = 1 if text.startswith(value_to_find, left) else 0

    if text.startswith(value_to_find, left):
        left += len(value_to_find)
    else:
        left += 1

    return count_substrings_helper(text, value_to_find, left) + count
```

Python shortcut Conveniently, this functionality is already built into Python. Therefore, a call to the built-in functionality count() for strings would be much simpler. However, the point here is to look at variants and see how to avoid too many temporary strings.

In practice, please use calls like the following, here for the inputs from the example of this task:

```
print("xhixhix".count("x"))
print("xhixhix".count("hi"))
print("mic".count("mic"))
print("haha".count("ho"))
print("xxxxyz".count("xx"))
```

Verification

The following inputs show the correct operation for the three variants. You find the same entries here in the first and last test cases. You have, therefore, already outsourced this to a function to avoid duplication.

```
def create_inputs_and_expected():
    return [("xhixhix", "x", 3), ("xhixhix", "hi", 2), ("mic", "mic", 1),
            ("haha", "ho", 0), ("xxxxyz", "xx", 2), ("xxxx", "xx", 2),
            ("xx-xxx-xxxx-xxxxx-xxxxxx", "xx", 9),
            ("xx-xxx-xxxx-xxxxx-xxxxxx", "xxx", 5)]

@pytest.mark.parametrize("input, search_for, expected",
                         create_inputs_and_expected())
def test_count_substrings(input, search_for, expected):
    assert count_substrings(input, search_for) == expected

@pytest.mark.parametrize("input, search_for, expected",
                         [("xhixhix", "x", 3), ("xhixhix", "hi", 2),
                          ("mic", "mic", 1), ("haha", "ho", 0),
                          ("xxxxyz", "xx", 3), ("xxxx", "xx", 3),
                          ("xx-xxx-xxxx-xxxxx-xxxxxx", "xx", 15),
                          ("xx-xxx-xxxx-xxxxx-xxxxxx", "xxx", 10)])
def test_count_substrings_v2(input, search_for, expected):
    assert count_substrings_v2(input, search_for) == expected

@pytest.mark.parametrize("input, search_for, expected",
                         create_inputs_and_expected())
def test_count_substrings_optimized(input, search_for, expected):
    assert count_substrings_optimized(input, search_for) == expected
```

3.3.13 Solution 13: Ruler (★★☆☆☆)

In the introduction, I showed how to draw a simple shape of a ruler as well as a stylized snowflake (see Figure 3-3) using recursion. In this exercise, you want to imitate an English-style ruler. This involves dividing an area of one inch into 1/2 and 1/4 and 1/8. In doing so, the length of the strokes decreases by one each time.

Example

The output should look somewhat like the following:

```
---- 0
-
--
-
---
-
--
-
---- 1
-
--
-
---
-
--
-
---- 2
```

Algorithm The drawing of the full inch markers is done in a loop. The intermediate lines are generated in function `draw_interval()`. This, in turn, takes advantage of the recursive nature of the distribution of lines. A shorter line is drawn around each slightly longer centerline. This is repeated as long as the line length is greater than or equal to 1.

```
def draw_ruler(major_tick_count, max_length):
    draw_line(max_length, "0")

    for i in range(1, major_tick_count + 1):
        draw_interval(max_length - 1)
        draw_line(max_length, i)
```

Finally, you need two helper functions for drawing an interval and a line of the specified length, including an optional marker (for the full inch numbers):

```
def draw_interval(center_length):
    if center_length > 0:
        draw_interval(center_length - 1)
        draw_line(center_length, "")
        draw_interval(center_length - 1)

def draw_line(count, label):
    print(("-" * count) + " " + str(label))
```

Verification

For testing, you call the draw_ruler() function as follows:

```
>>> draw_ruler(3, 4)
---- 0
-
--
-
---
-
--
-
---- 1
-
--
-
---
-
```

```
- -
-
---- 2
-
- -
-
---
-
- -
-
---- 3
```

3.4 Summary: What You Learned

This introductory chapter laid the foundation for a good understanding of recursion. The exercises expanded your knowledge on how to use recursion to solve problems. This is crucial to be able to implement recursive solutions in the following chapters in an efficient way and with a solid basis.

Now let's move on to sequences of characters, also known as strings. Very few program can live without them—time to get into it.

CHAPTER 4

Strings

Strings model character sequences and possess the type str, which offers a variety of functions. In this chapter, you will learn about this topic through various exercises.

4.1 Introduction

Strings consist of single characters and, like lists, are sequential data types (see section 5.1.1), which is why many actions can be performed analogously, such as slicing. Unlike other languages, Python does not have a data type for individual characters, so they are simply represented as strings of length 1.

Strings can be created as character sequences in double or single quotes, as shown by the following two lines:

```
str1 = "DOUBLE QUOTED STRING"
str2 = 'SINGLE QUOTED STRING'
```

4.1.1 Practically Relevant Functions

For strings, I'll go over the most common functions that are useful in practice. Let's assume that the variable str is a string. Then you can call the following functions:

- **len(str)** gets the length of the string. This is a general Python function for querying the length of sequential data types such as lists or tuples, etc., but also strings.

- **str[index]** provides index-based access to individual letters.

© Michael Inden 2022
M. Inden, *Python Challenges*, https://doi.org/10.1007/978-1-4842-7398-2_4

- **str[start:end]/str[start:end:step]** extracts the characters between the positions start and end - 1. As a special feature, a stepwidth can be specified. Interestingly, even the range specification can be omitted and with [::-1] only a negative step size can be used, resulting in a new string with the reverse letter order of the original string.

- **str[:end]** extracts the characters between the beginning and the position end - 1.

- **str[start:]** extracts the characters between the position start and the end of the string.

- **str.lower()/str.upper()** creates a new string consisting of lowercase or uppercase letters. Numbers and punctuation marks are not converted.

- **str.strip()** removes whitespace at the beginning and end of text and returns this as a new string. As a special feature, you can pass a character that will be removed instead of whitespace.

- **str.isalpha()/str.isdigit()/...** checks if all characters of the string are alphanumeric, digits, etc.

- **str.startswith(other)/str.endswith(other)** checks whether the string starts or ends with the given string.

- **str.find(other)/str.rfind(other)** searches for the supplied string and returns the index of the first occurrence or -1 on nonexistence. The function rfind() searches from the end. As a special feature, it is possible to specify an index range in both cases.

- **str.index(other, start, end)/str.rindex(other, start, end)** returns the index of the first or last occurrence of other. Unlike find(), an exception is thrown if the index is not present.

- **str.count(text)** counts how many times text occurs in the string.

- **str.replace(old, new)** creates a new string in which all occurrences of old are replaced by new.

- **str.split(delim)** returns a list of substrings resulting from splitting the original string. The delimiter is *no* regular expression[1]. Without specifying a delimiter, a text is split with respect to whitespace.

- **str.join(list)** does the opposite of split(). Specifically, the elements passed as a list are joined to the string as a delimiter.

- **str.capitalize()/str.title()** converts the first character to uppercase. With title() additionally within a string, the beginning of each new word is converted to uppercase.

4.1.2 Example Conversions and Extractions

Let's take an introductory look at simple actions on strings such as converting to lowercase or uppercase and splitting:

```
name = "Carl Heinz Miller"
print(name.lower())
print(name.upper())

print(name.split())

time = '20:26:45'
hrs, mins, secs = time.split(':')
print(hrs, mins, secs)
```

This results in the following output:

```
carl heinz miller
CARL HEINZ MILLER
['Carl', 'Heinz', 'Miller']
20 26 45
```

In addition, you can repeat text with * and remove text components, often whitespace, from the margins with strip(). As you can see, you can even pass in characters.

```
print("-repeater-" * 3)
```

---

[1] https://en.wikipedia.org/wiki/Regular_expression

```
with_whitespace = "  --CONTENT--  "
stripped1 = with_whitespace.strip()
stripped2 = stripped1.strip("-")
print("strip1:", stripped1, "length:", len(stripped1))
print("strip2:", stripped2, "length:", len(stripped2))
```

This results in the following output:

```
-repeater--repeater-repeater-
strip1:
--CONTENT-- length: 11
strip2: CONTENT length: 7
```

4.1.3 Equality

Now let's look at the definition of two strings and how they can be compared, in particular the effects of == (content equality) and is (reference equality):

```
str1 = 'String with same contents but different quotes'
str2 = "String with same contents but different quotes"
str3 = "String with same contents but XXX quotes".replace("XXX",
"different")
print("str1:", str1)
print("str2:", str2)
print("str3:", str3)

if str1 == str2:
    print("same content")
if str1 is str2:
    print("same reference str1 / str2")
if str1 == str3:
    print("same content")
if str1 is str3:
    print("same reference str1 / str3")
```

You get the following output:

```
str1: String with same contents but different quotes
str2: String with same contents but different quotes
```

```
str3: String with same contents but different quotes
same content
same reference str1 / str2")
same content
```

That the output of references `str1` and `str2` is the same may be surprising at first. Why is that? As an optimization, Python sometimes groups identical objects together.

However, this behavior is not guaranteed. At the latest, when actions are performed on the strings, like above the `replace()` references are no longer the same, but the content is in this case, of course, identical.

4.1.4 Slicing—Access to Individual Characters and Substrings

In the following code you use powerful slicing operations to access single characters, whole components, and even non-contiguous ranges. After that, you count occurrences and simulate a search and research. Finally, you replace a text component.

```
strange_message= "a message containing only a message"

mid_chars = strange_message[10:20]
last_seven_chars = strange_message[-7:]
print("mid_chars:", mid_chars, " / last_seven_chars:", last_seven_chars)

first_char = strange_message[0]
print(first_char, "count:", strange_message.count(first_char))
print(last_seven_chars, "count:", strange_message.count(last_seven_chars))

# search and continue searching
print("find message:", strange_message.find("message"))
print("find next message:", strange_message.find("message", 3))

# replace (all)
print("replace by info:", strange_message.replace("message", "info"))
```

This results in the following output:

```
mid_chars: containing  / last_seven_chars: message
a count: 5
```

```
message count: 2
find message: 2
find next message: 28
replace by info: a info containing only a info
```

4.1.5 Converting a String into a List of Characters

Sometimes you want to process text as single characters. A call to list() can be helpful for this:

```
print(list("Text als Liste"))
```

This results in the following outputs:

```
['T', 'e', 'x', 't', ' ', 'a', 'l', 's', ' ', 'L', 'i', 's', 't', 'e']
```

4.1.6 Iteration

There are several variants when looping through the individual characters of a string. First, it is possible to work indexed with a for loop and len() in combination with range(). However, this is the least adequate way in Python. It is better to work with enumerate(), which provides access to both the index and the value. Sometimes you don't need access to the index at all; then the third variant with in is recommended.

```
message = "Python has several loop variants"
for i in range(len(message)):
    print(i, message[i], end=',')
print()

for i, current_char in enumerate(message):
    print(i, current_char, end=',')
print()

for current_char in message:
    print(current_char, end=',')
print()
```

These loops produce the following output:

```
0 P,1 y,2 t,3 h,4 o,5 n,6  ,7 h,8 a,9 s,10  ,11 s,12 e,13 v,14 e,15 r,16 a,17 l
,18  ,19 l,20 o,21 o,22 p,23  ,24 v,25 a,26 r,27 i,28 a,29 n,30 t,31 s,
0 P,1 y,2 t,3 h,4 o,5 n,6  ,7 h,8 a,9 s,10  ,11 s,12 e,13 v,14 e,15 r,16 a,17 l
,18  ,19 l,20 o,21 o,22 p,23  ,24 v,25 a,26 r,27 i,28 a,29 n,30 t,31 s,
P,y,t,h,o,n, ,h,a,s, ,s,e,v,e,r,a,l, ,l,o,o,p, ,v,a,r,i,a,n,t,s,
```

4.1.7 Formatted Output

The following calls to `capitalize()` and `title()`

```
text = "this is a very special string"
print(text.capitalize())
print(text.title())
```

result in this output:

```
This is a very special string
This Is A Very Special String
```

Python offers different ways of formatting output with placeholders. In the simplest case, you specify the values in a comma-separated way in `print()`. Alternatively, you can specify placeholders in the text using {}, which will then be filled with the values of the call to of `format()`. There is also the variant with placeholders like %s and %d as well as the modulo operator in combination with a tuple that provides the values. Finally, an explicitly formatted string with f"text" and named parameters can be used.

```
product = "Apple iMac"
price = 3699
```

```
# variants of the formatted output
print("the", product, "costs", price)
print("the {} costs {}".format(product, price))
print(f"the %s costs %d" % (product, price))
print(f"the {product} costs {price}")
```

This results in the following output for all four variants:

```
the Apple iMac costs 3699
```

4.1.8 Character Processing

If you need to process single characters, the functions ord() and chr() can be useful. Here chr() converts a numerical value into a string of length 1 and ord() converts such a such a string into an int value:

```
>>> ord("A")
65
>>> chr(65)
'A'
>>> ord("0")
48
>>> chr(48)
'0'
```

4.1.9 Example: String Processing

As a final example of string processing, you want to count the number of occurrences of each letter in a string, treating lowercase and uppercase letters equally. For the text "Otto," you expect 2 x t and 2 x o due to the conversion to lowercase letters. Such a processing is also called a **histogram**. This is a representation of the distribution of objects, often numerical values. It is also known from photography for the brightness distribution of a picture. The following is about the distribution or determination of the frequencies of letters for a text. To do this, you first convert the input to lowercase with lower() and then iterate through this string. By calling isalpha() you make sure that you only include letters in your count.

```
from operator import itemgetter

def generate_character_histogram(word):
    char_count_map = {}

    for current_char in list(word.lower()):
        if current_char.isalpha():
            if current_char in char_count_map:
                char_count_map[current_char] += 1
            else:
```

```
        char_count_map[current_char] = 1

    return dict(sorted(char_count_map.items(), key=itemgetter(0)))
```

Let's try this out in the Python command line:

```
>>> generate_character_histogram("Otto")
{'o': 2, 't': 2}

>>> generate_character_histogram("Hello Micha")
{'a': 1, 'c': 1, 'e': 1, 'h': 2, 'i': 1, 'l': 2, 'm': 1, 'o': 1}

>>> generate_character_histogram("Python Challenges, Your Python Training")
{'a': 2, 'c': 1, 'e': 2, 'g': 2, 'h': 3, 'i': 2, 'l': 2, 'n': 5, 'o': 3,
'p': 2, 'r': 2, 's': 1, 't': 3, 'u': 1, 'y': 3}
```

4.2 Exercises

4.2.1 Exercise 1: Number Conversions (★★☆☆☆)

Based on a string, implement a validation for binary numbers and a conversion to it. Repeat both for hexadecimal numbers.

Note   The conversion can be solved with `int(value, radix)` and base 2 for binary numbers and base 16 for hexadecimal numbers. Do not use these explicitly; implement them yourself.

Examples

Input	Method	Result
"10101"	is_binary_number()	True
"111"	binary_to_decimal()	7
"AB"	hex_to_decimal()	171

Exercise 1a (★☆☆☆☆)

Write function is_binary_number(number) that checks that a given string consists only of the characters 0 and 1 (i. e., represents a binary number).

Exercise 1b (★★☆☆☆)

Write function binary_to_decimal(number) that converts a (valid) binary number represented as a string to the corresponding decimal number.

Exercise 1c (★★☆☆☆)

Write the entire conversion again, but this time for hexadecimal numbers.

4.2.2 Exercise 2: Joiner (★☆☆☆☆)

Write function join(values, delimiter) that joins a list of strings with the given delimiter and returns it as one string. Implement this yourself without using any special Python functionality like join() provided by type str.

Example

Input	Separator	Result
["hello", "world", "message"]	" +++ "	"hello +++ world +++ message"

4.2.3 Exercise 3: Reverse String (★★☆☆☆)

Write function reverse(text) that reverses the letters in a string and returns it as a result. Implement this yourself; in other words, do not use any special Python functionality, such as [::-1].

Examples

Input	Result
"ABCD"	"DCBA"
"OTTO"	"OTTO"
"PETER"	"RETEP"

4.2.4 Exercise 4: Palindrome (★★★☆☆)

Exercise 4a (★★☆☆☆)

Write function `is_palindrome(text)` that checks whether a given string is a palindrome regardless of case. A palindrome is a word that reads the same from the front and the back.

Note   You can easily solve the verification with `[::-1]`. Explicitly do not use Python components; implement the functionality yourself.

Examples

Input	Result
"Otto"	True
"ABCBX"	False
"ABCXcba"	True

Exercise 4b (★★★☆☆)

Write an extension that does not consider spaces and punctuation as relevant, allowing whole sentences to be checked, such as this one:

Was it a car or a cat I saw?

4.2.5 Exercise 5: No Duplicate Chars (★★★☆☆)

Determine if a given string contains duplicate letters. Uppercase and lowercase letters should not make any difference. Write function check_no_duplicate_chars(text) for this purpose.

Examples

Input	Result
"Otto"	False
"Adrian"	False
"Micha"	True
"ABCDEFG"	True

4.2.6 Exercise 6: Remove Duplicate Letters (★★★☆☆)

Write function remove_duplicates(text) that keeps each letter only once in a given text, thus deleting all subsequent duplicates regardless of case. However, the original order of the letters should be preserved.

Examples

Input	Result
"bananas"	"bans"
"lalalamama"	"lam"
"MICHAEL"	"MICHAEL"
"AaBbcCdD"	"ABcd"

4.2.7 Exercise 7: Capitalize (★★☆☆☆)

Exercise 7a (★★☆☆☆)

Write function `capitalize(text)` that converts a given text into an English title format where each word starts with a capital letter. You must explicitly not use the built-in function `title()` of the type `str`.

Examples

Input	Result
"this is a very special title"	"This Is A Very Special Title"
"effective java is great"	"Effective Java Is Great"

Exercise 7b: Modification (★★☆☆☆)

Assume now that the input is a list of strings and that a list of strings should be returned, with the individual words and then starting with a capital letter.

Exercise 7c: Special treatment (★★☆☆☆)

In headings, it is common to encounter special treatment of words. For example, "is" and "a" are not capitalized. Implement this as function `capitalize_special_2(words, ignorable_words)`, which gets the words excluded from the conversion as the second parameter.

Example

Input	Exceptions	Result
["this", "is", "a", "title"]	["is", "a"]	["This", "is", "a", "Title"]

145

4.2.8 Exercise 8: Rotation (★★☆☆☆)

Consider two strings, str1 and str2, where the first string is supposed to be longer than the second. Figure out if the first one contains the other one. In doing so, the characters within the first string may also be rotated. Characters can be moved from the beginning or the end to the opposite position (even repeatedly). To do this, create function contains_rotation(str1, str2), which is case-insensitive during the check.

Examples

Input 1	Input 2	Result
"ABCD"	"ABC"	True
"ABCDEF"	"EFAB"	True ("ABCDEF" < x 2 ⇒ "CDEFAB" contains "EFAB")
"BCDE"	"EC"	False
"Challenge"	"GECH"	True

4.2.9 Exercise 9: Well Formed Braces (★★☆☆☆)

Write function check_braces(text) that checks whether the sequence of round braces passed as a string contains matching (properly nested) pairs of braces.

Examples

Input	Result	Comment
"(())"	True	
"()()"	True	
"(())) ((())"	False	Although it has the same amount of opening and closing braces, it is not properly nested
"((()"	False	No suitable bracing

4.2.10 Exercise 10: Anagram (★★☆☆☆)

The term *anagram* is used to describe two strings that contain the same letters in the same frequency. Here, uppercase and lowercase should not make any difference. Write function is_anagram(str1, str2).

Examples

Input 1	Input 2	Result
"Otto"	"Toto"	True
"Mary"	"Army"	True
"Ananas"	"Bananas"	False

4.2.11 Exercise 11: Morse Code (★★☆☆☆)

Write function to_morse_code(text) that is capable of translating a given text into Morse code characters. They consist of sequences of one to four short and long tones per letter, symbolized by a dot (.) or a dash (-). It is desirable for easier distinguishability to place a space between each tone and three spaces between each sequence of letter tones. Otherwise, S (...) and EEE (...) would not be distinguishable from each other.

For simplicity, limit yourself to the letters E, O, S, T, W with the following encoding:

Letter	Morse code
E	.
O	- - -
S	. . .
T	-
W	. - -

Examples

Input	Result
SOS	... - - - ...
TWEET	- .-- . . -
WEST	.-- . ... -

Bonus Try to find out the corresponding Morse code for all letters of the alphabet so you can convert your name. You can find the necessary hints for this at https://en.wikipedia.org/wiki/Morse_code.

4.2.12 Exercise 12: Pattern Checker (★★★☆☆)

Write function matches_pattern(pattern, text) that examines a space-separated string (second parameter) against the structure of a pattern passed in the form of individual characters as the first parameter.

Examples

Input pattern	Input text	Result
"xyyx"	"tim mike tim"	True
"xyyx"	"tim mike tom tim"	False
"xyxx"	"tim mike tim"	False
"xxxx"	"tim tim"	True

4.2.13 Exercise 13: Tennis Score (★★★☆☆)

Write function tennis_score(score, player1_name, player2_name) that makes an announcement in a familiar style such as Fifteen Love, Deuce, or Advantage Player X, based on a textual score for two players, PL1 and PL2. The score is given in the format <PL1 points>:<PL2 points>.

The following counting rules apply to a game in tennis:

- A game is won (Game <PlayerX>) when a player reaches four or more points and is ahead by at least two points.

- Points from zero to three are named Love, Fifteen, Thirty, and Forty.

- In case of at least three points and a tie, this is called Deuce.

- With at least three points and a one-point difference, this is called Advantage <PlayerX> for the one who has one more point.

Examples

Input	Score
"1:0", "Micha", "Tim"	"Fifteen Love"
"2:2", "Micha", "Tim"	"Thirty Thirty"
"2:3", "Micha", "Tim"	"Thirty Forty"
"3:3", "Micha", "Tim"	"Deuce"
"4:3", "Micha", "Tim"	"Advantage Micha"
"4:4", "Micha", "Tim"	"Deuce"
"5:4", "Micha", "Tim"	"Advantage Micha"
"6:4", "Micha", "Tim"	"Game Micha"

4.2.14 Exercise 14: Version Numbers (★★☆☆☆)

Write function `compare_versions(version1, version2)` that compares version numbers in the format *MAJOR.MINOR.PATCH* with each other. Thereby the specification of *PATCH* is optional. In particular, the return value should be represented in the form of the characters <, =, and >.

Examples

Version 1	Version 2	Result
1.11.17	2.3.5	<
2.1	2.1.3	<
2.3.5	2.4	<
3.1	2.4	>
3.3	3.2.9	>
7.2.71	7.2.71	=

4.2.15 Exercise 15: Conversion str_to_number (★★☆☆☆)

Convert a string into an integer. To do this, write function str_to_number(text) on your own.

Note   The conversion can be easily achieved with int(value). Do not use this explicitly, but implement the entire conversion yourself.

Examples

Input	Result
"+123"	123
"-123"	-123
"7271"	7271
"ABC"	ValueError
"0123"	83 (for bonus task)
"-0123"	-83 (for bonus task)
"0128"	ValueError (for bonus task)

Bonus Enable the parsing of octal numbers.

4.2.16 Exercise 16: Print Tower (★★★☆☆)

Write function print_tower(n) that represents a tower of *n* slices stacked on top of each other as ASCII graphics, symbolized by the character #. Also, draw a lower boundary line.

Example

A tower of height three should look something like this:

```
      |
   #  |#
  ##  |##
 ###  |###
----------
```

4.2.17 Exercise 17: Filled Frame (★★☆☆☆)

Write function print_box(width, height, fillchar) that draws a rectangle of the specified size as an ASCII graphic and fills it with the passed-in fill character.

Examples

Below you see two rectangles filled differently:

```
+-----+      +-------+
|*****|      |$$$$$$$|
|*****|      |$$$$$$$|
|*****|      |$$$$$$$|
+-----+      |$$$$$$$|
             |$$$$$$$|
             +-------+
```

4.2.18 Exercise 18: Guessing Vowels (★★☆☆☆)

Write function translate_vowel(text, replacement) that replaces all vowels in a given text with a character or string. This can be used for a little guessing quiz, for example, or to determine word similarities based on consonants only.

Input	Replacement	Result
"guide"	"?"	"g??d?"
"lawnmower"	"-"	"l-wnm-w-r"
"quiz"	"_"	"q z"
"lawnmower"	""	"lwnmwr"

4.3 Solutions

4.3.1 Solution 1: Number Conversions (★★☆☆☆)

Based on a string, implement a validation for binary numbers and a conversion to it. Repeat both for hexadecimal numbers.

Note   The conversion can be solved with int(value, radix) and base 2 for binary numbers and base 16 for hexadecimal numbers. Do not use these explicitly; implement them yourself.

Examples

Input	Method	Result
"10101"	is_binary_number()	True
"111"	binary_to_decimal()	7
"AB "	hex_to_decimal()	171

Solution 1a (★☆☆☆☆)

Write function is_binary_number(number) that checks that a given string consists only of the characters 0 and 1 (i. e., represents a binary number).

Algorithm The brute force and index-based version iterates through the string character by character from the beginning to the end, checking whether the current character is 0 or 1. If another character is detected, the loop terminates and then `False` is returned.

```python
def is_binary_number(number):
    is_binary = True
    i = 0

    while i < len(number) and is_binary:
        current_char = number[i]
        is_binary = (current_char == "0" or current_char == "1")
        i += 1

    return is_binary
```

This can also be formulated as a search problem but needs some thought here when returning:

```python
def is_binary_number_v2(number):
    i = 0
    while i < len(number) and number[i] in ["0", "1"]:
        i += 1

    return i >= len(number)
```

Python shortcut The whole thing can be implemented in an easier and more understandable way with Python specifics:

```python
def is_binary_number_short_cut(word):
    for current_char in word:
        if current_char not in ["0", "1"]:
            return False

    return True
```

PYTHON STYLE: DON'T ASK FOR PERMISSION, ASK FOR FORGIVENESS

There is—as indicated in the task —still the possibility to use int(). Then you follow the Python motto of "Don't ask for permission, ask for forgiveness." In this case, it means trying potentially dangerous actions, like index accesses with the wrong index and reacting appropriately if they fail. With a strong Java background, I take a rather critical view of this habit—sure, the approach is often practical, but sometimes it is a bit risky. But let's look at this stylistically perfectly good variant of the check:

```python
def is_binary_number_v3(number):
    try:
        int(number, 2)
        return True
    except ValueError:
        return False
```

Solution 1b (★★☆☆)

Write function binary_to_decimal(number) that converts a (valid) binary number represented as a string to the corresponding decimal number.

Algorithm You traverses the string character by character from left to right and processes each character as a binary digit. The current character is used to calculate the value by multiplying the previously converted value by 2 and adding the current value. It is possible to formulate the algorithm more clearly, meaning without special treatments, because a valid input is ensured by the previously implemented function is_binary_number(number).

```python
def binary_to_decimal(number):
    if not is_binary_number(number):
        raise ValueError(number + " is not a binary number")

    decimal_value = 0
    for current_char in number:
        value = int(current_char)
        decimal_value = decimal_value * 2 + value

    return decimal_value
```

Solution 1c (★★☆☆☆)

Write the entire conversion again, but this time for hexadecimal numbers.

Algorithm For hexadecimal numbers, the factor has to be changed to 16. In addition, the letters A to F are now permitted in both lowercase and uppercase. Their value is determined by a subtraction ord(current_char.upper()) - ord("A") + 10— thus forming "A" to "F" to the values 0 to 5 and add 10, which then gives the correct value.

```python
def hex_to_decimal(number):
    if not is_hex_number(number):
        raise ValueError(number + " is not a hex number")

    decimal_value = 0
    for current_char in number:

        if current_char.isdigit():
            value = int(current_char)
        else:
            value = ord(current_char.upper()) - ord("A") + 10

        decimal_value = decimal_value * 16 + value


    return decimal_value
```

The check for valid hexadecimal numbers uses a tricky check with in under the specification of all possible digits and letters for hexadecimal numbers:

```python
def is_hex_number(number):
    for current_char in number:
        if current_char not in "0123456789ABCDEFabcdef":
            return False

    return True
```

Verification

For testing, use the following inputs, which show the correct functionality:

```python
@pytest.mark.parametrize("value, expected",
                    [("10101", True), ("222", False), ("12345",
                    False)])
```

```
def test_is_binary_number(value, expected):
    assert is_binary_number(value) == expected

@pytest.mark.parametrize("value, expected",
                         [("111", 7), ("1010", 10), ("1111", 15),
                          ("10000", 16)])
def test_binary_to_decimal(value, expected):
    assert binary_to_decimal(value) == expected

@pytest.mark.parametrize("value, expected",
                         [("7", 7), ("A", 10), ("F", 15), ("10", 16)])
def test_hex_to_decimal(value, expected):
    assert hex_to_decimal(value) == expected
```

4.3.2 Solution 2: Joiner (★☆☆☆☆)

Write function join(values, delimiter) that joins a list of strings with the given delimiter and returns it as one string. Implement this yourself without using any special Python functionality like join() provided by type str.

Example

Input	Separator	Result
["hello", "world", "message"]	" +++ "	"hello +++ world +++ message"

Algorithm Traverse the list of values from front to back. Insert the text into a string, add the separator string, and repeat this until the last value. As a special treatment, no separator string may be added after this.

```
def join(values, delimiter):
    result = ""
    for i, current_value in enumerate(values):
        result += current_value
        # no separator after last occurrence
```

```
    if i < len(values) - 1:
        result += delimiter

  return result
```

Python shortcut String joining can be written in a compact and understandable way and without special handling using the appropriate function `join()`:

```
result = delimiter.join(values)
```

A variant with `reduce()` from module `functools` looks like this:

```
import functools

result = functools.reduce(lambda str1, str2: str1 + delimiter +
str2, values)
```

By the way, the function `join()` is also handy when you want to convert the values of a list into a string. For this purpose, you use an empty string as a delimiter.

```
"".join(values)    # trick: Convert list to string
```

Verification

For testing, use the following inputs, which show the correct functionality:

```
@pytest.mark.parametrize("values, delimiter, expected",
                         [(["hello", "world", "message"], " +++ ",
                           "hello +++ world +++ message")])
def test_join(values, delimiter, expected):
    assert join(values, delimiter) == expected
```

4.3.3 Solution 3: Reverse String (★★☆☆☆)

Write function `reverse(text)` that reverses the letters in a string and returns it as a result. Implement this yourself; in other words, without using any special Python functionality, such as `[::-1]`.

Examples

Input	Result
"ABCD"	"DCBA"
"OTTO"	"OTTO"
"PETER"	"RETEP"

Algorithm Initially, an idea could be to traverse the original string character by character from the end and add the respective character to the result:

```python
def reverse(text):
    reversed_text = ""

    for i in range(len(text) - 1, -1, -1):
        current_char = text[i]
        reversed_text += current_char

    return reversed_text
```

A bit messy is the `for` loop with the multiple -1. The built-in functionality `reversed()` allows you to run through the text character by character from back to front, which is more readable:

```python
def reverse_nicer(text):
    reversed_text = ""

    for current_char in reversed(text):
        reversed_text += current_char

    return reversed_text
```

However, a small problem exists. The string concatenations with += are potentially expensive because strings are immutable in Python and thereby new string objects are created. Generally, each externally visible change creates a new string.

Optimized algorithm So how could it be more memory-efficient, for example, if very long strings are to be reversed extremely frequently?

The idea is to convert the string with `list()` into a list and work directly on it. In addition, you use two pointers, *left* and *right*, which initially point to the first and last character, respectively. Now you swap the individual letters, and the position pointers move inwards. Repeat the whole process as long as *left* < *right* is valid; if *left* >= *right,* the process is aborted.

Let's illustrate the procedure for the text ABCD, where l stands for *left* and r for *right*:

```
A B C D
l     r

D B C A
l     r

D C B A
  r l       => End
```

You implement the described procedure as follows:

```python
def reverse_inplace(text):
    original_chars = list(text)

    left = 0
    right = len(original_chars) - 1

    while left < right:
        left_char = original_chars[left]
        right_char = original_chars[right]

        original_chars[left] = right_char
        original_chars[right] = left_char
        left+=1
        right-=1

    # trick: convert list to string
    return "".join(original_chars)
```

Python shortcut Of course, the whole thing can be achieved much easier by the following two calls. Still, this exercise is about to get to know the character-by- character processing and possible optimizations.

```python
reversed_text = text[::-1])
reversed_text = "".join(reversed(text)))
```

Verification

Let's write a unit test to verify the desired functionality:

```
def input_and_expected():
    return [("ABCD", "DCBA"), ("OTTO", "OTTO"), ("PETER", "RETEP")]

@pytest.mark.parametrize("input, expected",
                            input_and_expected())
def test_reverse(input, expected):
    assert reverse(input) == expected

@pytest.mark.parametrize("input, expected",
                            input_and_expected())
def test_reverse_inplace(input, expected):
    assert reverse_inplace(input) == expected
```

4.3.4 Solution 4: Palindrome (★★★☆☆)

Solution 4a (★★☆☆☆)

Write function is_palindrome(text) that checks whether a given string is a palindrome
regardless of case. A palindrome is a word that reads the same from the front and
the back.

Note   You can easily solve the verification with [::-1]. Explicitly do not use
Python components; implement the functionality yourself.

Examples

Input	Result
"Otto"	True
"ABCBX"	False
"ABCXcba"	True

JOB INTERVIEW TIPS

In a job interview, here are possible questions you may ask to clarify the scope of the assignment:

- Should it be case-sensitive?

  ANSWER: No

- Are spaces relevant?

  ANSWER: First yes, later no, then to be ignored

Algorithm As in exercise 3, the string is represented as a list and you advance one position inward from the left and one position from the right, as long as the characters match and as long as the left position is still smaller than the right position:

```python
def is_palindrome(text):
    left = 0
    right = len(text) - 1

    lower_input = text.lower()
    is_same_char = True
    while left < right and is_same_char:
        is_same_char = (lower_input[left] == lower_input[right])
        left += 1
        right -= 1

    return is_same_char
```

Python shortcut Of course, the whole thing can be achieved in a straightforward way by calling the built-in functionality [::-1]. Still, this will generate an additional string.

```python
def is_palindrome_short(text):
    adjusted_input = text.lower()

    return adjusted_input == adjusted_input[::-1]
```

Algorithm with recursion How can you solve the palindrome problem recursively and without using a list as an auxiliary data structure? After reading Chapter 3 and working through some of the exercises on recursion given there, you should be able to implement this easily. With the strategy or the idiom of the helper function in mind, the following recursive implementation emerges, which, starting from the outside, always checks two characters. This is continued inward as long as the characters match and the left position is smaller than the right one.

```
def is_palindrome_rec(text):
    return is_palindrome_rec_in_range(text.lower(), 0, len(text) - 1)

def is_palindrome_rec_in_range(text, left, right):
    if left >= right:
        return True

    if text[left] == text[right]:
        return is_palindrome_rec_in_range(text, left + 1, right - 1)

    return False
```

An alternative way is always to shorten the string by the characters. Why is this logical solution not so good practically? The answer is obvious: This causes many temporary string objects to be created. Besides, a large number of copy actions would have to take place.

Solution 4b (★★★☆☆)

Write an extension that does not consider spaces and punctuation as relevant, allowing whole sentences to be checked, such as this one:

Was it a car or a cat I saw?

Algorithm You can incorporate special checks for whitespace into the algorithm. Still, it is easier to create a version of the function and replace all unwanted punctuation and whitespace therein before calling the original function.

```
def is_palindrome_special(text, ignore_spaces_and_punctuation):
    adjusted_input = text.lower()
    if ignore_spaces_and_punctuation:
        adjusted_input = adjusted_input.replace(" ", "")
        adjusted_input = adjusted_input.replace("!", "")
        adjusted_input = adjusted_input.replace(".", "")

    return is_palindrome_rec(adjusted_input)
```

Please note that `replace()` unfortunately does not support regular expression to remove the special characters. Here this is the case for a space, exclamation mark, and period. Therefore, you simply call this three times appropriately.

HINT: REGULAR EXPRESSIONS WITH PYTHON

If you prefer to use a regular expression after all, you can utilize the `re` module as follows:

```python
import re

def is_palindrome_special_with_reg_ex(text, ignore_spaces_and_punctuation):
    adjusted_input = text.lower()
    if ignore_spaces_and_punctuation:
        adjusted_input = re.sub(r"[ !\.\?]", "", adjusted_input)

    return is_palindrome_rec(adjusted_input)
```

Verification

To verify, you again write a unit test with the following inputs that show the correct operation:

```python
def palindrome_inputs_and_expecteds():
    return [("Otto", True),
            ("ABCBX", False),
            ("ABCXcba", True)]

@pytest.mark.parametrize("input, expected",
                          palindrome_inputs_and_expecteds())
def test_is_palindrome(input, expected):
    assert is_palindrome(input) == expected

@pytest.mark.parametrize("input, expected",
                          palindrome_inputs_and_expecteds())
def test_is_palindrome_rec(input, expected):
    assert is_palindrome_rec(input) == expected
```

```
@pytest.mark.parametrize("input, expected",
                              [("Was it a car or a cat i saw.", True),
                               ("This is not a Palindrome!", False)])
def test_is_palindrome_special(input, expected):
    ignore_spaces_and_punctuation = True
    assert is_palindrome_special(input,
                               ignore_spaces_and_punctuation) == expected
```

FINDINGS: PAY ATTENTION TO COMPREHENSIBILITY

It is absolutely natural for strings to choose an iterative solution due to their API and position/index-based access. This would no longer be convenient if you had to determine the palindrome property for the digits of a number. This can be done with recursion and some consideration even without the detour via conversion shown as exercise 10 in section 3.3.10. Having developed the functionality reverse() in the previous exercise, you can profitably use it here as follows:

```
def is_palindrome_with_reverse(text):
    adjusted_input = text.lower()

    return adjusted_input == reverse(adjusted_input)
```

This demonstrates that problem- and context-aware programming enables the creation of comprehensible and maintainable solutions. The properties of understandability, maintainability, and changeability are of high importance in practice since source code is usually modified far more frequently due to changing or new requirements than created completely from scratch.

4.3.5 Solution 5: No Duplicate Chars (★★★☆☆)

Determine if a given string contains duplicate letters. Uppercase and lowercase letters should not make any difference. Write function check_no_duplicate_chars(text) for this purpose.

Examples

Input	Result
"Otto"	False
"Adrian"	False
"Micha"	True
"ABCDEFG"	True

Algorithm When solving the task, you might get the idea of storing the individual characters in a set. You run through the input character by character from front to back. For each character, you check whether it is already in the set. If so, you have encountered a duplicate character and abort processing. Otherwise, you insert the character into the set and continue with the next character until you reach the end of the input or detect a duplicate character.

```python
def check_no_duplicate_chars(text):
    contained_chars = set()

    for current_char in text.upper():
        if current_char in contained_chars:
            return False

        contained_chars.add(current_char)

    return True
```

Python Shortcut Although the implementation shown is quite straightforward, other even more compact alternatives exist. They take advantage of the fact that any string can be converted into a list or set using the functions list() or set(). If there are no duplicates, the number of characters must be equal to the length of the string. Many words, but few instructions ... the whole thing can be formulated as follows:

```python
def check_no_duplicate_chars_v2(text):
    upper_case_input = text.upper()
    return len(upper_case_input) == len(set(upper_case_input))
```

Verification

You again use a unit test to verify the desired functionality:

```python
@pytest.mark.parametrize("input, expected",
                         [("Otto", False), ("Adrian", False),
                          ("Micha", True), ("ABCDEFG", True)])
def test_check_no_duplicate_chars(input, expected):
    assert check_no_duplicate_chars(input) == expected
```

4.3.6 Solution 6: Remove Duplicate Letters (★★★☆☆)

Write function remove_duplicates(text) that keeps each letter only once in a given text, thus deleting all subsequent duplicates regardless of case. However, the original order of the letters should be preserved.

Examples

Input	Result
"bananas"	"bans"
"lalalamama"	"lam"
"MICHAEL"	"MICHAEL"
"AaBbcCdD"	"ABcd"

Algorithm Again, you run through the string character by character and store the respective letters in a set called already_seen. If the current character is not yet contained there, it will be included in both the set and the result text. However, if such a character already exists, you continue with the next character of the input.

```python
def remove_duplicates(text):
    result = ""
    already_seen = set()

    for current_char in text:
        if not current_char.lower() in already_seen:
```

```
        already_seen.add(current_char.lower())
        result += current_char

    return result
```

Verification

Check the removal of duplicate letters using the following unit test:

```
@pytest.mark.parametrize("input, expected",
                    [("bananas", "bans"),
                     ("lalalamama", "lam"),
                     ("MICHAEL", "MICHAEL"),
                     ("AaBbCcDd", "ABcd")])
def test_remove_duplicates(input, expected):
    assert remove_duplicates(input) == expected
```

4.3.7 Solution 7: Capitalize (★★☆☆☆)
Exercise 7a (★★☆☆☆)

Write function `capitalize(text)` that converts a given text into an English title format where each word starts with a capital letter. You must explicitly not use the built-in function `title()` of the type `str`.

Examples

Input	Result
"this is a very special title"	"This Is A Very Special Title"
"effective java is great"	"Effective Java Is Great"

Algorithm Because strings are immutable, initially you copy the contents into a list upon which you make the modifications. You traverse this list from front to back, looking for the beginning of a new word. As an indicator, you use a `boolean` flag `capitalize_next_char`. This indicates that the first letter of the next word has to be capitalized. Initially, this flag is `True`, so the current (first) character is converted into a capital letter. This happens only for letters, not for numbers. After the conversion, the flag gets reset and letters are skipped until a space is found. You then reset the flag to True. This procedure gets repeated until the end of the list is reached. Finally, a new string is created from the list containing the modifications.

```python
def capitalize(text):
    input_chars = list(text)

    capitalize_next_char = True
    for i, current_char in enumerate(input_chars):
        if current_char.isspace():
            capitalize_next_char = True
        elif capitalize_next_char and current_char.isalpha():
            input_chars[i] = current_char.upper()
            capitalize_next_char = False

    return "".join(input_chars)
```

Let's try the whole thing in the Python command line:

```python
>>> capitalize("seems to be okay")
'Seems To Be Okay'
```

Now, however, you may wonder about the behavior that is supposed to occur for letters after digits or other non-letters:

```python
>>> capitalize("what should happen with -a +b 1c")
'What Should Happen With -A +B 1C'
```

HINT: SPECIAL TREATMENT VARIANT

A moment ago, I brought up a special case. It is a matter of definition how to deal with it. If letters after special characters should not be converted to uppercase, this can be achieved easily. The difference compared to before is subtle: You remove the `isalpha()` check and call `upper()` in every case. This is possible because the function can handle not only letters but also other characters.

```python
def capitalize_special(text):
    input_chars = list(text)
```

```
    capitalize_next_char = True
    for i, current_char in enumerate(input_chars):

        if current_char.isspace():
            capitalize_next_char = True
        elif capitalize_next_char:
            input_chars[i] = current_char.upper()
            capitalize_next_char = False

    return "".join(input_chars)
```

This then yields the following output:

```
>>> capitalize_special("what should happen with -a +b 1c")
'What Should Happen With -a +b 1c'
```

Behavior for whitespace It is also interesting to see how whitespace is handled:

```
print(capitalize("This is a text"))
print(capitalize("This \t is    a    text"))
```

This returns the following, not entirely without surprise—which is not to be considered further for your task:

```
This is a text
This    is    a    text
```

Python shortcut The desired functionality can be implemented as follows with list comprehension and split():

```
def capitalize_shorter(text):
    converted = [word[0].upper() + word[1:] for word in text.split()]
    return " ".join(converted)
```

This provides for the two inputs the same result:

```
>>> print(capitalize_shorter("This is a text"))
This Is A Text
>>> print(capitalize_shorter("This \t is    a    text"))
This Is A Text
```

Exercise 7b: Modification (★★☆☆☆)

Assume now that the input is a list of strings and that a list of strings should be returned, with the individual words and then starting with a capital letter.

Algorithm First, create a list to store the converted words. Then iterate through all elements of the given list and process each one by calling the function `capitalize_word()`. To convert the first character to a capital letter, retrieve it indexed with `[0]` and then call `upper()`. The remaining characters are returned by slicing with `[1:]`. A new word is formed from both and inserted into the result. To make the function `capitalize_word()` error-tolerant, it handles an empty input with a sanity check.

```python
def capitalize_words(words):
    return [capitalize_word(word) for word in words]

def capitalize_word(word):
    if not word:
        return ""

    return word[0].upper() + word[1:]
```

Exercise 7c: Special treatment (★★☆☆☆)

In headings, it is common to encounter special treatment of words. For example, "is" and "a" are not capitalized. Implement this as function `capitalize_special_2(words, ignorable_words)` that gets the words excluded from the conversion as the second parameter.

Example

Input	Exceptions	Result
["this", "is", "a", "title"]	["is", "a"]	["This", "is", "a", "Title"]

Algorithm The previously developed functionality is extended by a list of words that should not be converted. When traversing, you check if the current word is one from the negative list. If so, it is added to the result without modification. Otherwise, you perform the actions as before.

```python
def capitalize_special_2(words, ignorable_words):
```

```
    capitalized_words = []

    for word in words:
        if word in ignorable_words:
            capitalized_words.append(word)
        else:
            capitalized_words.append(capitalize_word(word))

    return capitalized_words
```

Verification

For testing, use the following inputs, which show the correct functionality:

```
@pytest.mark.parametrize("input, expected",
                         [("this is a very special title",
                           "This Is A Very Special Title"),
                          ("effective java is great",
                           "Effective Java Is Great")])
def test_capitalize(input, expected):
    assert capitalize(input) == expected

@pytest.mark.parametrize("words, expected",
                         [(["this", "is", "a", "very", "special", "title"],
                           ["This", "Is", "A", "Very", "Special", "Title"]),
                          (["effective", "java", "is", "great"],
                           ["Effective", "Java", "Is", "Great"])])
def test_capitalize_words(words, expected):
    assert capitalize_words(words) == expected

@pytest.mark.parametrize("words, expected",
                         [(["this", "is", "a", "very", "special", "title"],
                           ["This", "is", "a", "Very", "Special", "Title"]),
                          (["effective", "java", "is", "great"],
                           ["Effective", "Java", "is", "Great"])])
def test_capitalize_special_2(words, expected):
    assert capitalize_special_2(words, ["a", "is"]) == expected
```

4.3.8 Solution 8: Rotation (★★☆☆☆)

Consider two strings, str1 and str2, where the first string is supposed to be longer than the second. Figure out if the first one contains the other one. In doing so, the characters within the first string may also be rotated. Characters can be moved from the beginning or the end to the opposite position (even repeatedly). To do this, create function contains_rotation(str1, str2), which is case-insensitive during the check.

Examples

Input 1	Input 2	Result
"ABCD"	"ABC"	True
"ABCDEF"	"EFAB"	True ("ABCDEF" < x 2 ⇒ "CDEFAB" contains "EFAB")
"BCDE"	"EC"	False
"Challenge"	"GECH"	True

JOB INTERVIEW TIPS: POSSIBLE QUESTIONS AND SOLUTION IDEAS

In a job interview, here are possible questions you may ask to clarify the assignment:

- Is the direction of the rotation known ← / →?

  ANSWER: No, arbitrary

- Should the rotation check be case-sensitive?

  ANSWER: No, treat as same

Idea 1: Brute Force As a first idea, you could try all combinations. You start without rotation. Then you rotate string str1 to the left and check if this rotated string is contained in str2. In the worst case, this procedure is repeated up to n times. This is extremely inefficient.

Idea 2: First check if rotation makes sense Another idea for solving this is to collect all characters in a Set per string in advance and then use issubset() to check if all needed letters are included. But even this is laborious and does not really reflect well the problem to be solved.

Idea 3: Procedure in reality Think for a while and consider how you might solve the problem on a piece of paper. At some point, you get the idea to write the word twice in a sequence:

```
ABCDEF        EFAB
ABCDEFABCDEF  EFAB
```

Algorithm Checking whether one string can be present in the other if rotated can be solved very elegantly with the simple trick of writing the longer string behind the other. In the combination, you check whether the string to be searched for is contained there. With this approach, the solution is both surprisingly short and extremely simple:

```python
def contains_rotation(str1, str2):
    new_doubled_str1 = (str1 + str1).lower()

    return str2.lower() in new_doubled_str1
```

Verification

For testing, use the following inputs, which show the correct operation:

```python
@pytest.mark.parametrize("str1, str2, expected",
                         [("ABCD", "ABC", True),
                          ("ABCDEF", "EFAB", True),
                          ("BCDE", "EC", False),
                          ("Challenge", "GECH", True)])
def test_contains_rotation(str1, str2, expected):
    assert contains_rotation(str1, str2) == expected
```

4.3.9 Solution 9: Well Formed Braces (★★☆☆☆)

Write function check_braces(text) to check whether the sequence of round braces passed as string contains matching (properly nested) pairs of braces.

Examples

Input	Result	Comment
"(())"	True	
"()()"	True	
"(())) ((())"	False	Although it has the same amount of opening and closing braces, it is not properly nested.
"((()"	False	No suitable bracing

Algorithm Without much consideration, you might be tempted to try all possible combinations. After some thinking, you probably come to the following optimization: You only count the number of opening braces and compare it with the number of closing braces. You have to consider the detail of a closing brace before an opening one. Proceed as follows: Traverse the string from front to back. If the current character is an opening brace, increase the counter for opening braces by one. If it is a closing brace, reduce the counter by one. If the counter fall below 0, you encounter a closing brace without a corresponding opening brace. In the end, the counter must be equal to 0, so that it represents a correct bracing.

```python
def check_braces(text):
    opening_count = 0

    for ch in text:
        if ch == "(":
            opening_count += 1
        elif ch == ")":
            opening_count -= 1
            if opening_count < 0:
                return False

    return opening_count == 0
```

Verification

Test your newly developed check for correct bracing with the following inputs for a parameterized test—using an additional hint parameter as a trick, which is not used for testing, but only for preparing an informative output:

```
@pytest.mark.parametrize("input, expected, hint",
                    [("(())", True, "ok"),
                     ("()()", True, "ok"),
                     ("(()))(())", False, "not properly nested"),
                     ("(()", False, "no matching parenthesis"),
                     (")()", False, "starts with closing
                     parenthesis")])
def test_check_braces(input, expected, hint):
    assert check_braces(input) == expected
```

4.3.10 Solution 10: Anagram (★★☆☆☆)

The term "anagram" is used to describe two strings that contain the same letters in the same frequency. Here, uppercase and lowercase should not make any difference. Write function is_anagram(str1, str2).

Examples

Input 1	Input 2	Result
"Otto"	"Toto"	True
"Mary	"Army"	True
"Ananas"	"Bananas"	False

Algorithm The description of the task provides hints on how you can proceed. First, you convert the words with function calc_char_frequencies(text) into a histogram. Here, you run character by character through the respective word and fill a dictionary. This is done for both words. Afterwards, to find a deviation, the resulting two dictionaries are compared with each other.

```
def is_anagram(str1, str2):
    char_counts1 = calc_char_frequencies(str1)
    char_counts2 = calc_char_frequencies(str2)

    return char_counts1 == char_counts2

def calc_char_frequencies(text):
    char_counts = {}

    for current_char in text.upper():
        if current_char in char_counts:
            char_counts[current_char] += 1
        else:
            char_counts[current_char] = 1

    return char_counts
```

Python shortcut The creation of the histogram (i. e., the counting of the letter frequencies) can be written a bit more compactly—but less comprehensibly for my taste. So let's take advantage of the fact that setdefault() returns the current value for the key or else the default value given here in case of non-existence.

```
def calc_char_frequencies_shorter(text):
    char_counts = {}

    for current_char in text.upper():
        char_counts[current_char] = char_counts.setdefault(current_
        char, 0) + 1

    return char_counts
```

Verification

For testing, use the following inputs, which show the correct functioning:

```
@pytest.mark.parametrize("str1, str2, expected",
                         [("Otto", "Toto", True),
                          ("Mary", "Army", True),
                          ("Ananas", "Bananas", False)])
def test_is_anagram(str1, str2, expected):
    assert is_anagram(str1, str2) == expected
```

4.3.11 Solution 11: Morse Code (★★☆☆☆)

Write function `to_morse_code(text)` that is capable of translating a given text into Morse code characters. They consist of sequences of one to four short and long tones per letter, symbolized by a dot (.) or dash (-). It is desirable for easier distinguishability to place a space between each tone and three spaces between each sequence of letter tones. Otherwise, S (...) and EEE (...) would not be distinguishable from each other.

For simplicity, limit yourself to the letters E, O, S, T, W with the following encoding:

Letter	Morse code
E	.
O	- - -
S	. . .
T	-
W	. - -

Examples

Input	Result
SOS	... - - - ...
TWEET	- . - - . . -
WEST	. - - . ... -

Algorithm The string is traversed character by character and the current character is mapped to the corresponding Morse code. The function `convert_to_morse_code(current_char)` performs this task.

```python
def to_morse_code(text):
    converted_msg = ""

    for current_char in text.upper():
        converted_letter = convert_to_morse_code(current_char)
```

```
        converted_msg += converted_letter
        converted_msg += " "

    return converted_msg.strip()
```

While in other programming languages the mapping of single letters is accomplished using a switch, in Python there is a trick with a dictionary:

```
def convert_to_morse_code(current_char):
    chars_to_morse = {"E": ".",
                      "O": "- - -",
                      "S": ". . .",
                      "T": "-",
                      "W": ". - -"}

    return chars_to_morse[current_char]
```

Modern Python and match In many languages, case distinctions may be expressed using the if statement as well as the switch statement. The latter was missing in Python for a long time. With Python 3.10 comes match, an even more powerful variant for case discrimination with which we can now finally also realize the switch statement. Please consult section D.2 in Appendix D for more details.

As mentioned, you can use the new keywords match and case to formulate case distinctions like the following:

```
def convert_to_morse_code(current_char):
    value = "?"
    match current_char:
        case "E": value = "."
        case "O": value = "- - -"
        case "S": value = ". . ."
        case "T": value = "-"
        case "W": value = ". - -"

    return value
```

Bonus

Experiment and research a little bit to find out the corresponding Morse code for all letters of the alphabet so you can convert your name. You can find the necessary hints for this at https://en.wikipedia.org/wiki/Morse_code.

Verification

Let's check it using a unit test as follows:

```
@pytest.mark.parametrize("input, expected",
                         [("SOS", ". . .  - - -  . . ."),
                          ("TWEET", "-  . - -  .  .  -"),
                          ("OST", "- - -  . . .  -"),
                          ("WEST", ". - -  .  . . .  -")])
def test_to_morse_code(input, expected):
    assert to_morse_code(input) == expected
```

4.3.12 Solution 12: Pattern Checker (★★★☆☆)

Write function matches_pattern(pattern, text) that examines a space-separated string (second parameter) against the structure of a pattern passed in the form of individual characters as the first parameter.

Examples

Input pattern	Input text	Result
"xyyx"	"tim mike tim"	True
"xyyx"	"tim mike tom tim"	False
"xyxx"	"tim mike tim"	False
"xxxx"	"tim tim tim"	True

JOB INTERVIEW TIPS: PROBLEM SOLVING STRATEGIES

With exercises like this, you should always ask a few questions to clarify the context and gain a better understanding. For this example, possible questions include the following:

1. Is the pattern limited to the characters x and y?

   ANSWER: No, but only one letter each as a placeholder

2. Is the pattern always only four characters long?

   ANSWER: No, arbitrary

3. Does the pattern ever contain spaces?

   ANSWER: No

4. Is the input always separated with exactly one space?

   ANSWER: Yes

Algorithm As always, it is important first to understand the problem and identify appropriate data structures. You may recognize the pattern specification as a sequence of characters and the input values as space-separated words. They can be transformed into a corresponding list of individual values using split(). Initially, you check whether the length of the pattern and the list of input values match. Only in this case you run through the pattern character by character, as you have done so many times before. As an auxiliary data structure, you use a dictionary, which maps individual characters of the pattern to words. Now you check whether another word has already been inserted for a pattern character. With the help of this trick, you can easily detect mapping errors.

```
def matches_pattern(pattern, text):
    # perparation
    values = text.split(" ")
    if len(values) != len(pattern) or (len(values) == 1 and not values[0]):
        return False

    placeholder_to_value_map = {}
```

```
# run through all characters
for i, pattern_char in enumerate(pattern):
    value = values[i]

    # add, if not already there
    if pattern_char not in placeholder_to_value_map:
        placeholder_to_value_map[pattern_char] = value

    # does stored value match current string?
    assigned_value = placeholder_to_value_map[(pattern_char)]
    if not assigned_value == value:
        return False

return True
```

In the code, before the actual check, you still need to verify the special case of an empty input explicitly, since `"".split(" ")` results in a list of length 1.

Verification

For testing, use the following inputs, which show the correct functionality:

```
@pytest.mark.parametrize("pattern, input, expected",
                         [("x", "", False),
                          ("", "x", False)])
def test_matches_pattern_special_cases(pattern, input, expected):
    assert matches_pattern(pattern, input) == expected

@pytest.mark.parametrize("pattern, input, expected",
                         [("xyyx", "tim mike mike tim", True),
                          ("xyyx", "time mike tom tim", False),
                          ("xyxx", "tim mike mike tim", False),
                          ("xxxx", "tim tim tim tim", True)])
def test_matches_pattern(pattern, input, expected):
    assert matches_pattern(pattern, input) == expected
```

4.3.13 Solution 13: Tennis Score (★★★☆☆)

Write function tennis_score(score, player1_name, player2_name) that makes an announcement in a familiar style such as Fifteen Love, Deuce, or Advantage Player X based on a textual score for two players, PL1 and PL2. The score is given in the format <PL1 points>:<PL2 points>.

The following counting rules apply to a game in tennis:

- A game is won (Game <PlayerX>) when a player reaches four or more points and is ahead by at least two points.

- Points from zero to three are named Love, Fifteen, Thirty, and Forty.

- In case of at least three points and a tie, this is called Deuce.

- With at least three points and one point difference, this is called Advantage <PlayerX> for the one who has one more point.

Examples

Input	Score
"1:0", "Micha", "Tim"	"Fifteen Love"
"2:2", "Micha", "Tim"	"Thirty Thirty"
"2:3", "Micha", "Tim"	"Thirty Forty"
"3:3", "Micha", "Tim"	"Deuce"
"4:3", "Micha", "Tim"	"Advantage Micha"
"4:4", "Micha", "Tim"	"Deuce"
"5:4", "Micha", "Tim"	"Advantage Micha"
"6:4", "Micha", "Tim"	"Game Micha"

Algorithm In this case, it is a two-step algorithm:

1. First, a score in terms of two int values should be obtained from the textual representation.

2. Afterwards, it is your task to generate the corresponding textual score names based on these values.

When parsing the score, you can rely on standard functionality such as split() and int(). In addition, for reusable functionality, it is reasonable to include certain security checks. First, both values should be positive. After that, the specifics on the scores are to be tested. The player who reaches four points first wins the match, but only if they lead at least with two points. If both players have three or more points, then the point difference must be less than three. Otherwise, it is not a valid state in tennis. You extract the parsing with the checks into the function extract_points(score).

```python
def extract_points(score):
    values = score.strip().split(":")

    if len(values) != 2:
        raise ValueError("illegal format -- score has not" +
                         "format <points>:<points>, e.\,g. 7:6")

    score1 = int(values[0])
    score2 = int(values[1])

    # sanity check
    if score1 < 0 or score2 < 0:
        raise ValueError("points must be > 0")

    # prevents both e. g. 6:3 and 5:1
    if (score1 > 4 or score2 > 4) and abs(score1 - score2) > 2:
        raise ValueError("point difference must be < 3, " +
                         "otherwise invalid score")

    return score1, score2
```

After extracting the two scores separated by ':' from the input, you proceed with the conversion. Again, you use a multi-step decision procedure. According to the rules, a simple mapping comes into play for scores below three. This is perfectly described in terms of a dictionary. Starting from three points, a tie, advantage, or game win can occur. It is also possible for one player to win with four points if the other scores a maximum of two points. For the winning message, it is only necessary to determine which of the two players has more points. The described logic is implemented as follows:

```python
def tennis_score(score, player1_name, player2_name):
    points = extract_points(score)
```

```
    score1 = points[0]
    score2 = points[1]

    if score1 >= 3 and score2 >= 3:
        return generate_info(score1, score2, player1_name, player2_name)
    elif score1 >= 4 or score2 >= 4:
        return "Game " + (player1_name if (score1 > score2) else
        player2_name)
    else:
        # special naming
        point_names = {0: "Love", 1: "Fifteen", 2: "Thirty", 3: "Forty"}

        return point_names[score1] + " " + point_names[score2]
```

Only one last detail remains, namely the generation of the hint text for advantage or victory:

```
def generate_info(score1, score2, player1_name, player2_name):
    score_difference = abs(score1 - score2)

    player_name = player1_name if (score1 > score2) else player2_name

    if score1 == score2:
        return "Deuce"
    if score_difference == 1:
        return "Advantage " + player_name
    if score_difference == 2:
        return "Game " + player_name

    raise ValueError("Unexpected difference: " + score_difference)
```

Verification

Let's test the tennis scoring functionality with an imaginary gameplay:

```
@pytest.mark.parametrize("score, expected",
                         [("1:0", "Fifteen Love"),
                          ("2:2", "Thirty Thirty"),
                          ("2:3", "Thirty Forty"),
                          ("3:3", "Deuce"),
```

```
                        ("4:3", "Advantage Micha"),
                        ("4:4", "Deuce"),
                        ("5:4", "Advantage Micha"),
                        ("6:4", "Game Micha")])
def test_tennis_score_hard_win(score, expected):
    assert tennis_score(score, "Micha", "Tim") == expected
```

You should add more imaginary game sequences to neatly cover the edge cases of a close victory and an unchallenged victory:

```
@pytest.mark.parametrize("score, expected",
                        [("1:0", "Fifteen Love"),
                        ("2:2", "Thirty Thirty"),
                        ("3:2", "Forty Thirty"),
                        ("4:2", "Game Micha")])
def test_tennis_score_normal_win(score, expected):
    assert tennis_score(score, "Micha", "Tim") == expected

@pytest.mark.parametrize("score, expected",
                        [("1:0", "Fifteen Love"),
                        ("2:0", "Thirty Love"),
                        ("3:0", "Forty Love"),
                        ("4:0", "Game Micha")])
def test_tennis_score_straight_win(score, expected):
    assert tennis_score(score, "Micha", "Tim") == expected
```

4.3.14 Solution 14: Version Numbers (★★☆☆☆)

Write function `compare_versions(version1, version2)` that permits you to compare version numbers in the format *MAJOR.MINOR.PATCH* with each other, thereby the specification of *PATCH* is optional. In particular, the return value should be represented in the form of the characters <, =, and >.

Examples

Version 1	Version 2	Result
1.11.17	2.3.5	<
2.1	2.1.3	<
2.3.5	2.4	<
3.1	2.4	>
3.3	3.2.9	>
7.2.71	7.2.71	=

Algorithm Split the textual version numbers into a list containing version number components by calling `split()`. Loop through them and convert them to a version number using `int()`. Then compare in pairs using a separate function `compare()` starting at *MAJOR*, then *MINOR* and *PATCH* if necessary. If one input has more values than the other, then the single last number is not used except when the version number matches up to that component, such as for 3.1 and 3.1.7.

```
def compare_versions(version1, version2):
    v1_numbers = version1.split(".")
    v2_numbers = version2.split(".")

    pos = 0
    compare_result = "="
    while pos < len(v1_numbers) and
        pos < len(v2_numbers) and compare_result == "=":

      current_v1 = int(v1_numbers[pos])
      current_v2 = int(v2_numbers[pos])
      compare_result = compare(current_v1, current_v2)
      pos += 1

    # same start about 3.1 and 3.1.7
    if compare_result == "=":
        return compare(len(v1_numbers), len(v2_numbers))

    return compare_result
```

```
def compare(val1, val2):
    if val1 < val2:
        return "<"
    if val1 > val2:
        return ">"
    return "="
```

Verification

Test the comparison of version numbers with the following inputs for a parameterized test:

```
@pytest.mark.parametrize("version1, version2, expected",
                    [("1.11.17", "2.3.5", "<"),
                     ("2.3.5", "2.4", "<"),
                     ("2.1", "2.1.3", "<"),
                     ("3.1", "2.4", ">"),
                     ("3.3", "3.2.9", ">"),
                     ("7.2.71", "7.2.71", "=")])
def test_compare_versions(version1, version2, expected):
    assert compare_versions(version1, version2) == expected
```

HINT: HANDLING OF TRAILING ZEROS

The assignment did not specify a special case, namely the treatment of additional zeros in version numbers, such as for 3.1 and 3.1.0 or 3 and 3.0.0. You will find an extension that handles these special features in the accompanying sources.

4.3.15 Solution 15: Conversion str_to_number (★★☆☆☆)

Convert a string into an integer. To do this, write function str_to_number(text) on your own.

Note   The conversion can be easily achieved with int(value). Do not use this explicitly, but implement the entire conversion yourself.

Examples

Input	Result
"+123"	123
"-123"	-123
"7271"	7271
"ABC"	ValueError
"0123"	83 (for bonus task)
"-0123"	-83 (for bonus task)
"0128"	ValueError (for bonus task)

Algorithm Let's start brute force without looking for all details. So the initial step is checking if the first character is +/- and set flag is_negative accordingly. You also check if the first character is a sign (+ or -) to start processing the digits one position later if necessary. Then run through all characters and convert them to digits. The previous value is multiplied by 10 each time, and at the end, the corresponding numeric value results.

```python
def str_to_number_first_try(text):
    is_negative = text[0] == "-"
    value = 0

    startpos = 1 if starts_with_sign(text) else 0

    for pos in range(startpos, len(text)):
        digit_value = ord(text[pos]) - 48
        value = value * 10 + digit_value

    return -value if is_negative else value

def starts_with_sign(text):
    return text[0] in ["-", "+"]
```

Corrected algorithm Even without a more thorough analysis, it is clear that the above variant does not work correctly when mixing letters with digits. In this case, it is reasonable to throw a ValueError when a check with isdigit() fails:

```python
def str_to_number(text):
    is_negative = text[0] == "-"
    value = 0

    startpos = 1 if starts_with_sign(text) else 0

    for pos in range(startpos, len(text)):
        if not text[pos].isdigit():
            raise ValueError(text + " contains not only digits")

        digit_value = ord(text[pos]) - 48
        value = value * 10 + digit_value

    return -value if is_negative else value
```

HINT: VARIANT

A variant would be to abort processing upon finding the first character that is not a digit, as implemented in Perl, for example. Then the number string "123ab4567" would become 123.

Verification

To test the functionality, use three numbers: one with a positive sign, one with a negative sign, and one without. The positive sign should just be ignored during the conversion. Check the reaction to input with letters instead of numbers separately and expect a ValueError.

```python
@pytest.mark.parametrize("input, expected",
                        [("+123", 123), ("-123", -123),
                         ("123", 123), ("7271", 7271)])
def test_str_to_number(input, expected):
    assert str_to_number(input) == expected

def test_str_to_number_invalid_input():
    with pytest.raises(ValueError):
        str_to_number("ABC")
```

Bonus: Enable the Parsing of Octal Numbers

Octal numbers are identified in Python by a leading prefix 0 or, since Python 3.8, 0o and, according to their name, have base 8 rather than base 10. To support octal numbers, you must first determine whether the leading prefix exists. If this is the case, the factor for the positions in the number system must be changed to 8. Finally, with base 8, the two digits 8 and 9 are no longer allowed. Therefore, you add another check in the loop for processing the values. All in all, the source code is a bit bloated by the special treatments. The complexity is just manageable, especially because you use problem- adapted auxiliary functions with speaking names here.

```python
def str_to_number_bonus(text):
    is_negative = text[0] == "-"
    is_octal = text[0:2] == '0o' or \
               (starts_with_sign(text) and text[1:3] == "0o")

    value = 0
    factor = 8 if is_octal else 10

    startpos = calc_start_pos(text, is_octal)

    for pos in range(startpos, len(text)):
        if not text[pos].isdigit():
            raise ValueError(text + " contains not only digits")

        digit_value = ord(text[pos]) - 48
        if is_octal and digit_value >= 8:
            raise ValueError(text + " found digit >= 8")

        value = value * factor + digit_value

    return -value if is_negative else value

def calc_start_pos(text, is_octal):
    pos = 0
    if is_octal:
        pos = 3 if starts_with_sign(text) else 2
    elif starts_with_sign(text):
        pos = 1
    return pos
```

Verification

To test the functionality, use three numbers: one with a positive, one with a negative sign, and one without. The positive sign should just be ignored during the conversion. In addition, check a positive and negative octal number. In a separate test, it is ensured that digits greater than or equal to 8 must not occur in octal numbers.

```python
@pytest.mark.parametrize("input, expected",
                         [("+123", 123), ("-123", -123),
                          ("123", 123), ("7271", 7271),
                          ("+0o77", 63), ("-0o77", -63),
                          ("0o77", 63), ("+0o123", 83),
                          ("-0o123", -83), ("0o123", 83)])
def test_str_to_number_bonus(input, expected):
    assert str_to_number_bonus(input) == expected

def test_str_to_number_bonus_invalid_input():
    with pytest.raises(ValueError) as excinfo:
        str_to_number_bonus("0o128")

    assert str(excinfo.value).find("found digit >= 8") != -1
```

4.3.16 Solution 16: Print Tower (★★★☆☆)

Write function print_tower(n) that represents a tower of *n* slices stacked on top of each other as ASCII graphics, symbolized by the character #. Also, draw a lower boundary line.

Example

A tower of height three should look something like this:

```
    |
  # | #
 ## | ##
### | ###
---------
```

Algorithm You can divide the drawing into three steps: draw the top bar, the slices, and then the bottom boundary. Thus, the algorithm can be described using three function calls:

```python
def print_tower(height):
    draw_top(height)
    draw_slices(height)
    draw_bottom(height)
```

You implement the drawing of the individual components of this tower in a couple of helper functions, as already indicated:

```python
def draw_top(height):
    print(" " * (height + 1) + "|")

def draw_bottom(height):
    print("-" * ((height + 1) * 2 + 1))
```

Drawing the slices of the tower is a bit more complex due to their different sizes and the required computation of the free space on the left and right side:

```python
def draw_slices(height):
    for i in range(height - 1, -1, -1):
        value = height - i
        padding = i + 1

        print(" " * padding + "#" * value + "|" + "#" * value)
```

It is obvious how the problem can be broken down into increasingly smaller subproblems. Each function becomes thereby short for itself and usually also well testable (if no console outputs, but computations with return take place).

Algorithm with recursion Interestingly, the drawing of the individual slices of the tower can also be expressed recursively as follows:

```python
def draw_slices_rec(slice, height):
    if slice > 1:
        draw_slices_rec(slice - 1, height)

    print(" " * (height - slice + 1) + "#" * slice + "|" + "#" * slice)
```

Then, the call must be minimally modified:

```
def print_tower_rec(height):
    draw_top(height)
    draw_slices_rec(height, height)
    draw_bottom(height)
```

Verification

To check the functionality, use the Python command line interpreter one more time— here to print a tower of height four:

```
>>> print_tower(4)
      |
    #|#
   ##|##
  ###|###
 ####|####
-----------
```

4.3.17 Solution 17: Filled Frame (★★☆☆☆)

Write function print_box(width, height, fillchar) that draws a rectangle of the specified size as an ASCII graphic and fills it with the passed-in fill character.

Examples

Below you see two rectangles filled differently:

```
+-----+        +-------+
|****|        |$$$$$$$|
|****|        |$$$$$$$|
|****|        |$$$$$$$|
+-----+        |$$$$$$$|
               |$$$$$$$|
               +-------+
```

Algorithm To draw the filled frame, you traverse all lines and likewise all positions in the x-direction. In this exercise, the main concern is to correctly solve the special treatments at the corners and the edges with the index positions. In addition, with print() it is crucial to set the end character to empty to avoid the otherwise usual line break.

```
def print_box(width, height, fillchar):
    for y in range(height):
        for x in range(width):
            if x == 0 and (y == 0 or y == height - 1):
                print("+", end="")
            elif x == width - 1 and (y == 0 or y == height - 1):
                print("+", end="")
            elif y == 0 or y == height - 1:
                print("-", end="")
            elif x == 0 or x == width - 1:
                print("|", end="")
            else:
                print(fillchar, end="")
        print()
```

Verification

To check the functionality, use the Python command line interpreter again:

```
>>> print_box(9, 7, "$")
+-------+
|$$$$$$$|
|$$$$$$$|
|$$$$$$$|
|$$$$$$$|
|$$$$$$$|
+-------+
```

4.3.18 Solution 18: Guessing Vowels (★★☆☆☆)

Write function translate_vowel(text, replacement) that replaces all vowels in a given text with a character or string. This can be used for a little guessing quiz, for example, or to determine word similarities based on consonants only.

Input	Replacement	Result
"guide"	"?"	"g??d?"
"lawnmower"	"-"	"l-wnm-w-r"
"quiz"	"_"	"q z"
"lawnmower"	""	"lwnmwr"

Algorithm To convert the given text, you traverse it character by character from front to back. You collect the result in a new string. If you find a vowel, you insert the given replacement string, otherwise the consonant (or more precisely, the original character, which could also be a digit or a punctuation mark).

```python
def translate_vowel(text, replacement):
    translated = ""

    for letter in text:
        if is_vowel(letter):
            translated += replacement
        else:
            translated += letter

    return translated

def is_vowel(letter):
    return letter in "AÄEIOÖUÜaäeioöuü"
```

Python shortcut Interestingly, strings in Python provide the method maketrans() to create a mapping dictionary and the function translate() to transform according to the passed mapping. Next, you implement the transformation as follows:

```python
def translate_vowel_shorter(text, replacement):
    vowels = "AÄEIOÖUÜaäeioöuü"

    trans_dict = text.maketrans(vowels, replacement * len(vowels))

    return text.translate(trans_dict)
```

Verification

To check the functionality, use the Python command line interpreter:

```
>>> print(translate_vowel("guide", "?"))
... print(translate_vowel("guide", "-"))
... print(translate_vowel("table tennis", "_"))
... print(translate_vowel("quiz", "_"))
... print(translate_vowel("lawnmower", ""))
g??d?
g--dt_
bl_ t_nn_s
q__z
lwnmwr
```

The chosen algorithm is even capable of transforming entire sentences:

```
>>> print(translate_vowel("the guide recommends Java", "-"))
th- g--d- r-c-mm-nds J-v-
>>>
>> print(translate_vowel("fit through the Python challenge", "-"))
f-t thr--gh th- Pyth-n ch-ll-ng-
```

4.4 Summary: What You Learned

Strings are an integral part of almost every program. You built up a sound understanding by solving simple tasks like palindrome checking and string reversing. Other tasks can be significantly simplified using suitable auxiliary data structures, such as sets or dictionaries. They help when checking for well-formed braces, converting a word into Morse code, and other tasks. I hope you feel that solving problems is becoming easier the more basic knowledge you have in different areas, especially data structures.

That's why you will have a deeper look into this topic in the next chapter, which introduces lists, sets, and dictionaries in more depth.

CHAPTER 5

Basic Data Structures: Lists, Sets, and Dictionaries

In Python, lists, sets, and key-value mappings (dictionaries) are provided directly in the language as ***container classes***. They manage objects of other classes (also potentially of different data types).

5.1 Introduction

In the following, I first describe sequential data types and especially their operations. After that, you briefly look at lists, sets, and dictionaries.

5.1.1 Sequential Data Types

In Python, sequential data types exist as the basis for various data containers, such as lists, tuples, and strings. The name derives from the fact that these data containers combine sequences of elements. This means that the elements have a defined order and can be addressed via an index. Among other things, the following operations are defined:

- **in**: `elem in values` checks if the element is in the sequence.

- **not in**: `elem not in values` checks if the element is *not* in the sequence.

- **+/+=**: `values1 + values2` and `values1 += values2` appends the sequence `values2` to the other sequence and returns a new sequence.

© Michael Inden 2022
M. Inden, *Python Challenges*, https://doi.org/10.1007/978-1-4842-7398-2_5

- *****: Repeats the sequence n times.

- **[index]**: values[index] leads to an indexed access and returns the ith element from values. Specifically, [-1] can be used to access the last element.

- **[start:end]**: values[start:end] performs slicing and returns the elements from position start to exclusive end from values as a new sequence. There are two interesting variants. On the one hand, [:] (i. e. without range specification) returns a copy of the entire sequence. On the other hand, [start:] and [:end] respectively return the parts starting at start to the end or from the beginning to the index end exclusive.

- **[start:end:step]**: values[start:end:step] results in slicing and returns the elements from position start to exclusive end with a step size of step from values as a new sequence. There is an interesting variant [::-1] without range specification and with negative step size, which creates a new sequence in reverse order of the original sequence.

- **len()**: len(values) returns the size (i. e. the number of elements in the data container).

- **min()/max()**: Calls to min(values) resp. max(values) gets the element with the smallest or largest value from values.

- **sum()**: sum(values) sums the values from values.

Example

Let's look at an example of these operations because understanding them is essential for solving tasks and everyday programming in Python. First, you define some lists and then perform indexed accesses and slicing on them:

```python
names1 = ["Micha", "Tim", "Tom", "Willi"]
names2 = ["Marcello", "Karthi", "Michael"]
names = names1 + names2

print(names)
print(names[-1])
```

```
print(names[::-1])
print(names[::2])
print("len: %d, min: %s, max: %s" % (len(names), min(names), max(names)))
```

This results in the following output:

```
['Micha', 'Tim', 'Tom', 'Willi', 'Marcello', 'Karthi', 'Michael']
Michael
['Michael', 'Karthi', 'Marcello', 'Willi', 'Tom', 'Tim', 'Micha']
['Micha', 'Tom', 'Marcello', 'Michael']
len: 7, min: Karthi, max: Willi
```

Custom implementation of rindex() A useful functionality, which unfortunately can only be found in strings but not in sequential containers, is the search from the end with rindex(). However, you can easily implement this as a function or lambda as follows by inverting the sequential container and getting the position there:

```
def rindex(values, item):
    reversed_values = values[::-1]
    return len(values) - reversed_values.index(item) - 1

last_index_of = lambda values, item: len(values) - values[::-1].
index(item) - 1
```

5.1.2 Lists

A list is a sequence of elements ordered by their position. Duplicates are allowed. Lists provide high-performance indexed access. Since the list is a sequential data type, it possesses all the previously described operators for sequences. In addition, the following indexed, 0-based accesses and operations can be performed on lists:

- **pop(i)** returns the ith element of the list and removes it from the list. By default (i. e., without specifying the index), the first element is returned.

- **list[i] = element** replaces the element at position i with the passed element.

- **append(element)** appends the element to the end of the list.

- **insert(i, element)** inserts the element at index i in the list.

- **extend(other_list)** appends the elements of other_list to the end of the list.

- **count(value)** counts how many times the value value occurs in the list.

- **index(value)** returns the index where the value value first occurs in the list.

- **remove(value)** removes the element with the value value from the list. Only the first one will be deleted if multiple elements with this value exist. If there is no such value, a ValueError is raised.

- **reverse()** reverses the order of the elements in the list.

- **sort()** sorts the list in ascending order. An inverse (descending) sort is obtained with sort(reverse=True).

Example

Let's consider an example of these operations. First, you define two lists and then add elements. You also remove one element and add several elements.

```
numbers = [1, 2, 3, 4]
names = ["Peter", "Tim", "Mike", "Tom", "Mike"]

names.append("Tom")
names.insert(1, "Carsten")
names.remove("Tom")
print(names)

names.extend(numbers)
names.reverse()
print(names)

print("pop:", names.pop())
print("Tom idx:", names.index("Tom"))
print("Mike count:", names.count("Mike"))
```

This results in the following output:

```
['Peter', 'Carsten', 'Tim', 'Mike', 'Mike', 'Tom']
[4, 3, 2, 1, 'Tom', 'Mike', 'Mike', 'Tim', 'Carsten', 'Peter']
pop: Peter
Tom idx: 4
Mike count: 2
```

List Comprehension

Python offers ***comprehensions*** as elegant possibilities for creating new data structures. A list comprehension is an expression that generates a new result list based on a sequence of values and a calculation rule to generate a new list of results:

```
>>> even = [n for n in range(10) if n % 2 == 0]
>>> even
[0, 2, 4, 6, 8]
```

More complex expressions can also be specified, such as the creation of tuples:

```
>>> [(x, y) for x in range(3) for y in range(5)]
[(0, 0), (0, 1), (0, 2), (0, 3), (0, 4), (1, 0), (1, 1), (1, 2), (1, 3),
(1, 4), (2, 0), (2, 1), (2, 2), (2, 3), (2, 4)]
```

```
>>> [(x, y, z) for x in range(3) for y in range(3) for z in range(3)]
[(0, 0, 0), (0, 0, 1), (0, 0, 2), (0, 1, 0), (0, 1, 1), (0, 1, 2), (0, 2, 0),
(0, 2, 1), (0, 2, 2), (1, 0, 0), (1, 0, 1), (1, 0, 2), (1, 1, 0), (1, 1, 1),
(1, 1, 2), (1, 2, 0), (1, 2, 1), (1, 2, 2), (2, 0, 0), (2, 0, 1), (2, 0, 2),
(2, 1, 0), (2, 1, 1), (2, 1, 2), (2, 2, 0), (2, 2, 1), (2, 2, 2)]
```

In addition, you saw the specification of a condition in the initial example. In general, you should avoid the complexity getting too large. This assists in ensuring understandability and maintainability.

Regardless, comprehensions are a compelling and helpful feature of Python that you should undoubtedly master.

Variant as set and dictionary comprehension Similar possibilities exist for sets and dictionaries. Two examples follow, one for the determination of all odd numbers up to 10 and another for the mapping of even numbers to their square:

```
>>> {i for i in range(10) if i % 2 != 0}
{1, 3, 5, 7, 9}

>>> {n: n ** 2 for n in range(10) if n % 2 == 0}
{0: 0, 2: 4, 4: 16, 6: 36, 8: 64}
```

Example: Custom Implementation of remove_all()

Removing all elements from a collection that match a certain value is a functionality that is unfortunately not built in. Different variants to solve this are shown below.

Inplace variants First, you start with inplace variants, which means that the original list gets modified and consequently nothing is returned. Therefore, you repeatedly call remove() until a ValueError occurs when the value to be deleted is no longer found.

```
# not optimal variant
def remove_all_inplace(list, value):
    try:
        while True:
            list.remove(value)
    except (ValueError):
        pass
```

With this variant, it may be perceived as unattractive that exceptions are used to regulate the control flow. Perhaps you come to the following alternative:

```
# not optimal variant
def remove_all_inplace_improved(values, item):
    while item in values:
        values.remove(item)
```

At first these solutions look quite good, but both variants iterate using the outer loop (while true/in) and a hidden inner one (by the implementation of remove()) resulting in a running time of $O(n^2)$.

Variant offering better performance There is a solution that offers a running time of $O(n)$: You traverse through the list, and for every value, you check whether it matches the one to be deleted. If this is not the case, you continue with the next entry. If you find an entry to be deleted, you copy the successor into the position given by the write counter. The write counter is always moved on if no match is found. Finally, all values up to the write counter correspond to the desired result. You extract this with slicing.

```python
def remove_all_fast(values, item):
    write_idx = 0
    for value in values:
        if value != item:
            values[write_idx] = value
            write_idx += 1

    return values[:write_idx]
```

Improved variants Next, you use a list comprehension that retains only the values that satisfy the condition specified in `if`. This does not change the original list but creates a new result list. Again, this solution offers a running time of $O(n)$ but uses slightly more memory.

```python
def remove_all_v2(values, item):
    return [value for value in values if value != item]
```

This also applies to the following variant. Here, you use the built-in function `filter()`. While in Python 2 this returns a list, in Python 3, you only get a `filter` object that provides a function `iter ()` and is thus iterable. You can, therefore, easily wrap this in a list—please see the following practical tip about the implications.

```python
def remove_all_v3(values, item):
    return list(filter(lambda x: x != item, values))
```

ATTENTION: WHY DOES FILTER() NO LONGER RETURN A LIST?

As convenient as it is for smaller datasets to get the data as a list, there are some reasons why this is not feasible for large datasets. First of all, it may require a lot of memory. Secondly, not all values have to be kept for different calculations. Thus, the change of the mode of operation on Lazy Evaluation in Python 3 helps to save memory and increase performance. If you want to process the data directly and need a list, a simple wrapping is appropriate, as shown above. The dataset described by the filter is converted into a list.

Example: Custom Implementation of collect_all()

Another useful functionality is to collect elements that match a certain condition. This can be solved as follows:

```python
# Iteration
def collect_all(values, condition):
    result = []
    for elem in values:
        if condition(elem):
            result.append(elem)
    return result

# List Comprehension
def collect_all_v2(values, condition):
    return [elem for elem in values if condition(elem)]

# Filter
def collect_all_v3(values, condition):
    return list(filter(condition, values))
```

Check Implementations

Let's try some of the implementations of the functionality once. First, three variants of remove_all() are tested to delete the entry Mike. Finally, collect_all() should keep all entries with the value Mike.

```python
>>> names = ["Tim", "Tom", "Mike", "Mike", "Mike"]
... remove_all_inplace(names, "Mike")
... print(names)
['Tim', 'Tom']

>>> print(remove_all_v2(["Tim", "Tom", "Mike", "Mike", "Mike"], "Mike"))
['Tim', 'Tom']

>>> print(remove_all_fast(["Tim", "Tom", "Mike", "Mike", "Mike"], "Mike"))
['Tim', 'Tom']
```

```
>>> names = ["Tim", "Tom", "Mike", "Mike", "Mike"]
... print(collect_all(names, lambda value: value == "Mike"))
['Mike', 'Mike', 'Mike']
```

5.1.3 Sets

Let's now explore sets. The mathematical concept states that they contain no duplicates. Thus, sets form an unordered data structure that does not contain duplicates, but also does not provide indexed access. Instead, some set operations exist such as a test for containment and computation of union, intersection, difference, and symmetric difference.[1] In addition, there are the following actions:

- **add(element)** adds an element to the set if it does not already exist.

- **update(elements)** inserts the elements `elements` from a list or tuple into a set if not already present in the original set.

- **remove(element)/discard(element)** deletes the element from the set. If the element does not exist, remove() will raise a KeyError. With discard(), on the other hand, nonexistence will be ignored and nothing will happen.

- **pop()** removes the first element from the set (as an iteration would return them).

- **clear()** deletes all elements from the set.

- **copy()** returns a (shallow) copy of the set.[2]

Example

As an example of sets, you start by defining a set of colors (more precisely, their names) in curly brackets. Then you add another set and then a single element.

```
color_set = {"RED", "GREEN", "BLUE"}
color_set.update(["YELLOW", "ORANGE"])
color_set.add("GOLD")
print(color_set)
```

---

[1] All elements contained in either A or B, but not both sets.
[2] This functionality can be found for lists too, but there slicing is often the better choice to copy data.

This results in the following output (showing that insertion order does not get preserved in sets):

```
{'RED', 'BLUE', 'YELLOW', 'GOLD', 'GREEN', 'ORANGE'}
```

Finally, you define two sets with numbers and calculate the typical set operations such as union, intersection, and difference:

```
number_set1 = {1, 2, 3, 4, 5, 6, 7, 8}
number_set2 = {2, 3, 5, 7, 9, 11, 13}
print("union: %s\nintersection: %s\ndiff 1-2: %s\nsym diff: %s" %
    ((number_set1 | number_set2), (number_set1 & number_set2),
     (number_set1 - number_set2), (number_set1 ^ number_set2)))
```

This results in the following output:

```
union: {1, 2, 3, 4, 5, 6, 7, 8, 9, 11, 13}
intersection: {2, 3, 5, 7}
diff 1-2: {8, 1, 4, 6}
sym diff: {1, 4, 6, 8, 9, 11, 13}
```

5.1.4 Key-Value Mappings (Dictionaries)

Let's now turn to mappings from keys to values. They are also called *dictionaries* or *lookup tables*; other terms are associative arrays and hashes, respectively. Regardless of the name, the underlying idea is to assign a value for a unique key. An intuitive example is a telephone directory where names are mapped to telephone numbers. A search by name (key) usually returns a phone number (value) quite quickly. If there is no mapping back from phone number to name, finding a name to a phone number becomes quite laborious.

Dictionaries store key-value pairs and offer, among others, the following functions and operations:

- **dictionary[key] = value** adds a mapping (from key to value) as an entry to this dictionary. If a value is already stored for the given key, it gets overwritten with the new value.

- **update(other_dictionary)** inserts all entries from the passed dictionary into this dictionary. This overwrites values of already existing entries analogous to the way simple assignment works.

- **items()** generates a list containing all key-value pairs of the dictionary as tuples.

- **keys()/values()** returns a list containing all keys or values stored in the dictionary.

- **get(key, default_value)** get the associated value for a key key. If no entry exists for the key, the default value default_value is returned. If no default value was specified in the call, None is returned.

- **pop(key)** deletes an entry (key and associated value) from the dictionary. The value associated with the key key is returned. If no entry was stored for this key, a KeyError is the result.

- **clear()** removes all entries of the dictionary.

Unfortunately, there are no functions like contains_key() or contains_value() to check if a special key or value is stored in the dictionary. However, this functionality can be easily recreated by querying with in, as you will see in the following example.

Example

Again, you implement an example to learn about some of the possibilities. To do this, you define a dictionary with an initial payload of names and ages. Then you add one as well as several values. For inspection, you print out the dictionary, its keys, its values, and its entries. Finally, you check for the existence of specific values in these results.

```
mapping = {"Micha" : 49, "Peter": 42, "Tom": 27}
mapping["NEW"] = 42
mapping.update({"Jim" : 37, "John": 55})
print(mapping)
print(mapping.items())
print(mapping.keys())
print(mapping.values())

# "contains key"
print("contains key Micha?", "Micha" in mapping)
print("Micha values:", mapping.pop("Micha"))
print("contains key Micha?", "Micha" in mapping.keys())
```

```
# "contains value"
print("contains value 55?", 55 in mapping.values())
```

This results in the following output:

```
{'Micha': 49, 'Peter': 42, 'Tom': 27, 'NEW': 42, 'Jim': 37, 'John': 55}
dict_items([('Micha', 49), ('Peter', 42), ('Tom', 27), ('NEW', 42),
('Jim', 37),
    ('John', 55)])
dict_keys(['Micha', 'Peter', 'Tom', 'NEW', 'Jim', 'John'])
dict_values([49, 42, 27, 42, 37, 55])
contains key Micha? True
Micha values: 49
contains key Micha? False
contains value 55? True
```

Example: Filtering Elements of a Dictionary in a General Way

Sometimes you want to find all key-value mappings whose values meet a particular
condition. This can be programmed in a generally appropriate and elegant way for later
reuse as follows:

```
def filter_dict(input_dict, key_value_condition):
    filtered_dict = dict()
    for key, value in input_dict.items():
        if key_value_condition((key, value)):
            filtered_dict[key] = value
    return filtered_dict

def filter_by_value(input_dict, value_condition):
    filtered_result = filter_dict(input_dict,
                                  lambda item : value_condition(item[1]))
    return filtered_result
```

You can either use the more general function, which gets a filter for key and value, or
the specific function designed directly for value filtering.

Let's define a mapping of cities to (approximate) population numbers and a filter condition on larger cities between 200,000 and 700,000 inhabitants to see the whole thing in action. The last call shows how easy it is to extract only the keys if only they are of interest.

```
cities_sizes = {"Cologne": 1_000_000, "Kiel": 250_000, "Bremen": 550_000,
                "Zurich": 400_000, "Oldenburg": 170_000}

print(filter_dict(cities_sizes, lambda item: 200_000 <= item[1] <= 700_000))
filtered_cities = filter_by_value(cities_sizes,
                                  lambda size: 200_000 <= size <= 700_000)

print(filtered_cities)
print(set(filtered_cities.keys()))
```

This results in the following output:

```
{'Kiel': 250000, 'Bremen': 550000, 'Zurich': 400000}
{'Kiel': 250000, 'Bremen': 550000, 'Zurich': 400000}
{'Bremen', 'Zurich', 'Kiel'}
```

5.1.5 The Stack as a LIFO Data Structure

In the following, I describe the data structure stack. It is not directly a part of Python, but it proves to be very practical for various use cases and can be easily implemented.

A stack is similar to a stack of paper or a desk tray in which you put things on top of a pile and from which you can only take things from the top. In addition, a view of the top element is possible. Beyond that, it offers size information or at least a check whether elements are present. This results in the following methods that form the API:

1. **push(element)** adds an element on top.

2. **pop()** picks and removes the top element.

3. **peek()** takes a peek at the top element.

4. **is_empty()** checks if the stack is empty.

These four methods are sufficient to use stacks profitably for various tasks in practice and for algorithms, for example, when sequences have to be reversed. This property is described in computer science by the term LIFO for Last In, First Out. Sometimes it is referred as FCFS for First Come, First Serve.

Exercise 2 is about implementing a stack on your own.

Example

After solving Exercise 2, you can put some elements on the stack, look at the top element, take elements from the top again, and finally, check if the stack is empty according to expectations:

```python
def main():
    stack = Stack()
    stack.push("first")
    stack.push("second")

    print("PEEK: " + stack.peek())
    print("POP: " + stack.pop())
    print("POP: " + stack.pop())
    print("ISEMPTY: " + str(stack.is_empty()))
```

This provides the following output:

```
PEEK: second
POP: second
POP: first
ISEMPTY: true
```

5.1.6 The Queue as a FIFO Data Structure

To conclude this introduction to basic data structures, I would like to talk about queues. They are also not a part of Python. Like a stack, a queue is often very useful and can also be easily implemented.

A queue is similar to a line at a cash register. People queue up, and the person who came first is served first, known in computer science as FIFO for First In, First Out.

Normally, only a few actions, such as adding and removing elements, benefit from a queue. In addition, a look at the element at the beginning is possible. Beyond that, it offers size information or at least a check whether elements are present. This results in the following methods that form the API:

1. **enqueue(element)** adds an element to the end of the queue.

2. **dequeue()** takes a look at the element at the beginning of the queue.

3. **peek()** takes a look at the element at the beginning of the queue.

4. **is_empty()** checks if the queue is empty.

These four methods are sufficient to create queues for various tasks in practice and for algorithms, such as if you intend to transform recursive algorithms into iterative ones.

Implementation

The method names reflect the concept described earlier. For this purpose, the implementation stores its elements in a list and inserts elements at the end. By using pop(0) or shorter pop() the foremost element is provided.

```python
class Queue:
    def __init__(self):
        self.values = []

    def enqueue(self, elem):
        self.values.append(elem)

    def dequeue(self):
        if self.is_empty():
            raise QueueIsEmptyException()

        return self.values.pop(0);

    def peek(self):
        if (self.is_empty()):
            raise QueueIsEmptyException()

        return self.values[0]
```

```python
    def is_empty(self):
        return len(self.values) == 0

class QueueIsEmptyException(Exception):
    pass
```

Example

To understand how it works, you can insert some elements into the queue and then process them as long as there are elements. In particular, reprocessing is aimed for the entry Michael.

```python
def main():
    waiting_persons = Queue()

    waiting_persons.enqueue("Marcello")
    waiting_persons.enqueue("Michael")
    waiting_persons.enqueue("Karthi")

    while not waiting_persons.is_empty():
        if waiting_persons.peek() == "Michael":
            # reprocess at the end
            waiting_persons.enqueue("Michael again")

        next_person = waiting_persons.dequeue()
        print("Processing " + next_person)
```

The small sample program provides the following output:

```
Processing Marcello
Processing Michael
Processing Karthi
Processing Michael again
```

NOTE: DOES IT NEED THE CUSTOM CREATIONS OF STACK AND QUEUE?

Let's recap: With a stack, you get the element stored last as the first element (that is, in reverse insertion order). This is why it is called **_Last-In-First-Out_** (**_LIFO_**). For insertion, as you know, you conceptually use a function called push() and for removal you use one called pop(). On the other hand, a queue represents a queue as we know it from shopping or ticket machines. Here, the person who was there first gets to go first. Accordingly, one speaks of **_First-In-First-Out_** (**_FIFO_**). Typically, the corresponding operations are called enqueue() and dequeue().

Easily emulate stack and queue with lists As mentioned, Python offers neither stack nor queue as a data structure by default, but does offer powerful lists in terms of functionality. With them, the functions of stack and queue previously mentioned can be implemented easily. In both cases you use the function append() to add elements, such as to emulate push() or enqueue(). In addition, the list provides the function pop(). It can optionally be passed an index that determines the position of the element to be removed—without index, simply the last element. Let's see how to emulate a stack and a queue with a list:

```
# List as Stack
stack_of_tasks = []

# Add "tasks" to the stack via append()
stack_of_tasks.append("Task 1")
stack_of_tasks.append("Task 2")
stack_of_tasks.append("Task 3")
stack_of_tasks.append("Task 4")

# Take the top 2 "tasks" from the stack via pop()
last_tasks = stack_of_tasks.pop()
second_last_tasks = stack_of_tasks.pop()
print("Top most:", last_tasks)
print("2nd from top:", second_last_tasks)

# List as Queue
queue_of_numbers = []

# Add 3 elements to the queue via append()
queue_of_numbers.append("First")
queue_of_numbers.append("Second")
```

```
queue_of_numbers.append("Third")
# Remove elements via pop(0) until the queue is empty
while len(queue_of_numbers) > 0:
print("Processing:", queue_of_numbers.pop(0))
```

The above program produces the following output:

```
Top most: Task 4
2nd from top: Task 3
Processing: First
Processing: Second
Processing: Third
```

Discussion: What is not optimal about this? First of all, it is pretty obvious that the function names of the list do not optimally match those commonly used for stacks and queues. Worse, if you accidentally specify no index or the wrong index for pop(), this leads to confusion. Even worse, stacks and queues conceptually do not allow indexed access to elements, but lists do. And this is only the beginning of possible problems. Because the above implementations (or to be precise, usages) are lists, you can also call arbitrary functions that have nothing to do with stacks and queues at all, such as insert() or remove(). If this is not clear enough, you could also sort the elements by calling sort() and thus probably mess up the desired order a lot. As you can see, the pitfalls are many.

Conclusion

Based on this reasoning and the need for intuitive handling without risk of misuse, the definition of your own classes for providing the specific data structures stack and queue becomes obvious.

5.2 Exercises

5.2.1 Exercise 1: Common Elements (★★☆☆☆)

Find the common elements of two lists, *A* and *B,* and return them as a set. Implement this, both with and without using matching functions from Python's sets. Write your own function find_common(values1, values2), which works like the Python function intersection().

Examples

Input A	Input B	Result
[1, 2, 4, 7, 8]	[2, 3, 7, 9]	{2, 7}
[1, 2, 7, 4, 7, 8]	[7, 7, 3, 2, 9]	{2, 7}
[2, 4, 6, 8]	[1, 3, 5, 7, 9]	∅ = set()

5.2.2 Exercise 2: Your Own Stack (★★☆☆☆)

Define the basic requirements for a stack and implement class Stack based on these requirements using a list.

5.2.3 Exercise 3: List Reverse (★★☆☆☆)

Exercise 3a: List Reverse (★☆☆☆☆)

Write function reverse(values) that returns the elements of the original list in reverse order—of course without calling the reverse() function of the list.

Examples

Input	Result
[1, 2, 3, 4]	[4, 3, 2, 1]
["A", "BB", "CCC", "DDDD"]	["DDDD", "CCC", "BB", "A"]

Exercise 3b: List Reverse Inplace (★★☆☆☆)

What is different if you want to implement reversing the order inplace to be memory-optimal for very large datasets? What should be given then?

Exercise 3c: List Reverse Without Performant Index Access (★★☆☆☆)

Now let's assume that no performant random index access is available. What happens if you want to reverse the order and any position-based access will result in $O(n)$ and therefore $O(n^2)$ for the complete reversal process. How do you avoid this?

Tip   Use a stack.

5.2.4 Exercise 4: Remove Duplicates (★★☆☆☆)

You are supposed to remove duplicate entries from a list. The constraint is that the original order should be preserved. Write function `remove_duplicates(values)`.

Examples

Input	Result
[1, 1, 2, 3, 4, 1, 2, 3]	[1, 2, 3, 4]
[7, 5, 3, 5, 1]	[7, 5, 3, 1]
[1, 1, 1, 1]	[1]

5.2.5 Exercise 5: Maximum Profit (★★★☆☆)

Imagine that you have a sequence of prices ordered in time and that you want to calculate the maximum profit. The challenge is to determine at which time (or value, in this case) it would be ideal to buy and to sell. Write function `max_revenue(prices)` for this purpose, where the temporal order is expressed by the index in the list.

Examples

Input	Result
[250, 270, 230, 240, 222, 260, 294, 210]	72
[0, 10, 20, 30, 40, 50, 60, 70]	70
[70, 60, 50, 40, 30, 20, 10, 0]	0
[]	0

5.2.6 Exercise 6: Longest Sequence (★★★☆☆)

Suppose you are modeling stock prices or altitudes of a track by a list of numbers. Find the longest sequence of numbers whose values ascend or at least stay the same. Write function find_longest_growing_sequence(values).

Examples

Input	Result
[7, 2, 7, 1, 2, 5, 7, 1]	[1, 2, 5, 7]
[7, 2, 7, 1, 2, 3, 8, 1, 2, 3, 4, 5]	[1, 2, 3, 4, 5]
[1, 1, 2, 2, 2, 3, 3, 3, 3]	[1, 1, 2, 2, 2, 3, 3, 3, 3]

5.2.7 Exercise 7: Well-Formed Braces (★★☆☆☆)

Write function check_parentheses(braces_input) that checks whether a sequence of braces is neatly nested in each case. This should accept any round, square, and curly braces but no other characters.

Examples

Input	Result	Comment
"(())"	True	
"({[]})"	True	
"((()"	False	Odd number of braces
"((a)"	False	Wrong character, no braces
"(])"	False	No matching braces

Bonus Extend the solution so that a clear assignment of error causes becomes possible. Start with the following enumeration:

```
from enum import Enum, auto

class CheckResult(Enum):
    OK = auto()
    ODD_LENGTH = auto()
    CLOSING_BEFORE_OPENING = auto()
    MISMATCHING_PARENTHESIS = auto()
    INVALID_CHAR = auto()
    REMAINING_OPENING = auto()
```

5.2.8 Exercise 8: Pascal's Triangle (★★★☆☆)

Write function pascal(n) that computes Pascal's triangle in terms of nested lists. As you know, each new line results from the previous one. If there are more than two elements in it, two values are added and the sums build the values of the new line. In each case, a 1 is appended to the front and back.

Example

For the value 5, the desired representation is as follows:

```
[1]
[1, 1]
[1, 2, 1]
[1, 3, 3, 1]
[1, 4, 6, 4, 1]
```

5.2.9 Exercise 9: Check Magic Triangle (★★★☆☆)

Write function is_magic_triangle(values) that checks whether a sequence of numbers forms a magic triangle. Such a triangle is defined as one where the respective sums of the three sides' values must all be equal.

Examples

The following shows this for one triangle each of side length three and side length four:

```
 1                   2
6 5                 8 5
2 4 3               4   9
                   3 7 6 1
```

This results in the following sides and sums:

Input	Values 1	Values 2
side 1	1 + 5 + 3 = 9	2 + 5 + 9 + 1 = 17
side 2	3 + 4 + 2 = 9	1 + 6 + 7 + 3 = 17
side 3	2 + 6 + 1 = 9	3 + 4 + 8 + 2 = 17

Tip Model the individual sides of the triangle as sublists.

5.2.10 Exercise 10: Most Frequent Elements (★★☆☆☆)

Write function value_count(values) that determines a histogram (i. e., the distribution of the frequencies of the numbers in the given list). Also write function sort_dict_by_value(dictionary) to sort the dictionary by its values instead of by keys. Thereby a descending sorting is to be realized so that smaller values are listed at the beginning.

Examples

Input	Result	Most frequent(s)
[1, 2, 3, 4, 4, 4, 3, 3, 2, 4]	{1=1, 2=2, 3=3, 4=4}	4=4
[1, 1, 1, 2, 2, 2, 3, 3, 3]	{1=3, 2=3, 3=3}	Depending on query, logically all

5.2.11 Exercise 11: Addition of Digits (★★★☆☆)

Consider two decimal numbers that are to be added. Sounds simple, but for this assignment, the numbers are interestingly represented as a list of digits. Write function list_add(values1, values2). Also, consider the special case where there is an overflow.

Exercise 11a: Addition (★★★☆☆)

In the first part of the task, the digits are to be stored in the order of their occurrence in the list.

Examples

Input 1	Input 2	Result
123 = [1, 2, 3]	456 = [4, 5, 6]	579 = [5, 7, 9]
927 = [9, 2, 7]	135 = [1, 3, 5]	1062 = [1, 0, 6, 2]

Exercise 11b: Addition Inverse (★★★☆☆)

What changes if the digits are stored in reverse order in the list?

Examples

Input 1	Input 2	Result
123 = [3, 2, 1]	456 = [6, 5, 4]	579 = [9, 7, 5]
927 = [7, 2, 9]	135 = [5, 3, 1]	1062 = [2, 6, 0, 1]

5.2.12 Exercise 12: List Merge (★★☆☆☆)

Given two lists of numbers, each sorted in ascending order, merge them into a result list according to their order. Write function merge(values1, values2).

Examples

Input 1	Input 2	Result
1, 4, 7, 12, 20	10, 15, 17, 33	1, 4, 7, 10, 12, 15, 17, 20, 33
2, 3, 5, 7	11, 13, 17	2, 3, 5, 7, 11, 13, 17
2, 3, 5, 7, 11	7, 11, 13, 17	2, 3, 5, 7, 7, 11, 11, 13, 17
[1, 2, 3]	∅ = []	[1, 2, 3]

5.2.13 Exercise 13: Excel Magic Select (★★☆☆☆)

If you have worked a little with Excel, then you have probably used the Magic Selection. It continuously populates a selected area with values based on the previous values. This works for numbers, weekdays, or dates, for example. To achieve something similar on your own, write function generate_following_values(current_value, sequence_length) that implements this for numbers. Create a variation suitable for weekdays and with the following signature: generate_following_values_for_-predefined(predefined_values, current_value, sequence_length).

Examples

Initial value	Count	Result
1	7	[1, 2, 3, 4, 5, 6, 7]
5	4	[5, 6, 7, 8]
FRIDAY	8	[FRIDAY, SATURDAY, SUNDAY, MONDAY, TUESDAY, WEDNESDAY, THURSDAY, FRIDAY]

5.2.14 Exercise 14: Stack-Based Queue (★★☆☆☆)

You learned about stack and queue data structures in the introduction and implemented a queue based on a list. Then in exercise 2, you implemented a stack itself. Now you are asked to build a queue based on the stack data structure.

Example

Please check the functionality with the following procedure:

```python
def main():
    waiting_persons = Queue()

    waiting_persons.enqueue("Marcello")
    waiting_persons.enqueue("Michael")
    waiting_persons.enqueue("Karthi")

    while not waiting_persons.is_empty():
        if waiting_persons.peek() == "Michael":
            # reprocess at the end
            waiting_persons.enqueue("Michael again")

        next_person = waiting_persons.dequeue()
        print("Processing " + next_person)
```

The small sample program should produce the following output:

```
Processing Marcello
Processing Michael
Processing Karthi
Processing Michael again
```

5.3 Solutions

5.3.1 Solution 1: Common Elements (★★☆☆☆)

Find the common elements of two lists, *A* and *B,* and return them as a set. Implement this, both with and without using matching functions from Python's sets. Write your own function find_common(values1, values2), which works like the Python function intersection().

Examples

Input A	Input B	Result
[1, 2, 4, 7, 8]	[2, 3, 7, 9]	{2, 7}
[1, 2, 7, 4, 7, 8]	[7, 7, 3, 2, 9]	{2, 7}
[2, 4, 6, 8]	[1, 3, 5, 7, 9]	∅ = set()

Algorithm Use dictionaries and manage a counter for being contained in list 1 or 2. You first run through all elements from list 1 and enter the value 1 in the dictionary. Now you run through all elements of the second list. You increase the counter if an entry already exists in the dictionary for the value. Thus, all elements contained in both lists receive the value 2 and with multiple occurrences, a higher value. On the other hand, elements exclusively from list 2 are never stored. Finally, you keep only those entries whose number is greater than or equal to 2.

```python
def find_common(values1, values2):
    results = {}
    populate_from_collection1(values1, results)
    mark_if_also_in_second(values2, results)

    return remove_all_just_in_first(results)

def populate_from_collection1(values1, results):
    for elem1 in values1:
        results[elem1] = 1

def mark_if_also_in_second(values2, results):
    for elem2 in values2:
        if elem2 in results:
            results[elem2] += 1

def remove_all_just_in_first(results):
    final_result = set()
    for key, value in results.items():
        if value >= 2:
            final_result.add(key)

    return final_result
```

Python shortcut With the help of set comprehension, the last function becomes a one-liner:

```python
def remove_all_just_in_first(results):
    return {key for key, value in results.items() if value >= 2}
```

Despite this improvement, it seems too complicated. How can you make it better?

Optimized algorithm In fact, the problem can be solved much more compactly and understandably. Check all elements from the first collection to see if they are contained in the second collection. If so, these values get included in the result set.

```python
def find_common_short(values1, values2):
    results = set()
    for elem1 in values1:
        if elem1 in values2:
            results.add(elem1)

    return results
```

Python shortcut With the help of set comprehension, this becomes a one-liner:

```python
def find_common_short_comprehension(values1, values2):
    return {elem1 for elem1 in values1 if elem1 in values2}
```

Built-in Python shortcut For your own projects, please use the built-in functionality in the form of `intersection()`:

```python
def find_common_build_in(values1, values2):
    return set(values1).intersection(values2)
```

Verification

Test the implementation through the following unit tests:

```python
def inputs_and_expected():
    return [([1, 2, 4, 7, 8], [2, 3, 7, 9], {2, 7}),
            ([1, 2, 7, 4, 7, 8], [7, 7, 3, 2, 9], {2, 7}),
            ([2, 4, 6, 8], [1, 3, 5, 7, 9], set())]

@pytest.mark.parametrize("values1, values2, expected",
                         inputs_and_expected())
```

```python
def test_find_common(values1, values2, expected):
    result = find_common(values1, values2)

    assert result == expected

@pytest.mark.parametrize("values1, values2, expected",
                         inputs_and_expected())
def test_find_common(values1, values2, expected):
    result = find_common_short(values1, values2)

    assert result== expected
```

5.3.2 Solution 2: Your Own Stack (★★☆☆☆)

Define the basic requirements for a stack and implement class Stack based on these requirements using a list.

Algorithm It is possible to implement a stack yourself, using a list as a data storage, but not providing direct access to it externally. Users just have access through the following methods typical of a stack:

1. push(element) adds an element on top.

2. pop() picks and removes the top element.

3. peek() takes a look at the top element.

4. is_empty() checks if the stack is empty.

Each call to push() adds an element at the end of the list. This way, you simulate the stack. When accessing the top element, it is checked upfront whether the stack is empty, in which case a StackIsEmptyException is thrown. Otherwise, the top element is returned.

```python
class Stack:
    def __init__(self):
        self.__values = []

    def push(self, elem):
        self.__values.append(elem)
```

```python
    def pop(self):
        if self.is_empty():
            raise StackIsEmptyException()

        return self.__values.pop()

    def peek(self):
        if self.is_empty():
            raise StackIsEmptyException()

        return self.__values[-1]

    def is_empty(self):
        return len(self.__values) == 0

class StackIsEmptyException(Exception):
    pass
```

Perhaps somewhat more comprehensible would be to add elements at the beginning of the list and take them from there. However, this would be unfavorable in terms of performance. Why? This would result in constant recopying of the internal data of the list.

In addition, one could argue that the Python online documentation[3] describes how to use lists as stacks. Even if possible, the interface is not restricted to the above methods. In my book *Der Weg zum Java-Profi* [Ind20] I discuss in detail what can be problematic about this.

HINT: VISIBILITIY/ACCESSIBILITY

While languages like Java or C++ have ***visibilities*** to control and protect access to private class components, this is not possible in Python. However, there are two variants with _ and to achieve something similar. What is this all about?

- If names start with _, then by convention, the one underscore means that this method or attribute is considered private and an implementation detail of the class. However, Python does not enforce this. Especially, access is not prevented. Instead, you must rely on other programmers to observe this fact.

---

[3] https://docs.python.org/3/tutorial/datastructures.html

- A double underscore (__) marks an internal method. When used for attributes, this attribute is no longer visible to the outside for other classes under its name. This is also true for methods.

Verification

You verify the correct working of the stack you just implemented using a predefined flow. First, you insert two elements. Then you look at the top one with peek(). After that, you remove elements twice with pop(). As expected, they are supplied in reverse order of insertion. Finally, you check to see if the stack is empty. Because this is the case, a subsequent inspection of the topmost element should throw a StackIsEmptyException—show here just as a comment.

```
def main():
    stack = Stack()
    stack.push("first")
    stack.push("second")

    print("PEEK: " + stack.peek())
    print("POP: " + stack.pop())
    print("POP: " + stack.pop())
    print("ISEMPTY: " + str(stack.is_empty()))
    # print("POP: " + stack.pop())
```

This results in the following output:

```
PEEK: second
POP: second
POP: first
ISEMPTY: true
```

5.3.3 Solution 3: List Reverse (★★☆☆☆)

Solution 3a: List Reverse (★☆☆☆☆)

Write function reverse(values) that returns the elements of the original list in reverse order—of course without calling the reverse() function of the list.

Examples

Input	Result
[1, 2, 3, 4]	[4, 3, 2, 1]
["A", "BB", "CCC", "DDDD"]	["DDDD", "CCC", "BB", "A"]

Algorithm A simple solution is to traverse a list from back to front and add the current element to a result list. This can be implemented index-based as follows:

```python
def reverse(values):
    result = []

    for i in range(len(values) - 1, -1, -1):
        result.append(values[i])

    return result
```

Python shortcut Using list comprehensions, the whole thing can be written shorter and more concisely. The first variant is still based on the realization shown above, while the second relies on an inverted iterator with reversed():

```python
def reverse_with_comprehension(values):
    return [values[i] for i in range(len(values) - 1, -1, -1)]

def reverse_with_comprehension_nicer(values):
    return [value for value in reversed(values)]
```

Using list() in combination with reversed() is even shorter and nicer:

```python
def reverse_with_list_nicer(values):
    return list(reversed(values))
```

In fact, with slicing, the whole thing can be written briefly as follows, where again the result is a new list with the contents reversed from the original:

```python
reversed = values[::-1]
```

Solution 3b: List Reverse Inplace (★★☆☆☆)

What is different if you want to implement reversing the order inplace to be memory-optimal for very large datasets? What should be given then?

Algorithm Based on indexed access, you proceed inwards from the beginning and the end, swapping the elements:

```python
def reverse_inplace(original):
    left = 0
    right = len(original) - 1

    # run from the left and right, swap the elements based on their
    positions
    while left < right:
        left_elem = original[left]
        right_elem = original[right]

        # swap
        original[left] = right_elem
        original[right] = left_elem

        left += 1
        right -= 1

    return original
```

Python shortcut Please keep in mind that in real projects, the standard functionality reverse() should be used, which works inplace:

```python
values.reverse()
```

Solution 3c: List Reverse Without Performant Index Access (★★☆☆☆)

Now let's assume that no performant random index access is available. What happens if you want to reverse the order and any position-based access will result in $O(n)$ and therefore $O(n^2)$ for the complete reversal process. How do you avoid this?

Tip   Use a stack.

Algorithm In the case that no performant indexed-based access is available and you still have to reverse the order with running time complexity of $O(n)$, a stack comes into play—just as for various other algorithms, including this one. You traverse the list from front to back and put the current element on the stack each time. Afterwards, you iteratively remove the top element from the stack and add it to a result list until the stack is empty.

```python
def list_reverse_with_stack(values):
    # Go through the list from front to back and fill a stack
    all_values = Stack()

    for element in values:
        all_values.push(element)

    # Empty the stack and fill a result list
    result = []
    while not all_values.is_empty():
        result.append(all_values.pop())

    return result
```

Verification

Let's experiment with the input values from the example and invoke the function you created earlier— in the accompanying project all variants will of course be tested:

```python
def list_reverse_inputs_and_expected():
    return [([1, 2, 3, 4], [4, 3, 2, 1]),
            (["A", "BB", "CCC", "DDDD"], ["DDDD", "CCC", "BB", "A"])]

@pytest.mark.parametrize("inputs, expected",
                         list_reverse_inputs_and_expected())
def test_reverse(inputs, expected):
    result = reverse(inputs)

    assert result == expected

@pytest.mark.parametrize("inputs, expected",
                         list_reverse_inputs_and_expected())
```

```
def test_reverse_inplace(inputs, expected):
    modifiable_inputs = list(inputs)

    reverse_inplace(modifiable_inputs)

    assert modifiable_inputs == expected
```

5.3.4 Solution 4: Remove Duplicates (★★☆☆☆)

You are supposed to remove duplicate entries from a list. The constraint is that the original order should be preserved. Write function remove_duplicates(values).

Examples

Input	Result
[1, 1, 2, 3, 4, 1, 2, 3]	[1, 2, 3, 4]
[7, 5, 3, 5, 1]	[7, 5, 3, 1]
[1, 1, 1, 1]	[1]

Algorithm Traverse the list from front to back and successively fill a set with the entries contained in the list. For each element of the list, check whether it is already contained in the set of entries found. If not, it will be included and also added to the result. Otherwise, the next element gets checked.

```
def remove_duplicates(values):
    result = []

    already_found_numbers = set()

    for elem in values:
        if elem not in already_found_numbers:
            already_found_numbers.add(elem)
            result.append(elem)

    return result
```

Optimized algorithm While implementing you might get the idea of simply deleting the duplicates by refilling them into a set. This works but potentially messes up the order of the elements. A workaround is to use a dictionary. Calling fromkeys() creates a dictionary based on the passed list and automatically removes duplicate keys. In addition, since Python 3.6, the insertion order is preserved. With this knowledge, implementing the removal of duplicates is a snap.

```
list_with_duplicates = ["a", "b", "a", "c", "d", "c", "d"]

# order may change
no_duplicates1 = list(set(list_with_duplicates))

# stable order
no_duplicates2 = list(dict.fromkeys(list_with_duplicates))
```

Python shortcut With this knowledge, create the following implementation of the removal of duplicates as a function:

```
def remove_duplicates_with_dict(values):
    return list(dict.fromkeys(values))
```

Verification

Again, you use the introductory example's values to verify the implementation. The tests for the two optimized versions are not shown below because they are, apart from the function call, identical.

```
def inputs_and_expected():
    return [([1, 1, 2, 3, 4, 1, 2, 3], [1, 2, 3, 4]),
            ([7, 5, 3, 5, 1], [7, 5, 3, 1]),
            ([1, 1, 1, 1], [1])]

@pytest.mark.parametrize("inputs, expected",
                         inputs_and_expected())
def test_remove_duplicates(inputs, expected):
    result = remove_duplicates(inputs)

    assert result == expected
```

```
@pytest.mark.parametrize("inputs, expected",
                         inputs_and_expected())
def test_remove_duplicates_with_dict(inputs, expected):
    result = remove_duplicates_with_dict(inputs)

    assert result == expected
```

5.3.5 Solution 5: Maximum Profit (★★★☆☆)

Imagine that you have a sequence of prices ordered by time and you want to calculate the maximum profit. The challenge is to determine at which time (or value in this case) it would be ideal to buy and to sell. Write function `max_revenue(prices)` for this purpose, where the temporal order is expressed by the index in the list.

Examples

Input	Result
[250, 270, 230, 240, 222, 260, 294, 210]	72
[0, 10, 20, 30, 40, 50, 60, 70]	70
[70, 60, 50, 40, 30, 20, 10, 0]	0
[]	0

Algorithm Initially, you may be tempted to determine the minimum and the maximum and simply return the difference. After a short reflection, it becomes clear that a time dimension has to be considered in this case. First, a purchase and then a sale at a higher price must take place to realize a profit.

The next idea is to run through the list twice. First, all minimum values are determined by looking to see if the current value is less than the current minimum. This is then added to the list of minimum values valid for the time. In the second run, you determine the largest difference by comparing element by element. If the current value is greater than the currently valid minimum value, then the profit thus obtained is the difference between the current value and the minimum value determined at the position. Finally, the maximum profit is calculated from the maximum of the current maximum and the current profit. For the above example 1, the result is as follows:

Value	255	260	250	240	228	270	300	210	245
Minimum	255	255	250	240	228	228	228	210	210
Difference	0	5	0	0	0	42	72	0	35
Max. Difference	0	5	5	5	5	42	72	72	72

According to this idea, you express the whole thing in Python by first determining all relevant minimum values and then, based on that, the maximum:

```python
def max_revenue(prices):
    relevant_mins = calc_relevant_mins(prices)

    return calc_max_revenue(prices, relevant_mins)
```

The actual work happens in the following two helper functions:

```python
def calc_relevant_mins(prices):
    relevant_mins = []
    current_min = sys.maxsize
    for current_price in prices:
        current_min = min(current_min, current_price)
        relevant_mins.append(current_min)

    return relevant_mins

def calc_max_revenue(prices, relevant_mins):
    max_revenue = 0
    for i, price in enumerate(prices):
        if price > relevant_mins[i]:
            current_revenue = price - relevant_mins[i]
            max_revenue = max(max_revenue, current_revenue)

    return max_revenue
```

Optimized algorithm The variation just shown requires two passes. As long as the accesses are made in memory, this hardly plays a crucial role in the performance. The situation is somewhat different if the data is determined each time, for example, via a REST call or from a database.

In fact, the number of necessary calls and loop iterations can be reduced. However, this optimization can probably only be achieved if the previous implementation has been completed first.

```python
def max_revenue_optimized(prices):
    current_min = sys.maxsize
    max_revenue = 0
    for current_price in prices:
        current_min = min(current_min, current_price)
        current_revenue = current_price - current_min
        max_revenue = max(max_revenue, current_revenue)

    return max_revenue
```

Verification

For testing, you again use the values from the introductory example:

```python
def prices_and_expected():
    return [([0, 10, 20, 30, 40, 50, 60, 70], 70),
            ([70, 60, 50, 40, 30, 20, 10], 0),
            ([], 0)]
```

```python
@pytest.mark.parametrize("prices, expected", prices_and_expected())
def test_max_revenue(prices, expected):
    result = max_revenue(prices)

    assert result == expected
```

5.3.6 Solution 6: Longest Sequence (★★★☆☆)

Suppose you are modeling stock prices or altitudes of a track by a list of numbers. Find the longest sequence of numbers whose values ascend or at least stay the same. Write function find_longest_growing_sequence(values).

Examples

Input	Result
[7, 2, 7, 1, 2, 5, 7, 1]	[1, 2, 5, 7]
[7, 2, 7, 1, 2, 3, 8, 1, 2, 3, 4, 5]	[1, 2, 3, 4, 5]
[1, 1, 2, 2, 2, 3, 3, 3, 3]	[1, 1, 2, 2, 2, 3, 3, 3, 3]

Algorithm Here a so-called **greedy** algorithm is used. The idea is to collect the subsequent elements starting from one element until the next element is smaller than the current one. A temporary list and a result list are used for this purpose. Both are initially empty and are successively filled: the temporary list at each element read that is greater than or equal to the predecessor and the result list whenever a smaller successor value is found. If a value is smaller, the temporary list is cleared and starts as a one-element list with the current value. If the result list at a flank change is shorter than the temporary list with the previously collected elements, then the temporary list becomes the new result list. This procedure is repeated until you reach the end of the initial list.

Let's look at a procedure for the input 1272134572:

Input	Current character	Temporary list	Result list
1272134572	1	1	
1**2**72134572	2	12	
12**7**2134572	7	127	
127**2**134572	2	2	127
1272**1**34572	1	1	127
12721**3**4572	3	13	127
127213**4**572	4	134	127
1272134**5**72	5	1345	127
12721345**7**7	7	13457	127
127213457**2**	2	2	13457

```python
def find_longest_growing_sequence(values):
    longest_subsequence = []
    current_subsequence = []

    last_value = sys.maxsize

    for current_value in values:
        if current_value >= last_value:
            last_value = current_value
            current_subsequence.append(current_value)
        else:
            # end of this sequence, start new sequence
            if len(current_subsequence) >= len(longest_subsequence):
                longest_subsequence = current_subsequence

            current_subsequence = []
            last_value = current_value
            current_subsequence.append(current_value)

    # important, because otherwise the last sequence might not be considered
    if len(current_subsequence) >= len(longest_subsequence):
        longest_subsequence = current_subsequence

    return longest_subsequence
```

Be sure to note the additional check after the for loop—otherwise, a final sequence would not be correctly returned as a result.

Mini optimization The check should be optimized a bit further. As you can see, assigning the value and adding it to the current temporary list happens in every case. Thus, these actions can be separated from the condition and written as follows:

```python
for current_value in values:
    if current_value < last_value:
        # end of this sequence, start new sequence
        if len(current_subsequence) >= len(longest_subsequence):
            longest_subsequence = current_subsequence

        current_subsequence = []

    last_value = current_value
    current_subsequence.append(current_value)
```

Procedure for sections of equal length When checking for the longest sequence, you can either compare with > or >=. If there are two or more sequences of the same length, in the first case with > the first one is taken as a result, with >= always the last one.

Alternative and optimized algorithm Sometimes creating temporary data structures can be rather undesirable, for example, when the subsections can become huge. In such a case, it offers itself to determine only the respective index borders. As a final step, you extract the appropriate part.

```python
def find_longest_growing_sequence_optimized(values):
    if len(values) == 0:
        return values

    longest = (0, 0)
    start_current = 0
    end_current = 0

    for end_current in range(1, len(values)):
        # flank change
        if values[end_current] < values[end_current - 1]:
            if end_current - start_current > len(longest):
                longest = (start_current, end_current)
            start_current = end_current

    if end_current - start_current > len(longest):
        longest = (start_current, end_current)

    return values[longest[0] : longest[1]]
```

Verification

Use the sequences of values from the introduction to compare the computed results with your expectations:

```python
@pytest.mark.parametrize("values, expected",
                         [([7, 2, 7, 1, 2, 5, 7, 1], [1, 2, 5, 7]),
                          ([7, 2, 7, 1, 2, 3, 8, 1, 2, 3, 4, 5],
                           [1, 2, 3, 4, 5]),
```

```
                    ([1, 1, 2, 2, 2, 3, 3, 3, 3],
                     [1, 1, 2, 2, 2, 3, 3, 3, 3]),
                    ([], [])])
def test_find_longest_growing_sequence(values, expected):
    result = find_longest_growing_sequence(values)

    assert result == expected
```

5.3.7 Solution 7: Well-Formed Braces (★★☆☆☆)

Write function check_parentheses(braces_input) that checks whether a sequence
of braces is neatly nested in each case. This should accept any round, square and curly
braces but no other characters.

Examples

Input	Result	Comment
"(())"	True	
"({[]})"	True	
"((())"	False	Odd number of braces
"((a)"	False	Wrong character, no braces
"([)"	False	No matching braces

Algorithm Traverse the string from front to back. If the current character is an
opening brace (that is, one of the characters (, [, or {), store it in a stack. If it is a closing
brace, try to match it with the last opening brace. If there is no opening brace yet, or if
the brace types do not match, False is returned. If they match, the next character is read.
If it is an opening brace, proceed as before. If it is a closing brace, get the top element
from the stack and compare it to the character just read. Check for matching the type of
braces, which are ( ), [ ], and { }. Let's look at a flow for the input (()):

Input	Current character	Stack	Comment
(()]			Start
(()]	(	(	Store
(()]	(	((	Store
[()]	)	(	Match
(()]	]	(	Mismatch

The implementation uses a stack and performs the checks and actions described above:

```python
def check_parentheses(braces_input):
    # odd length cannot be a well-formed bracing
    if len(braces_input) % 2 != 0:
        return False

    opening_parentheses = Stack()
    for char in braces_input:
        if is_opening_parenthesis(char):
            opening_parentheses.push(char)
        elif is_closing_parenthesis(char):
            if opening_parentheses.is_empty():
                # closing before opening brace
                return False

            last_opening_parens = opening_parentheses.pop()
            if not is_matching_parenthesis_pair(last_opening_parens, char):
                # different pairs of braces
                return False
        else:
            # invalid character
            return False

    return opening_parentheses.is_empty()
```

Once again, it is recommended to extract helper functions such as is_opening_parenthesis() to be able to implement the actual algorithm at a higher level of abstraction and thus more clearly. Finally, let's take an examining look at the three helper functions—for the closing braces, here is an elegant Python variant with in for a list of characters instead of a character-by-character check with or and:

```python
def is_opening_parenthesis(ch):
    return ch == '(' or ch == '[' or ch == '{'

def is_closing_parenthesis(ch):
    return ch in [")", "]", "}"]

def is_matching_parenthesis_pair(opening, closing):
    return (opening == '(' and closing == ')') or \
           (opening == '[' and closing == ']') or \
           (opening == '{' and closing == '}')
```

Checking for matching pair of braces can also be written more elegantly using a list of tuples containing the opening and closing braces:

```python
# Alternative variant using tuple notation
def is_matching_parenthesis_pair(opening, closing):
    return (opening, closing) in [('(', ')'), ('[', ']'), ('{', '}')]
```

Verification

Use the values from the introduction to see your just-implemented functionality in action:

```python
@pytest.mark.parametrize("values, expected",
                [("()", True), ("()[]{}", True),
                 ("[((()[]{}))]", True),
                 ("(()", False), ("((})", False),
                 ("(()}", False), (")()(", False),
                 ("()((", False), ("()A(", False)])
def test_check_parentheses(values, expected):
    result = check_parentheses(values)

    assert result == expected
```

Let's look again at the implementation of the check and the return values. Several comments exist why True or False is returned. Wouldn't it be more intuitive to express this with a suitable enumeration as a return? Let's take a look at that now in the bonus.

Bonus

Extend the solution so that a clear assignment of error causes becomes possible. Start with the following enumeration:

```
from enum import Enum, auto

class CheckResult(Enum):
    OK = auto()
    ODD_LENGTH = auto()
    CLOSING_BEFORE_OPENING = auto()
    MISMATCHING_PARENTHESIS = auto()
    INVALID_CHAR = auto()
    REMAINING_OPENING = auto()
```

By using the enumeration, possible error causes may be communicated more clearly. Besides, you can omit the comments on the return values in the source code since the enumeration values adequately describe them.

```
def check_parentheses_v2(braces_input):
    # odd length cannot be well-formed braces
    if len(braces_input) % 2 != 0:
        return CheckResult.ODD_LENGTH

    opening_parentheses = Stack()

    for current_char in braces_input:
        if is_opening_parenthesis(current_char):
            opening_parentheses.push(current_char)
        elif is_closing_parenthesis(current_char):
            if opening_parentheses.is_empty():
                return CheckResult.CLOSING_BEFORE_OPENING
```

```
        last_opening_parens = opening_parentheses.pop()
        if not is_matching_parenthesis_pair(last_opening_parens,
                                            current_char):
            return CheckResult.MISMATCHING_PARENTHESIS
    else:
        return CheckResult.INVALID_CHAR

if opening_parentheses.is_empty():
    return CheckResult.OK

return CheckResult.REMAINING_OPENING
```

Verification

Using enumeration not only increases the readability of the application's source code but also adds clarity and conciseness to the unit test. As usual, use the values from the introductory example to see your just implemented functionality in action:

```
@pytest.mark.parametrize("values",
                        [("()"), ("()[]{}"), ("[((()[]{}))]")])
def test_check_parentheses_v2(values):
    result = check_parentheses_v2(values)

    assert result == CheckResult.OK

@pytest.mark.parametrize("values, expected",
                        [("(()", CheckResult.ODD_LENGTH),
                         ("((})", CheckResult.MISMATCHING_PARENTHESIS),
                         ("(()}", CheckResult.MISMATCHING_PARENTHESIS),
                         (")()(", CheckResult.CLOSING_BEFORE_OPENING),
                         ("()((", CheckResult.REMAINING_OPENING),
                         ("()A(", CheckResult.INVALID_CHAR)])
def test_check_parentheses_v2_errors(values, expected):
    result = check_parentheses_v2(values)

    assert result == expected
```

5.3.8 Solution 8: Pascal's Triangle (★★★☆☆)

Write function `pascal(n)` that computes Pascal's triangle in terms of nested lists. As you know, each new line results from the previous one. If there are more than two elements in it, two values are added, and the sums build the values of the new line. In each case, a 1 is appended to the front and back.

Example

For the value 5, the desired representation is as follows:

```
[1]
[1, 1]
[1, 2, 1]
[1, 3, 3, 1]
[1, 4, 6, 4, 1]
```

Algorithm The determination of the individual lines is done recursively. For the first line, a one-element list with the value 1 is generated. For all others, you calculate the values by invoking helper function `calc_line(previous_line)` based on the predecessor line and then add the intermediate result to the overall result. It might be a bit irritating that the call is 1-based, but the list index is, of course, 0-based.

```python
def pascal(n):
    result = []
    __pascal_helper(n, result)
    return result

def __pascal_helper(n, results):
    if n == 1:
        # recursive termination
        results.append([1])
    else:
        # recursive descent
        previous_line = __pascal_helper(n - 1, results)

        # calculate based on previous line
        current_line = __calc_line(previous_line)
        results.append(current_line)

    return results[n - 1]
```

Computing a row's values based on the predecessor row is performed for all rows with $n \geq 2$ as follows: If there is more than one value stored in the predecessor row list, iterate through it and sum each. To complete the computation, the value 1 is appended at the front and the back.

Somewhat more formally it can be written as follows, where the index of the rows and columns starts from 1 and not as in Python from 0:

$$pascal(row, col) = \begin{cases} 1, & row = 1 \text{ and } col = 1 \text{ (top)} \\ 1, & \forall row \in \{1, n\} \text{ and } col = 1 \\ 1, & \forall row \in \{1, n\} \text{ and } col = row \\ pascal(row - 1, col) + & \\ pascal(row - 1, col - 1), & \text{otherwise (based on predecessors)} \end{cases}$$

The implementation is done directly and is much more understandable than the purely recursive definition for each value already presented in section 3.3.9.

```python
# each row is calculated from the values of the row above it,
# flanked in each case by a 1
def __calc_line(previous_line):
    current_line = [previous_line[i] + previous_line[i + 1]
                    for i in range(len(previous_line) - 1)]

    return [1] + current_line + [1]
```

Verification

To test the implementation, define a function where you compute Pascal's triangle for the passed value and then print it appropriately:

```python
def print_pascal(n):
    for line in pascal(n):
        print(line)
```

Let's try it out:

```python
>>> print_pascal(4)
...
[1]
[1, 1]
[1, 2, 1]
[1, 3, 3, 1]
```

If you like it a bit more formal, a matching unit test is provided:

```
@pytest.mark.parametrize("n, expected",
                         [(1, [[1]]),
                          (2, [[1], [1, 1]]),
                          (3, [[1], [1, 1], [1, 2, 1]]),
                          (4, [[1], [1, 1], [1, 2, 1], [1, 3, 3, 1]])])
def test_pascal(n, expected):
    result = pascal(n)

    assert result == expected
```

5.3.9 Solution 9: Check Magic Triangle (★★★☆☆)

Write function is_magic_triangle(values) that checks whether a sequence of numbers forms a magic triangle. Such a triangle is defined as one where the respective sums of the three sides' values must all be equal.

Examples

The following shows this for one triangle each of side length three and side length four:

```
  1                2
 6 5              8 5
2 4 3            4   9
                3 7 6 1
```

This results in the following sides and sums:

Input	Values 1	Values 2
side 1	$1 + 5 + 3 = 9$	$2 + 5 + 9 + 1 = 17$
side 2	$3 + 4 + 2 = 9$	$1 + 6 + 7 + 3 = 17$
side 3	$2 + 6 + 1 = 9$	$3 + 4 + 8 + 2 = 17$

Tip   Model the individual sides of the triangle as sublists.

HINT: PROBLEM SOLVING STRATEGIES FOR THE JOB INTERVIEW

If the problem is initially unclear, it is advisable to reduce the problem to one or two concrete value assignments and to find the appropriate abstractions based on these.

Using the triangle of side length three as an example, you can build the sides shown above. If you think for a while, you will find that the sides can be expressed as sublists. However, the last side requires special treatment. For closing the figure again, the value of position 0 has to be taken into account. Still, it is not part of the sublist. Here two tricks offer themselves. The first one is to duplicate the list and extend it by the 0th element:

```python
values_with_loop = list(values)
# close the triangle
values_with_loop.append(values[0])

side1 = values_with_loop[0:3]
side2 = values_with_loop[2:5]
side3 = values_with_loop[4:7]
```

Alternatively, create three slices and add the 0th element in the third to fit:

```python
side1 = values[0:3]
side2 = values[2:5]
side3 = values[4:6]
# close the triangle
side3.append(values[0])
```

Algorithm: For triangles with side length three With the previous knowledge gathered, you start implementing the check for the special case of a triangle of side length three. Therefore, you first determine the sides and then build and compare the partial sums of the numbers contained there:

```python
def is_magic6(values):
    values_with_loop = list(values)
    values_with_loop.append(values[0])  # close the triangle

    side1 = values_with_loop[0:3]
    side2 = values_with_loop[2:5]
    side3 = values_with_loop[4:7]

    return compare_sum_of_sides(side1, side2, side3)
```

You extract the summing of the values of the sides as well as their comparison into the following function:

```
def compare_sum_of_sides(side1, side2, side3):
    sum1 = sum(side1)
    sum2 = sum(side2)
    sum3 = sum(side3)

    return sum1 == sum2 and sum2 == sum3
```

Intermediate inspection Now you should at least check the implementation with some values before you move on to the generalization:

```
>>> is_magic6([1, 5, 3, 4, 2, 6])
True

>>> is_magic6([1, 2, 3, 4, 5, 6])
False
```

Algorithm, general variant With the knowledge gained from the concrete example, a general variant can be created. The variance resides in calculating the indices for the sides of the triangle. Additionally, you add a sanity check at the beginning of the function. This prevents you from working on potentially invalid data constellations.

```
def is_magic_triangle(values):
    if len(values) % 3 != 0:
        raise ValueError("Not a triangle!", len(values), "must be a
        factor of 3")

    side_length = 1 + len(values) // 3

    values_with_loop = list(values)
    # close the triangle
    values_with_loop.append(values[0])

    side1 = values_with_loop[0: side_length]
    side2 = values_with_loop[side_length - 1: side_length * 2 - 1]
    side3 = values_with_loop[(side_length - 1) * 2: side_length * 3 - 2]

    return compare_sum_of_sides(side1, side2, side3)
```

Verification

Let's check the implementation with the following unit test:

```
@pytest.mark.parametrize("values, expected",
                         [([1, 5, 3, 4, 2, 6], True),
                          ([1, 2, 3, 4, 5, 6], False),
                          ([2, 5, 9, 1, 6, 7, 3, 4, 8], True),
                          ([1, 2, 3, 4, 5, 6, 7, 8, 9], False)])
def test_is_magic_triangle(values, expected):
    result = is_magic_triangle(values)

    assert result == expected
```

Alternative algorithm Based on the generalization already done, it is possible to omit the extraction of the sublists. Therefore, you once again use the idea of a position counter and traverse the original list in two loops. The outer loop represents the current side; in an inner loop, the respective position is handled. Two tricks are used:

1. The variable pos models the current position within the list. The new position is determined by adding 1. However, you need to reaccess the list's first value at the end of the list, so a modulo operation is used here.

2. After adding up the values for one side, you must go back by one position since the end value of one side of the triangle is also the start value of the next side.

As usual, add a sanity check at the beginning of the method. This will prevent you from potentially invalid data constellations.

```
def is_magic_triangle_v2(values):
    if len(values) % 3 != 0:
        raise ValueError("Not a triangle: " + len(values))

    side_length = 1 + len(values) // 3
    pos = 0
    sum_of_sides = [0, 0, 0]
```

```
for current_side in range(3):
    for _ in range(side_length):
        sum_of_sides[current_side] += values[pos]

        # trick 1: with modulo => no special treatment
        pos = (pos + 1) % len(values)

    # trick 2: The sides overlap, end field = next start field
    pos -= 1

return sum_of_sides[0] == sum_of_sides[1] and \
        sum_of_sides[1] == sum_of_sides[2]
```

Verification

The verification is performed with a unit test analogous to the previous one and therefore not shown again.

5.3.10 Solution 10: Most Frequent Elements (★★☆☆☆)

Write function value_count(values) that determines a histogram (i. e., the distribution of the frequencies of the numbers in the given list). Also, write function sort_dict_by_value(dictionary) to sort the dictionary by its values instead of by keys. Thereby a descending sorting is realized, so that smaller values are listed at the beginning.

Examples

Input	Result	Most frequent(s)
[1, 2, 3, 4, 4, 4, 3, 3, 2, 4]	{4=4, 3=3, 2=2, 1=1}	4=4
[1, 1, 1, 2, 2, 2, 3, 3, 3]	{1=3, 2=3, 3=3}	Depending on query, logically all

Algorithm Based on the input values, you compute a histogram as a dictionary with frequency values:

```
def value_count(values):
    value_to_count = {}

    for elem in values:
```

```
    if elem not in value_to_count:
        value_to_count[elem] = 0

    value_to_count[elem] += 1

  return value_to_count
```

As a final step, you still need to sort the resulting dictionary by value. Conveniently, this can be done with sorted() and specifying how the values are accessed and inverted. However, this returns a list of value pairs that you transfer to a dictionary with dict().

```
def sort_dict_by_value(dictionary):
    return dict(sorted(dictionary.items(), key=itemgetter(1),
    reverse=True))
```

Verification

As usual, use the values from the introduction to check your just implemented functionality with unit tests:

```
@pytest.mark.parametrize("values, expected",
                        [([1, 2, 3, 4, 4, 4, 3, 3, 2, 4],
                          {1: 1, 2: 2, 3: 3, 4: 4}),
                         ([1, 1, 1, 2, 2, 2, 3, 3, 3],
                          {1: 3, 2: 3, 3: 3})])
def test_value_count(values, expected):
    result = value_count(values)

    assert result == expected

@pytest.mark.parametrize("dictionary, expected",
                        [({1: 1, 2: 2, 3: 3, 4: 4},
                          {4: 4, 3: 3, 2: 2, 1: 1})])
def test_sort_dict_by_value(dictionary, expected):
    result = sort_dict_by_value(dictionary)

    assert result == expected
```

5.3.11 Solution 11: Addition of Digits (★★★☆☆)

Consider two decimal numbers that are to be added. Sounds simple, but for this assignment, the numbers are interestingly represented as a list of digits. Write function list_add(values1, values2). Also, consider the special case where there is an overflow.

Solution 11a: Addition (★★★☆☆)

In the first part of the task, the digits are to be stored in the order of their occurrence in the list.

Examples

Input 1	Input 2	Result
123 = [1, 2, 3]	456 = [4, 5, 6]	579 = [5, 7, 9]
927 = [9, 2, 7]	135 = [1, 3, 5]	1062 = [1, 0, 6, 2]

Algorithm Start with a simplification, namely that the numbers have the same amount of digits. Analogous to adding on the blackboard, you go from back to front from position to position and add the digits in each case. There may be a carry, which you must take into account in the following addition. If there is also a carry at the end of the processing (so for you at the front-most position), you must add the value 1 to the result at the front position. See Figure 5-1.

$$
\begin{array}{r}
927 \\
+ \quad 135 \\
\underline{1\ 0\ 1} \\
1062
\end{array}
$$

Figure 5-1. *Example of an addition with carries*

You apply this procedure to two lists of digits and traverse them from back to front—at the beginning still simplifying lists of equal length, which avoids special treatments.

```
def list_add(values1, values2):
    result = []
    carry = 0
```

```python
    for i in range(len(values1) - 1, -1, -1):
        sum = values1[i] + values2[i] + carry
        result.insert(0, sum % 10)

        carry = 1 if sum >= 10 else 0

    # add a 1 at the front of a carryover
    if carry == 1:
        result.insert(0, 1)

    return result
```

A deviating implementation would be to use iterators, here not the forward variant with iter(), but the backward variant with reversed(). However, this implementation struggles with the same problem as before with input data of different lengths.

```python
def list_add_with_iter(values1, values2):
    result = []
    carry = 0

    backiterator1 = reversed(values1)
    backiterator2 = reversed(values2)
    while True:
        try:
            value1 = next(backiterator1)
            value2 = next(backiterator2)

            sum = value1 + value2 + carry
            result.insert(0, sum % 10)

            carry = 1 if sum >= 10 else 0
        except StopIteration:
            break

    # consider carryover
    if carry == 1:
        result.insert(0, 1)

    return result
```

HINT: POSSIBLE ALTERNATIVE WITH `ZIP()`**?**

You could also come up with the idea of combining the two sequences of values with `zip()` and traversing them backwards. However, then you still need a wrapping with `list()`, since `zip()` is not reversible. However, this variant also fails since `zip()` restricts the combination to the smallest length of the sequences passed. Thus, again, you cannot add sequences of numbers of different lengths.

Improved algorithm If you want to provide a generally valid addition, you have to add the digits again starting from the back. However, with unequal length, it is then at some point no longer possible to access any digits because one number has fewer digits than the other. The auxiliary function `safe_get_at()` helps to handle a potentially failing access and provides a fallback of 0 in this case.

```python
def list_add_improved(values1, values2):
    result = []
    carry = 0

    idx1 = len(values1) - 1
    idx2 = len(values2) - 1

    while idx1 >= 0 or idx2 >= 0:
        value1 = safe_get_at(values1, idx1)
        value2 = safe_get_at(values2, idx2)

        sum = value1 + value2 + carry
        result.insert(0, sum % 10)

        carry = 1 if sum >= 10 else 0

        idx1 -= 1
        idx2 -= 1

    # add a 1 at the front of a carryover
    if carry == 1:
        result.insert(0, 1)

    return result
```

Let's take a quick look at the implementation of the safe indexed access, which maps accesses outside the allowed index range to the value 0. I use the Python feature of two comparison operators.

```python
def safe_get_at(values, pos):
    if 0 <= pos < len(values):
        return values[pos]

    return 0
```

In the implementation, my Java origin can be spotted.

In Python, it is stylistically nicer to handle expected index exceptions as follows:

```python
def safe_get_at(values, pos):
    try:
        return values[pos]
    except IndexError:
        return 0
```

Verification

Use unit tests to verify that the implementation produces the desired result for a given sequence of numbers:

```python
@pytest.mark.parametrize("values1, values2, expected",
                        [([1, 2, 3], [4, 5, 6], [5, 7, 9]),
                         ([9, 2, 7], [1, 3, 5], [1, 0, 6, 2])])
def test_list_add_improved(values1, values2, expected):
    result = list_add_improved(values1, values2)

    assert result == expected
```

Let's also consider the special case of unequal lengths of numbers for both implementations—only the second improved variant handles this correctly:

```python
>>> list_add([7,2,1], [1,2,7,0,0,0])
[8, 4, 8]
```

```python
>>> list_add_improved([7, 2, 1], [1, 2, 7, 0, 0, 0])
[1, 2, 7, 7, 2, 1]
```

Solution 11b: Addition Inverse (★★★☆☆)

What changes if the digits are stored in reverse order in the list?

Examples

Input 1	Input 2	Result
123 = [3, 2, 1]	456 = [6, 5, 4]	579 = [9, 7, 5]
927 = [7, 2, 9]	135 = [5, 3, 1]	1062 = [2, 6, 0, 1]

Algorithm If the order of the digits in the list is reversed to that within the number, things get simpler. You can then add directly, and the handling of numbers with unequal amounts of digits becomes easier. Again, you use the function safe_get_at(). Moreover, in case of an overflow, it is only necessary to add in the natural direction.

```python
def list_add_inverse(values1, values2):
    result = []
    carry = 0

    idx = 0
    while idx < len(values1) or idx < len(values2):
        value1 = safe_get_at(values1, idx)
        value2 = safe_get_at(values2, idx)

        sum = value1 + value2 + carry
        carry = 1 if sum >= 10 else 0

        result.append(sum % 10)
        idx += 1

    # add a 1 as carry to the "front"
    if carry == 1:
        result.append(1)

    return result
```

Verification

Consider two numbers in the form of lists with single digits—the values are written the other way around than in the number. In particular, this variant allows the addition of numbers of different lengths without having to deal with two index values.

```
@pytest.mark.parametrize("values1, values2, expected",
                         [([3, 2, 1], [6, 5, 4], [9, 7, 5]),
                          ([7, 2, 9], [5, 3, 1], [2, 6, 0, 1])])
def test_list_add_inverse(values1, values2, expected):
    result = list_add_inverse(values1, values2)

    assert result == expected
```

5.3.12 Solution 12: List Merge (★★☆☆☆)

Given two lists of numbers, each sorted in ascending order, merge them into a result list according to their order. Write function merge(values1, values2).

Examples

Input 1	Input 2	Result
1, 4, 7, 12, 20	10, 15, 17, 33	1, 4, 7, 10, 12, 15, 17, 20, 33
2, 3, 5, 7	11, 13, 17	2, 3, 5, 7, 11, 13, 17
2, 3, 5, 7, 11	7, 11, 13, 17	2, 3, 5, 7, 7, 11, 11, 13, 17
[1, 2, 3]	∅ = []	[1, 2, 3]

Algorithm At first, the problem seems quite easy to solve. You start at the beginning of both lists. Then you compare the respective position's values, insert the smaller one into the result, and increase the position in the list from which the element originates. This looks like the following:

```
def merge_first_try(values1, values2):
    pos1 = 0
    pos2 = 0
    result = []
```

```
    while pos1 < len(values1) or pos2 < len(values2):
        value1 = values1[pos1]
        value2 = values2[pos2]

        if value1 < value2:
            result.append(value1)
            pos1 += 1
        else:
            result.append(value2)
            pos2 += 1

    return result
```

Although this solution seems to be intuitive and good, it still contains problems. To identify them, let's try the function once for the second combination of values:

```
>>> merge_first_try([2, 3, 5, 7], [11, 13, 17])
...
IndexError: list index out of range
```

As a quick fix, you could replace the or with an and, which eliminates problems with exceptions. But this leads to another problem: Not all of the elements of both lists are processed any longer, usually depending on the value distribution even different numbers. So this is not a universal solution, but still a good start. You only have to cover the special needs of the elements remaining in a list appropriately. They are added to the result for this purpose.

```
def merge(values1, values2):
    pos1 = 0
    pos2 = 0
    result = []

    while pos1 < len(values1) and pos2 < len(values2):
        value1 = values1[pos1]
        value2 = values2[pos2]

        if value1 < value2:
            result.append(value1)
            pos1 += 1
```

```
    else:
        result.append(value2)
        pos2 += 1

    add_remaining(result, values1, pos1)
    add_remaining(result, values2, pos2)

    return result
```

You move the functionality of appending the remaining elements into function add_remaining(). Interestingly, no special checks are required before calling it. This is indirectly given by supplying the respective index as well as the termination condition in the for loop.

```
def add_remaining(result, values, idx):
    for i in range(idx, len(values)):
        result.append(values[i])
```

Python shortcut for add_remaining() In fact, adding the remaining elements is done in a shorter and more understandable way using slicing, as follows:

```
def add_remaining(result, values, idx):
    result += values[idx:]
```

Python shortcut The sorted merging of two lists can be easily implemented using the + operator and with the help of sorted():

```
def merge(values1, values2):
    return sorted(values1 + values2)
```

Alternative algorithm One variant is to generate the result data structure in advance. However, this leads to more index variables, and the entire thing becomes confusing. How can you avoid index access?

Instead of the potentially error-prone index accesses, try a variant with iterators. You run through the two lists from front to back and insert the elements as usual. Also, the appending of the remaining part can be transferred quite easily to iterators.

```
def merge_with_iter(values1, values2):
    result = []

    iterator1 = iter(values1)
```

```
    iterator2 = iter(values2)
    while True:
        try:
            value1, iterator1 = peek(iterator1)
            value2, iterator2 = peek(iterator2)

            if value1 < value2:
                result.append(value1)
                next(iterator1)
            else:
                result.append(value2)
                next(iterator2)
        except StopIteration:
            break

    add_remaining_with_iter(result, iterator1)
    add_remaining_with_iter(result, iterator2)

    return result
```

The last thing you implement is the addition of the remaining elements. However, this is a little bit more complex with iterators than the two variants shown before.

```
def add_remaining_with_iter(result, it):
    while True:
        try:
            value = next(it)
            result.append(value)
        except StopIteration:
            break
```

Another difficulty is that you cannot simply read out both elements via next(), since only one element is transferred to the result at a time. Therefore, you use a trick and create the function peek(), which first determines the next element and then reconstructs the iterator. In the above algorithm, you first take a look at the respective elements, and after comparing the value, you consume the element from the matching input data.

```
def peek(it):
    first = next(it)
    return first, itertools.chain([first], it)
```

The built-in function chain() is used here, which links two iterables together (i.e., make one out of two). Here it is used to restore the original dataset of the iterator.

Verification

Test the functionality with the value combinations from the introduction:

```
def inputs_and_expected():
    return [([1, 4, 7, 12, 20], [10, 15, 17, 33],
             [1, 4, 7, 10, 12, 15, 17, 20, 33]),
            ([2, 3, 5, 7], [11, 13, 17],
             [2, 3, 5, 7, 11, 13, 17]),
            ([2, 3, 5, 7, 11], [7, 11, 13, 17],
             [2, 3, 5, 7, 7, 11, 11, 13, 17]),
            ([1, 2, 3], [], [1, 2, 3])]

@pytest.mark.parametrize("values1, values2, expected",
                         inputs_and_expected())
def test_merge(values1, values2, expected):
    result = merge(values1, values2)

    assert result == expected

@pytest.mark.parametrize("values1, values2, expected",
                         inputs_and_expected())
def test_merge_with_iter(values1, values2, expected):
    result = merge_with_iter(values1, values2)

    assert result == expected
```

5.3.13 Solution 13: Excel Magic Select (★★☆☆☆)

If you have worked a little with Excel, then you have probably used the Magic Selection. It continuously populates a selected area with values based on the previous values. This works for numbers, weekdays, or dates, for example. To achieve something similar on your own, write function generate_following_values(current_value, sequence_length) that implements this for numbers. Create a variation suitable for weekdays and with the following signature: generate_following_values_for_-predefined(predefined_values, current_value, sequence_length).

Examples

Initial value	Count	Result
1	7	[1, 2, 3, 4, 5, 6, 7]
5	4	[5, 6, 7, 8]
FRIDAY	8	[FRIDAY, SATURDAY, SUNDAY, MONDAY, TUESDAY, WEDNESDAY, THURSDAY, FRIDAY]

Algorithm At first, you might think that this is based on something very sophisticated. But when thinking a second time about the algorithm, you quickly realize that all you need is a list as the result data structure and a loop to populate it:

```python
def generate_following_values(current_value, sequence_length):
    result = []
    while sequence_length > 0:
        result.append(current_value)
        current_value += 1
        sequence_length -= 1

    return result
```

Python shortcut With list comprehension, you write it briefly as follows:

```python
def generate_following_values_v2(start_value, sequence_length):
    return [value for value in range(start_value,
                                     start_value + sequence_length)]
```

Alternatively, this can be implemented by combining various functionalities from the itertools module. However, I like the two previous variants much better in terms of readability and comprehensibility.

```python
def generate_following_values_built_in(start_value, sequence_length):
    return list(itertools.islice(itertools.count(start_value), sequence_
    length))
```

Modified algorithm It is similarly easy to fill in with days of the week or via a list of predefined values, which, unlike numerical values, always repeat according to the length of the sequence.

With this knowledge, you minimally modify the previously used algorithm:

```python
def generate_following_values_for_predefined(predefined_values,
                                             current_value, sequence_
                                             length):
    result = []
    current_pos = predefined_values.index(current_value)
    while sequence_length > 0:
        result.append(current_value)
        current_value, current_pos = next_cyclic(predefined_values,
        current_pos)
        sequence_length -= 1

    return result
```

This function is intended to allow the cyclical traversal of a list in the forward direction by starting again at the beginning after the last element:

```python
def next_cyclic(values, current_pos):
    next_pos = (current_pos + 1) % len(values)

    return values[next_pos], next_pos
```

Verification

To track completion, you use a parameterized test, among other things one starting on a Friday, to generate eight values:

```python
@pytest.mark.parametrize("start_value, sequence_length, expected",
                    [(1, 7, [1, 2, 3, 4, 5, 6, 7]),
                     (5, 4, [5, 6, 7, 8])])
```

```python
def test_generate_following_values(start_value, sequence_length, expected):
    result = generate_following_values(start_value, sequence_length)

    assert result == expected

def predefined_values():
    return ["Monday", "Tuesday", "Wednesday", "Thursday",
            "Friday", "Saturday", "Sunday"]

@pytest.mark.parametrize("predefined_values, current_value, "
                         "sequence_length, expected",
                         [(predefined_values(), "Monday", 3,
                           ["Monday", "Tuesday", "Wednesday"]),
                          (predefined_values(), "Friday", 8,
                           ["Friday", "Saturday", "Sunday", "Monday",
                            "Tuesday", "Wednesday", "Thursday",
                            "Friday"])])
def test_generate_following_values_for_predefined(predefined_values,
                                                  current_value,
                                                  sequence_length,
                                                  expected):
    result = generate_following_values_for_predefined(predefined_values,
                                                      current_value,
                                                      sequence_length)

    assert result == expected
```

5.3.14 Solution 14: Stack-Based Queue (★★☆☆)

You learned about stack and queue data structures in the introduction and implemented a queue based on a list. Then in exercise 2, you implemented a stack itself. Now you are asked to build a queue based on the stack data structure.

Example

Please check the functionality with the following procedure:

```python
def main():
    waiting_persons = Queue()

    waiting_persons.enqueue("Marcello")
    waiting_persons.enqueue("Michael")
    waiting_persons.enqueue("Karthi")

    while not waiting_persons.is_empty():
        if waiting_persons.peek() == "Michael":
            # reprocess at the end
            waiting_persons.enqueue("Michael again")

        next_person = waiting_persons.dequeue()
        print("Processing " + next_person)
```

The small sample program should produce the following output:

```
Processing Marcello
Processing Michael
Processing Karthi
Processing Michael again
```

Algorithm You have already learned that a stack is suitable for reversing a list's order. Suppose you combine two stacks appropriately, one as an input buffer and one as an output buffer. In this case, you can implement a queue quite easily as follows. The only thing that's a bit tricky is that you just transfer the data from the input buffer to the output buffer when the latter is empty.

```python
class Queue:
    def __init__(self):
        self._inbox = Stack()
        self._outbox = Stack()

    def enqueue(self, elem):
        self._inbox.push(elem)

    def dequeue(self):
        if self.is_empty():
            raise QueueIsEmptyException()
```

```
        self._transfer_inbox_to_outbox()

        return self._outbox.pop()
    def peek(self):
        if self.is_empty():
            raise QueueIsEmptyException()

        self.__transfer_inbox_to_outbox()

        return self._outbox.peek()
    def is_empty(self):
        return self._inbox.is_empty() and self._outbox.is_empty()
    def _transfer_inbox_to_outbox(self):
        if self._outbox.is_empty():
            # transfer inbox to outbox
            while not self._inbox.is_empty():
                self._outbox.push(self._inbox.pop())
```

Verification

To test your implementation of the stack-based queue, execute the `main()` function and see if the output is as expected.

5.4 Summary: What You Learned

This chapter deepened your knowledge of basic data structures like lists, sets, and dictionaries. This knowledge is essential in business applications. These structures are useful for solving many tasks, not only individually but also in combination, such as the deletion of duplicates from lists. In addition, the exercise of the magic triangle, for example, trained abstract thinking. A small delicacy was to program the auto-completion of Excel itself. It is quite surprising what an elegant implementation this results in. Finally, you developed some functionality for merging lists. This is an elementary component for Merge Sort.

CHAPTER 6

Arrays

Arrays are data structures that store values of the same data type in a contiguous memory area. Thus, arrays are more memory-optimal and perform better than lists but are not supported natively in Python. However, they are supported by the array and numpy modules. In the following, you will look at the processing of data with the help of additional modules and deepen it with the help of exercises.

6.1 Introduction

While arrays are basic building blocks in many other programming languages, they exist in Python only as extensions, such as in the array and numpy modules. Because the former has only one-dimensional arrays and a cryptic syntax like

```
>>> import array
>>> ints = array.array('i', [2, 4, 6, 8])
>>> ints
array('i', [2, 4, 6, 8])
```

the choice for the following descriptions falls on numpy,[1] whose array implementation is more elegant and more pleasant to handle. In particular, arrays can be created quite easily from lists, even multidimensional ones:

```
import numpy as np

numbers = np.array([1, 2, 3, 4, 5, 6, 7])
primes = np.array([2, 3, 5, 7, 11, 13, 17])
```

---

[1]Please remember to install numpy using the pip tool: `pip install numpy` (on Mac, use `pip3` instead of `pip`).

© Michael Inden 2022
M. Inden, *Python Challenges*, https://doi.org/10.1007/978-1-4842-7398-2_6

```
twodim = np.array([["A1", "A2"],
                   ["B1", "B2"],
                   ["C1", "C2"]])
```

NumPy almost feels like a built-in data type since many operations like slicing and index accesses or the standard function `len()` are possible. You'll look at what to consider for multidimensional arrays later.

By providing arrays as a stand-alone module, an import is necessary. But arrays, unlike many built-in data types in other languages, are not just simple data containers but can do much more in terms of functionality than in Java or C++, for example.

NumPy offers various mathematical functionalities. I will go into more detail about NumPy specialties later. Upfront you will investigate one-dimensional and multidimensional arrays in this introduction and build a basic understanding of arrays.

6.1.1 One-Dimensional Arrays

As an introduction to processing data with arrays and to build knowledge of possible interview questions, let's look at some examples.

Textual Output

Arrays provide an appealing textual output, which is greatly beneficial for following the upcoming examples, especially the two-dimensional ones.

```
>>> grades = np.array(["A1", "A2", "B1", "B2", "C1", "C2"])

>>> grades
array(['A1', 'A2', 'B1', 'B2', 'C1', 'C2'], dtype='<U2')
```

Example 1: Swapping Elements

A common functionality is swapping elements at two positions. This can be achieved in a simple and readable way by providing function swap(`values`, `first`, `second`) as follows:

```
def swap(values, first, second):
    value1 = values[first]
    value2 = values[second]
```

```
values[first] = value2
values[second] = value1
```

Of course, you can also solve this with only three assignments and a temporary variable. Still, I think the previous version is a bit more comprehensible.

```
def swap(values, first, second):
    tmp = values[first]
    values[first] = values[second]
    values[second] = tmp
```

In Python, there is the following variant based on a tuple assignment:

```
def swap_with_tuple(values, first, second):
    values[second], values[first] = values[first], values[second]
```

HINT: PREFER READABILITY AND COMPREHENSIBILITY

Please keep in mind that readability and understandability are the keys to correctness and maintainability. Besides, this often facilitates testability.

While the helper variable to save one assignment is pretty catchy here, there are definitely more elaborate traceable low-level optimizations in other use cases. They are usually more difficult to read and less comprehensible.

Example 2: Basic Functionality for Arrays

Now let's write the function find(values, search_for) to search for a value in a one-dimensional array or a list and return the position or -1 for *not found*:

```
def find(values, search_for):
    for i, current_value in enumerate(values):
        if current_value == search_for:
            return i

    return -1
```

This can be solved as a typical search problem with a `while` loop where the condition is given as a comment at the end of the loop:

```python
def find(values, search_for):
    pos = 0
    while pos < len(values) and not values[pos] == search_for:
        pos += 1

    # i >= len(values) or values[i] == search_for
    return -1 if pos >= len(values) else pos
```

Please note the following: The Python built-in function `len()` returns the length of a list, so also for arrays, as long as they are one-dimensional. Alternatively, NumPy provides the attribute `size` on the array. For two-dimensional arrays, the values differ, but more about this later.

Pythonic variant with `enumerate()` Indexed accesses can hardly be avoided when working on array elements and are often quite intuitive. However, such accesses via the index in combination with `range(len(values))` do not necessarily correspond to good style in Python. Sometimes there are more elegant ways, like the following one with `enumerate()`:

```python
def find_with_enumerate(values, search_for):
    for i, value in enumerate(values):
        if value == search_for:
            return i

    return -1
```

Example 3: Remove Duplicates

The following shows a sorted array of positive numbers, but with duplicate values. Removing the duplicates should provide the following result:

```
[1, 2, 2, 3, 3, 3, 4, 4, 4, 4] => [1, 2, 3, 4]
```

JOB INTERVIEW TIPS: PROBLEM-SOLVING STRATEGIES

For assignments like this, you should always ask a few questions to clarify the context and gain a better understanding. For this example, possible questions include the following:

1. Is it necessary to keep the order/sorting of the numbers?

2. May a new array be created or must the actions be processed inplace—within the original array?

3. For inplace there are further questions:

    a. What exactly should happen when removing/deleting?

    b. What value represents *no entry*?

Solution 1 for Example 3: New array and sorted input Suppose you are to return a new array as a result when eliminating duplicates.

Maybe when you implement it you get the idea to remove the duplicates simply by refilling in a set. However, this does not guarantee that the original order is preserved. To be on the safe side, it is recommended to use a dictionary to ensure that the insertion order of the keys is preserved. Using fromkeys(), a dictionary is created based on the passed list and duplicate keys are automatically removed. As a second step, you prepare a new array based on the keys. This procedure can be implemented as follows:

```python
def remove_duplicates_new_array(sorted_numbers):
    # order may change
    # unique_values = list(set(sorted_numbers))

    # stable order
    unique_values = list(dict.fromkeys(sorted_numbers))
    return np.array(unique_values)
```

Solution 2 for Example 3: Unsorted/arbitrary numbers The previous task of removing duplicates in sorted numbers was easy to solve with Python on-board facilities. But how should you proceed with non-sorted data, assuming that the original order has to be maintained? Specifically, the result shown on the right should then result from the left sequence of values.

[1, 4, 4, 2, 2, 3, 4, 3, 4] => [1, 4, 2, 3]

Interestingly, a set would not make sense as a result data structure in this case because it would mess up the original order. If you think for a moment, ask an experienced colleague, or browse through a good book, you might discover that you can use a set as an auxiliary data structure for already discovered numbers. To store the result, you use a list. This variant (combination) works just as well with already sorted data.

```python
def remove_duplicates_stable(numbers):
    return np.array(collect_unique_values_stable(numbers))

def collect_unique_values_stable(numbers):
    result = []
    unique_values = set()
    for value in numbers:
        if value not in unique_values:
            unique_values.add(value)
            result.append(value)

    return result
```

This example illustrates the advantages of programming small functionalities that are self-contained and follow the SRP (Single Responsibility Principle). Even more: Keeping public methods understandable and moving details to (preferably private) helper methods often allows you to keep subsequent changes as local as possible. By the way, I discuss the SRP in detail in my book *Der Weg zum Java-Profi* [Ind20].

As a special feature since Python 3.6, the order of the keys when creating a dictionary with fromkeys() corresponds to the later iteration order, so the collection can be written even shorter as follows:

```python
def collect_unique_values_stable_shorter(numbers):
    return list(dict.fromkeys(numbers))
```

Solution 3 for Example 3: Inplace Given this sorted array again

```python
sortedNumbers = [1, 2, 2, 3, 3, 3, 4, 4, 4, 4]
```

all duplicates are to be removed, but this time you're not allowed to create a new array. This implementation is a little bit more difficult. The algorithm is as follows: Run through the array, check for each element, whether it already exists, and whether it is a duplicate. This check can be performed by comparing the current element with its predecessor. This simplification is possible because sorting exists; without it, it would be much more complicated to solve. You start the processing at the frontmost position and proceed step by step. Thereby you collect all numbers without duplicates on the left side of the array. To know where to read or write in the array, you use position pointers named read_pos and write_pos, respectively. If you find a duplicate number, the read pointer moves on and the write pointer stays in place.

```python
def remove_duplicates_inplace_first_try(sorted_numbers):
    prev_value = sorted_numbers[0]
    write_pos = 1
    read_pos = 1

    while read_pos < len(sorted_numbers):
        current_value = sorted_numbers[read_pos]

        if prev_value != current_value:
            sorted_numbers[write_pos] = current_value
            write_pos += 1
            prev_value = current_value

        read_pos += 1
```

Let's call this function once:

```python
>>> sorted_numbers = np.array([1, 2, 2, 3, 3, 3, 4, 4, 4, 4])
>>> remove_duplicates_inplace_first_try(sorted_numbers)
>>> print(sorted_numbers)
```

This variant is functionally correct, but the result is confusing:

```
[1 2 3 4 3 3 4 4 4 4]
```

This is because you are working inplace here. There is no hint how the result can be separated, up to where the values are valid and where the invalid, removed values start. Accordingly, two things are recommended:

1.   You should return the length of the valid range.

2.   You should delete the following positions with a special value, like -1 for primitive number types or for reference types often None. This value must not be part of the value set. Otherwise, irritations and inconsistencies are inevitable.

The following modification solves both issues and also uses a for loop, which makes everything a bit more elegant and shorter:

```python
def remove_duplicates_inplace_improved(sorted_numbers):
    write_index = 1

    for i in range(1, len(sorted_numbers)):
        current_value = sorted_numbers[i]
        prev_value = sorted_numbers[write_index - 1]

        if prev_value != current_value:
            sorted_numbers[write_index] = current_value
            write_index += 1

    # delete the positions that are no longer needed
    for i in range(write_index, len(sorted_numbers)):
        sorted_numbers[i] = -1

    return write_index
```

An invocation of this function returns the length of the valid range (additionally, after the last valid index in the modified array, all values are set to -1). Let's check this by running the following lines:

```python
>>> sorted_numbers = np.array([1, 2, 2, 3, 3, 3, 4, 4, 4, 4])
>>> pos = remove_duplicates_inplace_improved(sorted_numbers)
>>> print("pos:", pos, " / values:", sorted_numbers)
pos: 4 / values: [ 1 2 3 4 -1 -1 -1 -1 -1 -1]
```

Interim conclusion The example illustrates several problematic issues. First, that it is often more complex to work inplace—that is, without creating new arrays, but directly within the original array. Second, to handle changes when values remain in the array but are no longer part of the result, you can either return a counter or erase the values with a neutral, special value. However, it is often more understandable and therefore recommended to use the variants shown, which create a new array.

JOB INTERVIEW TIPS: ALTERNATIVE WAYS OF LOOKING AT THINGS

As simple as the assignment may have sounded at first, it does hold some potential for different approaches and solution strategies. When removing duplicates, you could also come up with the idea of replacing elements by *no entry*—for object references the value None:

```
["Tim", "Tim", "Jim", "Tom", "Jim", "Tom"]
=>
["Tim", None, "Jim", "Tom", None, None]
```

For a non-sorted array, it is also possible to retain the values in the order of their original occurrence:

```
[1, 2, 2, 4, 4, 3, 3, 3, 2, 2, 3, 1] => [1, 2, 4, 3]
```

Alternatively, it is possible to remove only consecutive duplicates at a time:

```
[1, 2, 2, 4, 4, 3, 3, 3, 2, 2, 3, 1] => [1, 2, 4, 3, 2, 3, 1]
```

As you can see, there is more to consider, even for apparently simple tasks. This is why requirements engineering and the correct coverage of requirements are a real challenge.

Example 4: Rotation by One or More Positions

Let's look at another problem, namely rotating an array by n positions to the left or to the right, where the elements are then to be shifted cyclically at the beginning or the end, respectively, as visualized below, where the middle array is the starting point:

2	3	4	1	⇐	1	2	3	4	⇒	4	1	2	3

The algorithm for a rotation by one element to the right is simple: Remember the last element and then repeatedly copy the element that is one ahead in the direction of rotation to the one behind it. Finally, the cached last element is inserted at the foremost position.

Please note that the following two functions work inplace (on the passed array) so they do not return a value:

```python
def rotate_right(values):
    if len(values) < 2:
        return

    end_pos = len(values) - 1
    temp = values[end_pos]

    for i in range(end_pos, 0, -1):
        values[i] = values[i - 1]

    values[0] = temp
```

The rotation to the left works analogously:

```python
def rotate_left(values):
    if len(values) < 2:
        return

    end_pos = len(values) - 1
    temp = values[0]

    for i in range(end_pos):
        values[i] = values[i + 1]

    values[end_pos] = temp
```

Let's try the whole thing out in the Python command line:

```python
>>> numbers = np.array([1, 2, 3, 4])
>>> rotate_right(numbers)
>>> numbers
array([4, 1, 2, 3])
>>>
```

```
>>> numbers = np.array([1, 2, 3, 4])
>>> rotate_left(numbers)
>>> print(numbers)
[2 3 4 1]
```

In case you are wondering about the different console outputs, it should be noted that there is a difference between the formatting with __repr__() and __str__(). In the first case, you get the type info and then the values are comma-separated as output. In the second case, the output is the same as the standard of lists.

Rotation around *n* positions (simple) An obvious extension is to rotate by a certain number of positions. This can be solved using brute force by calling the just-developed functionality *n* times:

```
def rotate_right_by_n_simple(values, n):
    for i in range(n):
        rotate_right(values)
```

This solution is acceptable in principle, although not performant due to the frequent copy actions. How can it be more efficient?

HINT: OPTIMIZATION OF LARGE VALUES FOR *n*

There is one more small feature to consider. Namely, if *n* is larger than the length of the array, you don't have to rotate all the time; you can limit this to what is actually needed by using the modulo operation i < n % len(values).

Rotation around *n* positions (tricky) Alternatively, imagine that *n* positions are added to the original array. This is accomplished by using an independent buffer that caches the last *n* elements. It is implemented in the function fill_temp_with_last_n(). This first creates a suitably sized array and puts the last *n* values there. Then you copy the values as before, but with an offset of *n*. Finally, you just need to copy the values back from the buffer using copy_temp_buffer_to_start().

```
def rotate_right_by_n(values, n):
    adjusted_n = n % len(values)
    temp_buffer = fill_temp_with_last_n(values, adjusted_n)
```

```
    # copy n positions to the right
    for i in range(len(values) - 1, adjusted_n - 1, -1):
        values[i] = values[i - adjusted_n]

    copy_temp_buffer_to_start(temp_buffer, values)

    return values
def fill_temp_with_last_n(values, n):
    temp_buffer = np.arange(n)

    for i in range (n):
        temp_buffer[i] = values[len(values) - n + i]

    return temp_buffer
def copy_temp_buffer_to_start(temp_buffer, values):
    for i in range(len(temp_buffer)):
        values[i] = temp_buffer[i]
```

Here's another hint: The function just presented for rotation can be suboptimal in terms of memory, especially if the value of n is very large and the array itself is also huge, but for our examples, this does not matter. Interestingly, the simple version would then be better in terms of memory, although probably rather slow due to the frequent copy actions.

6.1.2 Multidimensional Arrays

In this section, I will briefly discuss multidimensional arrays. Because it is more common in practice and easy to imagine visually, I will just discuss two-dimensional arrays.[2]

Using a two-dimensional rectangular array, you can model a playfield, such as a Sudoku puzzle or a landscape represented by characters. For a better understanding and an introduction, let's consider an example. Suppose # represents a boundary wall, $ stands for an item to be collected, P stands for the player, and X stands for the exit from a level. These characters are used to describe a playfield as follows:

---

[2] In other languages, multidimensional arrays are often implemented as arrays of arrays and thus do not necessarily have to be rectangular. In Python, this is equally true for nested lists, but not for NumPy arrays, which are always rectangular.

```
################
##   P          ##
####     $ X  ####
###### $   ######
################
```

In Python, a two-dimensional array can be used for processing, which you can construct based on strings converted to lists as follows:

```python
def main():
    world = np.array([list("################"),
                      list("##   P          ##"),
                      list("####     $ X  ####"),
                      list("###### $   ######"),
                      list("################")])
    print_array(world)

def print_array(values):
    max_y, max_x = get_dimension(values)
    for y in range(max_y):
        for x in range(max_x):
            value = values[y][x]
            print(value, end=" ")
        print()

def get_dimension(values):
    if isinstance(values, list):
        return len(values), len(values[0])

    if isinstance(values, np.ndarray):
        return values.shape

    raise ValueError("unsupported type", type(values))
```

In the code above, you can see the helper function get_dimension(values) to determine the dimensions for both lists and NumPy arrays. This allows using one or the other without worrying. See subsection 6.1.4 for a broader explanation.

Let's run the module TWO_DIM_ARRAY_WORLD_EXAMPLE.PY to see the output functionality in action. In the following, I will refer to similar things from time to time. Besides debugging, the console output is quite helpful, especially for multidimensional arrays.

```
# # # # # # # # # # # # # # # #
# #     P                 # #
# # # #        $ X        # # # #
# # # # # #    $       # # # # # #
# # # # # # # # # # # # # # # #
```

Accessing values There are two variants of how to specify the coordinates when accessing: one is [x][y] and the other is [y][x] if you think in a more line-oriented way. Between different developers, this can lead to misunderstandings and discussions. A small remedy can be achieved if you write an access function, like get_at(values, x, y), and consider the respective preference there. I will use this access function in the introduction and later switch over to direct array accesses:

```
def get_at(values, x, y) :
    return values[y][x];
```

Introductory Example

Your task is to rotate an array by 90 degrees to the left or right. Let's take a look at this for two rotations to the right:

```
1111        4321        4444
2222   =>   4321   =>   3333
3333        4321        2222
4444        4321        1111
```

Let's try to formalize the procedure a bit. The easiest way to implement the rotation is to create a new array and then populate it appropriately. For the determination of the formulas, let's use concrete example data, which facilitates the understanding (xn and yn stand for the new coordinates; in the following, the rotation to the left and the rotation to the right is shown on the left/right):

```
        x   0123
        y   ----
        0   ABCD
        1   EFGH

  xn  01                   xn  01
yn   --                 yn   --
 0   DH                  0   EA
 1   CG                  1   FB
 2   BF                  2   GC
 3   AE                  3   HD
```

You see that a 4 × 2 array turns into a 2 × 4 array.

The rotation is based on the following calculation rules, where max_x and max_y are the respective maximum coordinates:

```
              Orig  ->  new_x        new_y
--------------------------------------------------------
rotate_left:  (x,y) ->  y            max_x - x
rotate_right: (x,y) ->  max_y - y    x
```

You proceed to the implementation with this knowledge: You first create a suitably large array by calling np.empty() and traverse the original array line by line and then position by position. Based on the formulas above, the rotation can be implemented as follows:

```python
class RotationDirection(Enum):
    LEFT_90 = auto()
    RIGHT_90 = auto()

def rotate(values, dir):
    orig_length_y, orig_length_x = values.shape

    rotated_array = np.empty((orig_length_x, orig_length_y), values.dtype)

    for y in range(orig_length_y):
        for x in range(orig_length_x):
            max_x = orig_length_x - 1
            max_y = orig_length_y - 1

            orig_value = values[y][x]
```

```
    if dir == RotationDirection.LEFT_90:
        new_x = y
        new_y = max_x - x
        rotated_array[new_y][new_x] = orig_value

    if dir == RotationDirection.RIGHT_90:
        new_x = max_y - y
        new_y = x
        rotated_array[new_y][new_x] = orig_value

return rotated_array
```

Let's take a look at the operations in the Python command line:

```
def main():
    letters = np.array([["A", "B", "C", "D"],
                        ["E", "F", "G", "H"]])

    left_rotated = rotate(letters, RotationDirection.LEFT_90)
    print(left_rotated)
    right_rotated = rotate(letters, RotationDirection.RIGHT_90)
    print(right_rotated)
```

Finally, the call to print() shows the arrays rotated by 90 degrees to the left and to the right:

```
[['D' 'H']
 ['C' 'G']
 ['B' 'F']
 ['A' 'E']]
[['E' 'A']
 ['F' 'B']
 ['G' 'C']
 ['H' 'D']]
```

Modeling Directions

You will encounter directions in a variety of use cases. They can, of course, be modeled simply using an enumeration. In the context of two-dimensional arrays, it is extremely convenient and contributes significantly to readability and comprehensibility to define all essential cardinal directions in the enumeration and, moreover, offsets in x- and y- directions. For better manageability of the delta values, I offer a to_dx_dy() function:

```python
class Direction(Enum):
    N = (0, -1)
    NE = (1, -1)
    E = (1, 0)
    SE = (1, 1)
    S = (0, 1)
    SW = (-1, 1)
    W = (-1, 0)
    NW = (-1, -1)

    def to_dx_dy(self):
        return self.value

    @classmethod
    def provide_random_direction(cls):
        random_index = randrange(len(list(Direction)))
        return list(Direction)[random_index]
```

HINT: RANDOM NUMBERS

In the example, you see the function randrange(), which generates random numbers in the range 0 to the specified boundary exclusive. An alternative is random.randint(). To get a random number greater than or equal to 0.0 and less than 1.0, use the call random.random(). For example, if you want to simulate the numbers of a dice, you could implement this as follows:

```python
dice_eyes = random.randint(1, 6)
```

Example: Random traversal To go a little deeper on processing with directions, let's develop a traversal for a playfield. Whenever you hit array boundaries, you randomly choose a new direction not equal to the old one:

```python
def main():
    world = np.array([list("ABCDEF"),
                      list("GHIJKL"),
                      list("MNOPQR"),
                      list("abcdef"),
                      list("ghijkl")])

    dir = Direction.provide_random_direction()
    print("Direction:", dir.name)

    pos_x = 0
    pos_y = 0
    steps = 0

    while steps < 25:
        print(world[pos_y][pos_x], " ", end="")
        dx, dy = dir.to_dx_dy()
        if not is_on_board(world, pos_x + dx, pos_y + dy):
            dir = select_new_dir(world, dir, pos_x, pos_y)
            dx, dy = dir.to_dx_dy()
            print("\nNew Direction:", dir.name)

        pos_x += dx
        pos_y += dy
        steps += 1

def select_new_dir(world, dir, pos_x, pos_y):
    old_dir = dir
    while True:
        dir = Direction.provide_random_direction()
        dx, dy = dir.to_dx_dy()
        if old_dir != dir and is_on_board(world, pos_x + dx, pos_y + dy):
            break

    return dir
```

In this assignment, you immediately get in touch with another useful function named is_on_board(). Its task is to check whether a passed x-y value is valid for the array, here assuming that the array is rectangular.[3]

```
def is_on_board(values, next_pos_x, next_pos_y):
    max_y, max_x = values.shape

    return 0 <= next_pos_x < max_x and 0 <= next_pos_y < max_y
```

If you start the module RANDOM_TRAVERSAL_DIRECTION_EXAMPLE.PY, you will get output like the following, which shows the direction changes very well. The output is limited by the maximum number of 25 steps. Therefore, only 3 letters are found at the end.

```
Direction: SE
A H O d k
New Direction: N
e Q K E
New Direction: SW
J O b g
New Direction: N
a M G A
New Direction: E
B C D E F
New Direction: SW
K P c
```

----
[3] While this is always true for NumPy array, this is not always given when simulating an array using nested lists.

| HINT: VARIATION WITH BUFFER FIELDS AT THE BORDER |

Especially for two-dimensional arrays and accesses to adjacent cells, it may be useful to add an unused element at each border field to avoid special cases, indicated below with a X:

XXXXXXXXX

X   X

X   X

X   X

XXXXXXXXX

Using this trick, you always have eight adjacent cells. This helps to avoid special treatments in your programs. This is also true, for example, when walking through the array. Instead of checking for the array boundaries, you can restrict yourself to checking if you reach a boundary field. Sometimes it is handy to use a neutral element, such as the value 0, since this does not affect computations.

6.1.3 Typical Errors

Not only when accessing arrays, but especially there, you find a multiplicity of potential sources of errors, in particular, the following:

- **Off-by-one:** Sometimes you are off by one element when accessing because, for example, the index calculation contains an error, such as adding or subtracting 1 to correct the index or comparing positions with <, <=, >, or >=.

- **Array bounds**: Similarly, the bounds of the array are sometimes inadvertently disregarded, for example, by incorrect use of <, <= or >, >= when comparing length or lower or upper bounds.[4]

- **Dimensions:** As mentioned, how x and y are represented depends on the chosen flavor. This quickly causes x and y to be interchanged for two-dimensional arrays.

---

[4] Therefore, thorough testing and a good selection of test cases are recommended in both cases. How to achieve this is described in my book *Der Weg zum Java-Profi* [Ind20].

- **Rectangular property**: Although an n × m array is assumed to be rectangular, this need not be the case in Python when using nested lists. You can specify a different length for each new row, but many of the examples below use rectangular arrays,[5] especially because they are only supported by NumPy. The reason lies in the arrangement in memory for maximum performance.

- **Neutral element:** What represents *no value*. Is it -1 or None? How do you deal with this if these are possible values?

6.1.4 Special Features

I would like to point out something extraordinary. Practically, almost all of our developed program modules can be used for NumPy arrays and lists without changing much in the algorithmic part of the functions. Often, all that is needed is the determination of the sizes shown below. This is a significant advantage in contrast to algorithms in, say, Java and C++, which must be developed specifically for lists and other types.

For many algorithms for two-dimensional arrays, you can use the function get_dimension(values) to determine the dimensions for both lists and NumPy arrays. A few examples require some manual work but rarely a completely new implementation.

```python
def get_dimension(values):
    if isinstance(values, list):
        return len(values), len(values[0])

    if isinstance(values, np.ndarray):
        return values.shape

    raise ValueError("unsupported type", type(values))
```

---

[5] In job interviews, you should clarify this by asking a question.

For nested lists, it returns the number of lines and the length of the first line. This corresponds exactly to the dimensions that can be obtained from NumPy via the shape attribute as a tuple:

```
nested_lists = [[0, 1, 2, 3],
                [4, 5, 6, 7],
                [8, 9, 10, 10]]
nested_lists_array = np.array(nested_lists)

print(get_dimension(nested_lists))
print(get_dimension(nested_lists_array))
```

This results in the following output:

```
(3, 4)
(3, 4)
```

Special Treatment for Generalizations

Sometimes you want to apply functionalities not only for special types but in general. In doing so, you occasionally need to initialize arrays with an empty value or query whether an array is empty. You will look at this in more detail in the solution part of exercise 6, where you want to be able to use arrays with letters in addition to arrays with numbers to model a playfield. An empty field is then indicated by, for example, the numerical value 0, a single space character, or an empty string. You could formulate this general-purpose check as function is_empty_cell(values2dim, x, y) as follows:

```
def is_empty_cell(values2dim, x, y):
    return is_empty(values2dim[y][x])

def is_empty(value):
    if type(value) is str:
        return value == " " or len(value) == 0

    return value == 0
```

6.1.5 Recapitulation: NumPy

So far, you have used NumPy in various examples without it being remarkably different in handling than lists. This is a big plus. Nevertheless, I would like to introduce a few things explicitly and point out others.

What is NumPy? NumPy stands for Numerical Python and is a module for processing arrays. Besides basic functionalities, there are mathematical extensions for linear algebra and matrices.

Creating NumPy Arrays Based on Lists

Let's take a quick look at how easy it is to create a corresponding NumPy array from a list:

```
numbers = [1, 2, 3, 4, 5, 6, 7]
numbers_array = np.array(numbers)

firstprimes = [2, 3, 5, 7, 11, 13, 17]
firstprimes_array = np.array(firstprimes)

print(numbers_array)
print(firstprimes_array)
```

You receive the following output:

```
[1 2 3 4 5 6 7]
[ 2  3  5  7 11 13 17]
```

The whole thing also works without problems with two-dimensional nested lists:

```
twodim = np.array([["A1", "A2"],
                   ["B1", "B2"],
                   ["C1", "C2"]])
print(twodim)
print(len(twodim))    # 3
print(twodim.size)    # 6
print(twodim.shape)   # (3, 2)
```

You get the following output of the array (lengths are not shown here):

```
[['A1' 'A2']
 ['B1' 'B2']
 ['C1' 'C2']]
```

Creating NumPy Arrays with Particular Values

Sometimes you want to preinitialize arrays with a special value; for numbers this is often the value 0 or the 1. NumPy offers specific functions for this purpose:

- zeros()
- ones()
- empty()

Let's call these functions to create arrays. Note that the first value corresponds to the number of rows and the second one corresponds to the number of columns. Additionally, you can optionally specify a data type.

```
array_with_zeros = np.zeros((2, 4), dtype='int')
print(array_with_zeros)

array_with_ones = np.ones((5, 10))
print(array_with_ones)

empty_strings_array = np.empty((3, 3), dtype="str")
print(empty_strings_array)
```

This leads to the following output, which illustrates that by default (here for the ones) float is chosen as the data type:

```
[[0 0 0 0]
 [0 0 0 0]]
[[1. 1. 1. 1. 1. 1. 1. 1. 1. 1.]
 [1. 1. 1. 1. 1. 1. 1. 1. 1. 1.]
 [1. 1. 1. 1. 1. 1. 1. 1. 1. 1.]
 [1. 1. 1. 1. 1. 1. 1. 1. 1. 1.]
 [1. 1. 1. 1. 1. 1. 1. 1. 1. 1.]]
[['' '' '']
 ['' '' '']
 ['' '' '']]
```

Such initializations can also be achieved with Python on-board tools as follows but the NumPy variant feels more comprehensible for me:

```
zeros_with_lists = [[0 for x in range(4)] for y in range(2)]
print(zeros_with_lists)
```

```
ones_with_lists = [[1 for x in range(10)] for y in range(5)]
print(ones_with_lists)
```

```
empty_string_with_list = [["" for x in range(3)] for y in range(3)]
print(empty_string_with_list)
```

ATTENTION: FAULTY VARIANT WITH LIST COMPREHENSION

Please note the following pitfall: You might like to create something similar to the above using list comprehensions:

```
width = 10
height = 5
```

```
# generates non-independent references board = [[0] * width] * height
print(board)
```

```
# Attention: modification happens in all lines! board[1][1] = 1
print(board)
```

The lists created in this way are not independent of each other, and changes have effects on the other lines.

Other Functionalities of NumPy Arrays

Previously I indicated that NumPy offers some mathematical functionalities out of the box. But not only that. There are various others, which you can explore in detail in https://numpy.org/doc/stable/reference/routines.array-manipulation.html. As an example, I'll demonstrate the vertical and horizontal flipping of the contents of an array, which you are supposed to rebuild by hand in exercise 2.

Let's look at how this works using two arrays, where the 1 stands for horizontal and 0 for vertical:

```
import numpy as np

numbers = np.array([[1, 2, 3, 4],
                    [1, 2, 3, 4],
                    [1, 2, 3, 4]])
print(np.flip(numbers, 1))

numbers2 = np.array([[1, 1, 1, 1],
                     [2, 2, 2, 2],
                     [3, 3, 3, 3]])
print(np.flip(numbers2, 0))
```

This results in the following output:

```
[[4 3 2 1]
 [4 3 2 1]
 [4 3 2 1]]
[[3 3 3 3]
 [2 2 2 2]
 [1 1 1 1]]
```

Advantages of NumPy

As is well known, lists in Python are very convenient and provide an ordered and changeable sequence of values. The values stored can be of different types (heterogeneous) or contain only the same types (homogeneous). Multidimensional structures are possible by nesting lists. NumPy allows only homogeneous value assignments, which is often an advantage rather than a disadvantage.

What are the indisputable advantages of using NumPy instead of the built-in lists?

- NumPy arrays fit seamlessly and are easy to use.

- NumPy arrays use (slightly) less memory.

- NumPy arrays are (much) faster than lists for various use cases.

However, the last point only applies when processing enormous amounts of data, especially when performing mathematical operations such as matrix multiplication. Normal array accesses are sometimes even slower than indexed list accesses. I will show this with an example later.

Memory Consumption

To compare the memory consumption of lists and NumPy arrays, I created a list and an array with 100,000 elements each. To determine the used memory, I used the getsizeof() functionality from the sys module.

```
import numpy as np
import sys

numbers = [i for i in range(100_000)]
print("Size of each element:", sys.getsizeof(numbers[0]))
print("Size of the list:", sys.getsizeof(numbers))

numbers_array = np.arange(100_000)
print("Size of each element:", numbers_array.itemsize)
print("Size of the Numpy array:", sys.getsizeof(numbers_array))
```

The following output occurred:

```
Size of each element: 24
Size of the list: 824456
Size of each element: 8
Size of the Numpy array: 800096
```

You can see that (on my machine[6]) each element in a list occupied 24 bytes, but in NumPy, only 8 bytes. With NumPy the total size resulted from the number of elements, their size in bytes, and the number of bytes for the NumPy array as management:

$$100.000 * 8 + 96 = 800.096$$

With lists, the output confused me. According to the number for a single element

$$100.000 * 24 + x = 2.400.000$$

should be occupied, but surprisingly I got around 824.000.

---

[6] Please note that this may vary from system to system.

Performance Comparison

Finally, let's compare lists and arrays concerning their performance. I started with the basic functionality of indexed access to recognize that lists have a slight advantage here. However, when it comes to actions on all elements of an array, particularly complex mathematical operations like matrix multiplication, the picture reversed massively. NumPy clearly showed its strengths. Let's have a closer look at this through examples in more detail.

Index based accesses For indexed accesses, NumPy was a bit slower than the built-in lists. This can be observed in the first example, the flipping of the content by single assignments:

```python
for size in (100, 1000, 10000, 100000, 1_000_000):

    print("performing idx assign for ", size, "elements")

    orig_values = range(size)
    array = np.asarray(orig_values)
    result_list = list(orig_values)
    result_array = array[:]

    start = time.process_time()
    for i in range(size):
        result_list[i] = orig_values[size - 1 - i]
    end = time.process_time()
    print("list idx assign took %.2f ms" % ((end - start) * 1000))

    start = time.process_time()
    for i in range(size):
        result_array[i] = array[size - 1 - i]
    end = time.process_time()
    print("array idx assign took %.2f ms" % ((end - start) * 1000))
```

Here, indexed reads and writes are especially in demand. I looked at the outputs and saw that in this case, the lists were about 20% faster on my iMac:

```
performing idx assign for all 100 elements
list idx assign took 0.02 ms
array idx assign took 0.03 ms
performing idx assign for all 1000 elements
```

```
list idx assign took 0.26 ms
array idx assign took 0.33 ms
performing idx assign for all 10000 elements
list idx assign took 2.75 ms
array idx assign took 3.44 ms
performing idx assign for all 100000 elements
list idx assign took 27.81 ms
array idx assign took 35.23 ms
performing idx assign for all 1000000 elements
list idx assign took 273.67 ms
array idx assign took 354.75 ms
```

I modified it slightly and added a constant value to each element in the data container as an action. In that case, NumPy provided a nice shorthand and was a bit faster from about 1.000 elements. The more elements I managed, the clearer the differences for these actions.

```
result_list = [i + 5 for i in range(size)]

result_array = array1 + 5
```

Matrix multiplication Let's look at one example where performance improvements are noticeable (more accurately, drastic) when using NumPy: the common matrix multiplication. This consists of row-by-row and then element-by-element multiplication (the mathematical details are not relevant here, as I only want to compare performance here):

```
def python_implementation(arr1, arr2):
    result = [[0 for _ in range(len(arr1))] for _ in range(len(arr2[0]))]

    for row in range(len(arr1)):
        for x1_y2 in range(len(arr2[0])):
            for y2 in range(len(arr2)):
                result[row][x1_y2] += arr1[row][y2] * arr2[y2][x1_y2]
    return result

def numpy_implementation(arr1, arr2):
    return np.array(arr1).dot(arr2)
```

I ran the two variants with the following source code snippet once:

```
max_x = 100
max_y = 50
arr1 = [[random.randrange(1, 100) for _ in range(max_x)] for _ in
range(max_y)]
arr2 = [[random.randrange(1, 100) for _ in range(max_y)] for _ in
range(max_x)]

start = time.process_time()
python_implementation(arr1, arr2)
end = time.process_time()
print("list perform dot product took %.2f ms" % ((end - start) * 1000))

start = time.process_time()
numpy_implementation(arr1, arr2)
end = time.process_time()
print("array perform dot product took %.2f ms" % ((end - start) * 1000))
```

Thus, I obtained the following output, which shows the clear speed advantages of NumPy by a factor of about 50–60%:

```
list perform dot product took 86.52 ms
array perform dot product took 1.85 ms
```

6.2 Exercises

6.2.1 Exercise 1: Even Before Odd Numbers (★★☆☆☆)

Write function order_even_before_odd(numbers). This is supposed to rearrange a given array or a list of int values so that the even numbers appear first, followed by the odd numbers. The order within the even and odd numbers is not of relevance.

Examples

Input	Result
[1, 2, 3, 4, 5, 6, 7, 8, 9, 10]	[2, 4, 6, 8, 10, 3, 7, 1, 9, 5]
[2, 4, 6, 1, 8]	[2, 4, 6, 8, 1]
[2, 4, 6, 8, 1]	[2, 4, 6, 8, 1]

6.2.2 Exercise 2: Flip (★★☆☆☆)

Write generic functions for flipping a two-dimensional array horizontally with `flip_horizontally(values2dim)` and vertically with `flip_vertically(values2dim)`. The array should be rectangular, so no line should be longer than another.

Examples

The following illustrates how this functionality should work:

```
flip_horizontally()       flip_vertically()
-------------------       -----------------
123        321           1144        3366
456   =>   654           2255   =>   2255
789        987           3366        1144
```

6.2.3 Exercise 3: Palindrome (★★☆☆☆)

Write function `is_palindrome(values)` that checks an array of strings for whether its values form a palindrome.

Examples

Input	Result
["One", "Test", " – ", "Test", "One"]	True
["Max", "Mike", "Mike", "Max"]	True
["Tim", "Tom", "Mike", "Max"]	False

6.2.4 Exercise 4: Inplace Rotate (★★★☆☆)

Exercise 4a: Iterative (★★★☆☆)

In the introductory section, I showed how to rotate arrays. Now try this inplace without creating a new array. Your task is to rotate a two-dimensional, square-shaped array by 90 degrees clockwise. Write generic function `rotate_inplace(values2dim)` that iteratively implements this.

Example

For a 6 × 6 array, this is visualized below:

```
1 2 3 4 5 6      F G H I J 1
J K L M N 7      E T U V K 2
I V W X O 8  =>  D S Z W L 3
H U Z Y P 9      C R Y X M 4
G T S R Q O      B Q P O N 5
F E D C B A      A O 9 8 7 6
```

Exercise 4b: Recursive (★★★☆☆)

Write recursive function `rotate_inplace_recursive(values2dim)` that implements the desired 90-degree clockwise rotation.

6.2.5 Exercise 5: Jewels Board Init (★★★☆☆)

Exercise 5a: Initialize (★★★☆☆)

Initialize a two-dimensional rectangular array with random-based numbers representing various types of diamonds or jewels as numerical values. The constraint is that initially there must not be three diamonds of the same type placed horizontally or vertically in direct sequence. Write function `init_jewels_board(width, height, num_of_colors)` to generate a valid array of the given size and quantity of different types of diamonds.

Example

A random distribution of diamonds represented by digits may look like this for four different colors and shapes:

2 3 3 4 4 3 2
1 3 3 1 3 4 4
4 1 4 3 3 1 **3**
2 2 1 1 2 **3** 2
3 2 4 4 **3** 3 4

To illustrate this, Figure 6-1 shows another example.

Bonus: Diagonal Check (★★★☆☆) Add a check for diagonals. This should make the constellation from the example invalid, among other things, because of the diagonals marked in bold with the number 3 at the bottom right.

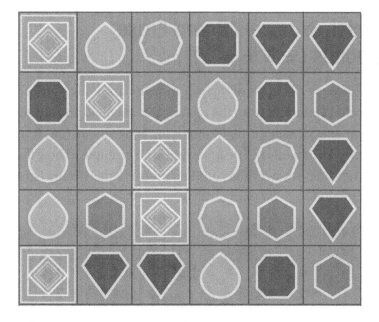

Figure 6-1. *Graphical representation of a Jewels board*

Exercise 5b: Validity Check (★★★☆☆)

In this subtask, you want to validate an existing playfield. As a challenge, a list of violations must be returned. Implement function check_board_validity(board2dim) for a rectangular array.

Example

To try out the validity check, use the playfield from the introduction, specially marked here:

```
values_with_errors = [[2, 3, 3, 4, 4, 3, 2],
                      [1, 3, 3, 1, 3, 4, 4],
                      [4, 1, 4, 3, 3, 1, 3],
                      [2, 2, 1, 1, 2, 3, 2],
                      [3, 2, 4, 4, 3, 3, 4]]
```

This should produce the following errors due to its diagonals:

```
['Invalid at x=3 y=2 hor=False, ver=False, dia=True',
 'Invalid at x=2 y=3 hor=False, ver=False, dia=True',
 'Invalid at x=4 y=4 hor=False, ver=False, dia=True']
```

6.2.6 Exercise 6: Jewels Board Erase Diamonds (★★★★☆)

The challenge is to delete all chains of three or more horizontally, vertically, or diagonally connected diamonds from the rectangular playfield and subsequently to fill the resulting empty spaces with the diamonds lying above them, (i.e., roughly in the same way gravity works in nature). The following is an example of how the erasing and then dropping is repeated several times until no more change occurs (spaces are shown as _ for better visibility):

Iteration 1:

```
1 1 1 2 4 4 3   erase   _ _ _ _ 4 4 _   fall down   _ _ _ _ _ _ _
1 2 3 4 2 4 3    =>     1 2 3 4 _ 4 _      =>        1 2 3 4 4 4 _
2 3 3 1 2 2 3           2 3 3 1 2 _ _                2 3 3 1 2 4 _
```

Iteration 2:

```
_ _ _ _ _ _ _   erase   _ _ _ _ _ _ _   fall down   _ _ _ _ _ _ _
1 2 3 4 4 4 _    =>     1 2 3 _ _ _ _      =>        1 2 3 _ _ _ _
2 3 3 1 2 4 _           2 3 3 1 2 4 _                2 3 3 1 2 4 _
```

Exercise 6a: Erase (★★★★☆)

Write function erase_chains(values2dim) that erases all rows of three or more contiguous diamonds in horizontal, vertical, and diagonal orientations from a rectangular playfield array.

Examples

An invocation of the method transforms the output array given on the left into the result shown on the right:

```
All chains without overlap     Special case: overlaps
1 2 3 3 3 4     0 0 0 0 0 0    1 1 1 2       0 0 0 2
1 3 2 4 2 4     0 3 0 4 2 0    1 1 3 4  =>  0 0 3 4
1 2 4 2 4 4 =>  0 0 4 0 4 0    1 2 1 3       0 2 0 3
1 2 3 5 5 5     0 0 3 0 0 0
1 2 1 3 4 4     0 0 1 3 4 4
```

Exercise 6b: Falling Down (★★★☆☆)

Write function fall_down(values2dim) working inplace that drops the diamonds from top to bottom, provided there is a space below their position.

Example

An invocation of the method transforms the output array given on the left into the result shown on the right:

```
0 1 3 3 0 0     0 0 0 0 0 0
0 1 0 0 0 0     0 0 0 0 0 0
0 0 3 3 0 0 =>  0 0 3 3 0 0
0 0 0 3 3 4     0 1 3 3 0 0
0 0 3 0 0 0     0 1 3 3 3 4
```

6.2.7 Exercise 7: Spiral Traversal (★★★★☆)

Write generic method `spiral_traversal(values2dim)` that traverses a two-dimensional rectangular array (or a nested list) in the form of a spiral and prepares it as a list. The start is in the upper left corner. First the outer layer is traversed and then the next inner layer.

Example

An example is shown in Figure 6-2.

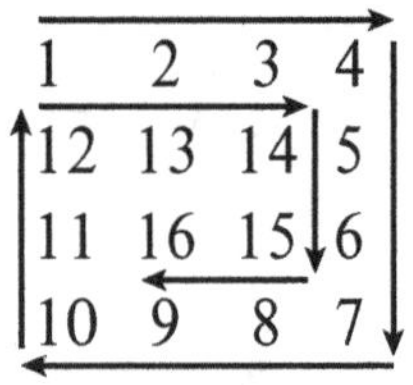

Figure 6-2. *Basic procedure for the spiral traversal*

For the following two arrays, the number or letter sequences listed below should be the results of a spiral traversal:

```
numbers = [[1, 2, 3, 4],
           [12, 13, 14, 5],
           [11, 16, 15, 6],
           [10, 9, 8, 7]]

letterPairs = [["AB", "BC", "CD", "DE"],
               ["JK", "KL", "LM", "EF"],
               ["IJ", "HI", "GH", "FG"]]
=>
```

[1, 2, 3, 4, 5, 6, 7, 8, 9, 10, 11, 12, 13, 14, 15, 16]

[AB, BC, CD, DE, EF, FG, GH, HI, IJ, JK, KL, LM]

6.2.8 Exercise 8: Add One to an Array as a Number (★★☆☆☆)

Consider an array or a list of numbers representing the digits of a decimal number. Write function add_one(digits) that performs an addition by the value 1 and is only allowed to use arrays as a data structure for the solution.

Examples

Input	Result
[1, 3, 2, 4]	[1, 3, 2, 5]
[1, 4, 8, 9]	[1, 4, 9, 0]
[9, 9, 9, 9]	[1, 0, 0, 0, 0]

6.2.9 Exercise 9: Sudoku Checker (★★★☆☆)

In this challenge, a Sudoku puzzle is examined to see if it is a valid solution. Let's assume a 9 × 9 array with int values. According to the Sudoku rules, each row and each column must contain all numbers from 1 to 9. Besides, all numbers from 1 to 9 must, in turn, occur in each 3 × 3 subarray. Write function is_sudoku_valid(board) for checking.

Example

The following is a valid solution:

1	2	3	4	5	6	7	8	9
4	5	6	7	8	9	1	2	3
7	8	9	1	2	3	4	5	6
2	1	4	3	6	5	8	9	7
3	6	5	8	9	7	2	1	4
8	9	7	2	1	4	3	6	5
5	3	1	6	4	2	9	7	8
6	4	2	9	7	8	5	3	1
9	7	8	5	3	1	6	4	2

Bonus While it is nice to be able to check a Sudoku board that is completely filled with digits for its validity, it is even better to be able to predict for a board with gaps (i.e., missing digits) whether a valid solution can emerge from it. This is of particular interest if you want to develop an algorithm for solving a Sudoku puzzle.

Example

Based on the example of the valid Sudoku playfield given above, I deleted the digits in random places. This surely results in a valid solution.

1	2		4	5		7	8	9
	5	6	7		9		2	3
7	8		1	2	3	4	5	6
2	1	4		6		8		7
3	6		8		7	2	1	4
	9	7		1	4	3	6	
5	3	1	6		2	9		8
6		2	9	7	8	5	3	1
9	7			3	1	6	4	2

6.2.10 Exercise 10: Flood Fill (★★☆☆☆)

Exercise 10a (★★☆☆☆)

Write function flood_fill(values2dim, start_x, start_y) that fills all free fields in an array or a two-dimensional nested list with a specified value.

Example

The following shows the filling process for the character *. The filling starts at a given position, such as the upper left corner. It then continues in all four compass directions until the boundaries of the array or a boundary represented by another character are found.

```
"    #  "      "***#  "       "   #   #  "         "    #******#  "
"     #"       "****#"        "   #   #"           "   #******#"
"#    #"  =>   "#***#"        "#  #   #  "  =>      "#  #*****#  "
"  # #  "      " #*#  "       "  # #   #  "         " # #******#  "
"   #   "      "  #  "        "   #   #   "         "  #*****#   "
```

Exercise 10b (★★☆☆☆)

Extend the function to fill any pattern passed as a rectangular array. However, spaces are not allowed in the pattern specification.

Example

The following is an impression of how a flood fill with a pattern could look. The pattern consists of several lines with characters:

```
.|.
-*-
.|.
```

If the filling starts at the bottom center, you get the following result:

```
    x             .|..|.x
   # #           -*--#--#
   ### #         .|.###.|#
#  ### #  =>  #|.###.|#
#   # #         #*--#--*#
 # #  #          #.#|..#
  #  #            #.|.#
```

6.2.11 Exercise 11: Array Min and Max (★★☆☆☆)

Exercise 11a: Min and Max (★☆☆☆☆)

Write two functions find_min(values) and find_max(values) that search for the minimum and maximum, respectively, of a given non-empty array using a self-implemented search, thus eliminating the usage of built-ins like min() and sort(). :-)

Example

Input	Minimum	Maximum
[2, 3, 4, 5, 6, 7, 8, 9, 1, 10]	1	10

Exercise 11b: Min und Max Pos (★★☆☆☆)

Implement two helper functions find_min_pos(values, start, end) and find-_max_pos(values, start, end) that seek and return the position of the minimum and maximum, respectively. Again, assume a non-empty array and additionally an index range of left and right boundaries. In the case of several identical values for minimum or maximum, the first occurrence should be returned.

To find the minimum and maximum values, respectively, write two functions find_min_by_pos(values, start, end) and find_max_by_pos(values, start, end) that use the helper function.

Examples

Method	Input	Range	Result	Position
find_min_xyz()	[5, 3, 4, 2, 6, 7, 8, 9, 1, 10]	0, 10	1	8
find_min_xyz()	[5, 3, 4, 2, 6, 7, 8, 9, 1, 10]	0, 7	2	3
find_min_xyz()	[5, 3, 4, 2, 6, 7, 8, 9, 1, 10]	2, 7	2	3
find_max_xyz()	[1, 22, 3, 4, 5, 10, 7, 8, 9, 49]	0, 10	49	9
find_max_xyz()	[1, 22, 3, 4, 5, 10, 7, 8, 9, 49]	0, 7	22	1
find_max_xyz()	[1, 22, 3, 4, 5, 10, 7, 8, 9, 49]	2, 7	10	5

6.2.12 Exercise 12: Array Split (★★★☆☆)

Say you have an array (or list) of arbitrary integers. For this task, the data structure is to be reordered so that all values less than a special reference value are placed on the left. All values greater than or equal to the reference value are placed on the right. The ordering within the subranges is not relevant and may vary.

Examples

Input	Reference element	Sample result
[4, 7, 1, 20]	9	[1, 4, 7, **9**, 20]
[3, 5, 2]	7	[2, 3, 5, **7**]
[2, 14, 10, 1, 11, 12, 3, 4]	7	[2, 1, 3, 4, **7**, 14, 10, 11, 12]
[3, 5, 7, 1, 11, 13, 17, 19]	11	[1, 3, 5, 7, **11**, 11, 13, 17, 19]

Exercise 12a: Array Split (★★☆☆☆)

Write function array_split(values, reference_element) to implement the functionality described above. In this first part of the exercise, it is allowed to create new data structures, such as lists.

Exercise 12b: Array Split Inplace (★★★☆☆)

Write function array_split_inplace(values, reference_element) that implements the functionality described inside the source array (i.e., inplace). It is explicitly not desirable to create new data structures. To be able to include the reference element in the result, the creation of an array is allowed once for the result. Because this has to be returned, it is permitted to return a value for an inplace function; indeed, it operates only partially inplace here.

Exercise 12c: Array Split Quick Sort Partition (★★★☆☆)

For sorting according to Quick Sort, you need a partitioning functionality similar to the one just developed. However, often the foremost element of the array is used as the reference element.

Based on the two previously developed implementations that use an explicit reference element, your task is to create corresponding alternatives such as the functions array_split_qs(values) and array_split_qs_inplace(values).

Examples

Input	Reference element	Sample result
[**9**, 4, 7, 1, 20]	9	[1, 4, 7, **9**, 20]
[**7**, 3, 5, 2]	7	[2, 3, 5, **7**]
[**7**, 2, 14, 10, 1, 11, 12, 3, 4]	7	[2, 1, 3, 4, **7**, 14, 10, 11, 12]
[**11**, 3, 5, 7, 1, 11, 13, 17, 19]	11	[1, 3, 5, 7, **11**, 11, 13, 17, 19]

6.2.13 Exercise 13: Minesweeper Board (★★★☆☆)

The chances are high that you've played Minesweeper in the past. To remind you, it's a nice little quiz game with a bit of puzzling. What is it about? Bombs are placed face down on a playfield. The player can choose any field on the board. If a field is uncovered, it shows a number. This indicates how many bombs are hidden in the neighboring fields. However, if you are unlucky, you hit a bomb field and you lose. Your task is about initializing such a field and preparing it for a subsequent game.

Solution 13a (★★☆☆☆)

Write function `place_bombs_randomly(width, height, probability)` that creates a playfield specified in size via the first two parameters, randomly filled with bombs, respecting the probability from 0.0 to 1.0 passed in.

Example

The following is a playfield of size 16 × 7 with bombs placed randomly. Bombs are represented by asterisks (`*`) and spaces by dots (`.`):

```
* * * . * * . * . * * . * . . .
. * * . * . . * . * * . . . . .
. . * . . . . . . . . * * * *
. . * . * * . * * . * * . . . .
* * . . . . * . * . . * . . . *
. . * . . * . * * . . * . * * *
. * . * * . * . * * * . . * * .
```

Exercise 13b (★★★☆☆)

Write function `calc_bomb_count(bombs)` that computes the number of adjacent fields based on the bomb fields passed in and returns a corresponding array.

Examples

A calculation for playfields of size 3 × 3 as well as size 5 × 5, including randomly distributed bombs results, is the following:

```
* . .          B 2 1          . * * . .          2 B B 3 1
. . *    =>     1 3 B          * . * * .          B 6 B B 1
. . *          0 2 B          * * . . .    =>     B B 4 3 2
                              * . . * .          B 6 4 B 1
                              * * * . .          B B B 2 1
```

Exercise 13c (★★☆☆☆)

Write function `print_board(bombs, bomb_symbol, bomb_counts)` that allows you to display a board as points and stars as well as numbers and B.

Example

The following is the above playfield of size 16 × 7 with all the calculated values for bomb neighbors:

```
B B B 4 B B 3 B 4 B B 3 B 1 0 0
3 B B 5 B 3 3 B 4 B B 4 3 4 3 2
1 3 B 4 3 3 3 4 4 4 4 B B B B
2 3 3 B 2 B B 4 B B 3 B B 4 4 3
B B 3 2 3 4 B 6 B 4 4 B 5 3 4 B
3 4 B 3 3 B 4 B B 5 4 B 4 B B B
1 B 3 B B 3 B 4 B B B 2 3 B B 3
```

6.3 Solutions

6.3.1 Solution 1: Even Before Odd Numbers (★★☆☆☆)

Write function order_even_before_odd(numbers). This is supposed to rearrange a given array or a list of int values so that the even numbers appear first, followed by the odd numbers. The order within the even and odd numbers is not of relevance.

Examples

Input	Result
[1, 2, 3, 4, 5, 6, 7, 8, 9, 10]	[2, 4, 6, 8, 10, 3, 7, 1, 9, 5]
[2, 4, 6, 1, 8]	[2, 4, 6, 8, 1]
[2, 4, 6, 8, 1]	[2, 4, 6, 8, 1]

Algorithm Traverse the array from the beginning. Skip even numbers. As soon as an odd number is found, search for an even number in the part of the array that follows. If such a number is found, swap it with the current odd number. The procedure is repeated until you reach the end of the array.

```
def order_even_before_odd(numbers):
    i = 0
    while i < len(numbers):
        value = numbers[i]

        if is_even(value):
            # even number, so continue with next number
            i += 1
        else:
            # odd number, jump over all odd ones, until the first even
            j = i + 1
            while j < len(numbers) and not is_even(numbers[j]):
                j += 1

            if j < len(numbers):
                swap(numbers, i, j)
```

```
        else:
            # no further numbers
            break

        i += 1
```

The helper functions for checking and swapping elements have already been implemented in earlier chapters or sections. They are shown here again to make it easier to try out the examples in the Python command line:

```python
def is_even(n):
    return n % 2 == 0

def is_odd(n):
    return n % 2 != 0

def swap(values, first, second):
    tmp = values[first]
    values[first] = values[second]
    values[second] = tmp
```

NOTE: VARIATION OF ODD BEFORE EVEN

A variation is to arrange all odd numbers before the even ones. Therefore, it is possible to write function order_odd_before_even(numbers) where again the ordering within the odd and even numbers is not important.

The algorithm is identical to that shown except for minimal differences in an inverted test. This modification is so simple that the function is not shown again here.

Optimized Algorithm: Improved Running Time

You recognize that your checks have quadratic running time, here $O(n \cdot m)$, because you should aim to reduce the running time of an algorithm to $O(1)$ in the best case, preferably $O(n)$ or at least $O(n \cdot log(n))$, ideally without reducing readability, so nested loops are used. This is not quite so dramatic for pure computations and comprehensibility. For an introduction to the O-notation, please consult Appendix C.

In this case, reducing the running time to $O(n)$ is actually fairly straightforward. As in many solutions to other problems, two position markers are used, here next_even and next_odd. In the beginning, it is assumed that the first element is even and the last odd. Now it is checked if the front number is really even, and the position marker is moved to the right. If the first odd number is encountered, it is swapped with the last element. Even if the last element were odd, it would be swapped again in the next step.

In contrast to the previous solution, this solution does not preserve the order of the even numbers; it also potentially shuffles the odd numbers to a greater extent.

```python
def order_even_before_odd_optimized(numbers):
    next_even = 0
    next_odd = len(numbers) - 1

    while next_even < next_odd:
        current_value = numbers[next_even]
        if is_even(current_value):
            next_even += 1
        else:
            swap(numbers, next_even, next_odd)

            next_odd -= 1
```

Let's take a look at the algorithm for the following unsorted numbers (2, 4, 3, 6, 1). Here e and o represent the position pointers for next_even and next_odd, respectively.

```
2 4 3 6 1
^       ^
e       o
  ^     ^
  e     o
    ^   ^
    e   o
--------- swap
    1 6 3
    ^ ^
    e o
--------- swap
```

```
6 1 3
^

eo
```

Finally, let's have a look at what happens for already sorted numbers. Let's use 1, 2, 3, 4 as examples.

```
1 2 3 4
^     ^

e     o
-------- swap
4 2 3 1
^   ^

E   o
  ^ ^

  e o
    ^

    eo
```

Optimized Algorithm: Less Copying

The previous optimization can be taken a little further. Instead of just skipping the even numbers from the left until you encounter an odd number, you can skip values starting two additional while loops. However, you still preserve a $O(n)$ running time from both sides as long as they are even in the front and odd in the back. This is required since you are traversing the same elements and not performing steps more than once (this insight requires some experience).

The following implementation applies what has been said and swaps elements only when it is unavoidable:

```python
def order_even_before_odd_optimized_v2(numbers):
    left = 0
    right = len(numbers) - 1

    while left < right:
        # run to the first odd number or to the end of the array
        while left < len(numbers) and is_even(numbers[left]):
            left += 1
```

313

```
# run to the first even number or to the beginning of the array
while right >= 0 and is_odd(numbers[right]):
    right -= 1

if left < right:
    swap(numbers, left, right)
    left += 1
    right -= 1
```

Verification

To try it out, use the following inputs that show how it works:

```
>>> import numpy as np

>>> values = np.array([1, 2, 3, 4, 5, 6, 7])
... order_even_before_odd(values)
... print(values)
[2 4 6 1 5 3 7]

>>> values = np.array([1, 2, 3, 4, 5, 6, 7])
... order_even_before_odd_optimized(values)
... print(values)
[6 2 4 5 3 7 1]

>>> values = np.array([1, 2, 3, 4, 5, 6, 7])
... order_even_before_odd_optimized_v2(values)
... print(values)
[6 2 4 3 5 1 7]
```

6.3.2 Solution 2: Flip (★★☆☆☆)

Write generic functions for flipping a two-dimensional array horizontally with flip_horizontally(values2dim) and vertically with flip_vertically(values2dim). The array should be rectangular (i.e., no line should be longer than another).

Examples

The following illustrates how this functionality should work:

```
flip_horizontally()     flip_vertically()
-------------------     -----------------
123       321           1144       3366
456  =>   654           2255  =>   2255
789       987           3366       1144
```

Horizontal flipping algorithm Traverse inwards from the left and right side of the array. To do this, use two position markers leftIdx and rightIdx. At each step, swap the values referenced by these positions and move inward until the positions overlap. The termination occurs at leftIdx >= rightIdx. Repeat the procedure for all lines.

The following sequence shows the described actions for one line, where l represents leftIdx and r represents rightIdx:

```
Step       Array values
---------------------
1          1 2 3 4
           ^     ^
           l     r

2          4 2 3 1
           ^     ^
           L     r

3          4 3 2 1
           ^     ^
           R     l
```

Algorithm for vertical flipping Move from the top and bottom towards the center until both positions overlap. Swap the values and repeat this for all columns. The implementation traverses the array in the x-direction and operates with two position markers on the vertical. After each swap, these position markers are moved towards each other until they cross. You then proceed with the next x-position.

The implementation uses two position pointers and swaps the respective values until the position pointers cross:

```python
def flip_horizontally(values2dim):
    max_y, max_x = get_dimension(values2dim)

    for y in range(max_y):
        left_idx = 0
        right_idx = max_x - 1

        while left_idx < right_idx:
            left_value = values2dim[y][left_idx]
            right_value = values2dim[y][right_idx]

            # swap
            values2dim[y][left_idx] = right_value
            values2dim[y][right_idx] = left_value

            left_idx += 1
            right_idx -= 1
```

Let's now take a look at the corresponding implementation of vertical flipping:

```python
def flip_vertically(values2dim):
    max_y, max_x = get_dimension(values2dim)
    for x in range(max_x):
        top_idx = 0
        bottom_idx = max_y - 1

        while top_idx < bottom_idx:
            top_value = values2dim[top_idx][x]
            bottom_value = values2dim[bottom_idx][x]

            # swap
            values2dim[top_idx][x] = bottom_value
            values2dim[bottom_idx][x] = top_value

            top_idx += 1
            bottom_idx -= 1
```

Here is the function for determining the dimensions of the two-dimensional array that returns the correct data for both nested lists and NumPy arrays, listed once again as a reminder:

```python
def get_dimension(values2dim):
    if isinstance(values2dim, list):
        return (len(values2dim), len(values2dim[0]))

    if isinstance(values2dim, np.ndarray):
        return values2dim.shape

    raise ValueError("unsupported type", type(values2dim))
```

Modified algorithm In fact, the implementation for flipping may be simplified a little bit. The number of steps can be directly computed in both cases: it is width/2 or height/2. For odd lengths, the middle element is not taken into account, resulting in a correct flip.

With these preliminary considerations, here's the implementation for horizontal flipping with a for loop as an example. In doing so, you make use of the auxiliary method developed in the introduction, swap(), for swapping two elements.

```python
def flip_horizontally_v2(values2dim):
    max_y, max_x = get_dimension(values2dim)
    for y in range(max_y):
        row = values2dim[y]
        for x in range(max_x // 2):
            swap(row, x, max_x - x - 1)
```

Optimized algorithm (only for lists) While the solutions shown so far have each made the swaps at the level of individual elements, you can benefit from reassigning entire lines for vertical flipping. This is significantly simpler both in terms of complexity and effort as well as in terms of the amount of source code and it also increases comprehensibility enormously.

```python
def flip_vertically_just_for_lists(values2dim):
    max_y, _ = get_dimension(values2dim)
    for y in range(max_y // 2):
        swap(values2dim, y, max_y - y - 1)
```

317

HINT: LIMITATION

This optimization is not possible for NumPy arrays since they operate purely on a contiguous piece of memory. You can read therein row by row, but you can't swap the references to these rows with each other. On the other hand, you can quickly turn a 4 × 4 array into a 2 × 8 array or 8 × 2 array with `reshape()`.

Verification

To test the functionality, use the inputs from the introductory example, which show the correct operation:

```
def test_flip_horizontally():
    hori_values = [[1, 2, 3],
                   [4, 5, 6],
                   [7, 8, 9]]

    flip_horizontally(hori_values)
    expected = [[3, 2, 1],
                [6, 5, 4],
                [9, 8, 7]]

    assert hori_values == expected

def test_flip_vertically():
    vert_values = [[1, 1, 4, 4],
                   [2, 2, 5, 5],
                   [3, 3, 6, 6]]

    flip_vertically(vert_values)

    expected = [[3, 3, 6, 6],
                [2, 2, 5, 5],
                [1, 1, 4, 4]]

    assert vert_values == expected
```

Both other functions are tested in exactly the same way as the previous ones so the associated test functions are not shown here again.

6.3.3 Solution 3: Palindrome (★★☆☆☆)

Write function is_palindrome(values) that checks an array of strings for whether its values form a palindrome.

Examples

Input	Result
["One", "Test", " – ", "Test", "One"]	True
["Max", "Mike", "Mike", "Max"]	True
["Tim", "Tom", "Mike", "Max"]	False

Algorithm The palindrome check can easily be expressed recursively. Again, two position pointers are used, which are initially located at the beginning and end of the array. It is checked whether the two values referenced by them are the same. If so, you continue to check recursively and move one position further to the middle on both sides with each recursion step until the positions overlap.

```
def is_palindrome_rec(values):
    return is_palindrome_rec_in_range(values, 0, len(values) - 1)

def is_palindrome_rec_in_range(values, left, right):
    # recursive termination
    if left >= right:
        return True

    # check if left == right
    if values[left] == values[right]:
        # recursive descent
        return is_palindrome_rec_in_range(values, left + 1, right - 1)

    return False
```

Optimized algorithm The palindrome check can be converted to an iterative variant based on the recursive solution without much effort:

```python
def is_palindrome_iterative(values):
    left = 0
    right = len(values) - 1

    same_value = True
    while left <= right and same_value:
        # check left == right and repeat until difference occurs
        same_value = values[left] == values[right]
        left += 1
        right -= 1

    return same_value
```

Besides this variant, you can also take advantage of the fact that the maximum number of steps is known, and you can terminate the loop directly in case of a violation of the palindrome property:

```python
def is_palindrome_short(values):
    for i in range(len(values) // 2):
        if values[i] != values[len(values) - 1 - i]:
            return False

    return True
```

Python shortcut Of course, the whole thing can be achieved a lot easier by calling the built-in functionality [::-1]:

```python
def is_palindrome_shorter(values):
    return values == values[::-1]
```

Please keep in mind that for this approach in the presumably rare case of very large amounts of data, an inverse variant of the original data is generated here and thus the memory is required twice.

Verification

For unit testing (again, shown only in excerpts for the recursive variant), use the inputs from the above example. The input and expected values are extracted as a function because they also serve as parameterization for the other two variants.

```python
def values_and_expected():
    return [(["A", "Test", " -- ", "Test", "A"], True),
            (["Max", "Mike", "Mike", "Max"], True),
            (["Tim", "Tom", "Mike", "Max"], False)]

@pytest.mark.parametrize("values, expected", values_and_expected())
def test_is_palindrome_rec(values, expected):
    result = is_palindrome_rec(values)

    assert result == expected
```

6.3.4 Solution 4: Inplace Rotate (★★★☆☆)

Solution 4a: Iterative (★★★☆☆)

In the introductory section, I showed how to rotate arrays. Now try this inplace (i.e., without creating a new array). Your task is to rotate a two-dimensional square shaped array by 90 degrees clockwise. Write generic function rotate_inplace(values2dim) that iteratively implements this.

Example

For a 6 × 6 array, this is visualized as follows:

```
1 2 3 4 5 6      F G H I J 1
J K L M N 7      E T U V K 2
I V W X 0 8  =>  D S Z W L 3
H U Z Y P 9      C R Y X M 4
G T S R Q 0      B Q P O N 5
F E D C B A      A 0 9 8 7 6
```

Algorithm Define four corner positions TL, TR, BL, and BR corresponding to the respective corners. Move from left to right and from top to bottom and copy logically as shown in Figure 6-3.

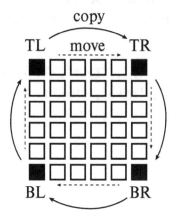

Figure 6-3. *Procedure for inplace rotation*

Repeat the procedure layer by layer for all neighbors of TL until TR is reached (analogously for the neighbors of the other corners). Then move one position inwards at a time until BL and BR intersect. Let's clarify the procedure again step by step.

Starting point Given the following array:

```
1 2 3 4 5 6
J K L M N 7
I V W X O 8
H U Z Y P 9
G T S R Q O
F E D C B A
```

Step 1: First, the outer layer is rotated by copying all values to the respective target position as shown here:

```
F G H I J 1
E K L M N 2
D V W X O 3
C U Z Y P 4
B T S R Q 5
A O 9 8 7 6
```

Step 2: Continue with one layer further inwards:

```
F G H I J 1
E T U V K 2
D S W X L 3
C R Z Y M 4
B Q P O N 5
A 0 9 8 7 6
```

Step 3: This continues until the innermost level is reached:

```
F G H I J 1
E T U V K 2
D S Z W L 3
C R Y X M 4
B Q P O N 5
A 0 9 8 7 6
```

For the processing steps shown, variable `offset` determines which layer you are in, so width/2 steps are required. Based on the layer, the number of positions to copy is obtained, for which an inner loop is used. The corresponding positions in the array are calculated based on their location, as indicated in the figure. Copying is also made easy by the use of helper variables.

```python
def rotate_inplace(values2dim):
    max_y, max_x = get_dimension(values2dim)
    height = max_y - 1
    width = max_x - 1

    offset = 0
    while offset <= width // 2:
        current_width = width - offset * 2

        for idx in range(current_width):
            # top, right, bottom, left
            lo_x = offset + idx
            lo_y = offset

            ro_x = width - offset
            ro_y = offset + idx
```

```
            ru_x = width - offset - idx
            ru_y = height - offset

            lu_x = offset
            lu_y = height - offset - idx

            lo = values2dim[lo_y][lo_x]
            ro = values2dim[ro_y][ro_x]

            ru = values2dim[ru_y][ru_x]
            lu = values2dim[lu_y][lu_x]

            # copy over
            values2dim[ro_y][ro_x] = lo
            values2dim[ru_y][ru_x] = ro
            values2dim[lu_y][lu_x] = ru
            values2dim[lo_y][lo_x] = lu

        offset += 1
```

Alternatively, you can omit helper variables and only cache the value of the upper left position. However, copying then becomes somewhat tricky because the order in the implementation must be exactly the other way around. This variant of the ring-shaped swap is implemented by the function rotate_elements(). To my taste, the previous variant is more understandable.

```
def rotate_inplace_v2(values2dim):
    side_length, _ = get_dimension(values2dim)

    start = 0
    while side_length > 0:
        for i in range(side_length):
            rotate_elements(values2dim, start, side_length, i)

        side_length = side_length - 2
        start += 1

def rotate_elements(values2dim, start, len, i):
    end = start + len - 1
    tmp = values2dim[start][start + i]
```

```
values2dim[start][start + i] = values2dim[end - i][start]
values2dim[end - i][start] = values2dim[end][end - i]
values2dim[end][end - i] = values2dim[start + i][end]
values2dim[start + i][end] = tmp
```

Solution 4b: Recursive (★★★☆☆)

Write recursive function rotate_inplace_recursive(values2dim) that implements the desired 90-degree clockwise rotation.

Algorithm You have already seen that you rotate layer by layer, going from the outer layer further to the inner layer. This literally screams for a recursive solution:

```
def rotate_inplace_recursive(values2dim):
    _, max_x = get_dimension(values2dim)

    __rotate_inplace_recursive_helper(values2dim, 0, max_x - 1)
```

The component *layer copy* is identical as before. Recursive calls replace only the while loop.

```
def __rotate_inplace_recursive_helper(values2dim, left, right):
    if left >= right:
        return

    current_width = right - left
    for i in range(current_width):
        lo = values2dim[left + i][left]
        ro = values2dim[right][left + i]
        ru = values2dim[right - i][right]
        lu = values2dim[left][right - i]

        values2dim[left + i][left] = ro
        values2dim[right][left + i] = ru
        values2dim[right - i][right] = lu
        values2dim[left][right - i] = lo

    __rotate_inplace_recursive_helper(values2dim, left + 1, right - 1)
```

Verification

You define the two-dimensional array shown at the beginning. Then you perform the rotation and compare the result with the expectation.

```python
def test_rotation():
    values = [['1', '2', '3', '4', '5', '6'],
              ['J', 'K', 'L', 'M', 'N', '7'],
              ['I', 'V', 'W', 'X', 'O', '8'],
              ['H', 'U', 'Z', 'Y', 'P', '9'],
              ['G', 'T', 'S', 'R', 'Q', '0'],
              ['F', 'E', 'D', 'C', 'B', 'A']]

    rotate_inplace(values)

    expected = [to_list("F G H I J 1"),
                to_list("E T U V K 2"),
                to_list("D S Z W L 3"),
                to_list("C R Y X M 4"),
                to_list("B Q P O N 5"),
                # this is how it would look by hand
                list("A 0 9 8 7 6".replace(" ", ""))]

    assert values == expected

def to_list(text):
    return list(text.replace(" ", ""))
```

I deliberately show several variants of how to convert a textual representation into a two-dimensional array. I prefer the second variant, especially if using the function to_list(text), which removes the spaces and then formats the string as a list.

6.3.5 Solution 5: Jewels Board Init (★★★☆☆)

Solution 5a: Initialize (★★★☆☆)

Initialize a two-dimensional rectangular array with random-based numbers representing various types of diamonds or jewels as numerical values. The constraint is that initially there must not be three diamonds of the same type placed horizontally or vertically in direct sequence. Write function `init_jewels_board(width, height, num_of_colors)`, which will generate a valid array of the given size and quantity of different types of diamonds.

Example

A random distribution of diamonds represented by digits may look like this for four different colors and shapes:

```
2 3 3 4 4 3 2
1 3 3 1 3 4 4
4 1 4 3 3 1 3
2 2 1 1 2 3 2
3 2 4 4 3 3 4
```

To illustrate this, Figure 6-4 shows another example.

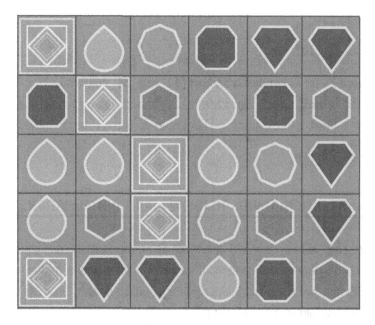

Figure 6-4. *Graphical representation of a Jewels board*

Algorithm First, you create a suitably sized array. Then you fill it row by row and position by position with random-based values using function select_valid_jewel(), which returns the numerical value for the type of diamond. In this method, you have to make sure that the random number just selected does not create a row of three horizontally or vertically.

```python
def init_jewels_board(width, height, num_of_colors):
    board = [[0 for x in range(width)] for y in range(height)]

    for y in range(height):
        for x in range(width):
            board[y][x] = select_valid_jewel(board, x, y, num_of_colors)

    return board

def select_valid_jewel(board, x, y, num_of_colors):
    next_jewel_nr = -1
    is_valid = False

    while not is_valid:

        next_jewel_nr = random.randint(1, num_of_colors)
        is_valid = not check_horizontally(board, x, y, next_jewel_nr) and \
                not check_vertically(board, x, y, next_jewel_nr)

    return next_jewel_nr
```

ATTENTION: THINGS TO KNOW ABOUT INITIALIZATION

The function select_valid_jewel() still needs optimization. At the moment, you can't determine that a valid number can be found for a position, for example, for the following constellation with only two types and the position *, for which neither 1 nor 2 is valid as a value, because both would lead to a row of three:

1221
2122
11*

However, the fact that a valid distribution is also available even for only two values gets obvious by the alternating distribution of the white and black squares of a chessboard. One way to fix the just-mentioned weakness is to choose a more powerful algorithm, such as one that uses backtracking.

There is another weak point: The generation of random numbers out of a small range of values often produces the same number several times, but this number has probably already been checked. This must be avoided. For this purpose, all previously selected random numbers can be stored in a set. Besides, you would have to check whether all expected and possible numbers have already been tried. This short list shows that it is much more complex than you might initially expect.

Now let's move on to checking the horizontal and vertical. At first, you could assume that starting from the current position, you would have to check to the left and right as well as up and down. However, if you reread the assignment more carefully, it says that no chains of length three or longer are allowed. Because you fill the playfield from top to bottom and from left to right, no diamonds to be checked can exist on the right and below the current position. Thus, you can limit yourself to checking to the left and to the top. Furthermore, you do not need to check for longer chains since they cannot occur if you have identified a chain of three.

With these preliminary considerations, you can use the two helper functions to check the respective neighboring fields horizontally and vertically by simply verifying that all of them have the same value as the initial field.

```python
def check_horizontally(board, x, y, jewel_nr):
    top1 = get_at(board, x, y - 1)
    top2 = get_at(board, x, y - 2)

    return top1 == jewel_nr and top2 == jewel_nr

def check_vertically(board, x, y, jewel_nr):
    left1 = get_at(board, x - 1, y)
    left2 = get_at(board, x - 2, y)

    return left1 == jewel_nr and left2 == jewel_nr
```

When accessing the array, the negative offsets may result in invalid array indices. Therefore, you implement function get_at(), which is mainly responsible for checking the boundaries and returns the value -1 for no longer being on the playfield. This value can never occur on the playfield, and thus it is counted as no chain when comparing. Furthermore, you use the function get_dimension() again.

```python
def get_at(values, x, y):
    max_y, max_x = get_dimension(values)
    if x < 0 or y < 0 or y >= max_y or x >= max_x:
        return -1

    return values[y][x]

def get_dimension(values2dim):
    if isinstance(values2dim, list):
        return (len(values2dim), len(values2dim[0]))
    if isinstance(values2dim, np.ndarray):
        return values2dim.shape

    raise ValueError("unsupported type", type(values2dim))
```

ATTENTION: LITTLE SOURCE CODE VS. SMALL BUT MANY METHODS

In this example, I follow the strategy of defining small helper functions, which on the one hand increases the amount of source code. On the other hand, functionalities can be described and tested very well in isolation. Moreover, this approach often allows expressing the source code on a comprehensible and conceptual level. In many cases, this allows extensions to be easily integrated.

Solution to the Bonus Task: Checking Diagonals (★★★☆☆)

Add a check for diagonals. This should make the constellation from the example invalid, among other things, because of the diagonals marked in bold with the number 3 at the bottom right.

Algorithm Checking the four diagonals from one position seems much more time-consuming than checking the horizontal and the vertical. Theoretically, there would be four directions for each position. As (almost) always, it is a good idea to think about a problem a little longer. If you follow this advice, you may come to the solution where in this case, starting from one position, it is sufficient to check only diagonally to the top left and right because, from the point of view of the positions above, this one corresponds to a check diagonally left and right below, as is indicated in the following:

```
X       X
 X   X
  X X
```

Thus, the diagonal check with two helper variables each for the positions of the compass directions northwest and northeast can be implemented as follows and invoked in the function select_valid_jewel():

```python
def check_diagonally(board, x, y, jewel_nr):
    up_left1 = get_at(board, x - 1, y - 1)
    up_left2 = get_at(board, x - 2, y - 2)

    up_right1 = get_at(board, x + 1, y - 1)
    up_right2 = get_at(board, x + 2, y - 2)

    return (up_left1 == jewel_nr and up_left2 == jewel_nr) or \
           (up_right1 == jewel_nr and up_right2 == jewel_nr)

def select_valid_jewel(board, x, y, num_of_colors):
    next_jewel_nr = -1
    is_valid = False

    while not is_valid:
        next_jewel_nr = random.randint(1, num_of_colors)

        is_valid = not check_horizontally(board, x, y, next_jewel_nr) and \
                   not check_vertically(board, x, y, next_jewel_nr) and \
                   not check_diagonally(board, x, y, next_jewel_nr)

    return next_jewel_nr
```

Verification

To verify that the correct playfields are being created now, let's generate and output one of size 5 × 3 with four types of diamonds as follows:

```
>>> import random
>>> import numpy as np
>>> board = init_jewels_board(5, 3, 4)
>>> np.array(board)
array([[3, 4, 3, 3, 2],
       [4, 4, 1, 2, 3],
       [1, 1, 3, 3, 2]])
```

Solution 5b: Validity Check (★★★☆☆)

In this subtask, you want to validate an existing playfield. As a challenge, a list of violations must be returned. Implement function check_board_validity(board2dim) for a rectangular array.

Example

To try out the validity check, use the playfield from the introduction, specially marked here:

```
values_with_errors = [[2, 3, 3, 4, 4, 3, 2],
                      [1, 3, 3, 1, 3, 4, 4],
                      [4, 1, 4, 3, 3, 1, 3],
                      [2, 2, 1, 1, 2, 3, 2],
                      [3, 2, 4, 4, 3, 3, 4]]
```

This should produce the following errors due to its diagonals:

```
['Invalid at x=3 y=2 hor=False, ver=False, dia=True',
 'Invalid at x=2 y=3 hor=False, ver=False, dia=True',
 'Invalid at x=4 y=4 hor=False, ver=False, dia=True']
```

332

Algorithm The validity check can be easily developed based on your previously implemented functions. You check for horizontal, vertical, and diagonal rows of three for each playfield position. If such a violation is found, you generate an appropriate error message.

```python
def check_board_validity(board2dim):
    errors = []

    max_y, max_x = get_dimension(board2dim)
    for y in range(max_y):
        for x in range(max_x):

            current_jewel = board2dim[y][x]

            has_chain_hor = check_horizontally(board2dim, x, y, current_jewel)
            has_chain_ver = check_vertically(board2dim, x, y, current_jewel)
            has_chain_dia = check_diagonally(board2dim, x, y, current_jewel)

            if has_chain_hor or has_chain_ver or has_chain_dia:
                error_msg = "Invalid at x={} y={} hor={}, ver={}, dia={}". \
                    format(x, y, has_chain_hor, has_chain_ver, has_chain_dia)
                errors.append(error_msg)

    return errors
```

Verification

To try out the validity check, you first use the playfield from the introduction and create a NumPy array from it:

```python
>>> values_with_errors = [[2, 3, 3, 4, 4, 3, 2],
                          [1, 3, 3, 1, 3, 4, 4],
                          [4, 1, 4, 3, 3, 1, 3],
                          [2, 2, 1, 1, 2, 3, 2],
                          [3, 2, 4, 4, 3, 3, 4]]

>>> array_with_errors = np.array(values_with_errors)
```

Your functionality should produce the following error messages due to the three faulty diagonals. This is the case for both calls.

```
>>> check_board_validity(values_with_errors)
['Invalid at x=3 y=2 hor=False, ver=False, dia=True',
 'Invalid at x=2 y=3 hor=False, ver=False, dia=True',
 'Invalid at x=4 y=4 hor=False, ver=False, dia=True']

>>> check_board_validity(array_with_errors)
['Invalid at x=3 y=2 hor=False, ver=False, dia=True',
 'Invalid at x=2 y=3 hor=False, ver=False, dia=True',
 'Invalid at x=4 y=4 hor=False, ver=False, dia=True']
```

Subsequently, you replace the problematic digits with a yet unused digit, such as number 5, and retest the function, expecting no conflicts:

```
def test_check_board_validity_no_conflicts():
    values = [[2, 3, 3, 4, 4, 3, 2],
              [1, 3, 3, 1, 3, 4, 4],
              [4, 1, 4, 5, 3, 1, 3],
              [2, 2, 5, 1, 2, 3, 2],
              [3, 2, 4, 4, 5, 3, 4]]

    errors = check_board_validity(values)

    assert errors == []
```

6.3.6 Solution 6: Jewels Board Erase Diamonds (★★★★☆)

The challenge is to delete all chains of three or more horizontally, vertically, or diagonally connected diamonds from the rectangular playfield and subsequently to fill the resulting empty spaces with the diamonds lying above them (i.e., roughly in the same way as gravity works in nature). The following is an example of how the erasing and then dropping is repeated several times until no more change occurs. Spaces are shown as _ for better visibility.

Iteration 1:

```
1 1 1 2 4 4 3   erase   _ _ _ _ 4 4 _   fall down   _ _ _ _ _ _ _
1 2 3 4 2 4 3    =>      1 2 3 4 _ 4 _      =>        1 2 3 4 4 4 _
2 3 3 1 2 2 3            2 3 3 1 2 _ _                2 3 3 1 2 4 _
```

Iteration 2:

```
_ _ _ _ _ _ _   erase   _ _ _ _ _ _ _   fall down   _ _ _ _ _ _ _
1 2 3 4 4 4 _    =>      1 2 3 _ _ _ _      =>        1 2 3 _ _ _ _
2 3 3 1 2 4 _            2 3 3 1 2 4 _                2 3 3 1 2 4 _
```

Solution 6a: Erase (★★★★☆)

Write function erase_chains(values2dim) that erases all rows of three or more contiguous diamonds in horizontal, vertical, and diagonal orientations from a rectangular playfield array.

Examples

An invocation of the method transforms the output array given on the left into the result shown on the right:

All chains without overlap

```
1 2 3 3 3 4        0 0 0 0 0 0
1 3 2 4 2 4        0 3 0 4 2 0
1 2 4 2 4 4   =>   0 0 4 0 4 0
1 2 3 5 5 5        0 0 3 0 0 0
1 2 1 3 4 4        0 0 1 3 4 4
```

Special case: overlaps

```
1 1 1 2        0 0 0 2
1 1 3 4   =>   0 0 3 4
1 2 1 3        0 2 0 3
```

Algorithm: Preliminary considerations As a first brute force variant, you could erase the values directly when finding them. In this case, you search for a chain of length 3 or more and then directly erase these fields. However, this has a crucial weakness: Single diamonds can be part of several chains, as shown in the example above. If you delete immediately, not all occurrences may be found; depending on which of the checks is done first, the other two fail in the following constellation.

```
XXX
XX
X X
```

A second idea is to modify the algorithm minimally by choosing an intermediate representation that symbolizes the deletion request, such as negative numbers, instead of deletion. After all entries in the array have been processed, the deletion takes place in a separate pass. Specifically, you remove all negative values from the array by replacing them with the numerical value 0.

Algorithm The second idea is implemented by function `erase_chains(values2dim)`. It starts with marking all the fields to be deleted using the function `mark_elements_for_removal(values2dim)`. Then they are deleted using the function `erase_all_marked(values2dim)`. For both methods you work position by position. First you have to detect chains of length 3 or more. Function `find_chains(values2dim, x, y)` is responsible for this. Once a chain has been found, it is marked by calling `mark_chains_for_removal(values2dim, x, y, dirs_with_chains)`. The next action is to determine whether each field is marked for deletion. In this case, the stored value is replaced with the value 0 (here by calling the function `blank_value(values2dim)`; details about this seemingly superfluous indirection will be considered later).

```python
def erase_chains(values2dim):
    mark_elements_for_removal(values2dim)

    return erase_all_marked(values2dim)

def mark_elements_for_removal(values2dim):
    max_y, max_x = get_dimension(values2dim)

    for y in range(max_y):
        for x in range(max_x):
            dirs_with_chains = find_chains(values2dim, x, y)

            mark_chains_for_removal(values2dim, x, y, dirs_with_chains)

def erase_all_marked(values2dim):
    erased_something = False

    max_y, max_x = get_dimension(values2dim)
    for y in range(max_y):
        for x in range(max_x):
            if is_element_marked_for_removal(values2dim[y][x]):
                values2dim[y][x] = blank_value(values2dim)
                erased_something = True

    return erased_something
```

```
def is_element_marked_for_removal(value):
    return value < 0

def blank_value(values2dim):
    return 0
```

Now let's move on to the two trickier implementations and start picking up and recognizing chains of three or more similar diamonds. For this, you check for all relevant directions if there is a chain (again with the optimization that you must check diagonally only to the lower right and left). For this, you traverse the fields, count the similar elements, and stop at a deviation. If you find three or more equal values, then that direction is included in the list dirs_with_chains. As a special feature, you check at the beginning of the function if the current field is empty; you don't want to collect chains of blanks.

```
def find_chains(values2dim, start_x, start_y):
    orig_value = values2dim[start_y][start_x]
    if orig_value == 0: # ATTENTION to think of such special cases
        return []

    dirs_with_chains = []

    relevant_dirs = (Direction.S, Direction.SW, Direction.E, Direction.SE)
    for current_dir in relevant_dirs:
        length = 1

    dx, dy = current_dir.value
    next_pos_x = start_x + dx
    next_pos_y = start_y + dy
    while is_on_board(values2dim, next_pos_x, next_pos_y) and \
            is_same(orig_value, values2dim[next_pos_y][next_pos_x]):
        length += 1
        next_pos_x += dx
        next_pos_y += dy

        if length >= 3:
            dirs_with_chains.append(current_dir)

    return dirs_with_chains
```

```python
def is_on_board(values2dim, next_pos_x, next_pos_y):
    max_y, max_x = get_dimension(values2dim)
    return 0 <= next_pos_x < max_x and 0 <= next_pos_y < max_y

def is_same(val1, val2):
    return abs(val1) == abs(val2)
```

In fact, you are almost there. The only thing missing is the function for marking for deletion. Did you think at the beginning that this assignment is so complex? Probably not :-) Let's get to work. You now traverse all chains and convert the original values into one marked for deletion. To accomplish this, you rely on helper function mark_element_for_removal(orig_value), which for the sake of simplicity converts the value to a negative value (with type str, for example, you can use a conversion to lowercase).

```python
def mark_chains_for_removal(values, start_x, start_y, dirs_with_chains):
    orig_value = values[start_y][start_x]

    for current_dir in dirs_with_chains:
        dx, dy = current_dir.value
        next_x = start_x
        next_y = start_y

        while is_on_board(values, next_x, next_y) and \
                is_same(orig_value, values[next_y][next_x]):
            values[next_y][next_x] = mark_element_for_removal(orig_value)

            next_x += dx
            next_y += dy

def mark_element_for_removal(value):
    return -value if value > 0 else value
```

I want to point out that the functionalities are solved using side effects. Here, you are operating directly on the passed data, so this is not bad because the data is not passed further out. Instead, it is all internal functionalities.

Verification

After this exhausting implementation, let's test the deletion as well:

```python
def test_erase_chains():
    values2dim = [[1, 1, 1, 2, 4, 4, 3],
                  [1, 1, 3, 4, 2, 4, 3],
                  [1, 3, 1, 1, 2, 2, 3]]

    deleted = erase_chains(values2dim)

    expected_board = [[0, 0, 0, 0, 4, 4, 0],
                      [0, 0, 3, 4, 0, 4, 0],
                      [0, 3, 0, 1, 2, 0, 0]]

    assert deleted is True
    assert values2dim == expected_board

def test_erase_chains_example_1():
    values2dim = [[1, 2, 3, 3, 3, 4],
                  [1, 3, 2, 4, 2, 4],
                  [1, 2, 4, 2, 4, 4],
                  [1, 2, 3, 5, 5, 5],
                  [1, 2, 1, 3, 4, 4]]

    deleted = erase_chains(values2dim)

    expected_board = [[0, 0, 0, 0, 0, 0],
                      [0, 3, 0, 4, 2, 0],
                      [0, 0, 4, 0, 4, 0],
                      [0, 0, 3, 0, 0, 0],
                      [0, 0, 1, 3, 4, 4]]

    assert deleted is True
    assert values2dim == expected_board
```

Solution 6b: Falling Down (★★★☆☆)

Write function fall_down(values2dim) working inplace that drops the diamonds from top to bottom, provided there is a space below their position.

Example

An invocation of the function transforms the output array given on the left into the result shown on the right:

```
0 1 3 3 0 0        0 0 0 0 0 0
0 1 0 0 0 0        0 0 0 0 0 0
0 0 3 3 0 0   =>   0 0 3 3 0 0
0 0 0 3 3 4        0 1 3 3 0 0
0 0 3 0 0 0        0 1 3 3 3 4
```

Algorithm At first, the task seems to be relatively easy to solve. However, the complexity increases due to a few special characteristics.

As one possible implementation, let's begin with a brute force solution. From left to right, the following is checked for all x-positions in the vertical: Starting from the lowest row to the second highest one, you test whether they represent a blank in each case. If this is the case, the value from the line above is used. In this case, the value from the line above is exchanged with the blank (symbolized here as _, represented in the model with the value 0).

```
1         1         _
2   =>    _    =>   1
_         2         2
```

The procedure can be implemented as follows:

```python
def fall_down_first_try(values2dim):
    max_y, max_x = get_dimension(values2dim)

    for x in range(max_x):
        for y in range(max_y - 1, 0, -1):
            value = values2dim[y][x]
```

```python
        if is_blank(value):
            # fall down
            values2dim[y][x] = values2dim[y - 1][x]
            values2dim[y - 1][x] = blank_value(values2dim)

def is_blank(value):
    return value == 0
```

This works pretty passably, but unfortunately not quite for the following special case:

```
1      _
_  =>  1
_      _
```

You recognize that propagation is missing, and thus the numbers do not continue to fall all the way down, even if there is an empty place below.

As a next idea, you could start falling from the top, but this doesn't work in every case either! While with this procedure the previously problematic case

```
1      _
_  =>  _
_      1
```

is solved, problems occur now for the first constellation. These problems do not occur with the variant before.

```
1      1
2  =>  _
_      2
```

You now know that both of the variants discussed do not yet work quite correctly. Moreover, it was crucial to use the right set of test data to uncover just these specific problems.

To correct this, you need to implement continuous falling of stones to always move all values per column. The while loop is used for this:

```python
def fall_down(values2dim):
    max_y, max_x = get_dimension(values2dim)

    for x in range(max_x):
        for y in range(max_y - 1, 0, -1):
            current_y = y
            # fall down until there is no more empty space under it
            while current_y < len(values2dim) and \
                is_blank(values2dim[current_y][x]):
            # fall down
            values2dim[current_y][x] = values2dim[current_y - 1][x]
            values2dim[current_y - 1][x] = blank_value(values2dim)

            current_y += 1
```

Verification

Let' take the previously obtained result of the deletion as the starting point for the falling:

```python
def test_fall_down():
    values2dim = [[0, 1, 3, 3, 0, 0],
                  [0, 1, 0, 0, 0, 0],
                  [0, 0, 3, 3, 0, 0],
                  [0, 0, 0, 3, 3, 4],
                  [0, 0, 3, 0, 0, 0]]

    fall_down(values2dim)

    expected_board = [[0, 0, 0, 0, 0, 0],
                      [0, 0, 0, 0, 0, 0],
                      [0, 0, 3, 3, 0, 0],
                      [0, 1, 3, 3, 0, 0],
                      [0, 1, 3, 3, 3, 4]]

    assert values2dim == expected_board
```

Overall Verification

To experience your functions all together in action, use the example you used for deleting:

```python
def main():
    example_board = [[1, 1, 1, 2, 4, 4, 3],

                     [1, 1, 3, 4, 2, 4, 3],
                     [1, 3, 1, 1, 2, 2, 3]]

    print_array(example_board)
    while erase_chains(example_board):
        print("--------------------------------")
        fall_down(example_board)
        print_array(example_board)
```

Using the following helper function print_array(values) developed in the introduction

```python
def print_array(values2dim):
    max_y, max_x = get_dimension(values2dim)
    for y in range(max_y):
        for x in range(max_x):
            value = values2dim[y][x]
            print(str(value) + " ", end='')

        print()
```

gives the expected output:

```
1 1 1 2 4 4 3
1 1 3 4 2 4 3
1 3 1 1 2 2 3
----------------------------------
0 0 0 0 0 0 0
0 0 0 4 4 4 0
0 3 3 1 2 4 0
----------------------------------
0 0 0 0 0 0 0
0 0 0 0 0 0 0
0 3 3 1 2 4 0
----------------------------------
```

Modification to characters Now let's go one step further and use letters as an alternative to digits for modeling. You perform the actions on a prepared array of letters, which allows you to see different deletions and iterations very nicely. However, you must adapt some of the functions for the type str appropriately (see the following practical tip). Add the following lines to the above main() function as indicated by the comment:

```
# main as before

    jewels_test_deletion = [list("AACCDE"),
                            list("AA DE"),
                            list("ABCCDE"),
                            list("AB CCD"),
                            list("ABCDDD")]

    print_array(jewels_test_deletion)

    while erase_chains(jewels_test_deletion):
        print("---------------------------------")
        fall_down(jewels_test_deletion)
        print_array(jewels_test_deletion)
```

The desired and expected result should then look like this:

```
A A C C D E
A A     D E
A B C C D E
A B   C C D
A B C D D D
---------------------------------
    C C
  A C C
  A C C C D
---------------------------------

  A
  A       D
```

Implementing the supplementary processing based on characters is the subject of the following practical tip. You will probably also suddenly realize why a few seemingly unimportant auxiliary functions were created in the previous implementation.

HINT: VARIANTS WITH TYPE STR

Some readers may have wondered why I implement various helper functions when the functionality seems very simple. The reason is that this way it gets easier to use the algorithms almost unchanged for other types instead just by redefining the corresponding helper functions, for example these:

```python
def blank_value(values2dim):
    if type(values2dim[0][0]) is str:
        return " "

    return 0

def is_blank(value):
    if type(value) is str:
        return value == " " or value == "_" or len(value) == 0

    return value == 0

def is_same(val1, val2):
    if type(val1) is str:
        return val1.lower() == val2.lower()
    return abs(val1) == abs(val2)

def mark_element_for_removal(value):
    if type(value) is str:
        return value.lower()
    return -value if value > 0 else value

def is_element_marked_for_removal(value):
    if type(value) is str:
        return value.islower()
    return value < 0
```

Using the approach described ensures that the higher-level functions for determining which chains to delete, the actual deletion, and the falling of the diamonds don't even need to be adjusted.

345

6.3.7 Solution 7: Spiral Traversal (★★★★☆)

Write generic method `spiral_traversal(values2dim)` that traverses a two-dimensional rectangular array (or a nested list) in the form of a spiral and prepare it as a list. The start is in the upper left corner. First, the outer layer is traversed, and then the next inner layer.

Example

An example is shown in Figure 6-5.

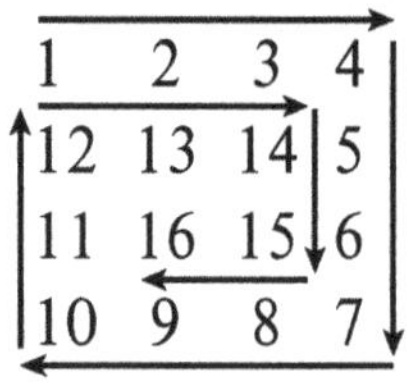

Figure 6-5. *Basic procedure for the spiral traversal*

For the following two nested lists of number and letter sequences, the results of a spiral traversal are shown:

```
numbers = [[1, 2, 3, 4],
           [12, 13, 14, 5],
           [11, 16, 15, 6],
           [10, 9, 8, 7]]

letter_pairs = [["AB", "BC", "CD", "DE"],
                ["JK", "KL", "LM", "EF"],
                ["IJ", "HI", "GH", "FG"]]

=>

[1, 2, 3, 4, 5, 6, 7, 8, 9, 10, 11, 12, 13, 14, 15, 16]
[AB, BC, CD, DE, EF, FG, GH, HI, IJ, JK, KL, LM]
```

JOB INTERVIEW TIPS: CLARIFY ASSUMPTIONS

Before proceeding with a solution, be sure to clarify any constraints or special requirements by asking questions. In this case, ask if the original data should be a rectangular. Assume that to be the case here.

Algorithm Let's start with an idea. For a spiral movement, you start going to the right until you reach the boundary, then change direction downward, and advance again until you reach the boundary. Then turn to the left and finally up to the boundary. For the spiral to narrow, the respective limits must be suitably reduced at each change of direction. Formulating the termination condition correctly is not quite easy when operating. The following observation helps: The total number of steps is given by $width * height - 1$ for a 4×3 sized data set, thus $4 * 3 - 1 = 12 - 1 = 11$. With these preliminary considerations, we implement the spiral traversal as follows:

```python
class Direction(Enum):
    RIGHT = (1, 0)
    DOWN = (0, 1)
    LEFT = (-1, 0)
    UP = (0, -1)

def spiral_traversal(values2dim):
    pos_x = 0
    pos_y = 0

    min_x = 0
    min_y = 1
    max_y, max_x = get_dimension(values2dim)

    results = []

    dir = Direction.RIGHT
    steps = 0

    all_steps = max_y * max_x
    while steps < all_steps:
        # action
        results.append(values2dim[pos_y][pos_x])
        if dir == Direction.RIGHT:
            if pos_x < max_x - 1:
                pos_x += 1
            else:
                dir = Direction.DOWN
                max_x -= 1
```

```
    if dir == Direction.DOWN:
        if pos_y < max_y - 1:
            pos_y += 1
        else:
            dir = Direction.LEFT
            max_y -= 1
    if dir == Direction.LEFT:
        if pos_x > min_x:
            pos_x -= 1
        else:
            dir = Direction.UP
            min_x += 1

    if dir == Direction.UP:
        if pos_y > min_y:
            pos_y -= 1
        else:
            dir = Direction.RIGHT
            min_y += 1

            # possible mistake: You now have to start one
            # position further to the right!
            pos_x += 1

    steps += 1

return results
```

After a complete traversal of one layer, you have to move the position pointer one position towards the center. This gets easily forgotten.

The algorithm presented works, but it requires quite a few special treatments.

Optimized algorithm Look at the figure again and then think a bit. You know that initially the whole array is a valid movement area. At each iteration, the outer layer is processed and you continues inwards. Now you can specify the valid range by four position markers as before. However, you proceed more cleverly when updating.

You notice that after moving to the right, the top line is processed so that you can increase the counter min_y by one. If you move down, then the rightmost side is traversed, and the counter max_x is decreased by one. Moving to the left, the bottom row is processed, and the counter max_y is decreased by one. Finally, when moving upwards, the counter min_x is increased by one. To detect when to increment, you implement utility function is_outside() or range checking.

Additionally, you can still take advantage of defining the direction constants according to the order in the spiral traversal and then implementing function next() in the enum that specifies the subsequent direction in each case. Likewise, you define there the offset values dx and dy as a tuple.

```python
class Direction(Enum):
    RIGHT = (1, 0)
    DOWN = (0, 1)
    LEFT = (-1, 0)
    UP = (0, -1)

    def next(self):
        keys = list(Direction.__members__.keys())
        pos = keys.index(self.name)
        return list(Direction)[(pos + 1) % len(keys)]
```

With these thoughts and preliminaries, you are now able to implement the spiral traversal in a readable and understandable way as follows:

```python
def spiral_traversal_optimized(values2dim):
    pos_x = 0
    pos_y = 0

    min_x = 0
    min_y = 0
    max_y, max_x = get_dimension(values2dim)
    results = []

    dir = Direction.RIGHT
    steps = 0
    all_steps = max_y * max_x
    while steps < all_steps:
        # action
        results.append(values2dim[pos_y][pos_x])
```

```
        dx, dy = dir.value
        if is_outside(pos_x + dx, pos_y + dy, min_x, max_x, min_y, max_y):
            if dir == Direction.RIGHT:
                min_y += 1
            if dir == Direction.DOWN:
                max_x -= 1
            if dir == Direction.LEFT:
                max_y -= 1
            if dir == Direction.UP:
                min_x += 1

            dir = dir.next()
            dx, dy = dir.value

        pos_x += dx
        pos_y += dy
        steps += 1

    return results

def is_outside(x, y, min_x, max_x, min_y, max_y):
    return x < min_x or x >= max_x or y < min_y or y >= max_y
```

Verification

Check if your algorithm as well as its optimized variant and really performs the expected traversal through the array or nested list for the inputs from the above example:

```
def values_and_expected():
    return [(([["A", "B", "C", "D"],
               ["J", "K", "L", "E"],
               ["I", "H", "G", "F"]],
              list("ABCDEFGHIJKL")),
             ([[1, 2, 3, 4],
               [12, 13, 14, 5],
               [11, 16, 15, 6],
               [10, 9, 8, 7]],
              [1, 2, 3, 4, 5, 6, 7, 8, 9, 10, 11, 12, 13, 14, 15, 16]))]
```

```
@pytest.mark.parametrize("values, expected", values_and_expected())
def test_spiral_traversal(values, expected):
    result = spiral_traversal(values)

    assert result == expected

@pytest.mark.parametrize("values, expected", values_and_expected())
def test_spiral_traversal_optimized(values, expected):
    result = spiral_traversal_optimized(values)

    assert result == expected
```

6.3.8 Solution 8: Add One to an Array as a Number (★★☆☆)

Consider an array or a list of numbers representing the digits of a decimal number. Write function add_one(digits) that performs an addition by the value 1 and is only allowed to use arrays as data structure for the solution.

Examples

Input	Result
[1, 3, 2, 4]	[1, 3, 2, 5]
[1, 4, 8, 9]	[1, 4, 9, 0]
[9, 9, 9, 9]	[1, 0, 0, 0, 0]

Algorithm You may remember back to your school days and use digit-oriented processing: traverse the values from back to front and then add the overflow value of the last addition to the respective digit value. Initially, you start with the assumption that there is an overflow. If the value 10 is reached again, the overflow must be propagated further. In the special case that the overflow propagates to the very front, the array must be increased by one position to accommodate the new leading 1.

```
def add_one(digits):
    if len(digits) == 0:
        raise ValueError("must be a valid non empty array / list")

    result = []
```

```
    # run from back to front and add, check for overflow
    overflow = 1
    for current_digit in reversed(digits):
        current_digit += overflow
        overflow = 1 if current_digit >= 10 else 0

        result.insert(0, current_digit % 10)

    if overflow == 1:
        result.insert(0, 1)

    return result
```

In the special case that the carry propagates all the way to the front, the array must be enlarged by one position to accommodate the new leading 1.

Verification

To check your implementation, use the three combinations of values from the introductory examples, which cover the three main cases of no propagation, propagation by one digit, and propagation over all digits. Additionally, add a test case for the propagation for two digits.

```
def values_and_expected():
    return [([1, 3, 2, 4], [1, 3, 2, 5]),
            ([1, 4, 8, 9], [1, 4, 9, 0]),
            ([1, 3, 9, 9], [1, 4, 0, 0]),
            ([9, 9, 9, 9], [1, 0, 0, 0, 0])]

@pytest.mark.parametrize("values, expected", values_and_expected())
def test_add_one(values, expected):
    result = add_one(values)

    assert result == expected
```

6.3.9 Solution 9: Sudoku Checker (★★★☆☆)

In this challenge, a Sudoku puzzle is examined to see if it is a valid solution. Let's assume a 9 × 9 array with int values. According to the Sudoku rules, each row and each column must contain all numbers from 1 to 9. Besides, all numbers from 1 to 9 must, in turn, occur in each 3 × 3 subarray. Write function is_sudoku_valid(board)for checking.

Example

The following is a valid solution:

1	2	3	4	5	6	7	8	9
4	5	6	7	8	9	1	2	3
7	8	9	1	2	3	4	5	6
2	1	4	3	6	5	8	9	7
3	6	5	8	9	7	2	1	4
8	9	7	2	1	4	3	6	5
5	3	1	6	4	2	9	7	8
6	4	2	9	7	8	5	3	1
9	7	8	5	3	1	6	4	2

Algorithm In Sudoku, three different types of checks have to be performed. They can be divided into three corresponding functions very well. First are the functions check_horizontally() and check_vertically(), which ensure horizontally and vertically that all digits from 1 to 9 always occur exactly once in a row or column, respectively. To check this, you collect all digits stored in the respective alignment in a list and compare them in the function all_desired_numbers() to see if they contain the desired numbers.

```
def check_horizontally(board):
    for row in range(9):
        # collect all values of a row in a list
        row_values = [board[row][x] for x in range(9)]

    if not all_desired_numbers(row_values):
        return False

    return True
```

```python
def check_vertically(board):
    for x in range(9):
        # collect all values of a column in a list
        column_values = [board[row][x] for row in range(9)]

        if not all_desired_numbers(column_values):
            return False

    return True
```

You might wonder whether it's preferable to collect the values in a set. Although this is obvious and works well for fully filled Sudoku puzzles, collecting data in a set complicates subsequent checking if you permit empty fields as well.

Regardless, both checks rely on the following helper function:

```python
def all_desired_numbers(all_collected_values):
    if len(all_collected_values) != 9:
        raise ValueError("not 9 values to process")

    one_to_nine = {1, 2, 3, 4, 5, 6, 7, 8, 9}
    values_set = set(all_collected_values)
    return one_to_nine == values_set
```

I would like to explicitly point out the elegance of the helper function all_desired-_numbers(). It unifies various things in its brevity: actually, you need to check that the collected values do not contain duplicates and that there are exactly nine different digits. Due to your implementation, you don't need to check the length. Still, you do it anyway to guard against careless errors with an exception. By converting the values into a set and comparing it to the set from the expected values, the process is nice and short.

Next, you need to check each of the nine subfields of size 3 × 3. This doesn't sound easy at first. But think a bit: You can use two nested loops to run off the 3 × 3 boxes. Two more nested loops run the respective x and y values for the boxes. Simple multiplications and additions are used to derive the corresponding index values in the original array. By following the previously presented idea of collecting the values into a list, which is finally checked against the expected target set of digits 1 to 9, the implementation loses its initial horror.

```python
def check_boxes(board):
    # 3 x 3 box
    for y_box in range(3):
        for x_box in range(3):
            # values per box
            box_values = collect_box_values(board, y_box, x_box)

            if not all_desired_numbers(box_values):
                return False

    return True
```

The picking up of digits within a 3 x 3 box is implemented as follows:

```python
def collect_box_values(board, y_box, x_box):
    box_values = []

    # inside the boxes each 3 x 3
    for y in range(3):
        for x in range(3):
            # actual index values
            real_y = y_box * 3 + y
            real_x = x_box * 3 + x
            box_values.append(board[real_y][real_x])

    return box_values
```

For a complete Sudoku check, you then need to combine these values all together by and:

```python
def is_sudoku_valid(board):
    return check_horizontally(board) and \
        check_vertically(board) and \
        check_boxes(board)
```

Verification

You first define the Sudoku playfield as shown in the introduction and then you test all three variants.

```python
def main():
    board = [[1, 2, 3, 4, 5, 6, 7, 8, 9],
             [4, 5, 6, 7, 8, 9, 1, 2, 3],
             [7, 8, 9, 1, 2, 3, 4, 5, 6],
             [2, 1, 4, 3, 6, 5, 8, 9, 7],
             [3, 6, 5, 8, 9, 7, 2, 1, 4],
             [8, 9, 7, 2, 1, 4, 3, 6, 5],
             [5, 3, 1, 6, 4, 2, 9, 7, 8],
             [6, 4, 2, 9, 7, 8, 5, 3, 1],
             [9, 7, 8, 5, 3, 1, 6, 4, 2], ]

    print("H: ", check_horizontally(board))
    print("V: ", check_vertically(board))
    print("B: ", check_boxes(board))
    print("S: ", is_sudoku_valid(board))
```

As expected, you get four times the value True as a result.

Bonus

While it is nice to be able to check a Sudoku board that is completely filled with digits for its validity, it is even better to be able to predict for a board with gaps (i.e., still missing digits) whether a valid solution can emerge from it. This is of particular interest if you want to develop an algorithm for solving a Sudoku puzzle.

Example

Based on the example of the valid Sudoku playfield given above, I deleted the digits in random places. This surely results in a valid solution.

1	2		4	5		7	8	9
	5	6	7		9		2	3
7	8		1	2	3	4	5	6
2	1	4		6		8		7
3	6		8		7	2	1	4
	9	7		1	4	3	6	
5	3	1	6		2	9		8
6		2	9	7	8	5	3	1
9	7			3	1	6	4	2

Algorithm A partially filled playfield can be checked for validity fairly easily if you take the previous implementation as a basis. First, you need modeling for the blank fields. In this case, the value 0 is a good choice. Based on this, you can leave the implementation for collecting the values horizontally, vertically, and in the boxes as it is. You only have to slightly modify the final check whether all values from 1 to 9 are included. First, you remove the value 0 from the collected values, if any. Then you make sure that there are no duplicates. Finally, you check whether the collected values are a subset of 1 to 9.

```python
def all_desired_numbers(all_collected_values):
    # remove irrelevant empty fields
    relevant_values = remove_all_occurences(all_collected_values, 0)

    # no duplicates?
    values_set = set(relevant_values)
    if len(relevant_values) != len(values_set):
        return False

    # only 1 to 9?
    one_to_nine = {1, 2, 3, 4, 5, 6, 7, 8, 9}

    return one_to_nine.issuperset(values_set)

def remove_all_occurences(values, item):
    return list(filter(lambda x: x != item, values))
```

The very best comes at the end. This function works for completely filled Sudoku puzzles and those containing blanks!

Verification

Again you define the Sudoku playfield with blanks, as shown before. After that, you check a slightly modified playfield, where the value 2 is inserted in the first line at position 3. Due to this, the playfield becomes invalid.

```python
def create_initialized_board():
    return [[1, 2, 0, 4, 5, 0, 7, 8, 9],
            [0, 5, 6, 7, 0, 9, 0, 2, 3],
            [7, 8, 0, 1, 2, 3, 4, 5, 6],
            [2, 1, 4, 0, 6, 0, 8, 0, 7],
            [3, 6, 0, 8, 9, 7, 2, 1, 4],
            [0, 9, 7, 0, 1, 4, 3, 6, 0],
            [5, 3, 1, 6, 0, 2, 9, 0, 8],
            [6, 0, 2, 9, 7, 8, 5, 3, 1],
            [9, 7, 0, 0, 3, 1, 6, 4, 2]]

def test_is_sudoku_valid():
    board = create_initialized_board()
    is_valid_sudoku = is_sudoku_valid(board)

    assert is_valid_sudoku is True

def test_is_sudoku_valid_for_invalid_board():
    board = create_initialized_board()
    # change it and make it invalid
    board[0][2] = 2

    is_valid_sudoku = is_sudoku_valid(board)

    assert is_valid_sudoku is False
```

The faulty playfield of the second test case looks like this and the problematic value is marked in bold:

```
1 2 2 4 5 0 7 8 9
0 5 6 7 0 9 0 2 3
7 8 0 1 2 3 4 5 6
2 1 4 0 6 0 8 0 7
3 6 0 8 9 7 2 1 4
0 9 7 0 1 4 3 6 0
5 3 1 6 0 2 9 0 8
6 0 2 9 7 8 5 3 1
9 7 0 0 3 1 6 4 2
```

6.3.10 Solution 10: Flood Fill (★★☆☆☆)

Exercise 10a (★★☆☆☆)

Write function flood_fill(values2dim, start_x, start_y) that fills all free fields in an array or a two-dimensional nested list with a specified value.

Example

The following shows the filling process for the character *. The filling starts at a given position, such as the upper left corner. It continues in all four compass directions until the boundaries of the array or a boundary represented by another character are found.

```
"   #  "     "***# "    "   #     # "     "   #******# "
"    #"      "****#"     "   #     #"      "   #******#"
"#   #" =>   "#***#"     "#   #    # " =>  "#   #*****# "
" # # "      " #*# "     " # #     # "     " # #******# "
"   # "      " # "       " # #     "       "   #*****#  "
```

Algorithm Recursively check the neighboring cells in the four cardinal directions. If a field is empty, it gets filled and the check it repeated. If you reach the array boundaries or a filled cell, you stop. This can be expressed recursively in an elegant way.

```python
def flood_fill(values2dim, x, y):
    max_y, max_x = get_dimension(values2dim)

    # recursive termination
    if x < 0 or y < 0 or x >= max_x or y >= max_y:
        return

    if values2dim[y][x] == ' ':
        values2dim[y][x] = '*'

    # recursive descent: fill all 4 directions
    flood_fill(values2dim, x, y - 1)
    flood_fill(values2dim, x + 1, y)
    flood_fill(values2dim, x, y + 1)
    flood_fill(values2dim, x - 1, y)
```

Verification

Now let's define the array shown in the introduction as a starting point and then perform a flood fill with different starting locations.

```python
def create_world_and_expected_fills():
    first_world = [list("   # "),
                   list("    #"),
                   list("#   #"),
                   list(" # # "),
                   list("  #  ")]
    first_filled = [list("***# "),
                    list("****# "),
                    list("#***# "),
                    list(" #*# "),
                    list("  #  ")]

    second_world = [list("   #    # "),
                    list("   #     #"),
                    list("#   #    # "),
                    list(" # #    # "),
                    list("  #   #   ")]
```

```
        second_filled = [list("  #******#"),
                         list("   #******#"),
                         list("#  #******# "),
                         list(" # #******#  "),
                         list("  #*****#    ")]

    return [(first_world, first_filled, 0, 0,),
            (second_world, second_filled, 4, 4)]

@pytest.mark.parametrize("world, expected, start_x, start_y",
                         create_world_and_expected_fills())
def test_flood_fill(world, expected, start_x, start_y):
    flood_fill(world, start_x, start_y)

    assert world == expected
```

Solution 10b (★★☆☆☆)

Extend the function to fill any pattern passed as a rectangular array. Spaces are not allowed in the pattern specification.

Example

The following is an impression of how a flood fill with a pattern could look. The pattern consists of several lines with characters:

```
.|.
-*-
.|.
```

If the filling starts at the bottom center, you get the following result:

```
       X               .|..|.x
     #   #            -*--#--#
    ###  #            .|.###.|#
#   ###  #   =>   #|.###.|#
#   #    #           #*--#--*#
 # #     #           #.#|..#
  #   #               #.|.#
```

Algorithm What needs to be changed to support a pattern? First of all, you must pass the desired pattern to the function. Interestingly, the fill algorithm remains almost the same and is only modified concerning the fill character's determination. Instead of a fixed value, the helper function find_fill_char() is invoked here, which determines the fill character relevant for the position. The recursive descent is expressed elegantly by using an enumeration for the directions as an alternative to the four individual calls show before.

```python
def flood_fill_with_pattern(values2dim, x, y, pattern):
    max_y, max_x = get_dimension(values2dim)

    # recursive termination
    if x < 0 or y < 0 or x >= max_x or y >= max_y:
        return

    if values2dim[y][x] == ' ':
        # determine appropriate fill character
        values2dim[y][x] = find_fill_char(y, x, pattern)

        # recursive descent in 4 directions
        for dir in Direction:
            dy, dx = dir.value

            flood_fill_with_pattern(values2dim, x + dx, y + dy, pattern)
class Direction(Enum):
    UP = (-1, 0)
    DOWN = (1, 0)
    LEFT = (0, -1)
    RIGHT = (0, 1)
```

Now let's determine the fill character based on the current position in relation to the width or the height of the playfield array using a simple modulo calculation:

```python
def find_fill_char(y, x, pattern):
    max_y, max_x = get_dimension(pattern)
    return pattern[y % max_y][x % max_x]
```

Verification

Analogous to before, you would like to fill the array with delimiters presented in the introduction with the pattern shown before. Therefore, you provide functions to generate patterns:

```python
def generate_pattern():
    return [list(".|."),
            list("-*-"),
            list(".|.")]

def generate_big_world():
    return [[" ", " ", " ", " ", " ", " ", "x", " ", " "],
            [" ", " ", " ", " ", "#", " ", " ", "#", " "],
            [" ", " ", " ", "#", "#", "#", " ", " ", "#"],
            ["#", " ", " ", "#", "#", "#", " ", " ", "#"],
            ["#", " ", " ", " ", "#", " ", " ", " ", "#"],
            [" ", "#", " ", "#", " ", " ", " ", "#", " "],
            [" ", " ", "#", " ", " ", " ", "#", " ", " "]]
```

For testing, you generate the initial pattern and call the flood fill with the pattern:

```python
>>> world = generate_big_world()
>>> flood_fill_with_pattern(world, 1, 1, generate_pattern())
```

For control purposes, you now print out the array. This allows you to examine the filling with the respective pattern.

```python
>>> print_array(world)
.|..|.x
-*--#--#
.|.###.|#
#|.###.|#
#*--#--*#
 #.#|..#
  #.|.#
```

```
def print_array(values2dim):
    max_y, max_x = get_dimension(values2dim)
    for y in range(max_y):
        for x in range(max_x):
            value = values2dim[y][x]
            print(str(value) + " ", end='')

        print()
```

6.3.11 Solution 11: Array Min and Max (★★☆☆☆)

Solution 11a: Min and Max (★☆☆☆☆)

Write two functions find_min(values) and find_max(values) that search for the
minimum and maximum, respectively, of a given non-empty array using a self-
implemented search, thus eliminating the usage of built-ins like min() and sort(). :-)

Example

Input	Minimum	Maximum
[2, 3, 4, 5, 6, 7, 8, 9, 1, 10]	1	10

Algorithm Loop through the array from the beginning. In both cases, assume that
the first element is the minimum or maximum. The array is traversed from front to back,
searching for a smaller or larger element. If such a candidate is found, the minimum or
maximum gets reassigned.

```
def find_min(values):
    if len(values) == 0:
        raise ValueError("find_min not supported for empty input")

    min = values[0]
    for i in range(1, len(values)):
        if values[i] < min:
            min = values[i]

    return min
```

```
def find_max(values):
    if len(values) == 0:
        raise ValueError("find_max not supported for empty input")

    max = values[0]
    for i in range(1, len(values)):
        if values[i] > max:
            max = values[i]

    return max
```

Due to the boundary condition of a non-empty output array, you can always start with the first element as minimum or maximum.

Solution 11b: Min und Max Pos (★★☆☆☆)

Implement two helper functions find_min_pos(values, start, end) and find-_max_pos(values, start, end) that seek and return the position of the minimum and maximum, respectively. Again, assume a non-empty array and additionally an index range of left and right boundaries. In the case of several identical values for minimum or maximum, the first occurrence should be returned.

To find the minimum and maximum values, respectively, write two functions find_min_by_pos(values, start, end) and find_max_by_pos(values, start, end) that use the helper function.

Examples

Method	Input	Range	Result	Position
find_min_xyz()	[5, 3, 4, 2, 6, 7, 8, 9, 1, 10]	0, 10	1	8
find_min_xyz()	[5, 3, 4, 2, 6, 7, 8, 9, 1, 10]	0, 7	2	3
find_min_xyz()	[5, 3, 4, 2, 6, 7, 8, 9, 1, 10]	2, 7	2	3
find_max_xyz()	[1, 22, 3, 4, 5, 10, 7, 8, 9, 49]	0, 10	49	9
find_max_xyz()	[1, 22, 3, 4, 5, 10, 7, 8, 9, 49]	0, 7	22	1
find_max_xyz()	[1, 22, 3, 4, 5, 10, 7, 8, 9, 49]	2, 7	10	5

Algorithm Based on the determined position of the minimum or maximum, the appropriate return of the corresponding element can be implemented trivially:

```python
def find_min_by_pos(values, start, end):
    min_pos = find_min_pos(values, start, end)
    return values[min_pos]

def find_max_by_pos(values, start, end):
    max_pos = find_max_pos(values, start, end)
    return values[max_pos]
```

To complete the process, you still need to determine the position of the minimum and maximum. For this, proceed as follows: To find the respective position of minimum and maximum, go through all elements, compare with the current value for minimum or maximum, and update the position if the value is smaller or larger.

```python
def find_min_pos(values, start, end):
    if len(values) == 0:
        raise ValueError("find_min_pos not supported for empty input")
    if start < 0 or start > end or end > len(values):
        raise ValueError("invalid range")

    min_pos = start
    for i in range(start + 1, end):
        if values[i] < values[min_pos]:
            min_pos = i

    return min_pos

def find_max_pos(values, start, end):
    if len(values) == 0:
        raise ValueError("find_max_pos not supported for empty input")
    if start < 0 or start > end or end > len(values):
        raise ValueError("invalid range")

    max_pos = start
    for i in range(start + 1, end):
        if values[i] > values[max_pos]:
            max_pos = i

    return max_pos
```

Verification

Test the functionality as usual with the inputs from the introduction:

```
def test_find_min_and_max():
    values = [ 2, 3, 4, 5, 6, 7, 8, 9, 1, 10 ]

    assert find_min(values) == 1
    assert find_max(values) == 10

@pytest.mark.parametrize("lower, upper, expected_pos, expected_value",
                         [(0, 10, 8, 1), (2, 7, 3, 2), (0, 7, 3, 2)])
def test_find_min_pos(lower, upper, expected_pos, expected_value):
    values = [ 5, 3, 4, 2, 6, 7, 8, 9, 1, 10 ]

    result_pos = find_min_pos(values, lower, upper)

    assert result_pos == expected_pos
    assert values[result_pos] == expected_value
@pytest.mark.parametrize("lower, upper, expected_pos, expected_value",
                         [(0, 10, 9, 49), (2, 7, 5, 10), (0, 7, 1, 22)])
def test_find_max_pos(lower, upper, expected_pos, expected_value):
    values = [ 1, 22, 3, 4, 5, 10, 7, 8, 9, 49 ]

    result_pos = find_max_pos(values, lower, upper)

    assert result_pos == expected_pos
    assert values[result_pos] == expected_value
```

6.3.12 Solution 12: Array Split (★★★☆☆)

Say you have an array (or list) of arbitrary integers. The data structure must be reordered so that all values less than a special reference value are placed on the left. All values greater than or equal to the reference value are placed on the right. The ordering within the subranges is not relevant and may vary.

Examples

Input	Reference element	Sample result
[4, 7, 1, 20]	9	[1, 4, 7, **9**, 20]
[3, 5, 2]	7	[2, 3, 5, **7**]
[2, 14, 10, 1, 11, 12, 3, 4]	7	[2, 1, 3, 4, **7**, 14, 10, 11, 12]
[3, 5, 7, 1, 11, 13, 17, 19]	11	[1, 3, 5, 7, **11**, 11, 13, 17, 19]

Solution 12a: Array Split (★★☆☆☆)

Write function array_split(values, reference_element) to implement the functionality described above. In this first part of the exercise, it is allowed to create new data structures, such as lists.

Algorithm To split an array according to a reference element into two halves with values less than or greater than or equal to the reference value, you define two result lists called lesser and bigger_or_equal. Afterwards, you iterate through the array. Depending on the comparison of the current element with the reference element, you populate one of the two lists. Finally, you only need to combine the lists and the reference element into one result list.

```
def array_split(values, reference_element):
    lesser = []
    bigger_or_equal = []

    for current in values:
        if current < reference_element:
            lesser.append(current)
        else:
            bigger_or_equal.append(current)

    return lesser + [reference_element] + bigger_or_equal
```

Pythonic algorithm In the solution shown, the for loop with the if and else is stylistically somewhat disturbing. With list comprehensions, this could be implemented a bit nicer as follows. In this alternative, however, the lists are traversed twice.

```
def array_split_nicer(values, reference_element):
    lesser = [value for value in values
                if value < reference_element]

    bigger_or_equal = [value for value in values
                        if value >= reference_element]

    return lesser + [reference_element] + bigger_or_equal
```

Solution 12b: Array Split Inplace (★★★☆☆)

Write function array_split_inplace(values, reference_element) that implements the functionality described inside the source array (i.e., inplace). It is explicitly not desirable to create new data structures. To be able to include the reference element in the result, the creation of an array is allowed once for the result. Because this has to be returned, it is permitted to return a value for an inplace function; indeed, it operates only partially inplace here.

Algorithm After you perform the simpler version, which improves your understanding of the processes, dare to try the inplace version! Here you cannot use auxiliary data structures. Rather, you implement the logic by swapping elements several times. Two position markers indicate which elements are to be swapped. The first position marker is increased as long as you encounter smaller values than the reference element, starting from the beginning. You do the same with the position marker for the upper part. As long as the values are larger than or equal to the reference element, you decrease the position. Finally, you swap the two values at the index positions found, but only if the position markers have not yet crossed. When crossing, you find no more mismatching elements. The last thing to do is to integrate the reference element at the correct position based on the newly arranged values. Some care has to be taken if the sequence of the higher elements is empty.

```
def array_split_inplace(values, reference_element):
    low = 0
    high = len(values) - 1

    while low < high:
        while low < high and values[low] < reference_element:
            low += 1
```

```
    while high > low and values[high] >= reference_element:
        high -= 1

    if low < high:
        swap(values, low, high)

if len(values[high + 1:]) == 0:
    return values[:high + 1] + [reference_element]
else:
    return values[:high] + [reference_element] + values[high:]
```

Solution 12c: Array Split Quick Sort Partition (★★★☆☆)

For sorting according to Quick Sort, you need a partitioning functionality similar to the one just developed. However, often the foremost element of the array is used as the reference element.

Based on the two previously developed implementations that use an explicit reference element, your task is to create corresponding alternatives such as the functions array_split_qs(values) and array_split_qs_inplace(values).

Examples

Input	Reference element	Sample result
[**9**, 4, 7, 1, 20]	9	[1, 4, 7, **9**, 20]
[**7**, 3, 5, 2]	7	[2, 3, 5, **7**]
[**7**, 2, 14, 10, 1, 11, 12, 3, 4]	7	[2, 1, 3, 4, **7**, 14, 10, 11, 12]
[**11**, 3, 5, 7, 1, 11, 13, 17, 19]	11	[1, 3, 5, 7, **11**, 11, 13, 17, 19]

Algorithm 1 When the element at position 0 acts as reference element, this is the only thing that must be taken into account in the implementation. Thus, the processing starts at index 1.

```
def array_split_qs(values):
    reference_value = values[0]

    lesser = [values[i] for i in range(1, len(values))
             if values[i] < reference_value]
```

```
bigger_or_equal = [values[i] for i in range(1, len(values))
                   if values[i] >= reference_value]

return lesser + [reference_value] + bigger_or_equal
```

Algorithm 2 The inplace variant also works with two position markers as before and swaps elements several times if necessary. This is repeated as long as the position markers have not yet crossed. In this particular situation, you no longer find any unsuitable elements. The last thing to do is to move the reference element from its position 0 to the crossover point (i.e., the matching position).

```
def array_split_qs_inplace(values):
    reference_value = values[0]

    low = 1
    high = len(values) - 1
    while low < high:
        while values[low] < reference_value and low < high:
            low += 1
        while values[high] >= reference_value and high >= low:
            high -= 1

        if low < high:
            swap(values, low, high)

    # important for two elements with values 1, 2 = > then 1 would be
      pivot, do
        not swap!

    if reference_value > values[high]:
        swap(values, 0, high)
```

Please remember that this function works inplace (meaning it operates directly on the passed data) and therefore does not return a result.

Verification

Test the functionality as usual with the inputs from the introduction:

```
>>> values = [2, 14, 10, 1, 11, 12, 3, 4]
```

```
>>> array_split(values, 7)
[2, 1, 3, 4, 7, 14, 10, 11, 12]
```

```
>>> array_split_inplace(values, 7)
[2, 4, 3, 1, 7, 12, 10, 14]
```

Let's have a look at the Quick Sort variants in action:

```
>>> values2 = [7, 2, 14, 10, 1, 11, 3, 12, 4]
```

```
>>> array_split_qs(values2)
[2, 1, 3, 4, 7, 14, 10, 11, 12]
```

```
>>> array_split_qs_inplace(values2)
```

```
>>> values2
[1, 2, 4, 3, 7, 11, 10, 12, 14]
```

Due to the slightly different algorithm, the elements in the first variant remain in the order in which they appear in the original array. The inplace variants swap elements, and thus there is a reshuffle. However, all smaller values are still found to the left of the reference element and all larger ones to the right.

6.3.13 Solution 13: Minesweeper Board (★★★☆☆)

Chances are high that you've played Minesweeper in the past. To remind you, it's a nice little quiz game with a bit of puzzling. What is it about? Bombs are placed face down on a playfield. The player can choose any field on the board. If a field is uncovered, it shows a number. This indicates how many bombs are hidden in the neighboring fields. However, if you are unlucky, you hit a bomb field and lose the game. Your task is about initializing such a field and preparing it for a subsequent game.

Solution 13a (★★☆☆☆)

Write function place_bombs_randomly(width, height, probability) that creates a playfield specified in size via the first two parameters, randomly filled with bombs, respecting the probability from 0.0 to 1.0 passed in.

Example

The following is a playfield of size 16 × 7 with bombs placed randomly. Bombs are represented by asterisks (*) and spaces by dots (.).

```
* * * . * * . * . * * . * . . .
. * * . * . . * . * * . . . . .
. . * . . . . . . . . * * * *
. . . * . * * . * * . * * . . .
* * . . . . * . * . . * . . . *
. . * . . * . * * . . * . * * *
. * . * * . * . * * * . . * * .
```

Algorithm Placing bombs randomly distributed in a playfield works as follows. For each position, a random number generated with `random.random()` and a given probability are used to determine whether a bomb should be placed on the playfield. As a result, a suitable nested list is generated. Here, a peculiarity is found, namely the playfield extends in all directions by one position each, as is covered in the following practical tip.

```python
def place_bombs_randomly(width, height, probability):
    bombs = [[False for x in range(width + 2)] for y in range(height + 2)]

    for y in range(1, len(bombs) - 1):
        for x in range(1, len(bombs[0]) - 1):
            bombs[y][x] = random.random() < probability

    return bombs
```

NOTE: PLAYFIELD WITH BORDER

For many two-dimensional algorithms, it is necessary to perform special checks at the borders. In some cases, it is helpful to place a special artificial border of one position around the actual playfield. In particular, this often simplifies calculations with neighboring cells in all compass directions, as is the case here with the bombs. But you have to assign a neutral value to the border cells. Here this is simply the value 0. Sometimes, however, special characters like # can be used with `str`-based playfields.

Some calculations become easier with this artificial boundary cell. However, you must then note that the bounds range from 1 to `len()` - 1—an additional stumbling block to the treacherous off-by-one errors commonly made with arrays.

Verification

Let's omit explicit testing here because, on the one hand, you are dealing with random numbers, and a unit test does not directly make sense for this. On the other hand, the algorithm is quite simple and the functionality is tested indirectly later.

Solution 13b (★★★☆☆)

Write function `calc_bomb_count(bombs)` that computes the number of adjacent fields based on the bomb fields passed and returns a corresponding array.

Examples

A calculation for playfields of size 3 × 3 as well as size 5 × 5, including randomly distributed bombs, results in the following:

```
*  .  .        B  2  1        .  *  *  .  .        2  B  B  3  1
.  .  *   =>   1  3  B        *  .  *  *  .        B  6  B  B  1
.  .  *        0  2  B        *  *  .  .  .   =>   B  B  4  3  2
                             *  .  .  *  .        B  6  4  B  1
                             *  *  *  .  .        B  B  B  2  1
```

Algorithm To calculate the number of neighboring cells with bombs, you again consider each cell in turn. Here you take advantage of the special margin, so you don't have to do range checks or special handling. First, you initialize a two-dimensional array of appropriate size with a value of 0 as an assumption that there are no bombs in the neighborhood. If a cell represents a bomb, you use the value 9 as an indicator. If it does not contain one, you must check all eight neighboring cells to see if they are home to a bomb. In this case, the bomb counter is increased by one. The calculation is facilitated by the use of the already known enumeration for the compass directions and their delta values in the x- and y-directions.

```
def calc_bomb_count(bombs):
    max_y, max_x = get_dimension(bombs)
    bomb_count = [[0 for x in range(max_x)] for y in range(max_y)]

    for y in range(1, max_y - 1):
        for x in range(1, max_x - 1):
            if not bombs[y][x]:
                for current_dir in Direction:
                    dx, dy = current_dir.to_dx_dy()
                    if bombs[y + dy][x + dx]:
                        bomb_count[y][x] += 1
            else:
                bomb_count[y][x] = 9

    return bomb_count
```

For better comprehension, the enumeration Direction is shown here again:

```
from enum import Enum

class Direction(Enum):
    N = (0, -1)
    NE = (1, -1)
    E = (1, 0)
    SE = (1, 1)
    S = (0, 1)
    SW = (-1, 1)
    W = (-1, 0)
    NW = (-1, -1)

    def to_dx_dy(self):
        return self.value
```

Verification

To check the implementation, use the 3 × 3 distribution, but you must consider the boundary cells accordingly. Until now, modeling of bombs was based on a two-dimensional nested list of bool. Wouldn't it be more practical to work on graphical representations and have them convert appropriately? Let's consider this as a unit test.

```python
def create_bomb_array_and_expected():
    bombs1 = ["*..",
              "..*",
              "..*"]

    result1 = ["B21",
                "13B",
                "02B"]

    bombs2 = [".**..",
              "*.**.",
              "**...",
              "*..*.",
              "***.."]

    result2 = ["2BB31",
                "B6BB1",
                "BB432",
                "B64B1",
                "BBB21"]

    return [(to_bool_array(bombs1), to_int_array(result1)),
        (to_bool_array(bombs2), to_int_array(result2))]

@pytest.mark.parametrize("bombs, expected",
                          create_bomb_array_and_expected())
def test_calc_bomb_count(bombs, expected):
    result = calc_bomb_count(bombs)

    assert result == expected
```

Let's look again at the helper functions. First, you have a textual representation of the distribution of bombs, which is converted into the required array data structure using to_bool_array(). In doing so, you don't have to worry about generating the boundary fields. The helper function to_int_array() goes one step further and converts the textual digits into the corresponding int values and takes into account the representation of bombs as B specifically.

The helper functions look like this:

```python
# hiding the border field logic and conversion
def to_bool_array(bombs):
    width = len(bombs[0])
    height = len(bombs)

    result = [[False for _ in range(width + 2)] for _ in range(height + 2)]

    for y in range(height):
        for x in range(width):
            if bombs[y][x] == '*':
                result[y + 1][x + 1] = True

    return result

def to_int_array(values):
    width = len(values[0])
    height = len(values)

    result = [[0 for _ in range(width + 2)] for _ in range(height + 2)]
    for y in range(height):
        for x in range(width):
            current_char = values[y][x]
            if current_char == 'B':
                result[y + 1][x + 1] = 9
            else:
                result[y + 1][x + 1] = int(current_char)

    return result
```

HINT: READABILITY AND COMPREHENSIBILITY IN TESTING

These two helper functions enable the creation of test cases to be kept simple and understandable. This makes it more likely that someone will extend the tests. If writing unit tests is rather tedious or even difficult, hardly anyone will bother to extend them.

Solution 13c (★★☆☆☆)

Write function print_board(bombs, bomb_symbol, bomb_counts) that allows you to display a board as points and stars as well as numbers and B.

Example

The following is the above playfield of size 16 × 7 with all the calculated values for bomb neighbors:

```
B B B 4 B B 3 B 4 B B 3 B 1 0 0
3 B B 5 B 3 3 B 4 B B 4 3 4 3 2
1 3 B 4 3 3 3 3 4 4 4 4 B B B B
2 3 3 B 2 B B 4 B B 3 B B 4 4 3
B B 3 2 3 4 B 6 B 4 4 B 5 3 4 B
3 4 B 3 3 B 4 B B 5 4 B 4 B B B
1 B 3 B B 3 B 4 B B B 2 3 B B 3
```

Algorithm For rendering, you use position-based processing. Since you want to implement both an output based on the bool model and, if passed, the values of the number of bomb neighbors in this function, a few cases have to be provided in addition to the loops nested for the x-direction and the y-direction.

```python
def print_board(bombs, bomb_symbol, solution):
    for y in range(1, len(bombs) - 1):
        for x in range(1, len(bombs[0]) - 1):
            if bombs[y][x]:
                print(bomb_symbol, end=" ")
            elif solution is not None and len(solution) != 0:
                print(solution[y][x], end=" ")
            else:
                print(".", end=" ")
        print()
    print()
```

Verification

Let's combine the three functions to experience the functionality in its entirety:

```
>>> import random
>>> from enum import Enum

>>> bombs = place_bombs_randomly(16, 7, 0.4)

>> print_board(bombs, '*', None)
. * * * * . * . * . * . * * . . .
. . * . * * . . . * * * . . * *
. . * . . . * . * * * * . . . .
* . . * . . . * * * . * * . * .
. . * . * . . . . . . * * * . *
* . . . . * * * . . * . . * * .
* * * . * . * * * * . . . . . *
```

```
>>> solution = calc_bomb_count(bombs)

>>> print_board(bombs, 'B', solution)
1 B B B B 4 B 2 B 4 B 4 B B 3 2
1 4 B 6 B B 3 4 4 B B B 4 3 B B
1 3 B 4 3 3 B 4 B B B B 4 3 3 3
B 3 3 B 2 2 2 B B B 6 B B 4 B 2
2 3 B 3 B 3 4 4 4 3 4 B B B 5 B
B 5 3 4 3 B B B 4 3 B 3 4 B B 3
B B B 2 B 4 B B B B 2 1 1 2 3 B
```

Summary: What You Learned

Just like strings, arrays are basic building blocks in many programming languages. In Python, lists are often favored, since arrays are not nicely supported in the language. However, there is a valid alternative with NumPy, with which arrays can be easily defined and which can offer significant performance improvements compared to lists. Anyway, it is important to avoid tricky off-by-one errors. In this chapter, you created small helper functions that, when used appropriately, can make algorithms more understandable. For two-dimensional arrays or nested lists, you learned, among other things, how to model directions and how this helps fill areas with patterns. More challenging tasks were the spiral traversal as well as the deletion and filling of a Jewels or Minesweeper playfield.

This chapter concludes the treatment of essential Python language tools and data structures. Now you turn to more complex topics and start with advanced techniques for recursion.

PART II

More Advanced and Tricky Topics

## CHAPTER 7

Advanced Recursion

In this chapter, you will explore some advanced aspects around recursion. You'll start with the optimization technique called memoization. After that, you'll look at backtracking as a problem-solving strategy that relies on trial and error and tries out possible solutions. Although this is not optimal in terms of performance, it can keep various implementations comprehensible.

7.1 Memoization

In Chapter 3, you saw that recursion is feasible for describing many algorithms and calculations in an understandable and, at the same time, elegant way. However, you also noticed that recursion sometimes leads to many self calls, which can harm performance. This applies, for example, to the calculation of Fibonacci numbers or of Pascal's triangle. How can this problem be overcome?

For this purpose, there is a useful technique called ***memoization***. It follows the same ideas as the caching or buffering of previously calculated values. It avoids multiple executions by reusing already calculated results for subsequent actions.

7.1.1 Memoization for Fibonacci Numbers

Conveniently, memoization can often be easily added to an existing algorithm and only requires minimal modification. Let's do this for the calculation of Fibonacci numbers.

Let's briefly repeat the recursive definition of ***Fibonacci numbers***:

$$fib(n) = \begin{cases} 1, & n = 1 \\ 1, & n = 2 \\ fib(n-1) + fib(n-2), & \forall n > 2 \end{cases}$$

© Michael Inden 2022
M. Inden, *Python Challenges*, https://doi.org/10.1007/978-1-4842-7398-2_7

The recursive implementation in Python follows the mathematical definition exactly:

```python
def fib_rec(n):
    if n <= 0:
        raise ValueError("n must be >= 1")

    # recursive termination
    if n == 1 or n == 2:
        return 1

    # recursive descent
    return fib_rec(n - 1) + fib_rec(n - 2)
```

So how do you add memoization? In fact, it is not too difficult. You need a helper function that calls the actual calculation function, and most importantly, a data structure to store intermediate results. In this case, you use a dictionary that is passed to the computation function.

```python
def fibonacci_optimized(n):
    return fibonacci_memo(n, {})
```

In the original function, you surround the actual computation with the actions for memoization. For every computation step, you first look in the dictionary to see if a suitable result already exists and return it if it does. Otherwise, you execute the algorithm as before, with the minimal modification that you store the computation result in a variable, to be able to deposit it at the end suitably in the lookup dictionary.

```python
def fibonacci_memo(n, lookup_map):
    if n <= 0:
        raise ValueError("n must be > 0")

    # MEMOIZATION: check if there is a suitable pre-calculated result
    if n in lookup_map:
        return lookup_map.get(n)

    # normal algorithm with helper variable for storing the result
    result = 0

    if n == 1 or n == 2:
        # recursive termination
        result = 1
```

```
else:
    # recursive descent
    result = fibonacci_memo(n - 1, lookup_map) + \
             fibonacci_memo(n - 2, lookup_map)

# MEMOIZATION: store calculated result
lookup_map[n] = result

return result
```

Performance comparison If you run both variants for the fortieth Fibonacci number, the purely recursive variant on my iMac 4GHz delivers a result after about 25 seconds, but the calculation of the forty-seventh Fibonacci number takes over 800 seconds, which corresponds to about 13 minutes! With memoization, on the other hand, you receive a result for both after a few milliseconds.

Notes   It should be noted that there is a variant of the Fibonacci calculation that starts at the value 0. Then $fib(0) = 0$ holds as well as $fib(1) = 1$ and afterwards recursively $fib(n) = fib(n - 1) + fib(n - 2)$. This produces the same sequence of numbers as the initial definition, only with the value for 0 added.

Furthermore, there are the following points to consider:

- **Data type**: The calculated Fibonacci numbers can get huge quite quickly. Conveniently, the Python number types scale, so unlike other languages, it should not be necessary to define a special type yourself so soon if necessary.

- **Recursive termination**: For implementation purposes, it's worth considering recursive termination before processing with memoization. This would probably be minimally more performant, but then the algorithm can't be reformulated that clearly from the existing one. Especially if you are not familiar with memoization yet, the shown variant seems a bit more catchy.

7.1.2 Memoization for Pascal's Triangle

Pascal's triangle is defined recursively, as are the Fibonacci numbers:

$$pascal(row, col) = \begin{cases} 1, & row = 1 \text{ and } col = 1 \text{ (top)} \\ 1, & \forall row \in \{1, n\} \text{ and } col = 1 \\ 1, & \forall row \in \{1, n\} \text{ and } col = row \\ pascal(row - 1, col) + \\ pascal(row - 1, col - 1), & \text{otherwise (all other positions)} \end{cases}$$

Let's first look at the purely recursive implementation again:

```python
def pascal_rec(row, col):
    # recursive termination: top
    if col == 1 and row == 1:
        return 1

    # recursive termination: borders
    if col == 1 or col == row:
        return 1

    # recursive descent
    return pascal_rec(row - 1, col) + pascal_rec(row - 1, col - 1)
```

For the computation of Pascal's triangle by using memoization, the original algorithm hardly changes. You merely surround it with the accesses to the lookup dictionary and the storage:

```python
def pascal_optimized(row, col):
    return calc_pascal_memo(row, col, {})

def calc_pascal_memo(row, col, lookup_map):
    # MEMOIZATION
    key = (row, col)
    if key in lookup_map:
        return lookup_map[key]
```

```
result = 0
# recursive termination: top
if col == 1 and row == 1:
    return 1

# recursive termination: borders
if col == 1 or col == row:
    return 1
else:
    # recursive descent
    result = calc_pascal_memo(row - 1, col, lookup_map) + \
            calc_pascal_memo(row - 1, col - 1, lookup_map)

# MEMOIZATION
lookup_map[key] = result

return result
```

A closer look reveals that you cannot use a basic type like int or str for the key but rather need a more special variant consisting of a row and a column due to the two-dimensional layout. For this purpose, you use a tuple consisting of row and column.

Performance comparison To compare the performance, I chose a call with the parameters for line 36 and column 12. The purely recursive variant requires a rather long running time of about 80 seconds for the selected values on an iMac with 4GHz. The optimized variant completes after a few milliseconds.

Conclusion

For the two examples presented here, the purely recursive definition results in many self calls. Without memoization, they cause the same intermediate results to be calculated and discarded over and over again. This is unnecessary and costs performance.

Memoization is a remedy that is as simple as it is ingenious and efficient. Additionally, many problems may still be solved elegantly with the help of a recursive algorithm, but without the need to accept the disadvantages in terms of performance. All in all, memoization can often reduce the running time (very) significantly.

NOTE: BACKGROUND KNOWLEDGE ON MEMOIZATION

The term "memoization," which seems a bit strange, goes back to Donald Michie (https://en.wikipedia.org/wiki/Memoization). As described earlier, it is a technique to optimize the processing of computations by caching partial results. In such a way, nested calls with the same input can be accelerated significantly. However, for memoization to be used, the wrapped recursive functions must be *pure functions*. This means that such a function returns the same value if it is called with a particular input. In addition, these functions must be free of any side effects.

7.1.3 Memoization with Python On-Board Tools

You know that memoization leads to a vast speedup of recursive computations. When implemented directly according to the purely recursive definition, there is exponential growth for the Fibonacci numbers in running time. In combination with the implementation of memoization, you can achieve enormous speed gains. For this purpose, data from previous calculations are cached, and each call is first checked to see if a result is already available. You use a dictionary to store the data. The explicit wrapping and subsequent calling of the actual functionality can be programmed by hand. However, the whole thing has the following (cosmetic) disadvantages:

1. **Separation of concerns**: Application code and auxiliary code are slightly interwoven. Although the two are quite easy to separate visually, clarity and elegance are somewhat lost.

2. **Source code duplication**: Memoization is actually a cross-cutting concern that should be solved in a general way. If, on the other hand, a separate implementation is made in each case, careless errors may creep in—even if this is unlikely due to the low complexity.

Python permits memoization to be implemented with less effort and in a standardized way. You will briefly look at the following techniques:

- Memoization using a decorator

- Built-in memoization with lru_cache from the module functools

The nice thing about these variants is that to implement memoization, you don't mix the application code with the source code. Better yet, this allows you to provide memoization as a cross-cutting concern. The prerequisite is an import as follows:

```
import functools
```

Memoization with a Decorator

As for the manual implementation, you again use an additional function, here decorate_ with_memo(func), which defines a data store. In contrast to the manual implementation, a helper function helper implements the memoization here. For this purpose, a function is returned, which is identical to the function func but enriched with memoization, or more precisely, which retrieves or stores its results in the dictionary. Here is a variant that is closer to the completely manual implementation as well as a slightly modified one where memoization is less visible.

```
# hand knitted
def decorate_with_memo(func):
    lookup_map = dict()

    @functools.wraps(func)
    def helper(n):
        # MEMOIZATION: check if precalculated result exists
        if n in lookup_map:
            return lookup_map[n]

        result = func(n)

        # MEMOIZATION: store calculated result
        lookup_map[n] = result
        return result

    return helper

# memoization not so obvious
def decorate_with_memo_shorter_one_param(func):
    lookup_map = dict()

    @functools.wraps(func)
    def helper(n):
```

```
    if n not in lookup_map:
        lookup_map[n] = func(n)

    return lookup_map[n]

return helper
```

The example uses the concept of decorators, which is briefly introduced in Appendix B. In general, decorators work like aspect-oriented programming or proxies, wrapping the original functionality with some functionality of their own. Therefore, the original function is passed to the decorator, and the decorator returns a modified function.

NOTE: USABLE TYPES

Since you use a dictionary to manage data, the keys stored there must be immutable. Thus, the arguments may only use immutable types, such as numbers, strings, or tuples.

Decorator for Fibonacci numbers In Appendix B I explain how to use decorators for argument checks, leaving the actual function code unaffected. Therefore, the problem to be solved is reflected as closely as possible without special treatments.

With the knowledge gained, you can implement the memoization-optimized version as follows—the source code reflects the mathematical (recursive) definition. The cross-cutting concern of parameter checking and memoization are implemented separately as independent decorators.

```
@check_argument_is_positive_integer
@decorate_with_memo_shorter_one_param
def fib_rec(n):
    # recursive termination
    if n == 1 or n == 2:
        return 1

    # recursive descent
    return fib_rec(n - 1) + fib_rec(n - 2)
```

Decorator for Pascal's triangle Your memoization decorator has been designed so far to accept one parameter. But how do you proceed if you need to support two parameters for Pascal's triangle computation and possibly even more for other functionalities?

It would be awkward and time-consuming to define a decorator with a suitable number of parameters each time. Conveniently, in Python, parameters can be evaluated and passed as tuples. Thus, you can implement the decorator in a general manner with the parameters (*args) as follows:

```python
def decorate_with_memo_shorter(func):
    lookup_map = dict()

    @functools.wraps(func)
    def helper(*args):
        if args not in lookup_map:
            lookup_map[args] = func(*args)

        return lookup_map[args]

    return helper
```

Let's take a quick look at the usage for Pascal's triangle:

```python
@decorate_with_memo_shorter
def pascal_rec(row, col):
    # recursive termination: top
    if col == 1 and row == 1:
        return 1

    # recursive termination: borders
    if col == 1 or col == row:
        return 1

    # recursive descent
    return pascal_rec(row - 1, col) + pascal_rec(row - 1, col - 1)
```

Built-in Memoization with lru_cache from the functools Module

You have seen wrapping with a decorator before. By using a LRU cache (Least Recently Used) from the functools module, the whole thing can be written even more elegantly and shorter. Moreover, there is no longer the danger of erroneous calls because the memoization functionality is not realized by yourself.

LRU cache for Fibonacci numbers As usual, you use the calculation of Fibonacci numbers as an example. They are also used in the description of the module `functools` online (`https://docs.python.org/3/library/functools.html`), here minimally adapted. By marking a function with `@lru_cache`, the caching of previous calculation results can be activated. Here the number may be limited by the argument `maxsize`. By default, the value is 128. Specifying None makes the size unlimited but also disables the LRU functionality.

```
>>> @functools.lru_cache(maxsize=None)
... @check_argument_is_positive_integer
... def fib_rec(n):
...     if n == 1 or n == 2:
...         return 1
...
...     return fib_rec(n-1) + fib_rec(n-2)
```

Let's try a few things. With `cache_info()` it is possible to output information about the cache. This is done before calling the function and after the calculation.

```
>>> fib.cache_info()
CacheInfo(hits=0, misses=0, maxsize=None, currsize=0)
>>> [fib(n) for n in range(1, 19)]
[1, 1, 2, 3, 5, 8, 13, 21, 34, 55, 89, 144, 233, 377, 610, 987, 1597, 2584]
>>> fib.cache_info()
CacheInfo(hits=32, misses=18, maxsize=None, currsize=18)
```

LRU cache for Pascal's triangle Memoization can also be added to Pascal's triangle calculation very easily as follows:

```
@functools.lru_cache(maxsize=None)
def pascal_rec(row, col):
    # recursive termination: top
    if col == 1 and row == 1:
        return 1

    # recursive termination: borders
    if col == 1 or col == row:
        return 1

    # recursive descent
    return pascal_rec(row - 1, col) + pascal_rec(row - 1, col - 1)
```

7.2 Backtracking

Backtracking is a problem-solving strategy based on trial and error, and it investigates all possible solutions. When detecting an error, previous steps are reset, hence the name *backtracking*. The goal is to reach a solution step by step. When an error occurs, you try another path to the solution. Thus, potentially all possible (and therefore perhaps also a lot of) ways are followed. However, this also has a disadvantage, namely a rather long running time until the problem is solved.

To keep the implementation manageable, backtracking is often used in combination with recursion for the following problems:

- Solving the n-Queens Problem

- Finding a solution to a Sudoku puzzle

- Finding a way out of a maze given as a 2D array or nested lists

7.2.1 The n-Queens Problem

The n-Queens Problem is a puzzle to be solved on an n × n board. Queens (from the chess game) must be placed so that no two queens can beat each other according to the chess rules. Thus, other queens may not be placed on the same row, column, or diagonals. As an example, here is the solution for a 4 × 4 board, where the queens are symbolized by a Q (for queen):

```
- - - - - - - - -
|  |Q|  |  |
- - - - - - - - -
|  |  |  |Q|
- - - - - - - - -
|Q|  |  |  |
- - - - - - - - -
|  |  |Q|  |
- - - - - - - - -
```

Algorithm

You start with a queen in row 0 and position 0 (upper left corner). After each placement, a check is made to ensure that there are no collisions in the vertical and diagonal left and right directions upwards with already placed queens. A check downwards is not necessary because no queens can be placed there yet since the filling is done from top to bottom. This is also the reason why a check in the horizontal direction is not necessary.

Provided the position is valid, move to the next row, trying all positions from 0 to $n - 1$. This procedure is repeated until you have finally placed the queen in the last row. If there is a problem in positioning a queen, use backtracking: remove the last placed queen and try again at the next possible position. If the end of the row is reached without a solution, this is an invalid situation, and the preceding queen must also be placed again. You can observe that backtracking sometimes goes back up one row, in extreme cases up to the first row.

Backtracking by example Let's look at the steps to the solution, where on the horizontal level, some intermediate steps are partly omitted and invalid positions are marked with x:

```
----------------          ----------------          ----------------
 Q |   |   |               Q |   |   |               Q |   |   |
----------------          ----------------          ----------------
   |   |   |               x | x | Q |                 |   | Q |
----------------    =>    ----------------    =>    ----------------
   |   |   |                 |   |   |               x | x | x | x
----------------          ----------------          ----------------
   |   |   |                 |   |   |                 |   |   |
----------------          ----------------          ----------------
```

=> **Backtracking**

No correct placement of a queen in the second row can be found with a queen in the first row and second position. So, a solution is tried at the following position in the first row like so:

```
----------------                ----------------                ----------------
 Q |   |   |                     Q |   |   |                     Q |   |   |
----------------                ----------------                ----------------
 x | x | x | Q                     |   |   | Q                     |   |   | Q
----------------      =>         ----------------      =>         ----------------
   |   |   |                     x | Q |   |                       | Q |   |
----------------                ----------------                ----------------
   |   |   |                       |   |   |                     x | x | x | x
----------------                ----------------                ----------------
```

=> **Backtracking**

Even with the queen in the third position in the first row, no valid position for a queen in the second row can be found. So, you have to go back not only one row but two rows and start the search again with the queen in row zero in position one:

```
----------------        ----------------        ----------------        ----------------
   | Q |   |               | Q |   |               | Q |   |               | Q |   |
----------------        ----------------        ----------------        ----------------
 x | x | x | Q             |   |   | Q             |   |   | Q             |   |   | Q
----------------  =>     ----------------  =>     ----------------  =>     ----------------
   |   |   |               |   |   |             Q |   |   |             Q |   |   |
----------------        ----------------        ----------------        ----------------
   |   |   |               |   |   |               |   |   |             x | x | Q |
----------------        ----------------        ----------------        ----------------
```

=> **Solution found**

Notice that you arrive at a solution through a few trial-and-error steps.

In the following, you will now take a rough look at the implementation of the algorithm.

Implementation of backtracking You again subdivide the previously described algorithm for solving the n-Queens Problem into a couple of functions so that one subproblem can be solved at a time.

First, think about how you want to model the playfield. A list of lists as a two-dimensional data model offers itself formally. Here, a Q represents a queen, and a blank means an empty board. To initially create a blank board, write function initialize_board(). Then you call the actual recursive backtracking function solve_n_queens(), which determines the solution inplace on the data model. If one is found, the helper function returns True, otherwise False. To allow callers to evaluate easily, you return a tuple with a solution flag and the playfield.

```python
def solve_n_queens(size):
    board = initialize_board(size)

    # Start the recursive solution finding
    solved = solve_n_queens_helper(board, 0)

    return solved, board  # (solved, board)

def initialize_board(size):
    return [[' ' for col in range(size)] for row in range(size)]
```

Now let's get back to the main task of finding a solution using recursion and backtracking. As described, the algorithm proceeds row by row and then tries the respective columns.

```python
def solve_n_queens_helper(board, row):
    max_row, max_col = get_dimension(board)

    # recursive termination
    if row >= max_row:
        return True

    solved = False
    col = 0
    while col < max_col and not solved:
        if is_valid_position((board, col, row):
            place_queen(board, col, row)

            # recursive descent
            solved = __solve_n_queens_helper(board, row + 1)

            # Backtracking, if no solution found
            if not solved:
                remove_queen(board, col, row)

        col += 1

    return solved
```

To keep the algorithm as free of details and list accesses as possible as well as thereby understandable, you define two helper functions place_queen() und remove_queen().

```python
def place_queen(board, col, row):
    board[row][col] = 'Q'
```

```python
def remove_queen(board, col, row):
    board[row][col] = ' '
```

Additionally, I want to mention how to process modifications in algorithms with backtracking. As one variation (used here), modifications made before the recursion steps are reverted. As a second variation, you can pass copies during the recursion step and perform the modification in the copy. Then no undo or delete is necessary anymore.

For the sake of completeness, the implementation of the initialization of the playfield is shown here:

```python
def get_dimension(values2dim):
    if (isinstance(values2dim, list)):
        return (len(values2dim), len(values2dim[0]))

    if (isinstance(values2dim, np.ndarray)):
        return values2dim.shape

    raise Exception("unsupported type", type(values2dim)) '
```

What Is Still Missing in the Implementation? What Is the Next Step?

As an exercise in Section 7.3.9 you are left with the task of implementing the is_valid_ position(board, col, row) function. This is to check whether a playfield is valid. Due to the chosen algorithm of the line-by-line approach and because only one queen can be placed per line, possible collisions may be excluded only vertically and diagonally.

7.3 Exercises

7.3.1 Exercise 1: Towers of Hanoi (★★★☆☆)

In the Towers of Hanoi problem, there are three towers or sticks named A, B, and C. At the beginning, several perforated discs are placed on stick A in order of size, with the largest at the bottom. The goal is now to move the entire stack (i. e., all the discs) from A to C. The discs must be placed on the top of the stack. The goal is to move one disk at a time and never place a smaller disc below a larger one. That's why you need the helper stick B. Write function `solve_tower_of_hanoi(n)` that prints the solution on the console in the form of the movements to be executed.

Example

The whole thing looks something like Figure 7-1.

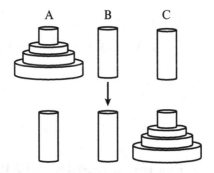

Figure 7-1. *Task definition for the Towers of Hanoi problem*

The following solution should be provided for three slices:

```
Tower Of Hanoi 3
A -> C
A -> B
C -> B
A -> C
B -> A
B -> C
A -> C
```

Bonus Create a console-based graphical format. For two slices, this would look something like this:

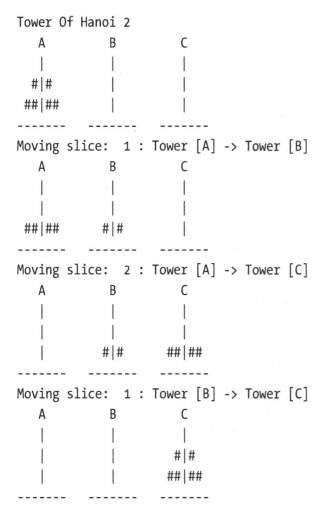

```
Tower Of Hanoi 2
    A           B           C
    |           |           |
  #|#           |           |
 ##|##          |           |
 -------     -------     -------
Moving slice:  1 : Tower [A] -> Tower [B]
    A           B           C
    |           |           |
    |           |           |
 ##|##        #|#           |
 -------     -------     -------
Moving slice:  2 : Tower [A] -> Tower [C]
    A           B           C
    |           |           |
    |           |           |
    |         #|#        ##|##
 -------     -------     -------
Moving slice:  1 : Tower [B] -> Tower [C]
    A           B           C
    |           |           |
    |           |         #|#
    |           |        ##|##
 -------     -------     -------
```

7.3.2 Exercise 2: Edit Distance (★★★★☆)

For two strings, compute how many changes they are—case-insensitive—apart; that is, how to transition one string to the other by applying any of the following actions one or more times:

- Add a character (+),

- Delete a character (−), or

- Change a character (↝).

Write function `edit_distance(str1, str2)` that tries the three actions character by character and checks the other part recursively.

Examples

The following modifications are required for the inputs shown:

Input 1	Input 2	Result	Actions
"Micha"	"Michael"	2	Micha $\underset{+e}{\rightarrow}$ Michae $\underset{+l}{\rightarrow}$ Michael
"rapple"	"tables"	4	rapple $\underset{+s}{\rightarrow}$ rapples $\underset{p\rightsquigarrow b}{\rightarrow}$ rapbles $\underset{-p}{\rightarrow}$ rables $\underset{r\rightsquigarrow t}{\rightarrow}$ tables

Bonus (★★★☆☆) Optimize Edit Distance with Memoization

7.3.3 Exercise 3: Longest Common Subsequence (★★★☆☆)

The previous exercise was about how many changes are needed to transform two given strings into each other. Another interesting problem is to find the longest common but not necessarily contiguous sequence of letters in two strings that occurs in two strings in the same sequence. Write function `lcs(str1, str2)` that recursively processes the strings from the back. In case of two parts of the same length, it uses the second one.

Examples

Input 1	Input 2	Result
"ABCE"	"ZACEF"	"ACE"
"ABCXY"	"XYACB"	"AB"
"ABCMIXCHXAEL"	"MICHAEL"	"MICHAEL"
"sunday-Morning"	"saturday-Night-Party"	"suday-ig"

Bonus Use Memoization for Longest Common Subsequence

7.3.4 Exercise 4: Way Out of a Labyrinth (★★★☆☆)

In this assignment, you are asked to find the way out of a maze. Assume a maze is given as a two-dimensional array or nested lists with walls symbolized by # and target positions (exits) symbolized by X. From any position, a path to all exits is supposed to be determined. If there are two exits in a row, only the first of the two has to be supplied. It is only allowed to move in the four compass directions, but not diagonally. Write function find_way_out(values, x, y) that logs each found exit with FOUND EXIT at ....

Example

A larger playfield with four target fields is shown below. The bottom figure shows each of the paths indicated by a dot (.). In between you see the logging of the found positions of the exits. For this example, the search starts from the upper left corner with coordinates x=1, y=1.ons of the exits. The search starts from the upper left corner with coordinates x=1, y=1.

```
##################################
# #         #    #    # #   X#X#
#  ##### #### ##   ##  # # ### #
#  ## #    # ## ## # #     # #
#   #  ###  # ## ##   #   ### # #
# #   ####    ## ##     ### # #
####   #     ####    # # #### #
######   #########  ##  # ### #
##     # X X####X # #  # ### ##
##################################
FOUND EXIT: x: 30, y: 1
FOUND EXIT: x: 17, y: 8
FOUND EXIT: x: 10, y: 8
```

```
###################################
#.#          #....#.....#  #...X#X#
#..##### ####.##...##..#  #.###  #
# .## #    #..## ## .# #..    # #
# ...#  ###..#.## ## ..#...### # #
# # ..####.....## ##.... ### # #
#### ..#... #### ....# # ####  #
#####...##########...##   # ### #
##     #..X X####X.# #  # ### ##
###################################
```

Based on the output, it is also clear that two of the target fields marked with X are not detected from the start position. One is the X at the very top right corner, which cannot be reached due to a missing link. The other is the lower middle X, which is behind another exit.

7.3.5 Exercise 5: Sudoku Solver (★★★★☆)

Write function solve_sudoku(board) that determines a valid solution, if any, for a partially initialized playfield passed as a parameter.

Example

A valid playfield with some blanks is shown here:

1	2		4	5		7	8	9
	5	6	7		9		2	3
7	8		1	2	3	4	5	6
2	1	4		6		8		7
3	6		8		7	2	1	4
	9	7		1	4	3	6	
5	3	1	6		2	9		8
6		2	9	7	8	5	3	1
9	7			3	1	6	4	2

This should be completed to the following solution:

1	2	3	4	5	6	7	8	9
4	5	6	7	8	9	1	2	3
7	8	9	1	2	3	4	5	6
2	1	4	3	6	5	8	9	7
3	6	5	8	9	7	2	1	4
8	9	7	2	1	4	3	6	5
5	3	1	6	4	2	9	7	8
6	4	2	9	7	8	5	3	1
9	7	8	5	3	1	6	4	2

7.3.6 Exercise 6: Math Operator Checker (★★★★☆)

This assignment is about a mathematically inclined puzzle. For a set of digits and another set of possible operators, you want to find all combinations that result in the desired value. The order of the digits cannot be changed. Still, it is possible to insert any operator from the possible operators between the digits, except before the first digit. Write function `all_combinations_with_value(n)` that determines all combinations that result in the value passed as parameter. Check this for the digits 1 to 9 and the operations + and −, and combining the digits. Start with function `find_all_combinations(values)`, which is passed the corresponding digits.

Examples

Let's consider two combinations only for the digits 1, 2, and 3:

$$1 + 2 + 3 = 6$$

$$1 + 23 = 24$$

In total, these digits allow the following different combinations to be formed:

Input	Result (`all_combinations()`)
[1, 2, 3]	{12−3=9, 123=123, 1+2+3=6, 1+2−3=0, 1−2+3=2, 1−23=−22, 1−2−3=−4, 1+23=24, 12+3=15}

Suppose you wanted to generate the value 100 from the given digits 1 to 9 and the set of available operators (+, −, and combining the digits). This is possible, for example, as follows:

$$1 + 2 + 3 - 4 + 5 + 6 + 78 + 9 = 100$$

In total, the following variants should be determined:

Input	Result (`allCombinationsWithValue()`)
100	[1+23−4+5+6+78−9, 123+4−5+67−89, 123−45−67+89, 12+3−4+5+67+8+9, 1+23−4+56+7+8+9, 12−3−4+5−6+7+89, 123−4−5−6−7+8−9, 1+2+34−5+67−8+9, 12+3+4+5−6−7+89, 123+45−67+8−9, 1+2+3−4+5+6+78+9]

7.3.7 Exercise 7: Water Jug Problem (★★★☆☆)

Let's say you have two jugs with capacities of m and n liters. Unfortunately, these jugs have no markings or indications of their fill level. The challenge is to measure x liters, where x is less than m or n. At the end of the procedure, one jug should contain x liters and the other should be empty. Write function `solve_water_jugs(size1, size2, desired_liters)`, which displays the solution on the console. If successful, it returns `True`, otherwise `False`.

Examples

For two jugs, one with a capacity of 4 liters and one with a capacity of 3 liters, you can measure 2 liters in the following way:

State	Action
Jug 1: 0/Jug 2: 0	Both jugs initial empty
Jug 1: 4/Jug 2: 0	Fill jug 1 (unnecessary, but due to the algorithm)
Jug 1: 4/Jug 2: 3	Fill jug 2
Jug 1: 0/Jug 2: 3	Empty jug 1
Jug 1: 3/Jug 2: 0	Pour jug 2 into jug 1

(continued)

State	Action
Jug 1: 3/Jug 2: 3	Fill jug 2
Jug 1: 4/Jug 2: 2	Pour jug 2 in jug 1
Jug 1: 0/Jug 2: 2	Empty jug 1
Solved	

On the other hand, measuring 2 liters is impossible with two jugs of 4 liters capacity each.

7.3.8 Exercise 8: All Palindrome Substrings (★★★★☆)

In this assignment, you want to determine for a given word whether it contains palindromes and, if so, which ones. Write recursive function `all_palindrome_parts_rec(input)` that determines all palindromes with at least two letters in the passed string and returns them sorted alphabetically.[1]

Examples

Input	Result
"BCDEDCB"	["BCDEDCB", "CDEDC", "DED"]
"ABALOTTOLL"	["ABA", "LL", "LOTTOL", "OTTO", "TT"]
"racecar"	["aceca", "cec", "racecar"]

Bonus Find the longest of all palindrome substrings. This time there is no requirement for maximum performance.

7.3.9 Exercise 9: The n-Queens Problem (★★★☆☆)

In the n-Queens Problem, n queens are to be placed on an n × n board in such a way that no two queens can beat each other according to chess rules. Thus, other queens must not be placed on the same row, column, or diagonal. To do this, extend the solution

---

[1] Of course, you are not interested in empty strings and single characters in this assignment, although of course, strictly speaking, they are also palindromes by definition.

shown in Section 7.2.1 and implement function `is_valid_position(board, col, row)`. Also write function `print_board(board)` to display the board as well as output the solution to the console.

Example

For a 4 × 4 playfield, there is the following solution, with the queens symbolized by a Q.

```
---------
| |Q| | |
---------
| | | |Q|
---------
|Q| | | |
---------
| | |Q| |
---------
```

7.4 Solutions

7.4.1 Solution 1: Towers of Hanoi (★★★☆☆)

In the Towers of Hanoi problem, there are three towers or sticks named A, B, and C. At the beginning, several perforated discs are placed on stick A in order of size, with the largest at the bottom. The goal is now to move the entire stack (i. e., all the discs) from A to C. The discs must be placed on the top of the stack. The goal is to move one disk at a time and never place a smaller disc below a larger one. That's why you need the helper stick B. Write function `solve_tower_of_hanoi(n)` that prints the solution on the console in the form of the movements to be executed.

Example

The whole thing looks something like Figure 7-2.

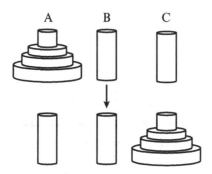

Figure 7-2. *Task definition for the Towers of Hanoi problem*

The following solution should be provided for three slices:

```
Tower Of Hanoi 3
A -> C
A -> B
C -> B
A -> C
B -> A
B -> C
A -> C
```

Algorithm The movement of the disks is implemented in function move_tower (n, source, helper, destination), which gets the number of slices to be moved, the initial source stick, the auxiliary stick, and the target stick. Initially you use n and 'A', 'B', and 'C' as initial parameters. The function move_tower() splits the problem into three smaller problems:

1. First, the tower, which is smaller by one slice, is transported from the source to the auxiliary stick.

2. Then, the last and largest slice is moved from the source to the target stick.

3. Finally, the remaining tower must be moved from the auxiliary to the target stick.

The action *move source to target* serves as a recursive termination when the height is 1. It gets a little tricky by swapping the source, target, and auxiliary stick during the actions.

```
def move_tower(n, source, helper, destination):
    if n == 1:
        print(source + " -> " + destination)
    else:
        # move all but last slice from source to auxiliary stick
        # destination thus becomes the new auxiliary stick
        move_tower(n - 1, source, destination, helper)

        # move the largest slice from source to target
        print(source + " -> " + destination)
        # move_tower(1, source, helper, destination); // unverständlicher

        # move tower reduced by one from auxiliary staff to target
        move_tower(n - 1, helper, source, destination)
```

In order to show fewer details, it is advisable to use the definition of the following function:

```
def solve_tower_of_hanoi(n):
    print("Tower Of Hanoi", n)
    move_tower(n, 'A', 'B', 'C')
```

To solve the problem, the function must be called with the desired number of slices, like this:

```
>>> solve_tower_of_hanoi(3)
Tower Of Hanoi 3
A -> C
A -> B
C -> B
A -> C
B -> A
B -> C
A -> C
```

HINT: RECURSION AS A TOOL

Although the problem sounds rather tricky at first, it can be solved quite easily with recursion. This assignment shows again that recursion is useful to reduce the difficulty by decomposing a problem into several smaller subproblems that are not so difficult to solve.

Bonus: Create a Console-Based Graphical Format

For two slices, this would look something like this:

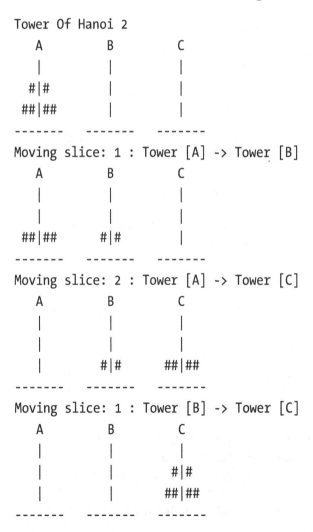

```
Tower Of Hanoi 2
    A           B           C
    |           |           |
  # | #         |           |
 ## | ##        |           |
-------     -------     -------
Moving slice: 1 : Tower [A] -> Tower [B]
    A           B           C
    |           |           |
    |           |           |
 ## | ##      # | #          |
-------     -------     -------
Moving slice: 2 : Tower [A] -> Tower [C]
    A           B           C
    |           |           |
    |           |           |
    |         # | #      ## | ##
-------     -------     -------
Moving slice: 1 : Tower [B] -> Tower [C]
    A           B           C
    |           |           |
    |           |         # | #
    |           |        ## | ##
-------     -------     -------
```

First, let's look at how the graphical output algorithm changes. This part for finding the solution remains absolutely the same. You just add class Tower to your implementation and an action that you pass as a lambda expression when solving. You modify the function solve_tower_of_hanoi(n) in such a way that three Tower objects are created there, and the desired number of disks is placed on the output tower accordingly.

```python
def solve_tower_of_hanoi_v2(n):
    print("Tower Of Hanoi", n)

    source = Tower("A")
    helper = Tower("B")
    destination = Tower("C")

    # Attention: reverse order: largest slice first
    for i in range(n, 0, -1):
        source.push(i)

    action = lambda: print_towers(n + 1, source, helper, destination)
    action()

    move_tower_v2(n, source, helper, destination, action)
```

The realization of move_tower_v2() only gets an action as another parameter. This allows an action to be executed at the recursive termination.

```python
def move_tower_v2(n, source, helper, destination, action):
    if n == 1:
        elem_to_move = source.pop()
        destination.push(elem_to_move)

        print("Moving slice:", elem_to_move, ":", source, "->", destination)
        action()
    else:
        move_tower_v2(n - 1, source, destination, helper, action)
        move_tower_v2(1, source, helper, destination, action)
        move_tower_v2(n - 1, helper, source, destination, action)
```

The class Tower Let's set about creating the Tower class, which uses a string for identification and a Stack to store the slices:

```
class Tower:
    def __init__(self, name):
        self.name = name
        self.__values = Stack()

    def __str__(self):
        return "Tower [" + self.name + "]"

    def push(self, item):
        self.__values.push(item)

    def pop(self):
        return self.__values.pop()
```

Additions in the class Stack You can reuse the class Stack built in Section 5.3.2, but you still have to add two functions:

```
def size(self):
    return len(self.__values)

def get_at(self, pos):
    return self.__values[pos]
```

Console output of towers In Chapter 4 on strings, you learned about a first variant for drawing towers in Section 4.2.16 in Exercise 16. Taking advantage of the knowledge gained there, you modify the implementation appropriately. First, you draw the top part of the tower with draw_top(). Then you draw the slices with draw_slices() and finally a bottom boundary line with draw_bottom().

```
    def print_tower(self, max_height):
        height = self.values.size() - 1

        visual = self.draw_top(max_height, height)
        visual += self.draw_slices(max_height, height)
        visual += self.draw_bottom(max_height)

        return visual

    def draw_top(self, max_height, height):
        visual = [" " * max_height + self.name + " " * max_height]
```

```
        for i in range(max_height - height - 1, 0, -1):
            visual.append(" " * max_height + "|" + " " * max_height)

        return visual

    def draw_slices(self, max_height, height):
        visual = []
        for i in range(height, -1, -1):
            value = self.values.get_at(i)
            padding = max_height - value

            visual.append(" " * padding + "#" * value + "|" +
                    "#" * value + " " * padding)

        return visual

    def draw_bottom(self, height):
        return ["-" * (height * 2 + 1)]
```

Output all towers Finally, you combine the output functionality in the following function to print the towers represented as three lists side by side:

```
def print_towers(max_height, source, helper, destination):
    tower1 = source.print_tower(max_height)
    tower2 = helper.print_tower(max_height)
    tower3 = destination.print_tower(max_height)

    for (a,b,c) in zip(tower1, tower2, tower3):
        print(a + "   " + b + "   " + c)
```

Verification

For testing, invoke the function. The output shows the correct operation:

```
>>> solve_tower_of_hanoi_v2(2)
Tower Of Hanoi 2
   A         B         C
   |         |         |
  #|#        |         |
 ##|##       |         |
-------   -------   -------
```

```
Moving slice: 1: Tower [A] -> Tower [B]
    A          B          C
    |          |          |
    |          |          |
  ##|##       #|#         |
  -------    -------    -------
Moving slice: 2: Tower [A] -> Tower [C]
    A          B          C
    |          |          |
    |          |          |
    |         #|#       ##|##
  -------    -------    -------
Moving slice: 1: Tower [B] -> Tower [C]
    A          B          C
    |          |          |
    |          |        #|#
    |          |       ##|##
  -------    -------    -------
```

7.4.2 Solution 2: Edit Distance (★★★★☆)

For two strings, compute how many changes they are—case-insensitive—apart; that is, how to transition one string to the other by applying any of the following actions one or more times:

- Add a character (+),

- Delete a character (−), or

- Change a character (~).

Write function edit_distance(str1, str2) that tries the three actions character by character and checks the other part recursively.

Examples

The following modifications are required for the inputs shown:

Input 1	Input 2	Result	Actions
"Micha"	"Michael"	2	Micha $\underset{+e}{\to}$ Michae $\underset{+l}{\to}$ Michael
"rapple"	"tables"	4	rapple $\underset{+s}{\to}$ rapples $\underset{p\leadsto b}{\to}$ rapbles $\underset{-p}{\to}$ rables $\underset{r\leadsto t}{\to}$ tables

Algorithm Let's start to consider how you can proceed here. If both strings match, then the edit distance is 0. If one of the two strings contains no (more) characters, then the distance to the other is the number of characters remaining in the other string. This means inserting the corresponding characters several times. This defines the recursive termination.

Otherwise, you check both strings from their beginning and compare them character by character. If they are the same, you go one position further towards the end of the string. If they are different, you check three different modifications:

1. **Insert**: Recursive call for the next characters

2. **Remove**: Recursive call for the next characters

3. **Replace**: Recursive call for the next characters

You examine three possible paths and then calculate the minimum from these three values.

Here's how you implement this:

```python
def edit_distance(str1, str2):
    return __edit_distance_helper(str1.lower(), str2.lower(),
                                  len(str1) - 1, len(str2) - 1)

def __edit_distance_helper(str1, str2, pos1, pos2):
    # recursive termination
    # if one of the strings is at the beginning and the other is
    # not yet, then take the length of the remaining string
    if pos1 < 0:
        return pos2 + 1
```

```
    if pos2 < 0:
        return pos1 + 1

    # check if the characters match and then advance to the next one
    if str1[pos1] == str2[pos2]:
        # recursive descent
        return __edit_distance_helper(str1, str2, pos1 - 1, pos2 - 1)
    else:
        # recursive descent: check for insert, delete, change
        insert_in_first = __edit_distance_helper(str1, str2, pos1,
        pos2 - 1)
        delete_in_first = __edit_distance_helper(str1, str2, pos1 - 1,
        pos2)
        change = __edit_distance_helper(str1, str2, pos1 - 1, pos2 - 1)

        # minimum from all three variants + 1
        return 1 + min(insert_in_first, delete_in_first, change)
```

Verification

For testing, you use the following inputs, which show the correct functionality:

```
@pytest.mark.parametrize("value1, value2, expected",
                         [("Micha", "Michael", 2),
                          ("rapple", "tables", 4)])
def test_edit_distance(value1, value2, expected):
    result = edit_distance(value1, value2)

    assert result == expected
```

Performance Test You also want to check the performance—because it is only a rough classification that matters, no sophisticated profiling is needed here, but the accuracy of time.process_time() is sufficient:

```
def main():
    inputs_tuples = [["Micha", "Michael"],
                     ["rapple", "tables"],
                     ["sunday-Morning", "saturday-Night"],
                     ["sunday-Morning-Breakfast", "saturday-Night-Party"]]
```

```python
for inputs in inputs_tuples:
    start = time.process_time()
    result = edit_distance(inputs[0], inputs[1])
    end = time.process_time()

    print(inputs[0] + " -> " + inputs[1] + " edits:", result)
    print("editDistance() took %.2f ms" % ((end - start) * 1000))
```

If you run the above lines with (a lot of) patience, you get approximately the following output. In fact, I stopped the last calculation after a few minutes, which is why it is not shown here.

```
Micha -> Michael edits: 2
editDistance() took 0.26 ms
rapple -> tables edits: 4
editDistance() took 0.35 ms
sunday-Morning -> saturday-Night edits: 10
editDistance() took 137443.89 ms
```

The running times increase significantly the more the two inputs differ. So how can you make it work better? The solution of the bonus task shows this.

Bonus: Optimize Edit Distance with Memoization (★★★☆☆)

At the beginning of the chapter, I described memoization as a technique and mentioned that one often uses a dictionary as a cache—so also here:

```python
def edit_distance_optimized(str1, str2):
    return __edit_distance_memo(str1.lower(), str2.lower(),
                                len(str1) - 1, len(str2) - 1, {})

def __edit_distance_memo(str1, str2, pos1, pos2, values):
    # recursive termination
    # if one of the strings is at the beginning and the other one
    # not yet, then take the length of the remaining string
    if pos1 < 0:
        return pos2 + 1
    if pos2 < 0:
        return pos1 + 1
```

```
# MEMOIZATION
if (pos1, pos2) in values:
    return values.get((pos1, pos2))

result = 0
# check if the characters match and then advance to the next one
if str1[pos1] == str2[pos2]:
    # recursive descent
    result = __edit_distance_memo(str1, str2, pos1 - 1, pos2 - 1, values)
else:
    # recursive descent: check for insert, delete, change
    insert = __edit_distance_memo(str1, str2, pos1, pos2 - 1, values)
    delete = __edit_distance_memo(str1, str2, pos1 - 1, pos2, values)
    change = __edit_distance_memo(str1, str2, pos1 - 1, pos2 - 1, values)

    # minimum from all three variants + 1
    result = 1 + min(insert_in_first, delete_in_first, change)

# MEMOIZATION
values[(pos1, pos2)] = result
```

Suppose you perform the same checks as before. Even with the last calculation of the Edit Distance of 16, only a minimum running time of less than one millisecond can be determined.

Using the memoization decorator In Section 7.1.3, you learned how to add memoization by using decorators to recursive functions to optimize running time.

For both the calculation of Fibonacci numbers and Pascal's triangle, it felt natural to annotate the decorator directly to the function calling itself. However, for Edit Distance, you have to think a bit. Here you have a two-step procedure, and it is not the initial function that must be annotated, but the one that performs the actual calculation.

```
# @decorate_with_memo_shorter
def edit_distance(str1, str2):
    return __edit_distance_helper(str1.lower(), str2.lower(),
                                  len(str1) - 1, len(str2) - 1)

@decorate_with_memo_shorter
def __edit_distance_helper(str1, str2, pos1, pos2):
    ....
```

Let's recap: An initial parameterization is done by the construct with the helper function. For all calls to edit_distance_helper(), the two inputs str1 and str2 remain unchanged. The variance is in the positions. Therefore, in the manual implementation, the key in the dictionary consists only of the positions. However, the universal variant cannot distinguish this and therefore uses a key consisting of all four parameter values.

7.4.3 Solution 3: Longest Common Subsequence (★★★☆☆)

The previous exercise was about how many changes are needed to transform two given strings into each other. Another interesting problem is to find the longest common but not necessarily contiguous sequence of letters in two strings that occurs in two strings in the same sequence. Write function lcs(str1, str2) to recursively process the strings from the back. In case of two parts of the same length, it uses the second one.

Examples

Input 1	Input 2	Result
"ABCE"	"ZACEF"	"ACE"
"ABCXY"	"XYACB"	"AB"
"ABCMIXCHXAEL"	"MICHAEL"	"MICHAEL"
"sunday-Morning"	"saturday-Night-Party"	"suday-ig"

Algorithm You move from the back to the front. If the characters match, the character is included in the result. If the characters differ, the check has to be repeated recursively for the strings shortened by one character.

```
def lcs(str1, str2):
    return __lcs_helper(str1, str2, len(str1) - 1, len(str2) - 1)

def __lcs_helper(str1, str2, pos1, pos2):
    # recursive termination
    if pos1 < 0 or pos2 < 0:
        return ""
```

```python
# are the characters the same?
if str1[pos1] == str2[pos2]:
    # recursive descent
    return __lcs_helper(str1, str2, pos1 - 1, pos2 - 1) + str1[pos1]
else:
    # otherwise take away one of both letters and try it
    # again, but neither letter belongs in the result
    lcs1 = __lcs_helper(str1, str2, pos1, pos2 - 1)
    lcs2 = __lcs_helper(str1, str2, pos1 - 1, pos2)

    return lcs1 if len(lcs1) > len(lcs2) else lcs2
```

Modified algorithm Alternatively, you can run from front to back until the end of the strings is reached. Interestingly, the same results are almost always produced because with the variant from the end, only for the second input combination, you get XY instead of AB as a result.

In this variant, if the letters are the same, you have to add them in front. In addition, the skipping of non-matching characters must now be simulated by increasing the respective position. All in all, the implementation changes as follows:

```python
def lcs_from_start(str1, str2):
    return __lcs__from_start_helper(str1, str2, 0, 0)

def __lcs__from_start_helper(str1, str2, pos1, pos2):
    #  recursive termination: one input is a the end
    if pos1 >= len(str1) or pos2 >= len(str2):
        return ""

    # are both character the same?
    if str1[pos1] == str2[pos2]:
        # recursive descent
        return str1[pos1] + \
                __lcs__from_start_helper(str1, str2, pos1 + 1, pos2 + 1)
    else:
        # otherwise take away one of both letters and try it
        # again, but neither letter belongs in the result
        lcs1 = __lcs__from_start_helper(str1, str2, pos1, pos2 + 1)
        lcs2 = __lcs__from_start_helper(str1, str2, pos1 + 1, pos2)

        return lcs1 if  len(lcs1) > len(lcs2) else lcs2
```

Verification

For testing, you use the following inputs, which show the correct operation:

```python
@pytest.mark.parametrize("value1, value2, expected",
                         [("ABCE", "ZACEF", "ACE"),
                          ("ABCXY", "XYACB", "AB"),
                          ("ABCMIXCHXAEL", "MICHAEL", "MICHAEL")])
def test_lcs(value1, value2, expected):
    result = lcs(value1, value2)

    assert result == expected
```

In the accompanying project, for the sake of completeness, you also test the variant with the LCS determination from the start (not shown here).

Performance test Again, you want to look at the performance. Here it is also true that `time.process_time()` is sufficient for classification.

```python
def main():
    inputs_tuples = [["ABCMIXCHXAEL", "MICHAEL"],
                     ["sunday-Morning", "saturday-Night-Party"],
                     ["sunday-Morning-Wakeup", "saturday-Night"]]

    for inputs in inputs_tuples:
        start = time.process_time()
        result = lcs(inputs[0], inputs[1])
        end = time.process_time()

        print(inputs[0] + " -> " + inputs[1] + " lcs:", result)
        print("lcs() took %.2f ms" % ((end - start) * 1000))
```

Measure the following execution times (they will vary slightly for you):

```
ABCMIXCHXAEL -> MICHAEL lcs: MICHAEL
lcs() took 0.03 ms
sunday-Morning -> saturday-Night-Party lcs: suday-ig
lcs() took 141523.38 ms
sunday-Morning-Wakeup -> saturday-Night lcs: suday-ig
lcs() took 280070.26 ms
```

Bonus: Use Memoization for Longest Common Subsequence

This results in long running times for more significant differences in the two inputs since many possible subsequences exist. Therefore, pure recursion is not performant. So how do you do it better? Again, you use memoization for performance optimization. This time you use two-dimensional nested lists of strings for data storage.

```python
def lcs_optimized(str1, str2):
    values = [[None for _ in range(len(str2))] for _ in range(len(str1))]

    return __lcs_with_memo(str1, str2, len(str1) - 1, len(str2) - 1, values)
```

The actual implementation uses memoization as follows:

```python
def __lcs_with_memo(str1, str2, pos1, pos2, values):
    # recursive termination
    if pos1 < 0 or pos2 < 0:
        return ""

    # MEMOIZATION
    if values[pos1][pos2] is not None:
        return values[pos1][pos2]

    lcs = ""

    # are the characters the same?
    if str1[pos1] == str2[pos2]:
        # recursive descent
        lcs = __lcs_with_memo(str1, str2, pos1 - 1, pos2 - 1, values) + \
            str1[pos1]
    else:
        # otherwise take away one of both letters and try it
        # again, but neither letter belongs in the result
        lcs1 = __lcs_with_memo(str1, str2, pos1, pos2 - 1, values)
        lcs2 = __lcs_with_memo(str1, str2, pos1 - 1, pos2, values)

        lcs = lcs1 if len(lcs1) > len(lcs2) else lcs2

    # MEMOIZATION
    values[pos1][pos2] = lcs

    return lcs
```

With this optimization, the running times can be reduced to a few milliseconds. For evaluation, start the module EX03_LCS_TIMING_MEMO.PY and compare your execution times with these values:

```
ABCMIXCHXAEL -> MICHAEL lcs: MICHAEL
lcs_optimized() took 0.03 ms
sunday-Morning -> saturday-Night-Party lcs: suday-ig
lcs_optimized() took 0.21 ms
sunday-Morning-Wakeup -> saturday-Night lcs: suday-ig
lcs_optimized() took 0.31 ms
```

Use of the memoization decorator As already described for Edit Distance, the two-step procedure of LCS requires you to annotate not the initial function but the one that performs the actual computation:

```
# @decorate_with_memo_shorter
def lcs(str1, str2):
    return __lcs_helper(str1, str2, len(str1) - 1, len(str2) - 1)

@decorate_with_memo_shorter
def __lcs_helper(str1, str2, pos1, pos2):
    ....
```

7.4.4 Solution 4: Way Out of a Labyrinth (★★★☆☆)

In this assignment, you are asked to find the way out of a maze. Assume a maze is given as a two-dimensional array or nested lists with walls symbolized by # and target positions (exits) symbolized by X. From any position, a path to all exits is supposed to be determined. If there are two exits in a row, only the first of the two has to be supplied. It is only allowed to move in the four compass directions, but not diagonally. Write function find_way_out(values, x, y) that logs each found exit with FOUND EXIT at ....

Example

A larger playfield with four target fields is shown below. The bottom part shows each of the paths indicated by a dot (.). In between you see the logging of the found positions of the exits. For this example, the search starts from the upper left corner with coordinates x=1, y=1.

```
####################################
# #          #    #     #  #   X#X#
#  ##### #### ##   ##   #  # ###  #
#  ## #    #  ## ##  #  #      # #
#    #  ###  # ## ##   #    ### # #
# #   ####    ##  ##      ###  # #
####   #      ####     #  # ####  #
######    #########    ##   # ###  #
##      #  X X####X # #   # ###  ##
####################################
FOUND EXIT: x: 30, y: 1
FOUND EXIT: x: 17, y: 8
FOUND EXIT: x: 10, y: 8
####################################
#.#          #....#.....#  #...X#X#
#..##### ####.##...##..#  #.###  #
# .## #    #..## ## .# #..    # #
# ...#  ###..#.## ##  ..#...### # #
# # ..####.....## ##.... ### # #
#### ..#...  #### ....#  # ####  #
######...#########...##   # ###  #
##      #..X X####X.# #  # # ### ##
####################################
```

Based on the outputs, it is also clear that two of the target fields marked with X are not detected from the start position. One is the X at the very top right corner, which cannot be reached due to a missing link. The other is the lower middle X, which is behind another exit.

Algorithm The algorithm for finding a way out of a labyrinth checks whether there is a way in the four compass directions, starting from the current position. To do this, neighboring fields that have already been visited are marked with the . character, just as you would do in reality with small stones, for example. The trial and error continues until you come to a X as a solution, a wall in the form of a #, or an already visited field (marked by .). If there is no possible direction left for a position, you use backtracking, resume the last chosen path, and try the remaining paths from there. This is implemented as follows:

```
def find_way_out(values, x, y):
    if x < 0 or y < 0 or x > len(values[0]) or y >= len(values):
        return False

    # recursive termination
    if get_at(values, x, y) == 'X':
        print("FOUND EXIT: x: {}, y: {}".format(x, y))
        return True

    # wall or already visited?
    if get_at(values, x, y) in '#.':
        return False

    # recursive descent
    if get_at(values, x, y) == ' ':
        # mark as visited
        values[y][x] = '.'

        # try all 4 cardinal directions
        up = find_way_out(values, x, y - 1)
        left = find_way_out(values, x + 1, y)
        down = find_way_out(values, x, y + 1)
        right = find_way_out(values, x - 1, y)

        found_a_way = up or left or down or right

        # backtracking because no valid solution
        if not found_a_way:
            values[y][x] = ' '    # wrong path, thus delete field marker

        return found_a_way

    raise ValueError("wrong char in labyrinth")
```

Note that you use the natural alignment of x and y coordinates in the functions. Still, when accessing the array or nested lists, the order is [y][x] because you are working in rows, as discussed in the introductory section of the chapter on arrays in Section 6.1.2.

Verification

To try it out, you define the maze from the introduction. Next, you call the function find_
way_out(), which logs the previously shown exits from the maze and finally visualizes
the ways with dots (.). Here you use a version of print_array() that leaves no white
space between characters to make the maze more recognizable.

```
def main():
    world_big = [list("###################################"),
                 list("# #            #    #      #  #    X#X#"),
                 list("#   ##### #### ##    ##   #   # ###   #"),
                 list("#   ## #    #  ## ## #  #      # #"),
                 list("#     #  ###  # ## ##    #    ### # #"),
                 list("# #    ####     ## ##       ###  # #"),
                 list("####    #      ####  ####  # ####   #"),
                 list("######    #########    ##   # ###   #"),
                 list("##      #  X X####X # #   # # ###   ##"),
                 list("###################################")]

    print_array(world_big)
    if find_way_out(world_big, 1, 1):
        print_array(world_big)
```

Alternative

The implementation shown nicely prepares the paths to the target fields graphically.
However, it has two minor disadvantages. On the one hand, it breaks off directly when an
exit is encountered and thus does not find an exit behind it. On the other hand, if there
are several paths to a target field, the program also logs the finding of an exit several
times. The latter could be solved quite easily by collecting all solution paths in a set.

   If you want to find all reachable exits, it is possible to modify the function shown
before so that visited fields are marked with a #. However, this way, the field is quite filled
up at the end and does not show the way anymore, which was an advantage of the initial
variant.

```
def find_way_out_v2(board, x, y):
    if board[y][x] == '#':
        return False
```

```
found = board[y][x] == 'X'
if found:
    print("FOUND EXIT: x: {}, y: {}".format(x, y))

board[y][x] = '#'

right = find_way_out_v2(board, x + 1, y)
left = find_way_out_v2(board, x - 1, y)
down = find_way_out_v2(board, x, y + 1)
up = find_way_out_v2(board, x, y - 1)

return found or right or left or down or up
```

Although the playing field is unrecognizable after that, four exits are found:

```
FOUND EXIT: x: 10, y: 8
FOUND EXIT: x: 12, y: 8
FOUND EXIT: x: 30, y: 1
FOUND EXIT: x: 17, y: 8
```

7.4.5 Solution 5: Sudoku Solver (★★★★☆)

Write function solve_sudoku(board) that determines a valid solution, if any, for a partially initialized playfield passed as a parameter.

Example

A valid playfield with some blanks is shown here:

1	2		4	5		7	8	9
	5	6	7		9		2	3
7	8		1	2	3	4	5	6
2	1	4		6		8		7
3	6		8		7	2	1	4
	9	7		1	4	3	6	
5	3	1	6		2	9		8
6		2	9	7	8	5	3	1
9	7			3	1	6	4	2

This should be completed to the following solution:

1	2	3	4	5	6	7	8	9
4	5	6	7	8	9	1	2	3
7	8	9	1	2	3	4	5	6
2	1	4	3	6	5	8	9	7
3	6	5	8	9	7	2	1	4
8	9	7	2	1	4	3	6	5
5	3	1	6	4	2	9	7	8
6	4	2	9	7	8	5	3	1
9	7	8	5	3	1	6	4	2

Algorithm To solve Sudoku, you use backtracking. As with other backtracking problems, Sudoku can be solved by step-by-step trial and error. In this case, that means trying different numbers for each of the empty squares. According to the Sudoku rules, the current digit must not already exist horizontally, vertically, or in a 3 × 3 block. If you find a valid value assignment, you can continue recursively at the next position to test whether you arrive at a solution. If none is found, then you try the procedure with the next digit. However, if none of the digits from 1 to 9 lead to a solution, you need backtracking to examine other possible paths to the solution.

You proceed as follows in the implementation:

1. Check if all rows have been processed; then you have a solution.

2. Find the next empty field. To do this, skip all fields that are already filled. This can also change lines.

3. If no empty field exist until the last row, you have found the solution.

4. Otherwise you try out the digits from 1 to 9.

    a. Is there a conflict? Then you have to try the next digit.

    b. The digit is a possible candidate. You call your function recursively for the following position (next column or even next row).

    c. If the recursion returns False, this digit does not lead to a solution and you use backtracking.

```python
def solve_sudoku(board):
    return __solve_sudoku_helper(board, 0, 0)
```

```python
def __solve_sudoku_helper(board, start_row, start_col):
    # 1) check if all rows have been processed, then you have a solution.
    if start_row > 8:
        return True

    row = start_row
    col = start_col

    # 2) skip fields with numbers until you reach the next empty field
    while board[row][col] != 0:
        col += 1
        if col > 8:
            col = 0
            row += 1
            # 3) already processed all lines?
            if row > 8:
                return True

    solved = False
    # 4) try for the current field all digits from 1 to 9 through
    for num in range(1, 10):
        board[row][col] = num

        # 4a) check if the whole field with the digit is still valid
        if is_valid_position(board):

            # 4b) recursive descent for the following field
            if col < 8:
                # recursive descent: next field in x-direction
                solved = __solve_sudoku_helper(board, row, col + 1)
            else:
                # recursive descent: next field in new line
                solved = __solve_sudoku_helper(board, row + 1, 0)

            # 4c) backtracking if recursion is not successful
            if not solved:
                # backtracking: no solution found
                board[row][col] = 0
```

```
        else:
            return True
    else:
        # try next digit
        board[row][col] = 0

    return False

def is_valid_position(board):
    return check_horizontally(board) and \
           check_vertically(board) and \
           check_boxes(board)
```

Looking at this implementation, you might already doubt whether this variant is really optimal, even without knowing the details of the helper functions shown in the following. Why? You keep checking the entire playfield for validity at every step, and even worse, doing that in combination with backtracking! I'll go into this in more detail later.

Let's first consider the three functions check_horizontally(board), check_vertically(board), and check_boxes(board). You implemented them in Exercise 9 in Section 6.3.9. They are shown again here for completeness:

```
def check_horizontally(board):
    for row in range(9):
        # collect all values of a row in a list
        row_values = [board[row][x] for x in range(9)]

        if not all_desired_numbers(row_values):
            return False

    return True

def check_vertically(board):
    for x in range(9):
        # collect all values of a column in a list
        column_values = [board[row][x] for row in range(9)]

        if not all_desired_numbers(column_values):
            return False

    return True
```

```
def check_boxes(board):
    for y_box in range(3):
        for x_box in range(3):
            box_values = collect_box_values(board, y_box, x_box)

            if not all_desired_numbers(box_values):
                return False

    return True
```

The following auxiliary functions still play an important role:

```
def collect_box_values(board, y_box, x_box):
    box_values = [ ]

    for y in range(3):
        for x in range(3):
            real_y = y_box * 3 + y
            real_x = x_box * 3 + x

            box_values.append(board[real_y][real_x])

    return box_values

def all_desired_numbers(all_collected_values):
    relevant_values = list(all_collected_values)

    # remove empty fields
    relevant_values = remove_all_occurences(relevant_values, 0)

    # check that there are no duplicates
    values_set = set(relevant_values)

    if len(relevant_values) != len(values_set):
        return False

    # only 1 to 9?
    return {1, 2, 3, 4, 5, 6, 7, 8, 9}.issuperset(values_set)

def remove_all_occurences(values, val):
    return [value for value in values if value != val]
```

```python
def print_array(values):
    for y in range(len(values)):
        for x in range(len(values[y])):
            print(values[y][x], end=" ")

        print()
```

Verification

Test this implementation with the example from the introduction:

```python
def main():
    board = [[1, 2, 0, 4, 5, 0, 7, 8, 9],
             [0, 5, 6, 7, 0, 9, 0, 2, 3],
             [7, 8, 0, 1, 2, 3, 4, 5, 6],
             [2, 1, 4, 0, 6, 0, 8, 0, 7],
             [3, 6, 0, 8, 9, 7, 2, 1, 4],
             [0, 9, 7, 0, 1, 4, 3, 6, 0],
             [5, 3, 1, 6, 0, 2, 9, 0, 8],
             [6, 0, 2, 9, 7, 8, 5, 3, 1],
             [9, 7, 0, 0, 3, 1, 6, 4, 2]]
    if solve_sudoku(board):
        print("Solved!")
    print_array(board)
```

This provides the following result:

```
Solved!
1 2 3 4 5 6 7 8 9
4 5 6 7 8 9 1 2 3
7 8 9 1 2 3 4 5 6
2 1 4 3 6 5 8 9 7
3 6 5 8 9 7 2 1 4
8 9 7 2 1 4 3 6 5
5 3 1 6 4 2 9 7 8
6 4 2 9 7 8 5 3 1
9 7 8 5 3 1 6 4 2
```

The solution is displayed within a few fractions of a second. So far, everything has worked really well. But what happens if the given playfield contains hardly any digits but lots of empty fields?

Playfields with more blanks When you tackle the challenge of trying to solve playfields with only a few given digits, there are many variations to be tried and a lot of backtracking comes into play. Suppose you wanted to solve something like the following playfield:

```
board2 = [
    [6, 0, 2, 0, 5, 0, 0, 0, 0],
    [0, 0, 0, 0, 0, 4, 0, 3, 0],
    [0, 0, 0, 0, 0, 0, 0, 0, 0],
    [4, 3, 0, 0, 0, 8, 0, 0, 0],
    [0, 1, 0, 0, 0, 0, 2, 0, 0],
    [0, 0, 0, 0, 0, 0, 7, 0, 0],
    [5, 0, 0, 2, 7, 0, 0, 0, 0],
    [0, 0, 0, 0, 0, 0, 0, 8, 1],
    [0, 0, 0, 6, 0, 0, 0, 0, 0],
]
```

In principle, this is already possible with your algorithm, but it takes several minutes. Although this is quite long, you probably couldn't solve difficult puzzles by hand in this time span—but with the computer, it should be even faster. So what can you improve?

Reasonable Optimizations

Idea 1: Optimization of the check Checking the entire playfield for validity in every step is neither useful, necessary, nor performant. As an optimization, you modify the check so that only a single column, row, and the relevant box are checked at a time. To do this, you first modify the function is_valid_position() slightly so that it receives a column and row as parameters:

```
def is_valid_position(board, row, col):
    return check_single_horizontally(board, row) and \
           check_single_vertically(board, col) and \
           check_single_box(board, row, col)
```

Then you create specific test methods such as the following:

```
def check_single_horizontally(board, row):
    column_values = [board[row][col] for col in range(9)]

    return all_desired_numbers(column_values)

def check_single_vertically(board, col):
    row_values = [board[row][col] for row in range(9)]

    return all_desired_numbers(row_values)
```

This optimization results in running times in the range of a few seconds—between 20 and 50 seconds for complicated playfields. This is already much better, but it can still be much more performant.

Idea 2: More clever testing If you look at the processes, you notice that you try all digits—this violates a bit of common sense. Wouldn't it make more sense to only use potentially valid paths, and to do so, check in advance whether the current digit is even usable in the context? You can then directly exclude all those digits that already exist in a row, column, or box. To do this, you need to modify the check as follows and pass the potential digit as parameter.

```
def is_valid_position(board, row, col, num):
    return check_num_not_in_column(board, col, num) and \
           check_num_not_in_row(board, row, num) and \
           check_num_not_in_box(board, row, col, num)

def check_num_not_in_column(board, col, num):
    for row in range(9):
        if board[row][col] == num:
            return False

    return True

def check_num_not_in_row(board, row, num):
    for col in range(9):
        if board[row][col] == num:
            return False

    return True
```

```
def check_num_not_in_box(board, row, col, num):
    adjusted_row = row // 3 * 3
    adjusted_col = col // 3 * 3

    for y in range(3):
        for x in range(3):
            if board[adjusted_row + y][adjusted_col + x] == num:
                return False

    return True
```

Idea 3: Optimized sequence of setting and checking Finally, you modify the trial and error so that only after determining that the digit is valid is it placed on the playfield. So far, in the solve_sudoku() function as step 4, you have tried all the digit as follows:

```
def __solve_sudoku_helper(board, start_row, start_col):
    ...

    solved = False
    # 4) for the current field, try all digits from 1 to 9
    for num in range(1, 10):
        board[row][col] = num

        # 4a) check if the whole playfield containing the digit is
        # still valid
        if is_valid_position(board, row, col, num):
    ...
```

You optimized this test twice. First, you changed the initial function is_valid_position(board) to is_valid_position(board, row, col) so that it also gets the row and column as parameters. As a further improvement, you pass the number to be checked is_valid_position(board, row, col, num).

Now you go one step further and change the order of inserting the value and checking. Therefore you switch only two lines, namely the assignment and the if with the call of the optimized variant of the validity check:

```
# 4) for the current field, try all digits from 1 to 9
for num in range(1, 10):
```

```
# 4a) check if the whole playfield containing the digit is still valid
if is_valid_position(board, row, col, num)
     board[row][col] = num
```

Results of the optimizations made Due to your optimizations—which, by the way, do not lead to any restrictions in readability or comprehensibility—you can save yourself from trying out many solution paths that never lead to the goal. The solutions were always determined in about 1 minute on my iMac (i7 4Ghz), even for more complex playing fields.

The naive way of implementation with the overall check of the board at each step led to running times of more than 20 minutes for more complex boards. While the first optimization finds a solution after about 3.5 minutes, the combination of ideas 2 and 3 leads to a running time of about 1 minute.

7.4.6 Solution 6: Math Operator Checker (★★★★☆)

This assignment is about a mathematically inclined puzzle. For a set of digits and another set of possible operators, you want to find all combinations that result in the desired value. The order of the digits cannot be changed. Still, it is possible to insert any operator from the possible operators between the digits, except before the first digit. Write function `all_combinations_with_value(n)` that determines all combinations that result in the value passed as parameter. Check it for the digits 1 to 9 and the operations +, −, and combining the digits. Start with function `find_all_combinations(values)` which is passed the corresponding digits.

Examples

Let's consider two combinations only for the digits 1, 2, and 3:

$$1 + 2 + 3 = 6$$

$$1 + 23 = 24$$

In total, these digits allow the following different combinations:

Input	Result (all_combinations())
[1, 2, 3]	{12−3=9, 123=123, 1+2+3=6, 1+2−3=0, 1−2+3=2, 1−23=−22, 1−2−3=−4, 1+23=24, 12+3=15}

Suppose you want to generate the value 100 from the given digits 1 to 9 and the set of available operators (+, −, and combining the digits). This is possible, for example, as follows:

$$1 + 2 + 3 - 4 + 5 + 6 + 78 + 9 = 100$$

In total, the following variants should be determined:

Input	Result (allCombinationsWithValue())
100	[1+23−4+5+6+78−9, 123+4−5+67−89, 123−45−67+89, 12+3−4+5+67+8+9, 1+23−4+56+7+8+9, 12−3−4+5−6+7+89, 123−4−5−6−7+8−9, 1+2+34−5+67−8+9, 12+3+4+5−6−7+89, 123+45−67+8−9, 1+2+3−4+5+6+78+9]

Algorithm First, you subdivide the problem at a high level by computing all possible combinations by calling the function all_combinations() and then using find_by_value() to search for those combinations whose evaluation yields the desired value:

```python
def all_combinations_with_value(base_values, desired_value):
    all_combinations = find_all_combinations(base_values)

    return find_by_value(all_combinations, desired_value)

def find_by_value(all_combinations, desired_value):
    return {key for key, value in all_combinations.items()
            if value == desired_value}
```

To calculate the combinations, the input is split into a left part and a right part. This results in three subproblems to be solved, namely $l + r$, $l - r$, and lr, where l and r stand for the left and right parts of the input. You compute the result with the function eval(). If there is only one digit left, this is the result and it constitutes the recursive termination.

```python
def find_all_combinations(digits):
    # recursive termination
    if len(digits) == 0:
        return {}
    if len(digits) == 1:
        last_digit = digits[0]
        return {last_digit: last_digit}

    # recursive descent
    left = digits[0]
```

```
    right = digits[1:]
    results = find_all_combinations(right)
    # create all combinations
    solutions = {}
    for expression, value in results.items():
        right_expr = str(expression)

        solutions[str(left) + "+" + right_expr] = \
            eval(str(left) + "+" + right_expr)
        solutions[str(left) + "-" + right_expr] = \
            eval(str(left) + "-" + right_expr)
        solutions[str(left) + right_expr] = \
            eval(str(left) + right_expr)

    return solutions
```

This variant is quite understandable but has the disadvantage that here again various partial lists are generated. Since the list with the digits is probably rather short, this does not matter. Nevertheless, as a mini-optimization, let's take a look at a variant that works with a position pointer.

```
def find_all_combinations(digits):
    return __all_combinations_helper(digits, 0)

def __all_combinations_helper(digits, pos):
    # recursive termination: last digit
    # no calculation needed, just digit
    if pos == len(digits) - 1:
        last_digit = digits[len(digits) - 1]
        return {last_digit: last_digit}

    # recursive descent
    results = __all_combinations_helper(digits, pos + 1)

    # create all combinations
    solutions = {}

    current_digit = digits[pos]
    left = str(current_digit)
    for expression, value in results.items():
        right = str(expression)
```

```
        solutions[left + "+" + right] = eval(left + "+" + right)
        solutions[left + "-" + right] = eval(left + "-" + right)
        solutions[left + right] = eval(left + right)

    return solutions
```

Verification

First, you write a unit test that checks the values shown in the introduction, namely the inputs 1 to 3, and which combinations can be built upon them.

```
@pytest.mark.parametrize("digits,  expected",
                         [([1, 2, 3],
                           {"12-3": 9,
                            "123": 123,
                            "1+2+3": 6,
                            "1+2-3": 0,
                            "1-2+3": 2,
                            "1-23": -22,
                            "1-2-3": -4,
                            "1+23": 24,
                            "12+3": 15})])
def test_all_combinations(digits, expected):
    result = find_all_combinations(digits)

    assert result == expected
```

Additionally, you want to verify the functionality for the result value 100.

```
@pytest.mark.parametrize("digits, value, expected",
                         [([1, 2, 3, 4, 5, 6, 7, 8, 9], 100,
                           {"1+23-4+5+6+78-9",
                            "12+3+4+5-6-7+89",
                            "123-45-67+89",
                            "123+4-5+67-89",
                            "123-4-5-6-7+8-9",
                            "123+45-67+8-9",
                            "1+2+3-4+5+6+78+9",
```

```
            "12+3-4+5+67+8+9",
            "1+23-4+56+7+8+9",
            "1+2+34-5+67-8+9",
            "12-3-4+5-6+7+89"})])
def test_all_combinations_with_value(digits, value, expected):
    result = all_combinations_with_value(digits, value)

    assert result == expected
```

7.4.7 Solution 7: Water Jug Problem (★★★☆☆)

Say you have two jugs with capacities of m and n liters. Unfortunately, these jugs have no markings or indications of their fill level. The challenge is to measure x liters, where x is less than m or n. At the end of the procedure, one jug should contain x liters and the other should be empty. Write function solve_water_jugs(size1, size2, desired_liters) to display the solution on the console and, if successful, return True, otherwise False.

Examples

For two jugs, one with a capacity of 4 liters and one with a capacity of 3 liters, you can measure 2 liters in the following way:

State	Action
Jug 1: 0/Jug 2: 0	Both jugs initial empty
Jug 1: 4/Jug 2: 0	Fill jug 1 (unnecessary, but due to the algorithm)
Jug 1: 4/Jug 2: 3	Fill jug 2
Jug 1: 0/Jug 2: 3	Empty jug 1
Jug 1: 3/Jug 2: 0	Pour jug 2 into jug 1
Jug 1: 3/Jug 2: 3	Fill jug 2
Jug 1: 4/Jug 2: 2	Pour jug 2 in jug 1
Jug 1: 0/Jug 2: 2	Empty jug 1
Solved	

On the other hand, measuring 2 liters is impossible with two jugs of 4 liters capacity each.

Algorithm To solve the water jug problem, you use recursion with a greedy algorithm. Here, at each point in time, you have the following next actions as possibilities:

- Empty jug 1 completely.

- Empty jug 2 completely.

- Fill jug 1 completely.

- Fill jug 2 completely.

- Fill jug 1 from jug 2 until the source jug is empty or the jug to be filled is full.

- Fill jug 2 from jug 1 until the source jug is empty or the jug to be filled is full.

Try these six variants step by step until one of them succeeds. To do this, you need to test each time whether there is the desired number of liters in one of the jugs and whether the other is empty.

```
def is_solved(current_jug1, current_jug2, desired_liters):
    return (current_jug1 == desired_liters and current_jug2 == 0) or \
           (current_jug2 == desired_liters and current_jug1 == 0)
```

Because trying out many solutions can be quite time-consuming, you remember for optimization the combinations you have already tried out. This speeds up the calculation by lengths but makes the implementation only minimally more complicated if you model the already calculated levels in the form of a tuple. To find the solution, you start with two empty jugs.

```
def solve_water_jugs(size1, size2, desired_liters):
    return __solve_water_jugs_rec(size1, size2, desired_liters, 0, 0, {})

def __solve_water_jugs_rec(size1, size2, desired_liters,
                           current_jug1, current_jug2, already_tried):

    if is_solved(current_jug1, current_jug2, desired_liters):
        print("Solved Jug 1:", current_jug1, " / 2:", current_jug2)
        return True
```

```
key = (current_jug1, current_jug2)
if key not in already_tried:
    already_tried[key] = True

    # try all 6 variants
    print("Jug 1:", current_jug1, " / 2: ", current_jug2)

    min_2_1 = min(current_jug2, (size1 - current_jug1))
    min_1_2 = min(current_jug1, (size2 - current_jug2))

    result = __solve_water_jugs_rec(size1, size2, desired_liters,
                                    0, current_jug2, already_tried) or \
            __solve_water_jugs_rec(size1, size2, desired_liters,
                                    current_jug1, 0, already_tried) or \
            __solve_water_jugs_rec(size1, size2, desired_liters,
                                    size1, current_jug2, already_tried) or \
            __solve_water_jugs_rec(size1, size2, desired_liters,
                                    current_jug1, size2, already_tried) or \
            __solve_water_jugs_rec(size1, size2, desired_liters,
                                    current_jug1 + min_2_1,
                                    current_jug2 - min_2_1,
                                    already_tried) or \
            __solve_water_jugs_rec(size1, size2, desired_liters,
                                    current_jug1 - min_1_2,
                                    current_jug2 + min_1_2,
                                    already_tried)

    already_tried[key] = result

    return result

return False
```

ATTENTION: POSSIBLE PITFALL

When implementing this, you might get the idea of simply examining all six variants independently, as you would do to determine all exits from a maze, for example. However, I'm afraid that's not right because it would allow multiple actions in one step. Therefore, only one step has to be examined at a time. Only in case of a failure do you proceed with another one. Thus, the following variant shown is not correct— it detects the solution, but additional, partly confusing steps are executed:

```
// Intuitive, BUT WRONG, because 2 or more steps possible
action_empty1 = __solve_water_jugs_rec(size1, size2, desired_liters,
                                    0, current_jug2, already_tried);
action_empty2 = __solve_water_jugs_rec(size1, size2, desired_liters,
                                    current_jug1, 0, already_tried);
action_fill1 = __solve_water_jugs_rec(size1, size2, desired_liters,
                                    size1, current_jug2, already_tried);
action_fill2 = __solve_water_jugs_rec(size1, size2, desired_liters,
                                    current_jug1, size2, already_tried);

min_2_1 = min(current_jug2, (size1 - current_jug1))
action_fillup1_from2 = __solve_water_jugs_rec(size1, size2, desired_liters,
                                        current_jug1 + min_2_1),
                                        current_jug2 - min_2_1,
                                        already_tried);

min_1_2 = min(current_jug1, (size2 - current_jug2))
action_fillup2_from1 = __solve_water_jugs_rec(size1, size2, desired_liters,
                                        current_jug1 - min_1_2),
                                        current_jug2 + min_1_2,
                                        already_tried);
```

Verification

Let's determine the solution for the combination from the example in the Python command line:

```
>>> print(solve_water_jugs(4, 3, 2))
Jug 1: 0 / 2:  0
```

```
Jug 1: 4  / 2:  0
Jug 1: 4  / 2:  3
Jug 1: 0  / 2:  3
Jug 1: 3  / 2:  0
Jug 1: 3  / 2:  3
Jug 1: 4  / 2:  2
Solved Jug 1: 0  / 2: 2
True
```

Let's try the counterexample with two 4-liter buckets and the target of 2 liters:

```
>>> print(solve_water_jugs(4, 4, 2))
Jug 1: 0  / 2:  0
Jug 1: 4  / 2:  0
Jug 1: 4  / 2:  4
Jug 1: 0  / 2:  4
False
```

7.4.8 Exercise 8: All Palindrome Substrings (★★★★☆)

In this assignment, you want to determine for a given word whether it contains palindromes and, if so, which ones. Write recursive function all_palindrome_parts_rec(input) that determines all palindromes with at least two letters in the passed string and returns them sorted alphabetically.[2]

Examples

Input	Result
"BCDEDCB"	["BCDEDCB", "CDEDC", "DED"]
"ABALOTTOLL"	["ABA", "LL", "LOTTOL", "OTTO", "TT"]
"racecar"	["aceca", "cec", "racecar"]

---

[2] Of course, you are not interested in empty strings and single characters in this assignment, although of course, strictly speaking, they are also palindromes by definition.

Algorithm This problem is broken down into three subproblems for texts of at least length 2:

1. Is the entire text a palindrome?

2. Is the part shortened on the left a palindrome (for all positions from the right)?

3. Is the right-shortened part a palindrome (for all positions from the left)?

For a better understanding, look at the procedure for the initial value LOTTOL:

```
1) LOTTOL
2) OTTOL, TTOL, TOL, OL
3) LOTTO, LOTT, LOT, LO
```

After that, you move both left and right inwards by one character and repeat the checks and this procedure until the positions overlap. For the example, the checks continue as follows:

```
1) OTTO
2) TTO, TO
3) OTT, OT
```

And finally, in the last step, only one check remains because the other substrings consist of only one character:

```
1) TT
2) T
3) T
```

As previously applied several times, a two-step variant is used here. In this case, the first method primarily initializes the result object and then starts the recursive call appropriately.

Based on this step-by-step procedure, let's implement the check for palindrome substrings as follows:

```python
def all_palindrome_parts_rec(input):
    results = set()

    __all_palindrome_parts_rec(input, 0, len(input) - 1, results)

    return results
```

```
def __all_palindrome_parts_rec(input, left, right, results):
    # recursive termination
    if left >= right:
        return

    # 1) check if the whole string is a palindrome
    complete_is_palindrome = is_palindrome_rec_in_range(input, left, right)
    if complete_is_palindrome:
        new_candidate = input[left:right + 1]
        results.add(new_candidate)

    # 2) check text shortened from left
    for i in range(left + 1, right):
        left_part_is_palindrome = is_palindrome_rec_in_range(input, i,
        right)
        if left_part_is_palindrome:
            new_candidate = input[i:right + 1]
            results.add(new_candidate)

    # 3) check text shortened from right
    for i in range(right - 1, left, -1):
        right_part_is_palindrome = is_palindrome_rec_in_range
        (input, left, i)
        if right_part_is_palindrome:
            new_candidate = input[left:i + 1]
            results.add(new_candidate)

    # recursive descent
    __all_palindrome_parts_rec_in_range(input, left + 1, right - 1,
    results)
```

Here you use the function is_palindrome_rec_in_range(input, left, right) created in Section 4.2.4 in Exercise 4 to check for palindromes on ranges of a string. This is shown again here for completeness:

```
def is_palindrome_rec_in_range(input, left, right):
    # recursive termination
    if left >= right:
        return True
```

```
    if input[left] == input[right]:
        # recursive descent
        return is_palindrome_rec_in_range(input, left + 1, right - 1)

    return False
```

Although the algorithm is quite comprehensible, it seems rather awkward with all the loops and index accesses. In fact, an exquisite solution exists.

Optimized algorithm Instead of painstakingly trying through all the shortened substrings, you can do much better by recursively invoking your function for a shortened part:

```
def all_palindrome_parts_rec_optimized(input):
    results = set()

    __all_palindrome_parts_rec_optimized(input, 0, len(input) - 1, results)

    return results

def __all_palindrome_parts_rec_optimized(input, left, right, results):
    # recursive termination
    if left >= right:
        return

    # 1) check if the whole string is a palindrome
    if is_palindrome_rec(input, left, right):
        results.add(input[left: right + 1])

    # recursive descent: 2) + 3) check from left / right
    __all_palindrome_parts_rec_optimized(input, left + 1, right, results)
    __all_palindrome_parts_rec_optimized(input, left, right - 1, results)
```

This can be made a bit more readable, but the performance is (slightly) worse due to the creation of substrings:

```
def all_palindrome_parts_rec_optimized_v3(input):
    results = set()

    __all_palindrome_parts_rec_optimized_v3(input, results)

    return results
```

```python
def __all_palindrome_parts_rec_optimized_v3(input, results):
    # recursive termination
    if len(input) < 2:
        return

    # 1) check if the whole string is a palindrome
    if is_palindrome_rec(input, 0, len(input) - 1):
        results.add(input)

    # recursive descent: 2) + 3) check from left / right
    __all_palindrome_parts_rec_optimized_v3(input[1:], results)
    __all_palindrome_parts_rec_optimized_v3(input[0:len(input) - 1],
    results)
```

Verification

For testing, you use the following inputs, which show the correct operation:

```python
def input_and_expected():
    return [("BCDEDCB",
             {"BCDEDCB", "CDEDC", "DED"}),
            ("ABALOTTOLL",
             {"ABA", "LL", "LOTTOL", "OTTO", "TT"}),
            ("racecar",
             {"aceca", "cec", "racecar"})]

@pytest.mark.parametrize("input, expected",
                         input_and_expected())
def test_all_palindrome_parts_recs(input, expected):
    result = all_palindrome_parts_rec(input)

    assert result == expected

@pytest.mark.parametrize("input, expected",
                         input_and_expected())
def test_all_palindrome_parts_recs_optimized(input, expected):
    result = all_palindrome_parts_rec_optimized(input)

    assert result == expected
```

```
@pytest.mark.parametrize("input, expected",
                         input_and_expected())
def test_all_palindrome_parts_recs_optimized_v3(input, expected):
    result = all_palindrome_parts_rec_optimized_v3(input)

    assert result == expected
```

Bonus: Find the Longest of All Palindrome Substrings

This time there is no requirement for maximum performance.

Algorithm After calculating all the palindrome substrings, finding the longest one is just a matter of traversing the values and using len() to find the longest one as follows:

```
def longest_palindrome_part(input):
    all_palindrome_parts = all_palindrome_parts_rec(input)

    longest = ''
    for word in all_palindrome_parts:
        if len(word) > len(longest):
            longest = word

    return longest
```

Verification

For testing, you use the following inputs, which show the correct operation:

```
@pytest.mark.parametrize("input, expected",
                         [("ABALOTTOLL", "LOTTOL"),
                          ("dreh_malam_herd", "dreh_malam_herd"),
                          ("abc_XYZYX_def", "_XYZYX_")])
def test_longest_palindrome(input, expected):
    longest = longest_palindrome_part(input)

    assert longest == expected
```

7.4.9 Solution 9: The n-Queens Problem (★★★☆☆)

In the n-Queens Problem, n queens are to be placed on an n × n board in such a way that no two queens can beat each other according to chess rules—thus, other queens must not be placed in the same row, column, or diagonal. To do this, extend the solution shown in Section 7.2.1 and implement the function is_valid_position(board, col, row). Also write function print_board(board) to display the board as well as output the solution to the console.

Example

For a 4 × 4 playfield, here is the following solution, with the queens symbolized by a Q:

```
- - - - - - - - -
|  | Q|  |  |
- - - - - - - - -
|  |  |  | Q|
- - - - - - - - -
| Q|  |  |  |
- - - - - - - - -
|  |  | Q|  |
- - - - - - - - -
```

Algorithm Let's recall and repeat the algorithm presented in the introduction.

You attempt to place the queens one after the other at different positions. You start with a queen in row 0 and position 0 (upper left corner). After each placement, a check is made to ensure that there are no collisions in the vertical and diagonal left and right directions upwards with queens that have already been placed. A check downwards is logically not necessary in any case because no queens can be placed there yet. After all, the filling is done from top to bottom. Since you also proceed line by line, a check in the horizontal direction is unnecessary.

Provided the position is valid, move to the next row, trying all positions from 0 to $n - 1$. This procedure is repeated until you have finally placed the queen in the last row. If there is a problem positioning a queen, use backtracking: remove the last-placed queen and try again at the next possible position. If the end of the row is reached without a solution, this is an invalid situation, and the previous queen must also be placed again. You can see that backtracking sometimes goes back up one row, in extreme cases to the first row.

Let's start with the easy part, namely recapping the introduction and creating the playfield and invoking the function to solve it:

```python
def solve_n_queens(size):
    board = initialize_board(size)

    # start the recursive solution finding
    solved = __solve_n_queens_helper(board, 0)

    return solved, board

def initialize_board(size):
    return [[' ' for col in range(size)] for row in range(size)]
```

To model the playfield, you use a nested list. A Q represents a queen, a space a free field. To keep the algorithm understandable, you extract the two functions, shown next, place_queen() and remove_queen() for placing and deleting the queens:

```python
def __solve_n_queens_helper(board, row):
    max_row, max_col = get_dimension(board)

    # recursive termination
    if row >= max_row:
        return True

    solved = False
    col = 0
    while col < max_col and not solved:
        if is_valid_position((board, col, row):
            place_queen(board, col, row)

            # recursive descent
            solved = __solve_n_queens_helper(board, row + 1)

            # Backtracking, if no solution found
            if not solved:
                remove_queen(board, col, row)
        col += 1

    return solved
```

The extraction of the following two functions leads to a better readability:

```
def place_queen(board, col, row):
    board[row][col] = 'Q'

def remove_queen(board, col, row):
    board[row][col] = ' '
```

As a reminder, get_dimension(values2dim) is shown again:

```
def get_dimension(values2dim):
    if (isinstance(values2dim, list)):
        return (len(values2dim), len(values2dim[0]))

    if (isinstance(values2dim, np.ndarray)):
        return values2dim.shape

    raise Exception("unsupported type", type(values2dim)) '
```

Start your own implementation Let's now get down to implementing the helper function. First, the one that checks whether a constellation is valid:

```
def is_valid_position(board, col, row):
    max_row, max_col = get_dimension(board)

    return check_horizontally(board, row, max_col) and \
           check_vertically(board, col, max_row) and \
           check_diagonally_left_up(board, col, row) and \
           check_diagonally_right_up(board, col, row, max_col)
```

Actually, the horizontal check is superfluous since you are just checking a new row where no other queen can be placed yet—for the sake of illustration, you implement and call the function anyway.

In the implementation, you use the following helper function to check in the x and y directions:

```
def check_horizontally(board, row, max_col):
    col = 0
    while col < max_col and board[row][col] == ' ':
        col += 1

    return col >= max_col
```

451

```
def check_vertically(board, col, max_row):
    row = 0
    while row < max_row and board[row][col] == ' ':
        row += 1

    return row >= max_roy
```

Since you fill the board from top to bottom, no queen can be placed below the current position yet. Thus, you limit yourself to the relevant diagonals to the top left and right:

```
def check_diagonally_right_up(board, col, row, max_col):
    diag_ru_free = True

    while col < max_col and row >= 0:
        diag_ru_free = diag_ru_free and board[row][col] == ' '
        row -= 1
        col += 1

    return diag_ru_free

def check_diagonally_left_up(board, col, row):
    diag_lu_free = True

    while col >= 0 and row >= 0:
        diag_lu_free = diag_lu_free and board[row][col] == ' '
        row -= 1
        col -= 1

    return diag_lu_free
```

The output of the stylized chessboard with n × n squares is implemented as follows—somewhat special is the calculation of the grid and of the cross lines:

```
def print_board(values):
    line = "-" * (len(values[0]) * 2 + 1)
    print(line)

    for y in range(len(values)):
        print("|", end='')
```

```
    for x in range(len(values[y])):
        print(values[y][x], end='|')

    print()
    print(line)
```

Verification

For two different sized playfields, you compute the solution to the n-Queens Problem using solve_n_queens(). Finally, you display the playfield determined as the solution in each case on the console.

```
def solve_and_print(size):
    solved_and_board = solve_n_queens(size)

    if solved_and_board[0]:
        print_board(solved_and_board[1])

def main():
    solve_and_print(4)
    solve_and_print(8)
```

For the playing fields of sizes 4 × 4 and 8 × 8 you get the following output (only the second one is shown):

```
- - - - - - - - - - - - - - - -
|Q| | | | | | | |
- - - - - - - - - - - - - - - -
| | | | |Q| | | |
- - - - - - - - - - - - - - - -
| | | | | | | |Q|
- - - - - - - - - - - - - - - -
| | | | | |Q| | |
- - - - - - - - - - - - - - - -
| | |Q| | | | | |
- - - - - - - - - - - - - - - -
| | | | | | |Q| |
- - - - - - - - - - - - - - - -
```

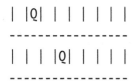

Alternative Solution Approach

Although the previously chosen representation as a two-dimensional array (or more precisely as two-dimensional nested lists) is absolutely catchy, there is an optimization. Because only one queen may be placed per row, it is possible to use a list for modeling the playfield and the queens' positioning, which simplifies a lot. Sounds strange at first. How is it supposed to work?

For the solution of the n-Queens Problem, you need in each case x- and y-coordinates. You reconstruct them by the following trick: The y-coordinate results from the position in the list. For the x-coordinate, you store a corresponding numerical value in the list. The presence of a queen, previously indicated by the character Q, can now be determined indirectly. If the list contains a numerical value greater than or equal to 0 at the position of the y-coordinate, then a queen is present.

With this knowledge, you can adjust the implementation of the algorithm in the appropriate places. In fact, the basic logic does not change, but the function signatures and position processing do. Conveniently, you also no longer need to generate a two-dimensional model of the playfield in advance. But let's look at the actual algorithm first:

```python
def solve_n_queens(size):
    board = [ ]
    solved = __solve_n_queens_helper(board, 0, size)

    return solved, board  # (solved, board)

def __solve_n_queens_helper(board, row, size):
    # recursive termination
    if row >= size:
        return True

    solved = False
    col = 0
```

```
    while col < size and not solved:
        if __is_valid_position(board, col, row, size):
            __place_queen(board, col, row)

            # recursive descent
            solved = __solve_n_queens_helper(board, row + 1, size)

            # backtracking, if no solution
            if not solved:
                __remove_queen(board, col, row)

        col += 1

    return solved
```

For better readability, you modify the following functions appropriately:

```
def __placeQueen(board, col, row):
    if len(board) != row:
        raise ValueError("invalid row" + str(row) + " col: " + str(col))

    board.append(col)

def __removeQueen(board, col, row):
    if board[row] != col:
        raise ValueError("invalid col" + str(col) + " row: " + str(row))

    board.remove(col)
```

The implementation of the check whether a constellation is valid becomes enormously simplified. For the vertical, it is checked whether the list already contains the same column. Only the check of the diagonals is still done in a separate helper method.

```
def __is_valid_position(board, col, row, size):
    yfree = col not in board

    return yfree and __check_diagonally(board, col, row, size)
```

Again, with the diagonals, you can apply the following trick: The difference in the x-direction must correspond to the difference in the y-direction for the queens located on a diagonal. For this, starting from the current position, only the coordinates have to be computed and compared:

```
(x - 2, y - 2)   X        X   (x + 2, y - 2)
                   \     /
(x - 1, y - 1)     X  X      (x + 1, y - 1)
                    \ /
                     X
                   (x,y)
```

You implement the whole thing as follows:

```python
def __check_diagonally(board, col, row, size):
    diag_lu_free = True
    diag_ru_free = True

    for y in range(row):
        x_pos_lu = col - (row - y)
        x_pos_ru = col + (row - y)

        if x_pos_lu >= 0:
            diag_lu_free = diag_lu_free and board[y] != x_pos_lu

        if x_pos_ru < size:
            diag_ru_free = diag_ru_free and board[y] != x_pos_ru

    return diag_ru_free and diag_lu_free
```

The output of the stylized chessboard with n × n squares is minimally adapted to the new data structure:

```python
def print_board(board, size):
    line = "-" * (size * 2 + 1)
    print(line)

    for y in range(size):
        print("|", end='')
        for x in range(size):
```

```
        value = 'Q' if x == board[y] else ' '
        print(value, end='|')

    print("\n" + line)
```

Verification

Again, for two playfields, you compute the solution to the n-Queens Problem using solve_n_queens(), which is supplied as a tuple, namely in the form of a bool variable as an indicator whether there is a solution, and as a list with the solution, if it exists. This is then output to the console:

```
def solve_and_print(size):
    solved_and_board = solve_n_queens(size)

    if solved_and_board[0]:
        print_board(solved_and_board[1], size)

def main():
    solve_and_print(4)
    solve_and_print(8)
```

The results are identical to the previous ones and are therefore not shown again.

7.5 Summary: What You Learned

Basic recursion is a very nice technique. When using it a bit more intensively, you see that simple recursion, besides the advantages, sometimes requires some patience due to long running times.

In this advanced chapter on recursion, you have significantly expanded your toolbox with memoization and backtracking. Memoization allows you to increase performance, and backtracking helps solve entertaining and amusing puzzles, such as Sudoku puzzles or the n-Queens problem. It is also possible to find a way out of a maze.

Now that you are fluent in recursion, you are well prepared to expand and use your knowledge for various algorithms on trees, which are special, very helpful, and exciting data structures suitable for various kinds of challenges. Let's get in touch.

CHAPTER 8

Binary Trees

While Python provides list, sets, and dictionaries as a rich variety of real-world data structures, it unfortunately does not include trees for direct use. However, they are helpful for various use cases and therefore desirable. Because the topic of trees is quite extensive and not to go beyond the scope of this book, I will deal mainly with binary trees and binary search trees as special cases.

Before you look at trees in more detail, I would like to mention some fields of usage:

- A file system is hierarchically structured and can be modeled as a tree. Here the nodes correspond to the directories and the leaves to the files.

- Mathematical calculations can be represented by trees. You will explore this in an exercise later.

- In the area of databases, B-trees[1] are used for efficient storage and search.

- In compiler construction, you can use an abstract syntax tree (AST) to represent the source code.[2]

8.1 Introduction

In this introduction, you'll first learn some terminology before briefly exploring binary tree and binary search trees. After that, I'll discuss traversal and some properties of trees. Finally, I'll introduce three trees that are used repeatedly in the text and the assignments.

---

[1] Please consult textbooks or the Internet for more info about B-trees. A good start is the following page: `www.geeksforgeeks.org/introduction-of-b-tree-2/`

[2] To be more precise, it's used to represent the abstract syntax structure of the source code—not the source code itself.

459

© Michael Inden 2022
M. Inden, *Python Challenges*, https://doi.org/10.1007/978-1-4842-7398-2_8

8.1.1 Structure, Terminology, and Examples of Use

Trees allow both structured storage and efficient access to data managed there. For this purpose, **trees** are strictly hierarchical and, as in real trees, no branch grows back into the trunk. A branching point is called **node** and stores a value. A node at the end of a branch is called **leaf**—values are also found there. The connecting branch pieces are called **edges**. Figure 8-1 gives a first impression.

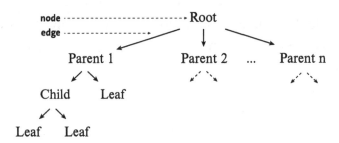

Figure 8-1. *A tree with some nodes and leaves*

The figure illustrates that trees consist of hierarchically organized nodes. They start from a root (which, interestingly enough, is located at the top in computer science), branch out into several children, which in turn can have any number of child nodes. Thus, they are parents and represent the roots of subtrees. Each node is referenced by exactly one other node.

8.1.2 Binary Trees

A binary tree is a special tree in which each node stores one value, and each node possesses at most two successors, often called left and right. This restriction makes it easier to express many algorithms. As a result, the binary tree is widely used in computer science. It also forms the basis for the binary search tree presented in the following.

Binary tree, homemade A binary tree can be realized with little effort by the following class called `BinaryTreeNode`:

```python
class BinaryTreeNode:

    def __init__(self, item):
        self.left = None
        self.right = None
        self.item = item
```

```
def is_leaf(self):
    return self.left is None and self.right is None

def __str__(self):
    return "BinaryTreeNode [item=%s, left=%s, right=%s]" %
            (self.item, self.left, self.right)
```

For the examples in this book, you do not need to model the binary tree as a standalone class called BinaryTree, but you will always use a special node as a root of the above type BinaryTreeNode. However, to further simplify the handling in your own and especially more complex business applications, the definition of a class BinaryTree is a good idea. There you can also provide various useful functionalities.

8.1.3 Binary Trees with Order: Binary Search Trees

Sometimes the terms "binary tree" and "binary search tree" (BST for short) are used interchangeably, but this is not correct. A binary search tree is indeed a binary tree, but one with the additional property that the nodes are arranged according to their values. The constraint is that the root's value is greater than that of the left successor and less than that of the right successor. This constraint applies recursively to all subtrees, as illustrated by Figure 8-2. Consequently, a BST does not contain any value more than once.

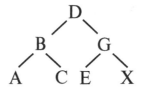

Figure 8-2. *Example of a binary search tree with letters*

Search in a BST A search in a BST can be performed in logarithmic time due to the ordering of the values. You implement the function find(startNode, searchFor) for this purpose. Depending on the comparison of the value with the current node's value, the search continues in the appropriate part of the tree until the value is found. If it is not found, None is returned.

```
def find(current_node, search_for):
    # recursive termination
```

```python
    if current_node is None:
        return None

    # recursive descent to the left or right depending on the comparison
    if current_node.item < search_for:
        return find(current_node.right, search_for)
    if current_node.item > search_for:
        return find(current_node.left, search_for)

    return current_node
```

Insertion into a BST The insertion into a BST may be expressed recursively as well. The insertion has to start at the root so that the ordering of values within the BST can be ensured.

```python
def insert(current_node, value):
    # recursive termination
    if current_node is None:
        return BinaryTreeNode(value)

    # recursive descent: to the left or right depending on the comparison
    if value < current_node.item:
        current_node.left = insert(current_node.left, value)
    elif value > current_node.item:
        current_node.right = insert(current_node.right, value)

    return current_node
```

Example of a BST The functions shown earlier are also part of the utility module for this chapter called tree_utils. With it, BSTs can be constructed quite easily and readably. In the following, you use the trick *underscore as a prefix* to keep the names of the nodes as speaking as possible. Besides, you only need the assignment to a variable if you want to continue working with the node. In particular, however, the root is always returned.

```python
_3 = BinaryTreeNode(3)
insert(_3, 1)
insert(_3, 2)
insert(_3, 4)
```

```
TreeUtils.nice_print(_3)
print("tree contains 2?", find(_3, 2))
print("tree contains 13?", find(_3, 13))
```

This generates the following output:

```
            3
      |-----+-----|
      1           4
      +--|
         2
tree contains 2? BinaryTreeNode [item=2, left=None, right=None]
tree contains 13? None
```

Problematic insertion order Please note that the sequence in which elements are added can greatly impact the performance of subsequent actions such as searches. I cover this briefly in Section 8.1.5. The following example demonstrates how quickly a tree degenerates into something like a list:

```
_4 = BinaryTreeNode(4)
insert(_4, 3)
insert(_4, 2)
insert(_4, 1)
TreeUtils.nice_print(_4)
```

This generates the following output:

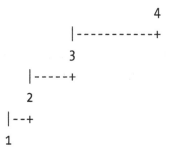

HINT: ASCII OUTPUT OF TREES

For the output of trees in the examples and exercises I call function `nice_print()`. Its implementation is developed in Exercise 13.

8.1.4 Traversals

When traversing a tree, a distinction is made between depth-first and breadth-first searches. Figure 8-3 illustrates both.

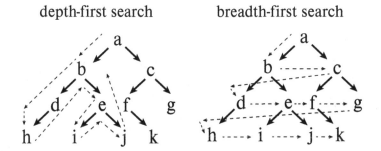

Figure 8-3. *Procedure for a depth-first search and a breadth-first search*

In a depth-first search, you traverse the tree as deeply as possible. With the breadth-first search, you move from the root node level by level through the tree. This is why it is also called level order or breadth-first.

Breadth-First/Level Order

The following sequence results for the tree from the example when traversing the levels from the root node downwards—the implementation is the subject of Exercise 5.

```
a b c d e f g h i j k
```

Conversion from tree to list A great advantage of the level order traversal is its good traceability and comprehensibility. If you have a tree in mind, you can easily predict this traversal and its result. This is an important and useful feature, especially when testing.

Let's assume that you have already solved Exercise 5 and thus have access to the implementation. Based on it, you can convert a tree into a list as follows:

```
def convert_to_list(node):
    result = []
    levelorder(node, lambda item: result.append(item))
    return result
```

Depth-First Searches

The three known depth-first search methods are preorder, inorder, and postorder. Preorder first processes the node itself and then those from the left and then the right subtree. For inorder, the processing order is first the left subtree, then the node itself, and then the right subtree. Postorder processes first the subtrees on the left, then on the right, and finally the node itself. The three depth-first search methods iterate through the previously shown values as follows:

```
Preorder:   a b d h e i j c f k g
Inorder:    h d b i e j a f k c g
Postorder:  h d i j e b k f g c a
```

The outputs are not quite as intuitive. In the case of a BST, the inorder traversal returns the nodes' values according to the order of their values. This yields 1 2 3 4 5 6 7 for the following tree:

```
          4
    |-----+----|
    2          6
 |--+--|    |--+--|
 1     3    5     7
```

Interestingly, these traversals can be easily implemented recursively. The action is highlighted in bold in each case:

```
def preorder(node):
    if node is None:
        return
```

```
    print(node.item)
    preorder(node.left)
    preorder(node.right)

def inorder(node):
    if node is None:
        return

    inorder(node.left)
    print(node.item)
    inorder(node.right)

def postorder(node):
    if node is None:
        return

    postorder(node.left)
    postorder(node.right)
    print(node.item)
```

NOTE: PRACTICAL RELEVANCE OF POSTORDER

Postorder is an important type of tree traversal for the following use cases:

- Delete: When deleting a root node of a subtree, you must always ensure that the child nodes are also deleted correctly. A postorder traversal is a good way to do this.

- Calculations of sizes: To determine the size of a directory or a hierarchical project's duration, postorder is best suited.

8.1.5 Balanced Trees and Other Properties

One speaks of *balanced trees* if in a binary tree the heights of the two subtrees differ by at most 1 (sometimes by some other constant value). The opposite is a *degenerated tree*, which arises from, among other things, inserting data in ways that are awkward for the tree, specifically when numbers are added in an ordered fashion into a binary search tree. This causes the tree to degenerate into a linear list, as you saw in an example in section 8.1.3.

Sometimes one or more rotation(s) restores the balance. For the tree from the introduction, a rotation to the left and one to the right is visualized in Figure 8-4. In the middle, you can see the balanced starting position.

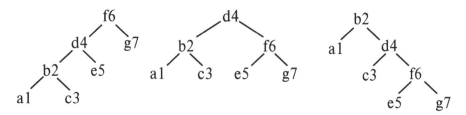

Figure 8-4. *Rotation to the left, original, rotation to the right*

The Properties Level and Height

As indicated in the introduction, trees are hierarchically structured and consist of nodes, which optionally have child nodes and may be nested arbitrarily deep. To describe this, the two terms *level* and *height* exist. The level is usually counted from 0 and starts at the root and then goes down to the lowest leaf. For height, the following applies. For a single node, it is 1. It is determined by the number of nodes on the way down to the lowest leaf for a subtree. This is visualized in Figure 8-5 where some nodes labeled as a child are, in fact, also the parent of others.

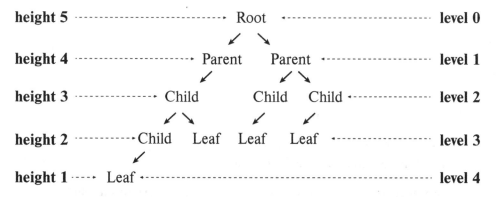

Figure 8-5. *Level and height of a tree*

The Properties Completeness and Perfectness

A complete binary tree is characterized by the fact that all levels must be completely filled, except for the last level. Moreover, all nodes have to be as far to the left as possible in the last level, so there are no gaps or all nodes are present.

In a ***complete binary tree,*** values may be missing on the right side (in algorithmics this is also called left-full):

```
      4
     / \
    2   6
   / \ /
  1  3 5
```

If all positions are occupied, this is called a ***perfect tree.***

```
      4
     / \
    2   6
   / \ / \
  1  3 5  7
```

The following constellation (here the missing 5 from the upper tree) is not allowed in a binary tree in the context of completeness (because the tree is then not left-full):

```
      4
     / \
    2   6
   / \   \
  1  3    7
```

Let's try something more formal:

- A ***perfect binary tree*** is one in which all leaves are on the same level and all nodes have two successors each.

- A ***complete binary tree*** is one in which all levels are completely filled—except for the last one, where nodes may be missing, but only as far to the right as possible.

- A *full binary tree* means that each node has either no children or two children, as shown in the following diagram:

```
  4
 / \
2   6
   / \
  5   7
```

This is the weakest requirement.

A graphical illustration for these definitions can be found online at `www.programiz.com/dsa/complete-binary-tree`.

8.1.6 Trees for the Examples and Exercises

Because you will repeatedly refer to some typical tree structures in the following, you implement three creation functions in the utility module `example_trees`.

Tree with Letters and Numbers

To try out tree traversal and other actions, construct a tree of seven nodes. Therefore you define objects of type `BinaryTreeNode`, which still have to be connected appropriately after their creation. For simplicity, the examples here are implemented without information hiding. Consequently, you directly access the attributes `left` and `right`.

```python
def create_example_tree():
    a1 = BinaryTreeNode("a1")
    b2 = BinaryTreeNode("b2")
    c3 = BinaryTreeNode("c3")
    d4 = BinaryTreeNode("d4")
    e5 = BinaryTreeNode("e5")
    f6 = BinaryTreeNode("f6")
    g7 = BinaryTreeNode("g7")

    d4.left = b2
    d4.right = f6
    b2.left = a1
```

```
    b2.right = c3
    f6.left = e5
    f6.right = g7

    return d4
```

This results in the following tree with root d4:

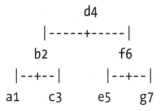

You may be surprised about the combination of letters and numbers. I chose this intentionally because it allows understanding some algorithms a bit easier—for example, to check traversals' order.

Trees with Textual and Real Digits

For some exercises, you also need a tree where the nodes' values consist only of digits (but textually as string). Because it is impossible to name the variables for the individual nodes with digits, let's use the trick of starting the variable name with an underscore.

To construct the tree, utilize the function `insert()`, which puts the value to be inserted in the appropriate place for it—this is only possible if you work with a BST and its order. As you can easily see, this will be much easier than the manual linking shown before.

```
def create_number_tree():
    _4 = BinaryTreeNode("4")
    insert(_4, "2")
    insert(_4, "1")
    insert(_4, "3")
    insert(_4, "6")
    insert(_4, "5")
    insert(_4, "7")

    return _4
```

This results in the following tree:

```
        4
  |-----+-----|
  2           6
|--+--|     |--+--|
1     3     5     7
```

Variant with integers The tree shown is generated as a variant for integers as follows:

```python
def create_integer_number_tree():
    _4 = BinaryTreeNode(4)
    insert(_4, 2)
    insert(_4, 1)
    insert(_4, 3)
    insert(_4, 6)
    insert(_4, 5)
    insert(_4, 7)

    return _4
```

8.2 Exercises

8.2.1 Exercise 1: Tree Traversal (★★☆☆☆)

Extend the functions presented in the introduction for the traversing trees so that they can perform any action on the current node during the traversal. To do this, add an action to the respective signature, such as for inorder: `inorder(node, action)`.

Bonus: Fill up a Tree into a List Build a representation of the values of the nodes in the form of a list. To do this, write function `to_list(node)` that returns the values based on an inorder traversal, and functions `to_list_preorder(node)` and `to_list_postorder(node)` that are based on a preorder and postorder traversal, respectively.

Example

When using the following tree

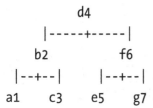

```
              d4
      |-----+-----|
      b2          f6
   |--+--|     |--+--|
  a1    c3    e5    g7
```

the conversions should result in something similar to

```
to_list: ['a1', 'b2', 'c3', 'd4', 'e5', 'f6', 'g7']
to_list_preorder: ['d4', 'b2', 'a1', 'c3', 'f6', 'e5', 'g7']
to_list_postorder: ['a1', 'c3', 'b2', 'e5', 'g7', 'f6', 'd4']
```

8.2.2 Exercise 2: Inorder, Preorder, and Postorder Iterative (★★★★☆)

In the introduction, you learned about inorder, preorder, and postorder as recursive variants. Now implement these types of traversals iteratively.

Example

Again, you use the following tree:

```
            d4
     |-----+-----|
     b2          f6
  |--+--|     |--+--|
 a1    c3    e5    g7
```

The three depth-first search methods traverse this tree as follows:

```
Preorder:    d4 b2 a1 c3 f6 e5 g7
Inorder:     a1 b2 c3 d4 e5 f6 g7
Postorder:   a1 c3 b2 e5 g7 f6 d4
```

8.2.3 Exercise 3: Tree Height (★★☆☆☆)

Implement function get_height(node) to determine the height for a tree and for subtrees with a single node as root.

Example

The following tree of height 4 is used as a starting point:

```
                        E
        |-----------+-----------|
        C                       G
    |-----|                 |-----+-----|
    A                       F           H
                                      |--|
                                       I
```

8.2.4 Exercise 4: Lowest Common Ancestor (★★★☆☆)

Compute the lowest common ancestor (LCA) for two nodes, A and B, hosted in an arbitrary binary search tree. The LCA denotes the node that is the ancestor of both A and B and is located as deep as possible in the tree—the root is always the ancestor of both A and B. Write function find_lca(start_node, value1, value2), which, in addition to the start node of the search (usually the root), also receives lower and upper limits, which indirectly describe the nodes that are closest to these values. If the values for the limits are outside the range of values, then there is no LCA and it returns None.

Example

The following binary tree is shown. If the lowest common ancestor is determined for the nodes with the values 1 and 5, this is the node with the value 4. In the tree, the respective nodes are circled and the ancestor is additionally marked in bold.

```
                        6
        |-----------+-----------|
        ④                       7
```

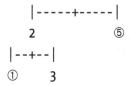

```
|-----+-----|
  2           ⑤
|--+--|
①     3
```

8.2.5 Exercise 5: Breadth-First (★★★☆☆)

In this exercise, you are asked to implement the breadth-first search, also called level order, using the function levelorder(start_node, action). The breadth-first search starts at the given node—usually the root—and then works its way through the tree level by level.

Note   Use a queue to store data on the nodes yet to be visited. The iterative variant is a bit easier to implement than the recursive one.

Examples

For the following two trees, the sequence 1 2 3 4 5 6 7 (for the left) and M I C H A E L (for the right) are to be determined as the result.

```
        1                        M
|-----+-----|            |-----+-----|
  2         3              I           C
|--+--|   |--+--|        |--+--|     |---+--|
4     5   6     7        H     A     E       L
```

8.2.6 Exercise 6: Level Sum (★★★★☆)

In the previous exercise, you implemented the breadth-first search. Now you want to sum up the values per level of a tree. For this purpose, let's assume that the values are natural numbers of type int. Write function level_sum(start_node).

Example

For the tree shown, the sums of the values of the nodes per level should be calculated and return the following result: {0=4, 1=8, 2=17, 3=16}.

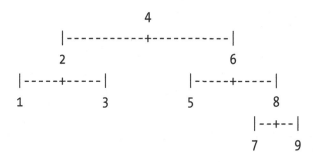

Level	Value(s)	Result
0	4	4
1	2, 6	8
2	1, 3, 5, 8	17
3	7, 9	16

8.2.7 Exercise 7: Tree Rotate (★★★☆☆)

Binary trees, especially binary search trees, may degenerate into lists if values are inserted only in ascending or descending order. An unbalance can be addressed by rotating parts of the tree. Write the functions rotate_left(node) and rotate_right(node) that rotate the tree around the node passed as parameter to the left or right, respectively.

Example

Figure 8-6 visualizes a rotation to the left and a rotation to the right with the balanced starting position in the middle.

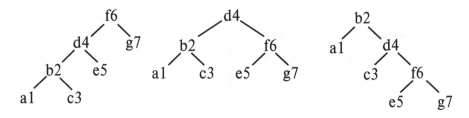

Figure 8-6. *Rotation to the left, original, rotation to the right*

8.2.8 Exercise 8: Reconstruction (★★★☆☆)

Exercise 8a: Reconstruction from a List (★★☆☆☆)

In this exercise, you want to reconstruct a binary search tree that is as balanced as possible from an ascending sorted list of natural numbers.

Example

For example, let these values be given:

```
\begin{lstlisting}
values = [1, 2, 3, 4, 5, 6, 7]
```

Then the following tree should be reconstructed from them:

```
            4
    |-----+-----|
    2           6
 |--+--|     |--+--|
 1     3     5     7
```

Exercise 8b: Reconstruction from Inorder/Preorder (★★★☆☆)

Suppose the sequence of values in preorder and inorder is given, each prepared as a list. This information about an arbitrary binary tree should be used to reconstruct the corresponding tree. Write function reconstruct(preorder_values, inorder_values).

Example

Two sequences of values of the traversals are as follows. Based on these values, you should reconstruct the tree shown in the previous part of the exercise.

```
preorder_values = [4, 2, 1, 3, 6, 5, 7]
inorder_values = [1, 2, 3, 4, 5, 6, 7]
```

8.2.9 Exercise 9: Math Evaluation (★★☆☆☆)

Consider using a tree to model mathematical expressions with the four operators +, −, /, and ∗. It is your task to compute the value of individual nodes, including in particular the value of the root node. For this purpose, write function `evaluate(node)`.

Example

Represent the expression 3 + 7 ∗ (7 − 1) by the following tree to compute the value 45 for the root node:

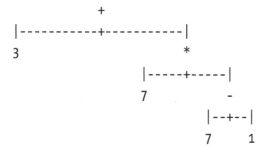

8.2.10 Exercise 10: Symmetry (★★☆☆☆)

Check if an arbitrary binary tree is symmetric in its structure. Therefore, write function `is_symmetric(node)`. In addition to the structural examination, you can also check for equality of values.

Examples

To check for symmetry, you use a binary tree that is symmetric in structure (left) and a binary tree that is also symmetric concerning values (right).

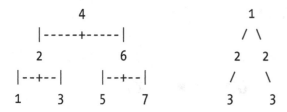

```
          4                            1
  |-----+-----|                       / \
  2           6                      2   2
|--+--|     |--+--|                 /     \
1     3     5     7                3       3
```

NOTE: THE SYMMETRY PROPERTY

In a symmetric binary tree, the left and right subtree are mirrored through the root along an imaginary vertical line (indicated by |):

```
      1
    / | \
   2  |  2
  /   |   \
 3    |    3
```

Depending on the definition, a comparison of the values can be omitted for the symmetry. In this case, only the structural organization can be counted as relevant.

Bonus: Mirror tree In the hint box, I indicated a mirror axis through the root. Create function `invert(node)` that mirrors the nodes of a tree at this implied line through the root.

Example

A mirroring looks like this:

```
          4                                    4
  |-----+-----|                        |-----+-----|
  2           6      =>                6           2
|--+--|     |--+--|                  |--+--|     |--+--|
1     3     5     7                  7     5     3     1
```

8.2.11 Exercise 11: Check Binary Search Tree (★★☆☆☆)

In this exercise, you are to check whether an arbitrary binary tree fulfills the property of a binary search tree (BST), so if the values in the left subtree are smaller than the root node's value and those in the right subtree are larger—and this holds for each subtree starting from the root. For simplification, assume int values. Write function is_bst(node).

Example

Use the following binary tree, which is also a binary search tree. For example, if you replace the number 1 with a larger number on the left side, it is no longer a binary search tree. However, the right subtree under the 6 is still a binary search tree.

```
        4
   |-----+-----|
   2           6
|--+--|     |--+--|
1     3     5     7
```

8.2.12 Exercise 12: Completeness (★★★★★)

Check the completeness of a tree. To do this, you initially solve the basics in the first two parts of the exercise and then proceed to the trickier completeness check.

Exercise 12a: Number of Nodes (★☆☆☆☆)

Count how many nodes are contained in any binary tree. To do this, write function count_nodes(node).

Example

For the binary tree shown, the value 7 should be determined. If you remove the right subtree, the tree consists of only 4 nodes.

```
            4
    |-----+-----|
    2           6
 |--+--|     |--+--|
 1     3     5     7
```

Exercise 12b: Check for Full/Perfect (★★☆☆☆)

For an arbitrary binary tree, check if all nodes have two successors or leaves each, and thus the tree is full. For perfection, all leaves must be at the same height. Write functions is_full(node) and is_perfect(node).

Example

The binary tree shown is both perfect and full. If you remove the two leaves below the 2, it is no longer perfect but still full.

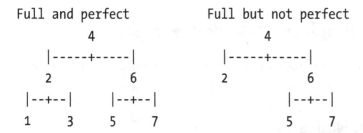

```
Full and perfect            Full but not perfect
            4                           4
    |-----+-----|               |-----+-----|
    2           6               2           6
 |--+--|     |--+--|                     |--+--|
 1     3     5     7                     5     7
```

Exercise 12c: Completeness (★★★★☆)

In this subtask, you are asked to check if a tree is complete as defined in the introduction, so a binary tree with all levels fully filled, with the allowed exception on the last level where nodes may be missing, but only with gaps as far to the right as possible.

Example

In addition to the perfect tree used so far, the following tree is also complete by definition. However, if you remove the children from node H, the tree is no longer complete.

```
                        F
            |------------+-----------|
          D                           H
      |-----+-----|               |-----+-----|
        B           E               G           I
    |--+--|
    A     C
```

Exercise 12d: Completeness Recursive (★★★★★)

In this last subtask, the following challenge remains to be mastered as a special treat. The check is to be solved without additional data structures and purely recursively. At first, this sounds hardly feasible, so I'll give a hint.

Tip   Develop the solution step by step. Create an auxiliary data structure that models whether or not a node exists for a certain position. Then traverse the tree and mark the positions appropriately. Afterwards, convert this implementation to a purely recursive one without the auxiliary data structure.

Example

As before, the following tree is complete by definition:

```
                        F
            |------------+-----------|
          D                           H
      |-----+-----|               |-----+-----|
        B           E               G           I
    |--+--|
    A     C
```

8.2.13 Exercise 13: Tree Printer (★★★★★)

In this exercise, you are to implement a binary tree's graphical output, as you have seen before in the examples. Therefore, you initially solve the basics in the first three parts of the assignment and then proceed to the trickier graphical presentation of trees.

Tip   Use a fixed grid of blocks of width three. This significantly contributes to a balanced representation and reduces complexity.

Example

The following tree should cover various special cases:

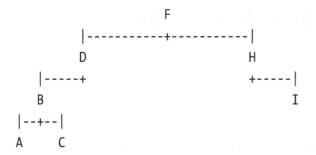

```
                        F
        |-----------+-----------|
        D                       H
      |-----+                 +-----|
      B                             I
    |--+--|
    A     C
```

Exercise 13a: Width of a Subtree (★★☆☆☆)

In this part of the exercise, you are asked to find the maximum width of a subtree of a given height using the function `subtree_width(height)`. For simplicity, you assume that a maximum of three characters represents the nodes. Besides, there is a distance of at least three characters between them. This is true for the leaves when the tree is full. On higher levels, there is naturally more space between the nodes of two subtrees.

Examples

On the left in Figure 8-7, you see a tree of height 2, and on the right, a tree of height 3. Based on the grid of 3, you get 9 and 21 as widths.

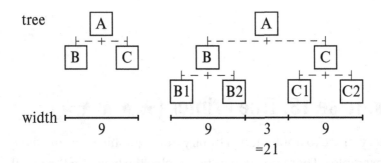

Figure 8-7. *Tree width*

Height	Total width	Width of subtree
1	3	0 (no subtree existing)
2	9	3
3	21	9
4	45	21

Exercise 13b: Draw Node (★★☆☆☆)

Write function draw_node(current_node, line_length) that creates a graphical output of a node, generating the given set of spaces appropriately. The node value should have a maximum of three characters and be placed in the middle.

Tip   Remember that if the current node has a left successor, the representation of the layer below starts on the left with the string ' |-'.

Example

The example in Figure 8-8 shows a single node with a spacing of five characters. Besides, the node value is center-aligned in a three-character box.

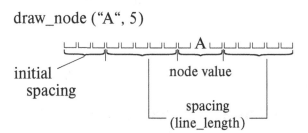

Figure 8-8. *Dimensions when drawing nodes*

Exercise 13c: Draw Connection Lines (★★☆☆☆)

Write function draw_connections(node, line_length) for building a graphical output of the connection lines of a node to its two successors. Missing successors have to be handled correctly.

Tip   The line length refers to the characters between the node representations. The parts representing the ends are still to be appended appropriately in each case, as well as the middle connector.

Example

The following figure visualizes all cases relevant in drawing, so with none, one, and two successor(s):

```
                        F
        |------------+-----------|
          D                       H
      |-----+                 +-----|
        B                         I
    |--+--|
    A     C
```

A schematic representation is shown again in Figure 8-9.

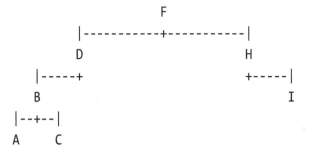

draw_connections (node, line_length)

Figure 8-9.   Schematic representation of the connecting lines

Exercise 13d: Tree Representation (★★★★★)

Combine all solutions of the parts of the exercise and complete the necessary steps to be able to print an arbitrary binary tree suitably on the console. To do this, write function nice_print(node).

Example

The output of the tree shown in the introductory example should look something like this through `nice_print()`:

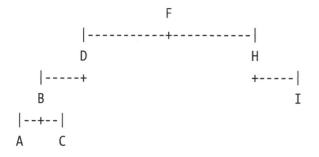

Also, check your algorithm with a real monster of a tree, which you can find in the sources. Here is a much-slimmed-down representative:

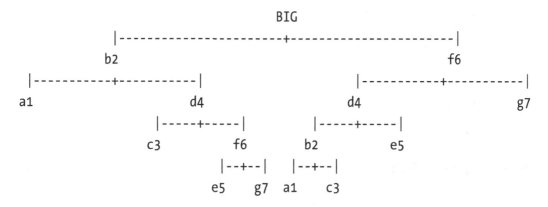

8.3 Solutions

8.3.1 Solution 1: Tree Traversal (★★☆☆☆)

Extend the functions already presented in the introduction for the traversing trees so that they can perform any action on the current node during the traversal. To do this, add an action to the respective signature, such as for inorder: `inorder(node, action)`.

Algorithm With this extension, each method for traversing the tree receives an additional parameter to define an action. Then this is called at the appropriate place instead of the console output.

```
def inorder(node, action):
    if node is None:
        return

    inorder(node.left, action)
    action(node.item)
    inorder(node.right, action)

def preorder(node, action):
    if node is None:
        return

    action(node.item)
    preorder(node.left, action)
    preorder(node.right, action)

def postorder(node, action):
    if node is None:
        return

    postorder(node.left, action)
    postorder(node.right, action)
    action(node.item)
```

Bonus: Fill up a Tree into a List

Build a representation of the values of the nodes in the form of a list. To do this, write function to_list(node) that returns the values based on an inorder traversal, and functions to_list_preorder(node) and to_list_postorder(node) that are based on a preorder and postorder traversal, respectively.

Example

When using the following tree

```
            d4
       |-----+-----|
      b2           f6
   |--+--|       |--+--|
  a1     c3     e5     g7
```

the conversions should result in something similar to

```
to_list: ['a1', 'b2', 'c3', 'd4', 'e5', 'f6', 'g7']
to_list_preorder: ['d4', 'b2', 'a1', 'c3', 'f6', 'e5', 'g7']
to_list_postorder: ['a1', 'c3', 'b2', 'e5', 'g7', 'f6', 'd4']
```

Algorithm Instead of the console output used so far as an action, the current value is added depending on the chosen traversal strategy. For the recursive descent, you use += to add the partial results and the method append() from list for the value of the current node.

```
def to_list(start_node):
    if start_node is None:
        return []

    result = []

    result += to_list(start_node.left)
    result.append(startNode.item)
    result += to_list(start_node.right)

    return result

def to_list_preorder(start_node):
    if start_node is None:
        return []

    result = []

    result.append(start_node.item)
    result += to_list_preorder((start_node.left)
    result += to_list_preorder((start_node.right)

    return result

def to_list_postorder(start_node):
    if start_node is None:
        return []

    result = []

    result += to_list_postorder(start_node.left)
```

```
    result += to_list_postorder(start_node.right)
    result.append(start_node.item)

    return result
```

Verification

Define a tree, perform an inorder traversal with the action passed, and finally populate two more lists from the tree:

```python
def main():
    def myprint(item):
        print(item, end=' ')

    root = example_trees.create_example_tree()
    TreeUtils.nice_print(root)

    print("\ninorder with action:")
    inorder(root, myprint)
    print("\npreorder with action:")
    preorder(root, myprint)
    print("\npostorder with action:")
    postorder(root, myprint)

    print("\nto_list:", to_list(root))
    print("to_list_preorder:", to_list_preorder(root))
    print("to_list_postorder:", to_list_postorder(root))
```

If you execute this main() function, you get the following output, which shows that your implementation works as expected:

```
          d4
     |-----+-----|
    b2          f6
 |--+--|     |--+--|
 a1    c3    e5    g7

inorder with action:
a1 b2 c3 d4 e5 f6 g7
preorder with action:
```

```
d4 b2 a1 c3 f6 e5 g7
postorder with action:
a1 c3 b2 e5 g7 f6 d4
to_list: ['a1', 'b2', 'c3', 'd4', 'e5', 'f6', 'g7']
to_list_preorder: ['d4', 'b2', 'a1', 'c3', 'f6', 'e5', 'g7']
to_list_postorder: ['a1', 'c3', 'b2', 'e5', 'g7', 'f6', 'd4']
```

8.3.2 Solution 2: Inorder, Preorder, and Postorder Iterative (★★★★☆)

In the introduction, you learned about inorder, preorder, and postorder as recursive variants. Now implement these types of traversals iteratively.

Example

Again, you use the following tree:

```
          d4
     |-----+-----|
     b2          f6
   |--+--|      |--+--|
  a1    c3     e5    g7
```

The three depth-first search methods traverse this tree as follows:

```
Preorder:    d4 b2 a1 c3 f6 e5 g7
Inorder:     a1 b2 c3 d4 e5 f6 g7
Postorder:   a1 c3 b2 e5 g7 f6 d4
```

Preliminary considerations for the algorithms For each of the iterative implementations, you need an auxiliary data structure. This is what I will now discuss in detail for the three variants.

Algorithm for inorder (★★★☆☆) When implementing an inorder traversal, you use a stack to temporarily store nodes that have to be processed later and variable current_node to store the current node. The basic idea is to start from the root, move to the bottom left of the tree, and put the current node on the stack until no successor is left. Then you take the uppermost node from the stack and process it (here by a simple console output). Now you continue with the right successor. Again, if there is no successor, process the top node from the stack.

The following sequence results for the tree of the example:

current_node	Stack	Action(s)	Direction of descent
d4	[ ]	Push d4	↙
b2	[d4]	Push b2	↙
a1	[b2, d4]	Push a1	↙
None	[a1, b2, d4]	Pop + action a1	↘
None	[b2, d4]	Pop + action b2	↘
c3	[d4]	Push c3	↙
None	[c3, d4]	Pop + action c3	↘
None	[d4]	Pop + action d4	↘
f6	[ ]	Push f6	↙
e5	[f6]	Push e5	↙
None	[e5, f6]	Pop + action e5	↘
None	[f6]	Pop + action f6	↘
g7	[ ]	Push g7	↙
None	[g7]	Pop + action g7	↘
None	[ ]	End	

Based on this, the iterative implementation of inorder looks like this:

```
def inorder_iterative(start_node, action):
    if start_node is None:
        return

    nodes_to_process = Stack()
    current_node = start_node

    # are there still nodes on the stack or is the current node not None?
    while not nodes_to_process.is_empty() or current_node is not None:
        if current_node is not None:
            # recursive descent to the left
            nodes_to_process.push(current_node)
            current_node = current_node.left
```

```
    else:
        # no left successor, then process current node
        current_node = nodes_to_process.pop()
        action(current_node.item)

        # continue with right successor
        current_node = current_node.right
```

Algorithm for preorder (★★☆☆☆) Interestingly, preorder is quite simple because the root of a subtree is always processed first. Then the left and right subtree are processed. For this, you again use a stack, which you fill initially with the current node. As long as the stack is not empty, you determine the top element and execute the desired action. Then you place the left and right successor nodes on the stack if they exist. It is important to note that the order of adding is opposite to that of reading. For the left subtree to be processed first, you must put the right node on the stack before the left one. This is repeated until the stack is empty. The following sequence results for the tree of the example:

current_node	Stack	Action(s)
	[d4]	Start: push d4
d4	[b2, f6]	Pop + action d4, push f6, push b2
b2	[a1, c3, f6]	Pop + action b2, push c3, push a1
a1	[c3, f6]	Pop + action a1
c3	[f6]	Pop + action c3
f6	[e5, g7]	pop + action f6, push g7, push e5
e5	[g7]	Pop + action e5
g7	[ ]	Pop + action g7
None	[ ]	End

This results in the following iterative preorder implementation, which is structurally very similar to the recursive variant:

```
def preorder_iterative(start_node, action):
    if start_node is None:
        return
```

```
nodes_to_process = Stack()
nodes_to_process.push(start_node)

while not nodes_to_process.is_empty():
    current_node = nodes_to_process.pop()

    if current_node is not None:
        action(current_node.item)

        # so that left is processed first, here order is reversed
        nodes_to_process.push(current_node.right)
        nodes_to_process.push(current_node.left)
```

To keep the analogy as strong as possible, it is helpful that collections can also store None values. This allows you to perform the None check once when extracting from the stack and otherwise keep the source code free of special handling.

Algorithm for postorder (★★★★☆) With postorder, you also use a stack for the intermediate storage of the nodes to be processed later. Of the three, however, this algorithm is the one with the greatest challenges and is tricky to implement because with postorder, although the traversal starts at the root, the action has to be executed after visiting the left and right subtree. Therefore, you have an interesting change compared to the previous two algorithms. In them, if an element is taken from the stack, then it is processed and not touched again. With the postorder implementation, an element is potentially inspected twice or more with peek() and later on removed only after that.

This time, you'll look at the source code first, and then I'll give further explanations:

```
def postorder_iterative(start_node, action):
    if start_node is None:
        return

    nodes_to_process = Stack()
    current_node = start_node
    last_node_visited = None

    while not nodes_to_process.is_empty() or current_node is not None:
        if current_node is not None:
            # descent to the left
            nodes_to_process.push(current_node)
            current_node = current_node.left
```

```
else:
    peek_node = nodes_to_process.peek()
    # descent to the right
    if peek_node.right is not None and \
        last_node_visited != peek_node.right:
        current_node = peek_node.right
    else:
        # sub root or leaf processing
        last_node_visited = nodes_to_process.pop()
        action(last_node_visited.item)
```

This is how the process works.: You start with the root node, put it on the stack, and continue in the left subtree. You repeat this until you no longer find a left successor. Now you have to move to the right successor. Only after that may the root be processed. Since you have saved all nodes on the stack, you now inspect the node from the stack. If this one has no right children and you have not just visited it, then you execute the passed action and remember this node as the last visited. For the other case, that there is a right subtree, you also traverse it as just described. This procedure is repeated until the stack is empty.

current_node	Stack	peek_node	Action
d4	[d4]		Push d4
b2	[b2, d4]		Push b2
a1	[a1, b2, d4]		Push a1
None	[a1, b2, d4]	a1	Action a1
None	[b2, d4]	b2	Peek + right
c3	[c3, b2, d4]		Push c3
None	[c3, b2, d4]	c3	Action c3
None	[b2, d4]	b2	Action b2
f6	[f6, d4]		Push f6
e5	[e5, f6, d4]		Push e5

(continued)

current_node	Stack	peek_node	Action
None	[f6, d4]	e5	Action e5
None	[f6, d4]	f6	Peek + right
g7	[g7, f6, d4]		Push g7
None	[g7, f6, d4]	g7	Action g7
None	[f6, d4]	f6	Action f6
None	[d4]	d4	Action d4
None	[]		

NOTE: ITERATIVE IMPLEMENTATION OF POSTORDER

While the implementations of the three traversals' recursive variants are all equally easy, and each is not very complex, this does not apply to the iterative implementations in any way. Preorder and inorder can still be implemented with a little thinking without major difficulties. With postorder, however, you really have to fight. Therefore, it is no shame to need a couple of attempts and to apply error corrections.

Don't worry. It's not always that tricky. Even the breadth-first traversal discussed later, which traverses level by level, is in my estimation much less complex to implement than the iterative postorder.

Recursion can be the key to simplicity in some cases. Sometimes, however, this comes at the expense of runtime. For optimization, you learned about memoization. However, very understandable iterative variants can also be found for some problems.

Verification

You define the tree from the introductory example and then traverse it each time using the desired procedure:

```python
def main():
    def myprint(item):
        print(item, end=' ')
```

```
root = example_trees.create_example_tree()
TreeUtils.nice_print(root)

print("inorder iterative:")
inorder_iterative(root, myprint)
print("\npreorder iterative:")
preorder_iterative(root, myprint)
print("\npostorder iterative:")
postorder_iterative(root, myprint)
```

If you execute the above main() function, you get the following output, which shows that your implementation does what it is supposed to do:

```
            d4
      |-----+-----|
     b2          f6
   |--+--|      |--+--|
  a1    c3    e5    g7

inorder iterative:
a1 b2 c3 d4 e5 f6 g7
preorder iterative:
d4 b2 a1 c3 f6 e5 g7
postorder iterative:
a1 c3 b2 e5 g7 f6 d4
```

Verification with unit test As an example, and because the implementation has already demanded quite a bit from you, I show the test for postorder. The other two tests are analogous and can be found in the sources of the companion project. For the test, iteratively the current value is filled into a list. After processing all values, the resulting list is then checked against the expected values.

```
def test_postorder_iterative():
    root = example_trees.create_example_tree()

    result = []
    postorder_iterative(root, lambda item: result.append(item))

    assert result == ["a1", "c3", "b2", "e5", "g7", "f6", "d4"]
```

Surprise Algorithm

While preorder was quite easy to design iteratively, it became a bit more difficult with inorder and even really tricky with postorder.

But then I got a tip from Prof. Dr. Dominik Gruntz on how to simplify the entire process iteratively. Many thanks to Dominik for this great algorithm suggestion. You keep the sequences analogous to the recursive ones, however, in reverse order, since you work with a stack. Besides, you integrate artificial new tree nodes.

```python
def inorder_iterative_v2(root):
    stack = Stack()
    stack.push(root)

    while not stack.is_empty():
        current_node = stack.pop()
        if not current_node is None:
            if current_node.is_leaf():
                print(current_node.item, end=" ")
            else:
                stack.push(current_node.right)
                stack.push(BinaryTreeNode(current_node.item))
                stack.push(current_node.left)

    print()
```

And better yet, you can turn it into a general-purpose function that allows all three traversal variations. To do this, you first define an enumeration and then the function traverse() that creates an artificial entry with a tree node at each appropriate point in the sequence. As mentioned, these special nodes ensure that the processing occurs at the right place.

```python
class Order(Enum):
    PREORDER = auto()
    INORDER = auto()
    POSTORDER = auto()

def traverse(root, order):
    stack = Stack()
    stack.push(root)
```

```
while not stack.is_empty():
    current_node = stack.pop()
    if not current_node is None:
        if current_node.is_leaf():
            print(current_node.item, end = " ")
        else:
            if order == Order.POSTORDER:
                stack.push(BinaryTreeNode(current_node.item))

            stack.push(current_node.right)

            if order == Order.INORDER:
                stack.push(BinaryTreeNode(current_node.item))

            stack.push(current_node.left)

            if order == Order.PREORDER:
                stack.push(BinaryTreeNode(current_node.item))
print()
```

HINT: INSIGHT

With the help of this example, it is easy to grasp that thorough thinking about a problem can lead to simpler, more comprehensible, and less complex source code. Besides, it is always good to get a second or third opinion if a solution is more complex than desired.

8.3.3 Solution 3: Tree Height (★★☆☆☆)

Implement function get_height(node) to determine the height for both a tree and for subtrees with a single node as root.

Example

The following tree of height 4 is used as a starting point:

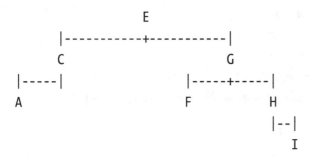

    Algorithm The tree height calculation uses a recursive algorithm, which determines the height of the left and the right subtree. Finally, you must compute the maximum from this and then add the value 1 for the current level.

```python
def get_height(parent):
    # recursive termination
    if parent is None:
        return 0

    # recursive descent
    left_height = get_height(parent.left)
    right_height = get_height(parent.right)

    return 1 + max(left_height, right_height)
```

Verification

You construct the tree from the example and then have the heights computed for some selected nodes:

```python
def main():
    e = BinaryTreeNode("E")
    insert(e, "C")
    insert(e, "A")
    insert(e, "G")
    insert(e, "F")
    insert(e, "H")
    insert(e, "I")
```

```
    TreeUtils.nice_print(e);

    print_infos(e.left, e, e.right, e.right.right.right)

def print_infos(c, e, g, i):
    print("\nHeight of root E:", get\_height(e))
    print("Height from left parent C: ", get\_height(c))
    print("Height from right parent G:", get\_height(g))
    print("Height from right child I: ", get\_height(i))
```

The following output occurs:

```
                    E
     |-----------+-----------|
         C                   G
   |-----+             |-----+-----|
   A                   F           H
                                 +--|
                                  I
```

```
Height of root E: 4
Height from left parent C: 2
Height from right parent G: 3
Height from right child I: 1
```

8.3.4 Solution 4: Lowest Common Ancestor (★★★☆☆)

Compute the lowest common ancestor (LCA) for two nodes, A and B, hosted in an arbitrary binary search tree. The LCA denotes the node that is the ancestor of both A and B and is located as deep as possible in the tree—the root is always the ancestor of both A and B. Write function find_lca(start_node, value1, value2) that, in addition to the start node of the search (usually the root), also receives lower and upper limits, which indirectly describe the nodes that are closest to these values. If the values for the limits are outside the range of values, then there is no LCA and it is supposed to return None.

Example

The following is a binary tree. If the lowest common ancestor is determined for the nodes with the values 1 and 5, this is the node with the value 4. In the figure, the respective nodes are circled and the ancestor is additionally marked in bold.

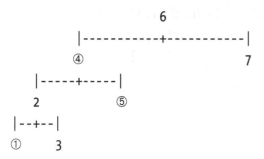

Algorithm Intuitively, you may be tempted to go up from the two nodes until the paths cross. Nevertheless, this is impossible whenever no backward direction exists in the node to the parent—like here. However, in your modeling of trees using the BinaryTreeNode class, you only use references to children, not to the parent node.

But there is a straightforward implementation starting from the root. From there, you proceed as follows: Let current_value be the value of the current node. In addition, let value1 and value2 be the passed node values (i. e. those of the two nodes of the potential successors). If value1 and value2 are smaller than current_value, then due to the sorting property within the binary search tree, both must be located in the left subtree—continue searching there. If both value1 and value2 are greater than current_value, then continue searching on the right. Otherwise for the cases value1 < current_value < value2 or value2 < current_value < value1, you have found the LCA; it is the current node.

```
def find_lca(start_node, value1, value2):
    # recursive termination
    if start_node is None:
        return None

    current_value = start_node.item

    # recursive descent
    if value1 < current_value and value2 < current_value:
        return find_lca(start_node.left, value1, value2)
```

```
if value1 > current_value and value2 > current_value:
    return find_lca(start_node.right, value1, value2)

# Here is value1 < current_value < value2 or
# value2 < current_value < value1
return start_node
```

Verification

You construct the tree shown in the example and invoke your method:

```python
@pytest.mark.parametrize("value1, value2, expected",
                         [(1, 3, 2), (1, 5, 4), (2, 5, 4),
                          (3, 5, 4), (1, 7, 6)])
def test_find_lca(value1, value2, expected):
    root = create_lca_example_tree()

    result = find_lca(root, value1, value2)

    assert result.item == expected

def test_find_lca_special():
    root = create_lca_example_tree()

    result = find_lca(root, 1, 2)
    assert result.item == 2
```

If you only check the quite obvious cases, everything works fine. If you consider checking two nodes in a parent-child relationship, namely the nodes with the values 1 and 2, you intuitively expect the node with the value 4. However, the node with the value 2 is calculated. According to the definition (among others in Wikipedia (https://en.wikipedia.org/wiki/Lowest_common_ancestor)), each node is also considered a successor of itself. Thus, the node with the value 2 is indeed the LCA in this case.

For the sake of completeness, the construction of the tree is shown:

```python
def create_lca_example_tree():
    _6 = BinaryTreeNode(6)
    insert(_6, 7)
    insert(_6, 4)
    insert(_6, 5)
```

```
insert(_6, 2)
insert(_6, 1)
insert(_6, 3)
```

return _6

8.3.5 Solution 5: Breadth-First (★★★☆☆)

In this exercise, you are asked to implement the breadth-first search, also called level order, using the function levelorder(start_node, action). The breadth-first search starts at the given node—usually the root—and then works its way through the tree level by level.

Note   Use a queue to store data on the nodes yet to be visited. The iterative variant is a bit easier to implement than the recursive one.

Examples

For the following two trees, the sequence 1 2 3 4 5 6 7 (for the left) and M I C H A E L (for the right) are to be determined as the result.

```
         1                        M
  |-----+-----|            |-----+-----|
  2           3            I           C
|--+--|     |--+--|      |--+--|     |--+--|
4     5     6     7      H     A     E     L
```

Algorithm For the breadth-first search, you use a queue as a cache for nodes to be processed later. First, you insert the root into the queue. Then you process elements as long as there are elements in the queue. This processing is divided into steps. First, perform the desired action for each element. Then put the left and right successor nodes into the queue if such a node exists. The algorithm checks in the processing whether the value in the queue is not equal to None. This avoids the special handling of missing successors when adding them.

```
def levelorder(start_node, action):
    if start_node is None:
        return

    to_process = Queue()
    to_process.enqueue(start_node)

    while not to_process.is_empty():
        current = to_process.dequeue()

    if current is not None:
        action(current.item)

        to_process.enqueue(current.left)
        to_process.enqueue(current.right)
```

To avoid special handling and None checks in the source code as much as possible, you benefit from the fact that None values can be stored in containers. This allows you to run the None check once when removing from the queue and not check it when adding the child nodes.

Instead of the while loop, you can also solve this by using recursive calls. If you are interested, study the source code in the companion project.

Let's clarify how the processes are in detail.

Queue	Action
[1]	1
[3, 2]	2
[5, 4, 3]	3
[7, 6, 5, 4]	4
[7, 6, 5]	5
[7, 6]	6
[7]	7
[ ]	End

Verification

You construct the tree with the numbers (the left one of the examples) and call your just created function to perform the level-order traversal:

```python
def create_level_order_example_tree():
    _1 = BinaryTreeNode("1")
    _2 = BinaryTreeNode("2")
    _3 = BinaryTreeNode("3")
    _4 = BinaryTreeNode("4")
    _5 = BinaryTreeNode("5")
    _6 = BinaryTreeNode("6")
    _7 = BinaryTreeNode("7")

    _1.left = _2
    _1.right = _3
    _2.left = _4
    _2.right = _5
    _3.left = _6
    _3.right = _7

    return _1

def main():
    root = create_level_order_example_tree()
    tree_utils.nice_print(root)

    print("Levelorder: ")
    levelorder(root, lambda item: print(item, end=' '))
    print("\nlevelorder_recursive: ")
    levelorder_recursive(root, lambda item: print(item, end=' '))
```

Then you get the following output—please note that the project sources contain a recursive implementation of level-order too:

```
           1
    |-----+-----|
    2           3
 |--+--|     |--+--|
 4     5     6     7
```

Levelorder:
1 2 3 4 5 6 7
levelorder_recursive:
1 2 3 4 5 6 7

Verification with unit test This can also be expressed quite simply as a unit test:

```
def test_levelorder():
    root = create_level_order_example_tree()

    result = []
    levelorder(root, lambda item: result.append(item))

    assert result == ["1", "2", "3", "4", "5", "6", "7"]
```

8.3.6 Solution 6: Level Sum (★★★★☆)

In the previous exercise, you implemented the breadth-first search. Now you want to sum up the values per level of a tree. For this purpose, let's assume that the values are natural numbers of type int. Write function level_sum(start_node).

Example

For the tree shown, the sums of the values of the nodes per level should be calculated and return the following result: {0=4, 1=8, 2=17, 3=16}.

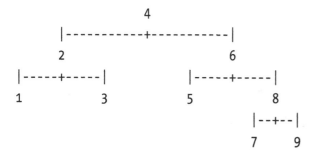

Level	Value(s)	Result
0	4	4
1	2, 6	8
2	1, 3, 5, 8	17
3	7, 9	16

Algorithm The breadth-first search provides a good basis. You are still missing a suitable data structure and a way to determine the current level to complete the solution. With a bit of thought, you come up with using a dictionary as the result data structure. The current level serves as the key. The value is formed by a tuple. You traverse the tree as you did with level order. To determine the levels, you cheat. Since you start from the root (of a subtree), you can assume level 0. Each change to a lower level increases the value. For this you use the second value from the tuple. This way, you always know on which level the currently processed node is located. With this information the summation can be formulated easily:

```python
def level_sum(start_node):
    if start_node is None:
        return {}
    result = {}

    to_process = Queue()
    # pretty cool, tuple (node, level)
    to_process.enqueue((start_node, 0))

    while not to_process.is_empty():
        current_node_and_level = to_process.dequeue()

        current_node = current_node_and_level[0]
        level = current_node_and_level[1]

    if level not in result:
        result[level] = 0

    result[level] += current_node.item
```

```
    if current_node.left is not None:
        to_process.enqueue((current_node.left, level + 1))

    if current_node.right is not None:
        to_process.enqueue((current_node.right, level + 1))

    return result
```

Algorithm with depth-first search Interestingly, the same can be easily implemented using depth-first search, regardless of the type of traversal. In the following, it is implemented with inorder, and the variants for preorder and postorder are indicated as comments:

```
def level_sum_depth_first(root):
    results = {}

    traverse_depth_first(root, 0, results)

    return dict(sorted(results.items()))

def traverse_depth_first(current_node, level, results):
    if current_node:
        # PREORDER
        # results[level] = results.get(level, 0) + current_node.item
        traverse_depth_first(current_node.left, level + 1, results)

    # INORDER
    results[level] = results.get(level, 0) + current_node.item

    traverse_depth_first(current_node.right, level + 1, results)

    # POSTORDER
    # results[level] = results.get(level, 0) + current_node.item
```

As before, you use a dictionary as a data structure, whose key is the level. If there is already an entry for the level, the value of the current node is added. Otherwise, the trick of specifying a default value in the call get(level, 0) ensures a starting value of 0.

Verification

Let's construct the tree from the example as usual and invoke the function you just implemented:

```python
def main():
    root = create_example_level_sum_tree()

    result = level_sum(root)
    print("\nlevel_sum:", result)

def create_example_level_sum_tree():
    _4 = BinaryTreeNode(4)
    insert(_4, 2)
    insert(_4, 1)
    insert(_4, 3)
    insert(_4, 6)
    insert(_4, 5)
    insert(_4, 8)
    insert(_4, 7)
    insert(_4, 9)
    return _4
```

Then you get the following output:

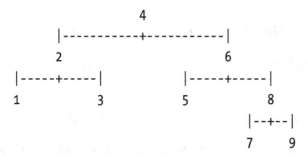

```
level_sum: {0=4, 1=8, 2=17, 3=16}
```

Verification with unit test This can also be expressed quite simply as a unit test:

```python
def test_level_sum():
    root = create_example_level_sum_tree()
```

```
result = level_sum(root)

assert result == {0: 4, 1: 8, 2: 17, 3: 16}

def test_level_sum_depth_first():
    root = create_example_level_sum_tree()

    result = level_sum_depth_first(root)

    assert result == {0: 4, 1: 8, 2: 17, 3: 16}
```

8.3.7 Solution 7: Tree Rotate (★★★☆☆)

Binary trees, especially binary search trees, may degenerate into lists if values are inserted only in ascending or descending order. A dysbalance can be addressed by rotating parts of the tree. Write functions rotate_left(node) and rotate_right(node) that will rotate the tree around the node passed as parameter to the left or right, respectively.

Example

Figure 8-10 visualizes a rotation to the left and a rotation to the right with the balanced starting position in the middle.

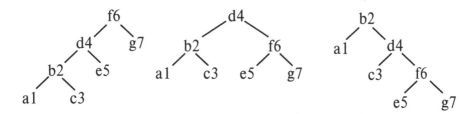

Figure 8-10. *Rotation to the left, original, rotation to the right*

   Algorithm At first, you might be frightened by the expected, but in fact only supposed, complexity of the undertaking. In general, it is a good idea to mentally go through the process using a simple example, such as the one above. Quite quickly you will realize that far fewer nodes are involved and actions are necessary than probably expected. To execute the respective rotation, you actually only have to consider the root and the left or right neighbor as well as a node from the level below, as shown in Figure 8-11.

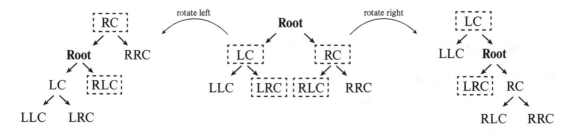

Figure 8-11. *Nodes affected during rotations*

Figure 8-11 illustrates that you just need to reassign two links in the tree to complete the rotation. To gain a better understanding of this, the relevant nodes are named accordingly. In the figure, LC and RC stand for Left Child and Right Child, LLC and LRC for Left Left Child and Left Right Child, and RLC and RRC for Right Left Child and Right Right Child.

With these preliminary considerations, the implementation of the rotations exactly follows the sequence illustrated in the diagrams:

```python
def rotate_left(node):
    if node.right is None:
        raise ValueError("can't rotate left, no valid root")

    rc = node.right
    rlc = node.right.left

    rc.left = node
    node.right = rlc

    return rc

def rotate_right(node):
    if node.left is None:
        raise ValueError("can't rotate right, no valid root")

    lc = node.left
    lrc = node.left.right

    lc.right = node
    node.left = lrc

    return lc
```

Please keep in mind that these functions change the subtrees' references and thus may affect previously cached nodes. The root is suddenly no longer the root but located one level below.

Verification

First, you define the tree in the middle, like the example. Then you rotate it first to the left and then twice to the right, which should correspond to a simple rotation to the right starting from the tree in the middle.

```
def main():
    root = example_trees.create_example_tree()
    TreeUtils.nice_print(root)

    print("\nRotate left")
    left_rotated_root = rotate_left(root)
    TreeUtils.nice_print(left_rotated_root)

    print("\nRotate right")
    right_rotated_root = rotate_right(rotate_right(left_rotated_root))
    TreeUtils.nice_print(right_rotated_root)
```

Execute the program to see that the rotations work correctly:

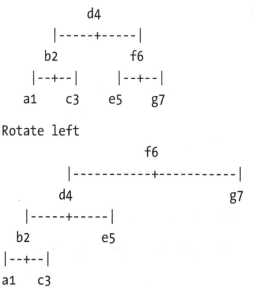

```
            d4
     |-----+-----|
    b2           f6
  |--+--|      |--+--|
  a1    c3    e5    g7
Rotate left
                  f6
        |-----------+-----------|
       d4                       g7
  |-----+-----|
  b2           e5
|--+--|
a1    c3
```

Rotate right

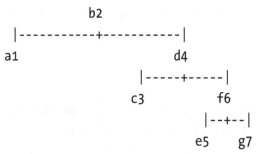

Verification with unit test Let's consider how you could test this using unit tests. Again, it depends on the appropriate idea and data structure. It would be difficult and costly to check the resulting trees for consistency structurally. It is much easier if you compare the result of a traversal with the expected values. But pay attention. When doing this, you have to avoid using the inorder traversal since it always produces the same node order for an arbitrary binary search tree, regardless of the tree's structure! Here either a preorder or a postorder or, better still, a level order traversal is suitable. The latter has the great advantage that the order can be easily derived from a graphical representation of the tree and is, therefore, best suited for the unit test because it remains comprehensible and understandable. You already implemented the conversion at the beginning in Section 8.1.4 as method convert_to_list().

```
def test_rotate_left():
    root = example_trees.create_example_tree()

    result = rotate_left(root)
    as_list = convert_to_list(result)
    assert as_list == ["f6", "d4", "g7", "b2", "e5", "a1", "c3"]

def test_rotate_right():
    root = example_trees.create_example_tree()

    result = rotate_right(root)
    as_list = convert_to_list(result)
    assert as_list == ["b2", "a1", "d4", "c3", "f6", "e5", "g7"]
```

As a reminder, the function for converting a tree into a list based on a level order is shown here again.

```
def convert_to_list(node):
    result = []
    levelorder(node, lambda item: result.append(item))
    return result
```

8.3.8 Solution 8: Reconstruction (★★★☆☆)

Solution 8a: Reconstruction from a List (★★☆☆☆)

In this exercise, you want to reconstruct a binary search tree that is as balanced as possible from an ascending sorted list of natural numbers.

Example

For example, use these values:

```
values = [1, 2, 3, 4, 5, 6, 7]
```

Then the following tree should be reconstructed from them:

```
          4
    |-----+-----|
    2           6
 |--+--|     |--+--|
 1     3     5     7
```

Algorithm Reconstructing a binary search tree from a sorted list in ascending order is not that difficult. Due to the sorting, you can split the list in half and use the value in the middle as the base for the new node. You construct the left and right subtree recursively from the list's left and right parts, respectively. You continue the bisection until the sublist has only the size 0 or 1.

```
def reconstruct(values):
    # recursive termination
    if not values: # len(values) == 0 not recommended by PEP 8
        return None

    mid_idx = len(values) // 2
    mid_value = values[mid_idx]

    new_node = BinaryTreeNode(mid_value)
```

```
    # recursive termination
    if len(values) == 1:
        return new_node

    # recursive descent
    left_part = values[0: mid_idx]
    right_part = values[mid_idx + 1:len(values)]

    new_node.left = reconstruct(left_part)
    new_node.right = reconstruct(right_part)

    return new_node
```

You could omit the query on length 1 in the middle of the function without changing the functionality. The function would then simply be called twice for an empty list and thus terminate directly. For me, this special treatment was a bit more understandable, but that's a matter of taste.

Verification

Let's see the implementation in action and supply an arbitrary but suitably sorted list of int values. With this, you invoke your function, which returns the root of the tree as a result. Finally, you verify that the tree is indeed correctly reconstructed by printing various information to the console.

```
def main():
    inputs = [[1, 2, 3, 4, 5, 6, 7],
              [1, 2, 3, 4, 5, 6, 7, 8]]

    for values in inputs:
        root = reconstruct(values)
        print_info(root)
```

The output function is simple to implement:

```
def print_info(root):
    TreeUtils.nice_print(root)

    print("Root: ", root)
    print("Left: ", root.left)
```

```
    print("Right:", root.right)
    print()
```

The following abbreviated output shows that the two trees are correctly reconstructed:

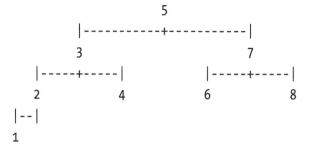

```
             4
      |-----+-----|
      2           6
   |--+--|     |--+--|
   1     3     5     7

Root:  BinaryTreeNode [item=4, left=BinaryTreeNode [item=2, ..
Left:  BinaryTreeNode [item=2, left=BinaryTreeNode [item=1, ...
Right: BinaryTreeNode [item=6, left=BinaryTreeNode [item=5, ...
```

```
                    5
        |-----------+-----------|
        3                       7
     |-----+-----|           |-----+-----|
     2           4           6           8
   |--|
   1

Root:  BinaryTreeNode [item=5, left=BinaryTreeNode [item=3, ...
Left:  BinaryTreeNode [item=3, left=BinaryTreeNode [item=2, ...
Right: BinaryTreeNode [item=7, left=BinaryTreeNode [item=6, ...
```

Verification with unit test Once again you use a level order traversal for the unit test to verify the reconstruction:

```
def test_reconstruct_from_list():
    inputs = [1, 2, 3, 4, 5, 6, 7]

    result_root = reconstruct(inputs)
    result = convert_to_list(result_root)

    assert result == [4, 2, 6, 1, 3, 5, 7]
```

Solution 8b: Reconstruction from Inorder/Preorder (★★★☆☆)

Suppose the sequence of values in preorder and inorder is given, each prepared as a list. This information about an arbitrary binary tree should be used to reconstruct the corresponding tree. Write function reconstruct(preorder_values, inorder_values).

Example

Two sequences of values of the traversals are given below. Based on these values, you should reconstruct the tree shown in the previous part of the exercise.

```
preorder_values = [4, 2, 1, 3, 6, 5, 7]
inorder_values = [1, 2, 3, 4, 5, 6, 7]
```

Algorithm For a better understanding of the need for two inputs and the algorithm, let's take another look at the values of a preorder and inorder traversal with the value of the root highlighted in bold as an example:

```
Preorder  4 2 1 3 6 5 7
Inorder   1 2 3 4 5 6 7
```

The preorder traversal always starts with the root, so based on the first value, you can create the root first. By searching for the value of the root in the value sequence of the inorder traversal, you determine how the values are divided into left and right subtrees. Everything in the inorder to the left of the value of the root represents the values of the left subtree. Analogously, this applies to the values to the right of it and the right subtree. This results in the following sublists:

```
Left:  1 2 3
Right: 5 6 7
```

To call your function recursively, you need to find the corresponding value sequences for preorder. How do you do this?

Let's take a detailed look at the values of a preorder and an inorder traversal. By looking closely, you can see the following pattern:

$$\begin{array}{cccc} & \overset{root}{4} & \overset{left}{213} & \overset{right}{657} \\ \textit{Preorder} & & & \\ \textit{Inorder} & \underset{left}{123} & \underset{root}{4} & \underset{right}{567} \end{array}$$

With this knowledge, you can implement the algorithm as follows, taking advantage of slicing to generate the appropriate chunks from the original and use them for the recursive descent:

```python
def reconstruct_clearer(preorder_values, inorder_values):
    # recursive termination
    # len(values) == 0 not recommended by PEP 8
    if not preorder_values or not inorder_values:
        return None

    root_value = preorder_values[0]
    root = BinaryTreeNode(root_value)

    # recursive termination
    if len(preorder_values) == 1 and len(inorder_values) == 1:
        return root

    # recursive descent
    index = inorder_values.index(root_value)

    # left and right part for inorder
    left_inorder = inorder_values[0: index]
    right_inorder = inorder_values[index + 1: len(inorder_values)]

    # left and right part for preorder
    left_preorder = preorder_values[1: 1 + index]
    right_preorder = preorder_values[index + 1: len(preorder_values)]

    root.left = reconstruct_clearer(left_preorder, left_inorder)
    root.right = reconstruct_clearer(right_preorder, right_inorder)

    return root
```

Verification

To understand the reconstruction, you provide the appropriate value sequences as three nested lists. As usual, Pytest automatically extracts the preorder and inorder values from each of these inputs. The result is given in the form of a level order traversal. This offers good traceability based on the graphical representation.

```
@pytest.mark.parametrize("preorder_values, inorder_values, expected",
                         [([4, 2, 1, 3, 6, 5, 7], [1, 2, 3, 4, 5, 6, 7],
                          [4, 2, 6, 1, 3, 5, 7]),
                         ([5, 4, 2, 1, 3, 7, 6, 8], [1, 2, 3, 4, 5, 6, 7, 8],
                          [5, 4, 7, 2, 6, 8, 1, 3])])
def test_reconstruct_from_pre_in_order(preorder_values, inorder_values,
                                       expected):

    result_root = reconstruct_clearer(preorder_values, inorder_values)
    result = convert_to_list(result_root)

    assert result == expected
```

HINT: THINGS TO KNOW ABOUT RECONSTRUCTION

Interestingly, using the algorithm shown, any binary tree can be reconstructed, regardless of whether it is also a binary search tree (for which its nodes follow an order). But it gets even more remarkable. If the values of the preorder traversal originate from a binary search tree, it is possible to reconstruct it based only on that, as follows:

```
def reconstruct_from_preorder_bst(preorder_values):
    # recursive termination
    if not preorder_values:
        return None

    root_value = preorder_values[0]
    root = BinaryTreeNode(root_value)

    # splitting
    left_values = [value for value in preorder_values if value < root_value]
    right_values = [value for value in preorder_values if value > root_value]

    # recursive descent
    root.left = reconstruct_from_preorder_bst(left_values)
    root.right = reconstruct_from_preorder_bst(right_values)

    return root
```

This is possible since, in a binary search tree, the values of the preorder traversal are first the value of the root, then the values smaller than the root, and finally the values of the right subtree, which are also larger than the value of the root. This condition also applies recursively. With the help of two filter conditions, all left and right subtree values can be easily extracted— as shown above—and used as input for the recursive call.

Try the reconstruction with the following dataset:

```
inputs = [[4, 2, 1, 3, 6, 5, 7],
          [5, 4, 2, 1, 3, 7, 6, 8]]
```

```
for values in inputs:
    root = reconstruct_from_preorder_bst(values)
    TreeUtils.nice_print(root)
```

The first input data generates the following tree:

```
            4
    |-----+-----|
    2           6
|--+--|     |--+--|
1     3     5     7
```

8.3.9 Solution 9: Math Evaluation (★★☆☆☆)

Consider using a tree to model mathematical expressions with the four operators +, −, /, and ∗. It is your task to compute the value of individual nodes, including in particular the value of the root node. For this purpose, write function evaluate(node).

Example

Represent the expression $3 + 7 * (7 - 1)$ by the following tree to compute the value 45 for the root node:

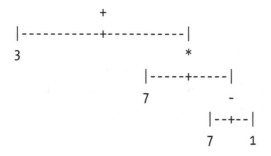

Algorithm The problem can be solved simply and clearly by a recursive call in combination with the appropriate operators as follows. It's a bit clumsy due to the fact that there is no switch in Python up to Python 3.9.

```python
def evaluate(node):
    value = node.item;

    if value == "+":
        return evaluate(node.left) + evaluate(node.right)
    if value == "-":
        return evaluate(node.left) - evaluate(node.right)
    if value == "*":
        return evaluate(node.left) * evaluate(node.right)
    if value == "/":
        return evaluate(node.left) / evaluate(node.right)
    else:
        return int(value)
```

Python 3.10 introduces match as a new keyword, which is more powerful than switch known from other programming languages. In combination with a dynamic evaluation, you can write the whole thing as follows:

```python
def evaluate_v2(node):
    value = node.item

    match value:
        case "+" | "-" | "*" | "/":
            val1 = evaluate_v2(node.left)
            val2 = evaluate_v2(node.right)
            return eval(str(val1) + value + str(val2))
        case _:
            return int(value)
```

Verification

Let's construct the tree from the example and invoke the above function:

```python
def main():
    plus = BinaryTreeNode("+")
    _3 = BinaryTreeNode("3")
```

```
mult = BinaryTreeNode("*")
_7 = BinaryTreeNode("7")
minus = BinaryTreeNode("-")
_1 = BinaryTreeNode("1")

plus.left = _3
plus.right = mult
mult.left = _7
mult.right = minus
minus.left = _7
minus.right = _1

tree_utils.nice_print(plus)

print("+:", evaluate(plus))
print("*:", evaluate(mult))
print("-:", evaluate(minus))

print("+:", evaluate_v2(plus))
print("*:", evaluate_v2(mult))
print("-:", evaluate_v2(minus))
```

If you execute this main() function, you get on the output of the tree as well as the results of the selected individual nodes:

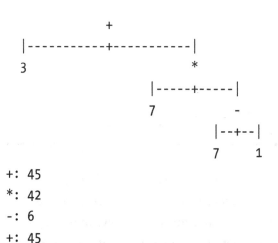

```
+: 45
*: 42
-: 6
+: 45
*: 42
-: 6
```

8.3.10 Solution 10: Symmetry (★★☆☆☆)

Check if an arbitrary binary tree is symmetric in its structure. Write function `is_symmetric(node)`. In addition to the structural examination, you can also check for equality of values.

Examples

To check for symmetry, you use a binary tree that is symmetric in structure (left) and a binary tree that is also symmetric concerning values (right).

```
        4                       1
  |-----+-----|               /   \
  2           6              2      2
|--+--|     |--+--|          /        \
1     3     5     7         3          3
```

NOTE: THE SYMMETRY PROPERTY

In a symmetric binary tree, the left and right subtree are mirrored through the root along an imaginary vertical line (indicated by |):

```
   1
  /|\
 2 | 2
 / | \
3  |  3
```

Depending on the definition, a comparison of the values can be omitted for the symmetry. In this case, only the structural organization can be counted as relevant.

Algorithm Once again, you benefit from a good basic knowledge of recursion. Starting from the root, you check the two opposite successor nodes. The simplest case is that for a node, no successor nodes exist. This constellation is always symmetrical. If, however, only one of the two successor nodes exists, then the tree is not symmetric. Accordingly, only the case for two successor nodes is to be considered. Here the respective left and right subtrees must be mirror-inverted. For this, you check recursively whether the right subtree of the left and the left subtree of the right node structurally fit each other, as well as the left subtree of the right and the right subtree of the left node.

```python
def is_symmetric(node):
    if node is None:
        return True

    return check_if_nodes_are_symmetric(node.left, node.right)

def check_if_nodes_are_symmetric(left, right):
    if left is None and right is None:
        return True
    if left is None or right is None:
        return False

    # descend both subtrees
    return check_if_nodes_are_symmetric(left.right, right.left) and \
        check_if_nodes_are_symmetric(left.left, right.right)
```

Advanced algorithm: Value symmetry In fact, the extension to value checking is simple if you have implemented the previous exercise correctly. Only a Boolean parameter check_value has to be added to the signature and evaluated at the appropriate place before the recursive descent:

```python
def check_if_nodes_and_values_are_symmetric(left, right, check_value):
    if left is None and right is None:
        return True
    if left is None or right is None:
        return False

    # check values
    if check_value and not left.item == right.item:
        return False

    # descend both subtrees
    return check_if_nodes_and_values_are_symmetric(left.right, right.left,
                                                   check_value) and \
            check_if_nodes_and_values_are_symmetric(left.left, right.right,
                                                    check_value)
```

Verification

You construct the two trees from the introduction and invoke the function you just created. The first tree is already known. The other one is explicitly created for this example with `create_symmetric_number_tree()`: After that, you add the node with the value 4, which deliberately breaks the symmetry.

```
def main():
    root = example_trees.create_number_tree()
    TreeUtils.nice_print(root)
    print("symmetric:", is_symmetric(root))

    root2 = create_symmetric_number_tree()
    TreeUtils.nice_print(root2)
    print("symmetric:", is_symmetric(root2))

    # modified tree: add a 4
    root2.right.left = BinaryTreeNode("4")
    TreeUtils.nice_print(root2)
    print("symmetric:", is_symmetric((root2))
```

In `create_symmetric_number_tree()` you create a root and then the symmetric structure with nodes with the values 2 and 3.

```
def create_symmetric_number_tree():
    root = BinaryTreeNode("1")
    root.left = BinaryTreeNode("2")
    root.right = BinaryTreeNode("2")
    root.left.left = BinaryTreeNode("3")
    root.right.right = BinaryTreeNode("3")
    return root
```

If you execute this `main()` function, you get the expected results:

```
          4
    |-----+-----|
    2           6
  |--+--|     |--+--|
  1     3     5     7
```

```
symmetric: True
          1
    |-----+-----|
    2           2
  |--+         +--|
  3               3
symmetric: True
          1
    |-----+-----|
    2           2
  |--+       |--+--|
  3          4     3
symmetric: False
```

Bonus: Mirror Tree

In the hint box, I indicated a mirror axis through the root. Create function invert(node) that mirrors the nodes of a tree at this implied line through the root.

Example

A mirroring looks like this:

```
        4                       4
  |-----+-----|           |-----+-----|
  2           6   =>       6           2
|--+--|     |--+--|      |--+--|     |--+--|
1     3     5     7      7     5     3     1
```

Algorithm At first, you might once again assume that the challenge is difficult to solve. But in fact, it is much easier to implement with the help of recursion than you initially think.

The algorithm proceeds from the root downwards and swaps the left and right subtrees. To do this, you store these subtrees in temporary variables and then assign them to the other side. That's really all there is to it!

You implement this in Python as follows:

```python
def invert(root):
    if root is None:
        return None

    inverted_right = invert(root.right)
    inverted_left = invert(root.left)

    root.left = inverted_right
    root.right = inverted_left

    return root
```

Python shortcut Using the tuple notation, you can implement the whole thing even more compactly as follows:

```python
def invert_clearer(root):
    if root is None:
        return None

    root.left, root.right = invert(root.right), invert(root.left)

    return root
```

Verification

You construct the left tree from the introduction and invoke the function you just created:

```python
def main():
    root = example_trees.create_number_tree()
    newroot = invert(root)
    TreeUtils.nice_print(newroot)

    newroot = invert_clearer(newroot)
    TreeUtils.nice_print(newroot)
```

If you execute this `main()` function, you get the expected mirroring and another one results again in the original:

```
                    4
            |-----+-----|
          6                 2
      |--+--|          |--+--|
      7     5          3     1
                    4
            |-----+-----|
          2                 6
      |--+--|          |--+--|
      1     3          5     7
```

8.3.11 Solution 11: Check Binary Search Tree (★★☆☆☆)

In this exercise, you check whether an arbitrary binary tree fulfills the property of a binary search tree (BST), so the values in the left subtree are smaller than the root node's value and those in the right subtree are larger—and this holds for each subtree starting from the root. For simplification, assume `int` values. Write function `is_bst(node)`.

Example

Use the following binary tree, which is also a binary search tree. For example, if you replace the number 1 with a larger number on the left side, it is no longer a binary search tree. However, the right subtree under the 6 is still a binary search tree.

```
              4
        |-----+-----|
        2                 6
    |--+--|          |--+--|
    1     3          5     7
```

Algorithm From the assignment, you recognize a recursive design. A tree with only one node is always a binary search tree. If there is a left or right successor or even both, you check their values for compliance with the value relation and perform this recursively for their successors, if they exist.

```python
def is_bst(node):
    # recursive termination
    if node is None:
        return True

    if node.is_leaf():
        return True

    # recursive descent
    is_left_bst = True
    is_right_bst = True
    if node.left is not None:
        is_left_bst = node.left.item < node.item and is_bst(node.left)
    if node.right is not None:
        is_right_bst = node.right.item > node.item and is_bst(node.right)

    return is_left_bst and is_right_bst
```

Verification

You construct the tree from the example and invoke the function you just created. You also apply two modifications and check again.

```python
def main():
    _4 = create_integer_number_tree()

    _2 = _4.left
    _6 = _4.right
    TreeUtils.nice_print(_4)
    print("is_bst(_4):", is_bst(_4))
    print("is_bst(_2):", is_bst(_2))
    print("is_bst(_6):", is_bst(_6))
```

```
# change the tree on the left in a wrong and on the right in a correct way
_2.left = BinaryTreeNode(13)
_6.right = None

TreeUtils.nice_print(_4)
print("is_bst(_4):", is_bst(_4))
print("is_bst(_2):", is_bst(_2))
print("is_bst(_6):", is_bst(_6))
```

If you execute this main() function, you get both the output of the tree and the results for selected individual nodes, whether these nodes themselves (but of course with their successors) represent a binary search tree.

However, if you carelessly store a larger value in the left subtree (e. g., 13), neither the whole tree nor the part with node 2 as root is a BST. For the right subtree, if you delete the node with the value 7, the right subtree with the node with the value 6 remains a BST.

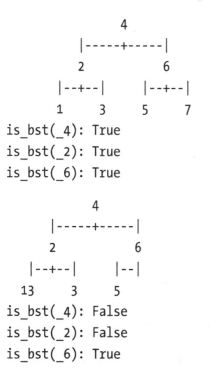

```
            4
      |-----+-----|
      2           6
    |--+--|     |--+--|
    1     3     5     7
is_bst(_4): True
is_bst(_2): True
is_bst(_6): True


            4
      |-----+-----|
      2           6
    |--+--|     |--|
   13     3     5
is_bst(_4): False
is_bst(_2): False
is_bst(_6): True
```

8.3.12 Solution 12: Completeness (★★★★★)

In this exercise, you check the completeness of a tree. To do this, you initially solve the basics in the first two parts of the exercise and then proceed to the trickier completeness check.

Solution 12a: Number of Nodes (★☆☆☆☆)

Count how many nodes are contained in any binary tree. To do this, write function count_nodes(node).

Example

For the binary tree shown, the value 7 should be determined. If you remove the right subtree, the tree consists of only 4 nodes.

```
            4
    |-----+-----|
    2           6
 |--+--|     |--+--|
 1     3     5     7
```

Algorithm The algorithm is really extremely straightforward if you express it recursively. Each node counts as 1, and then you continue counting in both its left and right subtrees and add their results until you hit a leaf.

```python
def count_nodes(node):
    if node is None:
        return 0

    return 1 + count_nodes(node.left) + count_nodes(node.right)
```

Solution 12b: Check for Full/Perfect (★★☆☆☆)

For an arbitrary binary tree, check if all nodes have two successors or leaves each, and thus the tree is full. For perfection, all leaves must be at the same height. Write functions is_full(node) and is_perfect(node).

Example

The binary tree shown is both perfect and full. If you remove the two leaves below the 2, it is no longer perfect but still full.

```
Full and perfect              Full but not perfect
        4                             4
|-----+-----|                 |-----+-----|
2           6                 2           6
|--+--|   |--+--|                       |--+--|
1   3   5   7                         5   7
```

Algorithm The check whether a tree is full is not that difficult if it is implemented recursively. Attention: Please do not confuse *full* and *complete* (see the introduction for definitions). A tree is full if it has no or two successors. Otherwise, it cannot be a full tree.

```python
def is_full(node):
    if node is None:
        return True

    return __is_full_helper(node.left, node.right)

def __is_full_helper(left_node, right_node):
    if left_node is None and right_node is None:
        return True

    if left_node is not None and right_node is not None:
        return is_full(left_node) and is_full(right_node)

    return False
```

This is a good start. Based on this, you need some smaller extensions to be able to check the perfectness. First, you must determine the height of the whole tree, starting from the root. This can easily be achieved, as you implemented it as solution of Exercise 8.3.3. After that, you proceed quite similar to is_full(), but now every node must have two successors. On the level of the leaves, you additionally have to check if they are at the correct level. You might stumble over the fact that the height of a leaf is 1. Therefore you still need the level on which they are located. For this, you cheat with an additional parameter current_level in your function. This results in the following implementation:

```
def is_perfect(node):
    if node is None:
        return True

    height = get_height(node)

    return is_perfect_helper(node.left, node.right, height, 1)

def is_perfect_helper(left_node, right_node, height, current_level):
    if left_node is None or right_node is None:
        return False

    if left_node.is_leaf() and right_node.is_leaf():
        return on_same_height(left_node, right_node, height, current_level)

    return is_perfect_helper(left_node.left, left_node.right, height,
                             current_level + 1) and \
        is_perfect_helper(right_node.left, right_node.right, height,
                          current_level + 1)

def on_same_height(left_node, right_node, height, current_level):
    # problem: height of the node is 1, therefore you must
    # take into account the current level here
    return get_height(left_node) + current_level == height and \
        get_height(right_node) + current_level == height
```

Verification

You construct the tree with numbers from the introduction and invoke the methods you just created. In addition, you modify the tree by deleting the reference to the right subtree. Then you invoke the functions again.

```
def main():
    _4 = example_trees.create_number_tree()
    TreeUtils.nice_print(_4)

    print("#nodes:", count_nodes(_4))
    print("is_full?:", is_full(_4))
    print("is_perfect?:", is_perfect(_4))
    print()
```

```
# delete nodes with values 1, 3
_2 = _4.left
_2.left = None
_2.right = None
TreeUtils.nice_print(_4)

print("#nodes:", count_nodes(_4))
print("is_full?:", is_full(_4))
print("is_perfect?:", is_perfect(_4))
print()
```

If you run this main() function, you get the expected results:

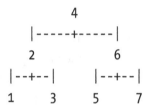

```
#nodes: 7
is_full?: True
is_perfect?: True
```

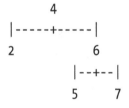

```
#nodes: 5
is_full?: True
is_perfect?: False
```

Solution 12c: Completeness (★★★★☆)

In this subtask, you check if a tree is complete as defined in the introduction—as a binary tree with all levels fully filled, with the allowed exception on the last level where nodes may be missing, but only with gaps as far to the right as possible.

Example

In addition to the perfect tree used so far, the following tree is also complete by definition. However, if you remove the children from node H, the tree is no longer complete.

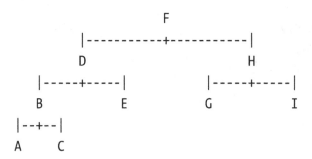

Algorithm At first, this seems to be a rather tricky task, much more complicated than the checks shown before. If you study the definition again, the tree is supposed to contain successors in pairs. Moreover, there must be no gaps in the tree, so no node with a missing left successor but with a right successor. If the tree is not fully filled, then only leaves from the right may be missing. On closer visual inspection, it is noticeable that you can traverse level by level, but nodes may be missing only in the last level.

Now the level order traversal comes to mind. You use this here and just add a few checks. For each node there must be no right successor without a left one. Besides, you check whether you have discovered a missing node in the meantime. How can this happen? This is possible whenever you want to add a node's successors to the queue, but there is only one left or right successor. This is expressed by the flag missing_node. So, if a missing successor has been detected, then the nodes processed afterwards must be leaves only.

```python
def levelorder_is_complete(start_node):
    if start_node is None:
        return False

    to_process = Queue()
    to_process.enqueue(start_node)

    # indicates that a node does not have two successors
    missing_node = False
```

```
while not to_process.is_empty():
    current = to_process.dequeue()

    # only descendants on the right side
    if current.left is None and current.right is not None:
        return False

    # if a missing node was previously detected,
    # then the next may be only a leaf
    if missing_node and not current.is_leaf():
        return False

    # include sub-elements, mark if not complete
    if current.left is not None:
        to_process.enqueue(current.left)
    else:
        missing_node = True
    if current.right is not None:
        to_process.enqueue(current.right)
    else:
        missing_node = True

# all nodes successfully tested
return True
```

Verification

You construct the tree from the example and invoke the function you just created. In addition, you modify the tree by removing the leaves below the H node and check again.

```
def main():
    F = create_completness_example_tree()
    TreeUtils.nice_print(F)
    print("levelorder_is_complete?", levelorder_is_complete(F))

    # remove leaves under H
    H = F.right
    H.left = None
    H.right = None
```

```
    TreeUtils.nice_print(F)
    print("levelorder_is_complete?", levelorder_is_complete(F))

def create_completness_example_tree():
    F = BinaryTreeNode("F")
    TreeUtils.insert(F, "D")
    TreeUtils.insert(F, "H")
    TreeUtils.insert(F, "B")
    TreeUtils.insert(F, "E")
    TreeUtils.insert(F, "A")
    TreeUtils.insert(F, "C")
    TreeUtils.insert(F, "G")
    TreeUtils.insert(F, "I")
    return F
```

If you execute this main() function, you get the expected results:

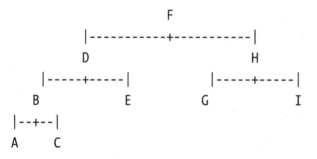

```
levelorder_is_complete? True
```

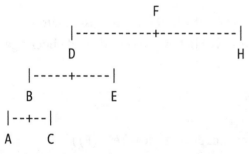

```
levelorder_is_complete? False
```

536

Solution 12d: Completeness Recursive (★★★★★)

In this last subtask, the following challenge remains to be mastered as a special treat. The check is to be solved without additional data structures and purely recursively. At first, this sounds hardly feasible, so I'll give a hint.

Tip   Develop the solution step by step. Create an auxiliary data structure that models whether or not a node exists for a certain position. Then traverse the tree and mark the positions appropriately. Afterwards, convert this implementation to a purely recursive one without the auxiliary data structure.

Example

As before, the following tree is complete by definition:

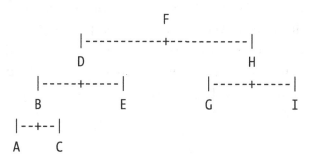

Algorithm In fact, the assignment sounds hardly manageable, but that is why it is a tough challenge. As like so often, it is worthwhile to start by developing a version that does not yet meet all the required properties and gradually refine it. You start with the ideas from the tip.

The idea is this: You traverse the tree, and for each node that exists, you mark exactly that in a list of bools When doing so, you number the positions according to level order from left to right and top to bottom. To determine the position of the current node in the list, you perform the following computation: For the position i, the left successor has the position $i * 2 + 1$ and the right successor has position $i * 2 + 2$.[3] Figure 8-12 illustrates this.

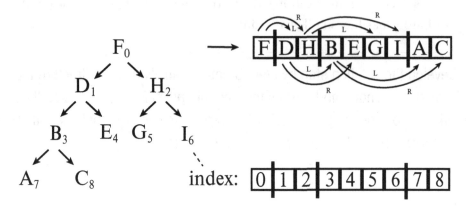

Figure 8-12. *Map a tree node to a position in the list/array*

Now you still need to know how large the result list needs to be. Theoretically, at most, it can contain 2^{height} elements. However, for very deep and thus expanding trees, many leaves might not exist at all. To optimize the memory consumption, you count the number of nodes to determine the actual size needed. This is where Exercise 12a helps you. Then you traverse all the tree elements using the `traverse_and_mark()` function. Finally, you summarize the data using `all_assigned()`.

```
def is_complete(start_node):
    node_count = count_nodes(start_node)

    node_exists = [False] * node_count

    # now you traverse the tree from the root downwards
    traverse_and_mark(start_node, node_exists, 0)

    return all_assigned((node_exists)
```

Let's move on to traversing the tree and filling the list. Interestingly, it doesn't matter whether you use preorder, inorder, or postorder here. The only important thing is that the positions are determined according to the mentioned computation rule.

---

[3] The computation gets a little bit easier if you assign the index 1 to the root. Then the children have positions $2i$ and $2i + 1$.

```
def traverse_and_mark(start_node, node_exists, pos):
    # recursive termination
    if start_node is None:
        return

    if pos >= len(node_exists):
        return

    # action
    node_exists[pos] = True

    # recursive descent
    traverse_and_mark(start_node.left, node_exists, pos * 2 + 1)
    traverse_and_mark(start_node.right, node_exists, pos * 2 + 2)
```

Finally, you need to check if there is a position in the list that is not occupied by True. In this case, you detect that the tree is not complete. This is implemented as follows:

```
def all_assigned(node_exists):
    for exists in node_exists:
        if not exists:
            return False

    return True
```

If you remember the built-in function all() you can shorten the implementation—I keep the helper function because it communicates the algorithm more clearly.

```
def all_assigned(node_exists):
    return all(node_exists)
```

Phew, that was quite a bit of work so far, and you needed several tricks. On a positive note, this algorithm works. I'll show that later along with the algorithm converted purely to recursive processing based on these ideas.

On the negative side, however, you need quite a bit of additional memory depending on the tree's size. Let's see how you can avoid this by using the purely recursive variant.

Recursive algorithm The goal is to eliminate the use of the list and work only recursively. Therefore, the previously created traverse_and_mark() function is a good starting point. Since you're not allowed to use a list as a data store, you need the number of nodes as a parameter.

```
def is_complete_rec(start_node):
    return __is_complete_rec_helper(start_node, 0, count_nodes(start_node))

def __is_complete_rec_helper(start_node, pos, node_count):
    if start_node is None:
        return True
    if pos >= node_count:
        return False

    if not __is_complete_rec_helper(start_node.left, 2 * pos + 1,
    node_count):
        return False
    if not __is_complete_rec_helper(start_node.right, 2 * pos + 2,
    node_count):
        return False

    return True
```

Without the intermediate steps, it would have been challenging—at least for me—to formulate the task recursively since the trick of the logic in the position calculation can hardly be derived without the list in mind. It is quite impressive what these few lines accomplish.

Verification

Again, you construct the tree and modify it after testing. If you take away the node H or I individually or both, then completeness is no longer given.

```
def main():
    F = create_completness_example_tree()
    TreeUtils.nice_print(F)
    print("is_complete?", is_complete(F))
    print("is_complete_rec?", is_complete_rec(F))

    # modification: remove leaves under H
    H = F.right
    H.left = None
    H.right = None
    TreeUtils.nice_print(F)
```

```
    print("is_complete?", is_complete(F))
    print("is_complete_rec?", is_complete_rec(F))
def create_completness_example_tree():
    F = BinaryTreeNode("F")
    TreeUtils.insert(F, "D")
    TreeUtils.insert(F, "H")
    TreeUtils.insert(F, "B")
    TreeUtils.insert(F, "E")
    TreeUtils.insert(F, "A")
    TreeUtils.insert(F, "C")
    TreeUtils.insert(F, "G")
    TreeUtils.insert(F, "I")
    return F
```

If you run this main() function, you get the expected results—moreover, they are consistent for the function variations:

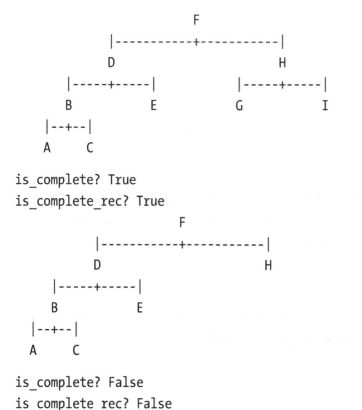

```
is_complete? True
is_complete_rec? True
```

```
is_complete? False
is_complete_rec? False
```

8.3.13 Solution 13: Tree Printer (★★★★★)

In this exercise, you implement a binary tree's graphical output, as you have seen before in the examples. Therefore, you initially solve the basics in the first three parts of the assignment and then proceed to the trickier graphical presentation of trees.

Tip   Use a fixed grid of blocks of width three. This significantly contributes to a balanced representation and reduces complexity.

Example

The following tree should cover various special cases:

```
                    F
       |-----------+-----------|
          D                   H
       |-----+              +-----|
        B                         I
      |--+--|
      A     C
```

Solution 13a: Width of a Subtree (★★☆☆☆)

In this part of the exercise, you are asked to find the maximum width of a subtree of a given height using the function subtree_width(height). For simplicity, you assume that a maximum of three characters represents the nodes. Besides, there is a distance of at least three characters between them. This is true for the leaves when the tree is full. On higher levels, there is naturally more space between the nodes of two subtrees.

Examples

Examples On the left, you see a tree of height 2, and on the right, a tree of height 3. Based on the grid of three, you get 9 and 21 as widths. See Figure 8-13.

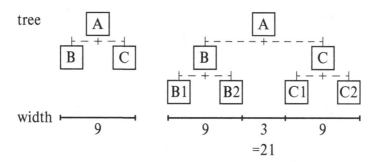

Figure 8-13. *Tree width*

Height	Total width	Width of subtree
1	3	0 (no subtree existing)
2	9	3
3	21	9
4	45	21

Algorithm In the diagram, you recognize that the lowest level of a binary tree can contain at most 2^n nodes, with n as the height of the tree. In order not to exceed the scope you want to ignore variable widths of the nodes. To determine the maximum width for a height, the total width is as follows:

$$max\_num\_of\_leaves * leaf\_width + (max\_num\_of\_leaves - 1) * spacing$$

This is the basis for the following implementation. Perhaps the last computation is a bit tricky. You have to subtract the spacing and divide by two since you only want to determine the maximum width of a subtree.

```python
def subtree_width(height):
    if height <= 0:
        return 0

    leaf_width = 3
    spacing = 3
```

```
max_num_of_leaves = pow(2, height - 1)
width_of_tree = max_num_of_leaves * leaf_width + \
                (max_num_of_leaves - 1) * spacing
width_of_subtree = (width_of_tree - spacing) // 2

return width_of_subtree
```

Solution 13b: Draw Node (★★☆☆☆)

Write function draw_node(current_node, line_length) that creates a graphical output of a node, generating the given set of spaces appropriately. The node value should have a maximum of three characters and be placed in the middle.

Tip   Remember that if the current node has a left successor, the representation of the layer below starts on the left with the string ' |-'.

Example

The example shows a single node with a spacing of five characters. Besides, the node value is center-aligned in a three-character box. See Figure 8-14.

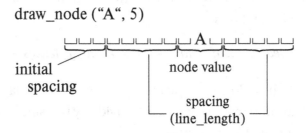

Figure 8-14. *Dimensions when drawing nodes*

Algorithm As usual, it is a good idea to reduce the complexity by subdividing an assignment into several smaller subtasks. Using function spacing() you create the required spacing both to the left and right of the node representation. Its preparation first checks for the special cases of no existence or no value in the node. Then this corresponds graphically to a free space of three characters. Otherwise, you pad the value converted to a string with spaces if it is shorter than three characters. If it is longer, you truncate the text to three characters. This is done in the function stringify_node_value(node). Because subsequent lines start with the text '|-' if a left successor exists, you add three more spaces to the front of your string representation.

```python
def draw_node(current_node, line_length):
    str_node = " "
    str_node += spacing(line_length)
    str_node += stringify_node_value(current_node)
    str_node += spacing(line_length)

    return str_node

def stringify_node_value(node):
    if node is None:
        return " "
    if node.item is None:
        return " "

    node_value = str(node.item)
    if len(node_value) == 1:
        return " " + node_value + " "
    if len(node_value) == 2:
        return node_value + " "

    return node_value[0:3]

def spacing(line_length):
    return " " * line_length
```

Solution 13c: Draw Connection Lines (★★☆☆☆)

Write function draw_connections(node, line_length) to build a graphical output of the connection lines of a node to its two successors. Missing successors must be handled correctly.

Tip   The line length refers to the characters between the node representations. The parts representing ends are still to be appended appropriately in each case, as well as the middle connector.

Example

The following figure visualizes all cases relevant in drawing, with none, one, and two successor(s).

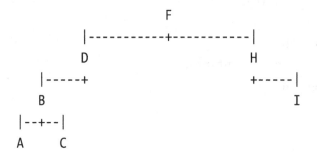

A schematic representation is shown again in Figure 8-15.

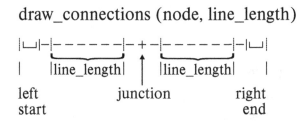

Figure 8-15. *Schematic representation of the connecting lines*

Algorithm When drawing the connecting lines below a node, all three variants with and without left or right successor are to be covered. Even a little more interesting is the fact that a non-existent node must also produce a corresponding output of blanks. This is needed if there are no children on the left side. Otherwise, the nodes on the right side would not be indented correctly.

You subdivide the drawing into three parts. First, you prepare the left part of the output with draw_left_connection_part(). After that, in draw_junction(node) you create the connection point respecting all special cases. Finally, with draw_right_connection_part() you prepare the right part.

```
def draw_connections(node, line_length):
    if node is None:
        return " " + spacing(line_length) + \
               " " + spacing(line_length) + " "
```

```
    connection = draw_left_connection_part(node, line_length)
    connection += draw_junction(node)
    connection += draw_right_connection_part(node, line_length)

    return connection

def draw_left_connection_part(node, line_length):
    if node.left is None:
        return " " + spacing(line_length)
    else:
        return " |-" + draw_line(line_length)

def draw_right_connection_part(node, line_length):
    if node.right is None:
        return spacing(line_length) + " "
    else:
        return draw_line(line_length) + "-| "

def draw_junction(node):
    if node.left is None and node.right is None:
        return " "
    elif node.left is None:
        return " +-"
    elif node.right is None:
        return "-+ "
    else:
        return "-+-"

def draw_line(line_length):
    return "-" * line_length
```

Solution 13d: Tree Representation (★★★★★)

Combine all solutions of the parts of the exercise and complete the necessary steps to be able to print an arbitrary binary tree suitably on the console. To do this, write function nice_print(node).

Example

The output of the tree shown in the introductory example should also look something like this through `nice_print()`:

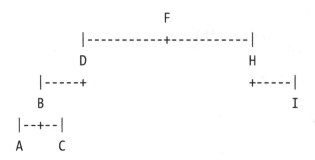

Also, check your algorithm with a real monster of a tree, which you can find in the sources. Here is a much-slimmed-down representative:

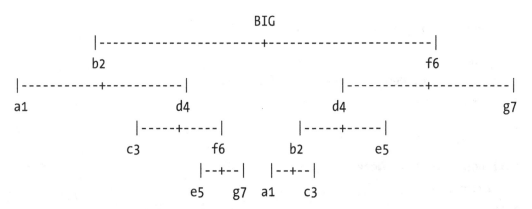

Algorithm In the previous task, you learned how to map binary trees to lists or arrays. Here, this has to be slightly modified because in the tree nodes can be missing at arbitrary places in contrast to completeness. For computing the size of the list, you need the height of the tree. This is also important for computing the corresponding distances and line lengths. In this case, the trick also helps determine the maximum width of a subtree and use it appropriately.

These ideas mentioned earlier may be picked up to create a suitable list in which the nodes are stored in a scattered manner. The following function will assist you in doing so:

```
def fill_nodes_into_list(start_node):
    height = get_height(start_node)
    nodes = [None] * pow(2, height)
```

```
    traverse_and_mark(start_node, nodes, 0)

    return nodes

def traverse_and_mark(start_node, nodes, pos):
    if start_node is None:
        return

    if pos >= len(nodes):
        return

    # action
    nodes[pos] = start_node

    # recursive descent
    traverse_and_mark(start_node.left, nodes, pos * 2 + 1)
    traverse_and_mark(start_node.right, nodes, pos * 2 + 2)
```

For drawing, the tree and the list are traversed level by level and the graphical representation is prepared. However, this has the disadvantage that very extensive trees also require quite a lot of additional memory when drawing since they are kept as an array or list.

There are still a few challenges waiting for you:

- As you start drawing at the top, you need to move the previously prepared lines for each new level by appropriate positions to the right.

- The distances between the nodes and the lengths of the connecting lines have to be computed and kept depending on the total height, the current level, and position. Thereby the lowest level still needs special treatment.

Figure 8-16 illustrates the grid and the different distances between the nodes per level and from one level to the next.

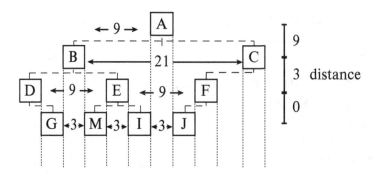

Figure 8-16. *Spacing between nodes*

The associated implementation benefits from the use of the helper functions:

```
def nice_print_v1(node):
    if node is None:
        return

    tree_height = get_height(node)
    all_nodes = fill_nodes_into_list(node)

    # traverse level by level
    offset = 0
    lines = []
    for level in range(tree_height):

        line_length = subtree_width(tree_height - 1 - level)

        # indent predecessor lines to the right
        for i in range(len(lines)):
            lines[i] = " " + spacing(line_length) + lines[i]

        nodes_per_level = pow(2, level)
        node_line = ""
        connection_line = ""

        for pos in range(nodes_per_level):
            current_node = all_nodes[offset + pos]

            node_line += draw_node(current_node, line_length)
            node_line += spacing_between_nodes(tree_height, level)
```

```
            connection_line += draw_connections(current_node, line_length)
            connection_line += spacing_between_connections
            (tree_height, level)

        lines.append(node_line)
        lines.append(connection_line)

        # jump forward in the list
        offset += nodes_per_level

    for line in lines:
        print(line)

def spacing_between_nodes(tree_height, level):
    spacing_length = subtree_width(tree_height - level)
    spacing = " " * spacing_length
    if spacing_length > 0:
        spacing += " "
    return spacing

def spacing_between_connections(tree_height, level):
    spacing_length = subtree_width(tree_height - level)
    return " " * spacing_length
```

Memory-optimized algorithm In the following, I would like to present a modification that does not need any additional memory. Instead, it renders the graphical representation of the tree with a level order traversal. You use a list with single lines, wherein those with nodes and connecting lines alternate. In my opinion, the previously shown version is somewhat clearer. The following version needs the special treatment of changing levels, which is performed more naturally in the first version.

Overall, however, it is still a clear level order traversal, whose action is a bit more extensive in this case.

```
def nice_print(start_node):
    if start_node is None:
        return

    to_process = Queue()
    # very cool: tuple (node, level)
    to_process.enqueue((start_node, 0))
```

```python
tree_height = get_height(start_node)
lines = []

level = 0
node_line = ""
connection_line = ""
additional_left_spacing = ""

while not to_process.is_empty() and level < tree_height:
    # levelorder
    current_node_and_level = to_process.dequeue()
    current_node = current_node_and_level[0]
    node_level = current_node_and_level[1]

    line_length = subtree_width(tree_height - 1 - level)

    # change in level
    if level != node_level:
        level = node_level
        line_length = subtree_width(tree_height - 1 - level)

        lines.append(node_line)
        lines.append(connection_line)

        for i in range(len(lines)):
            lines[i] = " " + additional_left_spacing + \
                        spacing(line_length) + lines[i]

        node_line = ""
        connection_line = ""

    node_line += draw_node(current_node, line_length)
    node_line += spacing_between_nodes(tree_height, level)
    connection_line += draw_connections(current_node, line_length)
    connection_line += spacing_between_connections(tree_height, level)

    # levelorder
    if current_node is not None:
        to_process.enqueue((current_node.left, level + 1))
        to_process.enqueue((current_node.right, level + 1))
```

```
        else:
            # artificial placeholders
            to_process.enqueue((None, level + 1))
            to_process.enqueue((None, level + 1))

    for line in lines:
        print(line)
```

Verification

You have developed quite a bit. Now you want to see the fruits of your labor. For this purpose, you use the trees from the introductory example. The first tree shows well the principle way of working. The second is a combination of the previous example trees, but rotated to the left and right and united under a new root with the value BIG.

```
def create_tree_print_example_tree():
    F = BinaryTreeNode("F")
    TreeUtils.insert(F, "D")
    TreeUtils.insert(F, "H")
    TreeUtils.insert(F, "B")
    TreeUtils.insert(F, "A")
    TreeUtils.insert(F, "C")
    TreeUtils.insert(F, "I")
    return F

def create_big_tree():
    d4a = example_trees.create_example_tree()
    d4b = example_trees.create_example_tree()
    BIG = BinaryTreeNode("BIG")
    BIG.left = rotate_right(d4a)
    BIG.right = rotate_left(d4b)
    return BIG
```

These functions result in the following trees:

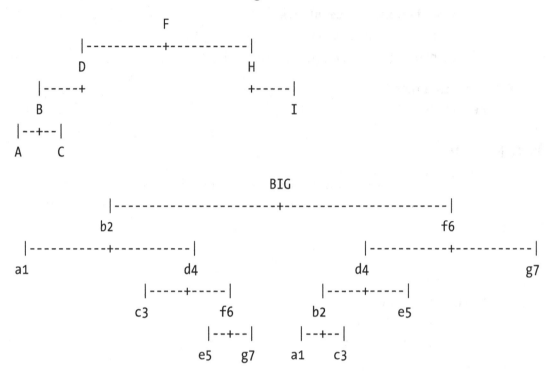

If you want to see how beautifully really expansive trees are rendered, call the function for the following construct:

```python
def create_monster_tree():
    mon = BinaryTreeNode("MON")
    mon.left = create_big_tree()
    mon.right = create_big_tree()
    return mon
```

In the companion project, you will find a double combination of this monster tree, which for fun I have named King Kong.

8.4 Summary: What You Learned

This chapter covered probably the most complex topic in this book, which is binary trees. As in many other languages, they are not part of standard Python. However, binary trees are suitable for solving numerous problems elegantly. Therefore, this chapter gave an introduction. Besides things like rotation, even mathematical calculations, for example, can be represented and processed very smartly using binary trees. Something challenging and to puzzle over was certainly the check for completeness and the graphical output of a binary tree.

In the next chapter, you continue with searching and sorting, which are essential topics in computer science like binary trees.

CHAPTER 9

Searching and Sorting

Searching and sorting are two elementary topics of computer science in the field of algorithms and data structures. Python provides efficient implementations for both of them and thus takes a lot of work off your shoulders. However, understanding the underlying algorithms helps in choosing the most suitable variant for a particular use case. I only skim over the topic of searching here since it is built in and does not offer a lot of variations, except for binary search, which is covered in section 9.1.1.

In this chapter, you will primarily dedicate yourself to some essential sorting algorithms because you will learn some algorithmic tricks in the meantime.

9.1 Introduction Search

When managing data, sometimes you need to search for items, such as customers with the first name "Carsten" or an invoice with specific order date. Conveniently, all containers like lists, sets and dictionaries offer various methods or functions, such as those with which you can search for elements.

9.1.1 Search with in(), index(), and count()

Sometimes you just need to check if certain data is present in a container. The keyword in helps with this. Occasionally you may also want to get the position of the element. Then you use index(), which triggers a ValueError in case of non-existence:

```
3 in [1, 2, 3] # => True

[1, 2, 3].index(2) # => 1
[1, 2, 3].index(4) # => ValueError
```

© Michael Inden 2022
M. Inden, *Python Challenges*, https://doi.org/10.1007/978-1-4842-7398-2_9

Furthermore, it is important to remember that index() always returns the index of the first occurrence. If there are several identical elements and all their occurrences are to be determined, then you can help yourself with a combination of in and enumerate(). If necessary, count() returns the number of identical elements.

```python
print([1, 2, 3, 2].index(2)) # => 1

print([i for i, val in enumerate([1, 2, 3, 2, 4, 2]) if val == 2]) # =>
[1, 3, 5]
print([1, 2, 3, 2, 4, 2].count(2)) # => 3
```

For dictionaries you can get the keys (keys()), the values (values()), or their combination with items(). For queries, there is another short form for the keys:

```python
programmers = {"Michael": "Python",
               "Tim": "C++",
               "Karthi": "Java"}

if "Karthi" in programmers.keys():
    print("Karthi is here")

# Python Shortcut
if "Karthi" in programmers:
    print("Karthi is here II")

if "C++" in programmers.values():
    print("someone knows C++")

if ("Michael", "Python") in programmers.items():
    print("Michael knows Python")
```

In addition, all() can be used to check whether a set of elements is included. With any() you can determine if there is a match.

```python
print(all(elem in [2, 3, 5, 7, 9] for elem in [7, 2]))  # => True
print(any(elem in [2, 3, 5, 7, 9] for elem in [7, 2]))  # => True
print(any(elem in [2, 3, 5, 7, 9] for elem in [4]))  # => False
```

9.1.2 Search with rindex() and rfind()

For strings, there are functions `rindex()` and `rfind()` to find the position of a desired element from the end of the string:

```
print("Hello".rindex("l")) # => 3
print("Hello".rfind("l")) # => 3
print("Hello".rfind("x")) # => -1
# print("Hello".rindex("x")) # => ValueError: substring not found
```

Unfortunately, there is no such thing for lists. However, you can program this quite easily yourself using the function named `last_index_of()`, which is known from Java and, in my opinion, is better understandable. If no element is found, the return value is -1.

```
def last_index_of(values, search_for):
    for pos in range(len(values) - 1, -1, -1):
        if values[pos] == search_for:
            return pos

    return -1

print(last_index_of([1, 2, 3, 2, 4, 2, 5, 2], 2))  # => 7
```

9.1.3 Binary Search

A brute-force way to search is to iterate over all elements until the desired element is found or you reach the end of the dataset, like this:

```
def find(values, search_for):
    for i, current_value in enumerate(values):
        if current_value == search_for:
            return i

    return -1
```

The same applies to the search methods just mentioned. Even if not directly visible, all of them iteratively look at all elements of the data structure until they find what they are looking for. They search all result in a linear running time. In contrast, there is an efficient search called ***binary search***, which offers logarithmic running time. But there is a prerequisite: ***binary search requires sorted data.*** If you have to sort data explicitly first, then the advantage over a linear search is hardly given, especially with small datasets.

For larger volumes of data, however, the logarithmic running time of a binary search is significantly better than that of a linear search. The low running time is achieved by the algorithm splitting the parts to be processed in half in each case and then continuing the search in the appropriate chunk. Figure 9-1 illustrates the principle procedure, with discarded parts marked in gray.

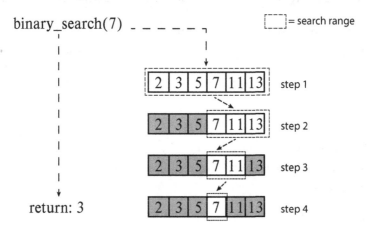

Figure 9-1. *Schematic sequence for binary search*

In the figure, the arrow points between the elements in the first step—depending on the implementation of `binary_search()`, the left or right element directly adjacent to the center is used for comparison if the number is even.

9.2 Introduction Sort

In this section, I introduce some sorting algorithms that form the basis for the later exercises.

9.2.1 Insertion Sort

Insertion Sort is illustrated the best by sorting a deck of cards in your hand. Typically, you start on the left side, then take the next card to the right, and insert it appropriately into the already sorted left part, which usually causes some cards to move to the right.

With this procedure, you can skip the first card since it is sorted by itself and start with the second card. Let's look at this for the number sequence 4, 2, 7, 9, 1. For this purpose, the respective new element to be sorted in is marked. The already sorted part on the left is separated with ‖ from the unsorted part on the right.

4 ‖ ② 7 9 1

2 4 ‖ ⑦ 9 1

2 4 7 ‖ ⑨ 1

2 4 7 9 ‖ ①

1 2 4 7 9

In the example, you start with the value 2. For each number, you have to determine the correct insertion position. There are two ways to do this, as described below.

Determine Insertion Position

Starting from the current position, move to the left as long as the compared values are larger. Alternatively, you can also start from the beginning and move one position to the right as long as the compared values are smaller.

```python
def find_insert_pos_from_current(values, current_pos):
    insert_pos = current_pos
    while insert_pos > 0 and values[insert_pos - 1] > values[current_pos]:
        insert_pos -= 1

    return insert_pos

def find_insert_pos_from_start(values, current_pos):
    insert_pos = 0
    while insert_pos < current_pos and values[insert_pos] <
    values[current_pos]:
        insert_pos += 1

    return insert_pos
```

| HINT: STABLE SORTING |

When sorting elements of the same value, keeping their original order in the collection is referred to as a **Stable Sort**. This is often a preferable behavior because it prevents data associated with the elements from getting out of order.

For the example, `find_insert_pos_from_current()` results in a stable sorting, but the second one does not. However, if you replace the < with <=, the resulting sorting algorithm also becomes stable:

```
while insert_pos < current_pos and \
        values[insert_pos] <= values[current_pos]:
```

This is due to the fact that a most recently found element of the same value is always placed behind all elements of the same value.

Implementation of Insertion Sort

After identifying the correct insertion position for a value, all values (up to the currently considered value) have to be shifted by one position to the right. Finally, the value is inserted at the determined position.

```
def insertion_sort(values):
    for current_pos in range(1, len(numbers)):
        current_val = numbers[current_pos]
        insert_pos = find_insert_pos_from_current(values, current_pos)

        move_right(values, current_pos, insert_pos)

        numbers[insert_pos] = current_val

def move_right(values, current_pos, insert_pos):
    move_pos = current_pos
    while move_pos > insert_pos:
        values[move_pos] = values[move_pos - 1]
        move_pos -= 1
```

This code shows a well-understandable implementation that focuses on comprehensibility and not on speed. In fact, it is possible to combine some actions cleverly and thus avoid multiple runs. Later, in Exercise 4, you will deal with exactly this optimization.

Let's try out the implementation on the command line:

```
>>> values = [ 4, 2, 7, 9, 1 ]
>>> insertion_sort(values)
>>> print(values)
[1, 2, 4, 7, 9]
```

9.2.2 Selection Sort

Selection Sort is another intuitive method for sorting. It offers two variations, one based on the minimum and the other on the maximum. In the minimum version, the values to be sorted are traversed from front to back. In each step, the minimum is determined from the section that is still unsorted. This is moved forward by swapping it with the current element. This causes the sorted area to grow from the front and the remaining unsorted section to shrink. For the version based on the maximum, the data to be sorted is processed from the back to the front. The respective maximum is placed at the end so that the sorted area grows from the back.

To gain a better understanding, let's reproduce this for a small set of values. For this purpose, the respective current minimum or maximum is specially marked. The sorted part is separated from the unsorted part with ||. You can easily observe how the sorted part grows.

```
    Min                      Max
    ->                       <-
    || 4 2 7 9 ①             4 2 7 ⑨ 1 ||
1:  1 || ② 7 9 4             4 2 ⑦ 1 || 9
2:  1 2 || 7 9 ④             ④ 2 1 || 7 9
3:  1 2 4 || 9 ⑦             1 ② || 4 7 9
4:  1 2 4 7 || 9             1 || 2 4 7 9
```

The implementation of the version concerning the minimum is as follows:

```python
def selection_sort_min(values):
    for i in range(len(values) - 1):
        min_idx = i

        # find minimum
        for j in range(i + 1, len(values)):
            if values[j] < values[min_idx]:
                min_idx = j

        # swap current value with minimum
        tmp = values[min_idx]
        values[min_idx] = values[i]
        values[i] = tmp
```

If you only look at algorithms at this low level, it is usually difficult to understand and comprehend them. Of course, the final algorithms used in frameworks must be as optimal as possible. This requires estimations with the O-notation. This is easier to perform on the low level than on the high level since then all constructs, including invoked functions or methods, must be considered. However, to learn and get started, it is much more suitable to program comprehensively first and then optimize in further steps.

Let's execute the sorting in the following main():

```python
def main():
    values = [4, 2, 7, 9, 1]
    selection_sort_min(values)
    print(values)
```

We get the expected output:

```
[1, 2, 4, 7, 9]
```

OPINION: START WITH COMPREHENSIBILITY

How can Selection Sort be described on a higher level of abstraction? To do this, let's use some auxiliary functions that you created for arrays. In the corresponding chapter's introduction, you learned about the method swap() for swapping elements and the function find_min_pos() for finding the position of the smallest element, which was created as solution for Exercise 11 in Section 6.3.11. Conveniently, they can also be used for lists without modification.

By using these functions, the actual procedure becomes almost immediately apparent. You traverse the values from the beginning and, in each case, find the minimum of the remaining part and swap it with the value of the current position:

```python
def selection_sort_min_readable(values):
    for cur_idx in range(len(values) - 1):
        min_idx = find_min_pos(values, cur_idx, len(values))
        swap(values, min_idx, cur_idx)
```

In the code, the two helper functions from the module array_utils marked in bold are used. As usual, the module array_utils bundles several helper functions developed in Chapter 6. The two helper functions called in the code above are shown again here to ease trying out the example with the command line:

```python
def find_min_pos(values, start_pos, end_pos):
    min_pos = start_pos
    for i in range(start_pos + 1, end_pos):
        if values[i] < values[min_pos]:
            min_pos = i

    return min_pos

def swap(values, pos1, pos2):
    temp = values[pos1]
    values[pos1] = values[pos2]
    values[pos2] = temp
```

9.2.3 Merge Sort

Merge Sort is based on a divide-and-conquer approach. It recursively splits the values to be sorted into smaller and smaller subparts of about half the original size until they consist of only one or possibly no element. Afterwards, the subparts are combined again. In this merging step, the sorting is done by the appropriate merging based on the respective values. The processes can be illustrated as shown in Figure 9-2.

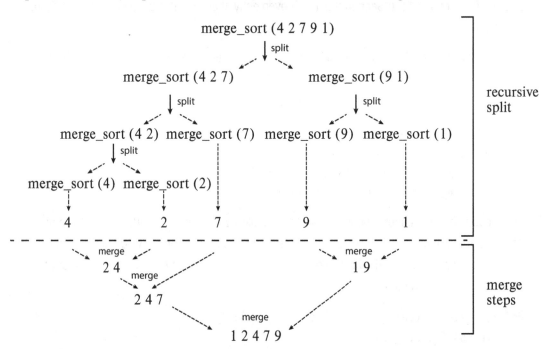

Figure 9-2. *Merge Sort procedure*

The splitting algorithm can be implemented recursively and well comprehensibly—though also somewhat inefficiently—as long as you are allowed to create new lists. The implementation of the function merge(values1, values2) was already presented as the solution to Exercise 12 in Section 5.3.12. It is used here:

```
def merge_sort(to_sort):
    # recursive termination: length 0 (only if initially empty array) or 1
    if len(to_sort) <= 1:
        return to_sort
```

```
# recursive descent: divide into two halves
mid_pos = len(to_sort) // 2
left = to_sort[0: mid_pos]
result_left = merge_sort(left)

right = to_sort[mid_pos: len(to_sort)]
result_right = merge_sort(right)

# combine the partial results into larger sorted data set
return merge(result_left, result_right)
```

Let's execute the sorting in the following main():

```
def main():
    unsorted_values = [4, 2, 7, 9, 1]
    sorted_values = merge_sort(unsorted_values)
    print(sorted_values)
```

You get the expected output:

```
[1, 2, 4, 7, 9]
```

HINT: ANALOGY FROM REAL LIFE LEADS TO OPTIMIZATION

The analogy to sorting a deck of cards is suitable for Merge Sort as well. If you need to sort a fairly large pile of cards, you can divide it into many, much smaller piles, sort them separately, and then merge them successively. However, instead of reducing the piles down to one card, it is a good idea to sort the smaller piles using another method, often Insertion Sort, which has a running time of $O(n)$ for small, ideally nearly ordered values. This is useful for fine-tuning. Ingeniously, Merge Sort makes this easy as pie:

```
def merge_sort_with_insertion_sort(to_sort):
    # recursive termination including mini-optimization
    if len(to_sort) < 5:
        insertion_sort(to_sort)
        return to_sort

    # recursive descent: divide into two halves
    mid_pos = len(to_sort) // 2
    left = to_sort[0: mid_pos]
```

```
result_left = merge_sort(left)

right = to_sort[mid_pos: len(to_sort)]
result_right = merge_sort(right)

# combine the partial results into larger sorted data set
return merge(result_left, result_right)
```

Finally, I would like to point out that the limit at which one should switch to Insertion Sort has been set here quite arbitrarily to the value 5. Presumably, values between 10 and 20 elements are quite practical. However, it would be best if you rely on the knowledge of algorithm professionals who create mathematically sound estimates for running times.

9.2.4 Quick Sort

Just like Merge Sort, Quick Sort is based on a divide-and-conquer approach and splits the values to be sorted into smaller and smaller subparts. A special element (called a *pivot*) is chosen that determines the grouping or processing. For simplicity, you can choose the first element of the subparts to be sorted as the pivot element, but other ways are conceivable. In Quick Sort, sorting is done based on this pivot element by arranging all elements of the parts according to their value to the left (less than or equal to) or to the right (greater than) of the pivot. This way, the pivot element is placed in the correct position. The whole process is repeated recursively for the left and right parts until the parts consist of only one element. The processes are shown in Figure 9-3.

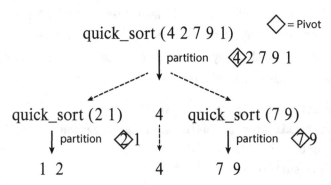

Figure 9-3. *Quick Sort*

Let's start with an implementation for lists since this is more easily accessible and understandable. As a result, breaking down the contents of a list into smaller and larger elements is easy to implement. Later, combining the results of the recursive computations is also straightforward. The whole implementation is intentional, not optimized for speed but for comprehensibility.

For partitioning, you collect all elements that are less than or equal to or greater than the value of the pivot element in respectively one separate result list. You skip the first element because it is the pivot element and then apply the appropriate filter condition within a list comprehension.

```python
def quick_sort(values):
    # recursive termination
    if len(values) <= 1:
        return values

    # collect less than or equal to / greater than pivot
    pivot = values[0]
    below_or_equals = [value for value in values[1:] if value <= pivot]
    aboves = [value for value in values[1:] if value > pivot]

    # recursive descent
    sorted_lowers_part = quick_sort(below_or_equals)
    sorted_uppers_part = quick_sort(aboves)

    # assemble
    return sorted_lowers_part + [pivot] + sorted_uppers_part
```

The whole thing is quite intuitive for lists and when not optimized for performance. It becomes considerably more awkward if you want to realize the partitioning for inplace (i. e., directly in the original array or list itself). You can see this for yourself later when solving Exercise 6. You will now take a look at the basic procedure.

Let's execute the sorting in the following main():

```python
def main():
    unsorted_values = [4, 2, 7, 9, 1]
    sorted_values = quick_sort(unsorted_values)
    print(sorted_values)
```

We get the expected output:

```
[1, 2, 4, 7, 9]
```

Inplace Implementation

The basic algorithm can be implemented as follows, although the realization of the partitioning, as already mentioned, will be a practice exercise:

```python
def quick_sort_inplace(values):
    quick_sort_in_range(values, 0, len(values) - 1)

def quick_sort_in_range(values, left, right):
    # recursive termination
    if left >= right:
        return

    partition_index = partition(values, left, right)

    # recursive descent
    quick_sort_in_range(values, left, partition_index - 1)
    quick_sort_in_range(values, partition_index + 1, right)
```

HINT: AVOIDING SIDE EFFECTS BY COPYING

If the original data set should be left unchanged, you can first create a copy of it and then call the inplace function:

```python
def quick_sort_with_copy(values):
    copied_values = values.copy()
    quick_sort_inplace(copied_values);

    return copied_values
```

9.2.5 Bucket Sort

Bucket Sort is an interesting sorting method whose algorithm is only outlined below since the implementation is the subject of Exercise 7.

Bucket Sort is a two-step procedure for sorting data. First, the values are collected in special containers called buckets. Then, these values are transferred appropriately into a sorted list. For the algorithm to be feasible, the elements to be sorted must have a limited set of values. For example, this applies to the age information of persons, where you can assume a range of values from 0 to 150.

```
ages = [10, 50, 22, 7, 42, 111, 50, 7]
```

This definition of a maximum number of different values means that a corresponding number of containers, the buckets, can store the values or, more precisely, their frequency. One bucket is provided for each possible value.

Step 1: Distribution to buckets At first, the initial set of data is traversed, and their occurrence is recorded in the buckets. For the age information above, the distribution is as follows:

```
bucket[7] = 2
bucket[10] = 1
bucket[22] = 1
bucket[42] = 1
bucket[50] = 2
bucket[111] = 1
```

All other buckets store the value 0.

Step 2: Preparation of the sorted result In a final step, the buckets are traversed from the beginning. The respective values are inserted into the result as many times as their number is stored in the bucket. This produces this sorting:

```
result = [7, 7, 10, 22, 42, 50, 50, 111]
```

9.2.6 Final Thoughts

Many of the more intuitive algorithms, such as Insertion Sort and Selection Sort, possess the disadvantage of having a running time of $O(n^2)$. However, Insertion Sort has a positive and remarkable feature: As long as the output data is (nearly) sorted, Insertion Sort becomes extremely performant with $O(n)$.

Quick Sort and Merge Sort are usually very efficient with a running time of $O(n \cdot log(n))$.[1] Still, they also have higher complexity of the source code, especially when working inplace. For frameworks and larger datasets, performance is essential. Potentially unfavorable for Merge Sort, on the other hand, is the creation of many copies of subranges. The same applies to Quick Sort and its partitioning. For both, however, some variants do this inplace. Interestingly, the respective divisions of the subranges to be sorted are quite easy to express by recursion, but the partitioning or merging part is then more complex and more difficult to implement. This holds in particular if you work inplace. For Merge Sort, you will find an example in the provided PyCharm project. For Quick Sort, you may try it in Exercise 6.

Bucket Sort remains. This algorithm sometimes runs even in linear running time, which is $O(n)$. However, in contrast to the other sorting algorithms presented, it is not generally applicable since it has the already mentioned restriction concerning the number of allowed values.

9.3 Exercises

9.3.1 Exercise 1: Contains All (★★☆☆☆)

The task is to create function `contains_all(values, search_values)` that checks if all passed values are present in the given list. Explicitly do not use the Python standard functionality of `all()`. Program this yourself.

Examples

Input	Search values	Result
[0, 1, 2, 3, 4, 5, 6, 7, 8, 9]	[7, 2]	True
[0, 1, 2, 3, 4, 5, 6, 7, 8, 9]	[5, 11]	False

---

[1] Strictly speaking and very formal, Quick Sort gets a running time of $O(n^2)$ assigned since for very rare special cases its running time can get quadratic.

9.3.2 Exercise 2: Partitioning (★★★★☆)

The challenge is to suitably sort or arrange a mixed sequence of the letters A and B in a single pass so that all As occur before the Bs. This can also be extended to three letters.

Examples

Input	Result
"ABAABBBAAABBBA"	"AAAAAAABBBBBBB"
"ABACCBBCAACCBBA"	"AAAAABBBBBCCCCC"

Exercise 2a: Partitioning Two Letters (★★★☆☆)

Write function `partition2(text)` that takes a given sequence built out of the two letters A and B and turns it into an ordered sequence where all As occur before the Bs.

Exercise 2b: Partitioning Three Letters (★★★★☆)

Write function `partition3(text)` that partitions a sequence built of the three letters A, B, and C given as `str` into an ordered sequence where all As occur before Bs and they in turn before Cs. Instead of letters, this can be thought of for colors of a flag. Then it is known as the Dutch Flag Problem.

9.3.3 Exercise 3: Binary Search (★★☆☆☆)

Exercise 3a: Binary Search Recursive (★★☆☆☆)

Write recursive function `binary_search(values, search_for)` that performs a search for the desired value in a sorted list.

Examples

Input	Search values	Result
[1, 2, 3, 4, 5, 7, 8, 9]	5	True
[1, 2, 3, 4, 5, 7, 8, 9]	6	False

Exercise 3b: Binary Search Iterative (★★☆☆☆)

Your task is to convert the recursive function into an iterative one. As a modification it should return the position of the search value or -1 for not found instead of True or False. Additionally, it should be named `binary_search_iterative(values, search_value)`.

Examples

Input	Search values	Result
[1, 2, 3, 4, 5, 7, 8, 9]	5	4
[1, 2, 3, 4, 5, 7, 8, 9]	6	-1

9.3.4 Exercise 4: Insertion Sort (★★☆☆☆)

The introductory Section 9.2.1 showed a simplified, easy-to-follow realization of Insertion Sort. In this exercise, the goal is to optimize the whole thing by now finding the insertion position and performing the necessary swapping and insertion in one go. Write an optimized version of `insertion_sort(values)`.

Example

Input	Result
[7, 2, 5, 1, 6, 8, 9, 4, 3]	[1, 2, 3, 4, 5, 6, 7, 8, 9]

9.3.5 Exercise 5: Selection Sort (★★☆☆☆)

Write a variation of Selection Sort that uses the maximum instead of the minimum and has the following signature: `selection_sort_max_inplace(values)`.

What needs to be modified so that the sort algorithm leaves the original data unchanged and returns a new sorted list? Implement this requirement in function `selection_sort_max_copy(values)`.

Example

Input	Result
[7, 2, 5, 1, 6, 8, 9, 4, 3]	[1, 2, 3, 4, 5, 6, 7, 8, 9]

9.3.6 Exercise 6: Quick Sort (★★★☆☆)

I described Quick Sort in the introductory Section 9.2.4. Whereas the splitting into two ranges with values less than or equal to the pivot elements can be implemented very easily when creating new lists, this is more challenging for lists when performing inplace. You need to implement the partitioning with the function partition(values, left, right). In the following, the already existing source code is shown once again:

```
def quick_sort_inplace(values):
    quick_sort_in_range(values, 0, len(values) - 1)

def quick_sort_in_range(values, left, right):
    # recursive termination
    if left >= right:
        return

    partition_index = partition(values, left, right)

    # recursive descent
    quick_sort_in_range(values, left, partition_index - 1)
    quick_sort_in_range(values, partition_index + 1, right)
```

Examples

Input	Result
[5, 2, 7, 1, 4, 3, 6, 8]	[1, 2, 3, 4, 5, 6, 7, 8]
[5, 2, 7, 9, 6, 3, 1, 4, 8]	[1, 2, 3, 4, 5, 6, 7, 8, 9]
[5, 2, 7, 9, 6, 3, 1, 4, 2, 3, 8]	[1, 2, 2, 3, 3, 4, 5, 6, 7, 8, 9]

9.3.7 Exercise 7: Bucket Sort (★★☆☆☆)

In the introductory Section 9.2.5, a Bucket Sort algorithm was described. In this exercise, you want to create function bucket_sort(values, expected_max) that implements this sorting algorithm for a list of values and an expected maximum value.

Example

Input	Maximum value	Result
[10, 50, 22, 7, 42, 111, 50, 7]	150	[7, 7, 10, 22, 42, 50, 50, 111]

9.3.8 Exercise 8: Search in Rotated Data (★★★★☆)

In this exercise, your task is to implement an efficient binary search in a sorted sequence of integer values. The challenge is that the values are ordered but rotated within themselves. According to that, the smallest element may not be at the front of the data. Additionally, the largest element does often not reside at the end of the data (except in the special case of a rotation by 0 positions).

Tip   Be careful also to check the special case of a rotation of 0 or a multiple of the length of the data set that would again correspond to a rotation for the value 0.

Exercise 8a: Flank Change Efficient (★★★★☆)

Write function find_flank_pos(values) that efficiently finds the position of a flank change in a given sorted sequence of n integer values, say 25, 33, 47, 1, 2, 3, 5, 11 in logarithmic time, which is $O(log(n))$. Write two functions min_value(values) and max_value(values) based on find_flank_pos(values) that, according to their names, determine the minimum and maximum, respectively, from the given sorted but rotated sequence of values.

Examples

Input	Flank position	Minimum	Maximum
[25, 33, 47, 1, 2, 3, 5, 11]	3	1	47
[5, 11, 17, 25, 1, 2]	4	1	25
[6, 1, 2, 3, 4, 5]	1	1	6
[1, 2, 3, 4, 5, 6]	0 (special case)	1	6

Exercise 8b: Binary Search in Rotated Data (★★★★☆)

Write function binary_search_rotated(values, search_for) that efficiently searches in a sorted sequence of integer values, say the number sequence 25, 33, 47, 1, 2, 3, 5, 11, for a given value and returns its position or -1 if not found.

Examples

Input	Flank position	Search value	Result
[25, 33, 47, 1, 2, 3, 5, 11]	3	47	2
[25, 33, 47, 1, 2, 3, 5, 11]	3	3	5
[25, 33, 47, 1, 2, 3, 5, 11]	3	13	-1
[1, 2, 3, 4, 5, 6, 7]	0 (special case)	5	4
[1, 2, 3, 4, 5, 6, 7]	0 (special case)	13	-1

9.4 Solutions

9.4.1 Solution 1: Contains All (★★☆☆☆)

The task is to create function contains_all(values, search_values) that checks if all passed values are present in the given list. Explicitly do not use the Python standard functionality of all(). Program this yourself.

Examples

Input	Search values	Result
[0, 1, 2, 3, 4, 5, 6, 7, 8, 9]	[7, 2]	True
[0, 1, 2, 3, 4, 5, 6, 7, 8, 9]	[5, 11]	False

Algorithm For your implementation, you call the test with `in` repeatedly, for all elements passed to be checked for containment:

```python
def contains_all(values, search_values):
    for current in search_values:
        if current not in values:
            return False

    return True
```

Python shortcut Of course this can be written more compactly with the help of `all()`. Nevertheless, a helper function is probably useful to keep the calling source code as understandable as possible.

```python
def contains_all_v2(values, search_values):
    return all(elem in values for elem in search_values)
```

Verification

Let's define a list with the numbers from 0 to 9 and check if the values 7 and 2, as well as 5 and 11, are present there:

```python
@pytest.mark.parametrize("values, search_values, expected",
                         [([0, 1, 2, 3, 4, 5, 6, 7, 8, 9], [7, 2], True),
                          ([0, 1, 2, 3, 4, 5, 6, 7, 8, 9], [5, 11], False)])
def test_contains_all(values, search_values, expected):
    assert contains_all(values, search_values) == expected

@pytest.mark.parametrize("values, search_values, expected",
                         [([0, 1, 2, 3, 4, 5, 6, 7, 8, 9], [7, 2], True),
                          ([0, 1, 2, 3, 4, 5, 6, 7, 8, 9], [5, 11], False)])
def test_contains_all_v2(values, search_values, expected):
    assert contains_all_v2(values, search_values) == expected
```

9.4.2 Solution 2: Partitioning (★★★★☆)

The challenge is to suitably sort or arrange a mixed sequence of the letters A and B in a single pass so that all As occur before the Bs. This can also be extended to three letters.

Examples

Input	Result
"ABAABBBAAABBBA"	"AAAAAAABBBBBBB"
"ABACCBBCAACCBBA"	"AAAAABBBBBCCCCC"

Solution 2a: Partitioning Two Letters (★★★☆☆)

Write function partition2(text) that takes a given sequence built out of the two letters A and B and turns it into an ordered sequence where all As occur before the Bs.

Algorithm Although you may be initially tempted to compare all possible positions, an ingenious and performant solution exists that solves the task in one pass. Work with two position pointers, low and high, which mark the front and back positions, in this case, the valid range given by the rearmost A and the foremost B. This area is initially empty and grows until you reach the end of the text. The following procedure is used: When an A is found, its position pointer (low) is incremented. When a B is found, it is swapped to the back. Afterwards, the position pointer of the Bs (high) is decreased, expanding the already correctly divided area.

```python
def partition2(char_values):
    low = 0
    high = len(char_values) - 1

    while low <= high:
        if char_values[low] == 'A':
            low += 1
        else:
            swap_positions(char_values, low, high)
            high -= 1
            # low must remain, because theoretically also a
            # B can be exchanged to the front
```

```
    return "".join(char_values)

def swap_positions(list, pos1, pos2):
    list[pos1], list[pos2] = list[pos2], list[pos1]
```

Because a B may also move to the front when swapping, the lower position pointer must stay unchanged. In one of the next steps, the B will then move to the back again. This tricky algorithm makes it possible to arrange all As in front of the Bs in a single pass.

Solution 2b: Partitioning Three Letters (★★★★☆)

Write function partition3(text) that partitions a sequence built of the three letters A, B, and C given as str into an ordered sequence where all As occur before Bs and they in turn before Cs. Instead of letters, this can be thought of for colors of a flag. Then it is known as the Dutch Flag Problem.

Algorithm The extension from two to three letters (or colors) employs similar ideas as before, but with a few more tricks and special treatments. You start again at the beginning of the array or list but use the three position markers low, mid, and high. Initially, they are located for the first and middle character at position 0, the one for high at the end position. If an A is found, the positions for low and mid shift by one to the right. Before that, the last character from the lower range is swapped with the current (middle) one. If you read a B, only the middle position is shifted towards the end. If the current character is a C, this is swapped to the back. The position marker for the upper area is then reduced by 1.

```
def partition3(char_values):
    low = 0
    mid = 0
    high = len(char_values) - 1

    while mid <= high:
        if char_values[mid] == 'A':
            swap_positions(char_values, low, mid)
            low += 1
            mid += 1
        elif char_values[mid] == 'B':
            mid += 1
```

```
        else:
            swap_positions(char_values, mid, high)
            high -= 1
            # low, mid must remain unchanged, because also a B or C
            # can be swapped to the front

    return "".join(char_values)
```

Verification

To check functionality, you use two strings consisting of a shuffled sequence of the letters A and B or A, B, and C, respectively:

```
def test_partition2():
    assert partition2(list("ABAABBBAAABBBA")) == "AAAAAAABBBBBB"

def test_partition3():
    assert partition3(list("ABACCBBCAACCBBA")) == "AAAAABBBBBCCCCC"
```

9.4.3 Solution 3: Binary Search (★★☆☆☆)

Solution 3a: Binary Search Recursive (★★☆☆☆)

Write recursive function binary_search(values, search_for) that performs a search for the desired value in a sorted list.

Examples

Input	Search values	Result
[1, 2, 3, 4, 5, 7, 8, 9]	5	True
[1, 2, 3, 4, 5, 7, 8, 9]	6	False

Algorithm Divide the list into two halves. Determine the value in the middle and see if you need to search further in the top or bottom half. This can be easily determined based on the given sort order.

$$Value_{center} == search\_for \Rightarrow found, end$$

$$Value_{center} < search\_for \Rightarrow continue \ searching \ in \ lower \ part$$

$$Value_{center} > search\_for \Rightarrow continue \ searching \ in \ upper \ part$$

The implementation in Python strictly follows the description. As usual, be especially careful at the boundaries of the list or array to avoid making careless mistakes.

```python
def binary_search(sorted_values, search_for):

    mid_pos = len(sorted_values) // 2

    # recursive termination
    if search_for == sorted_values[mid_pos]:
        return True

    # there are still at least 2 numbers
    if len(sorted_values) > 1:
        if search_for < sorted_values[mid_pos]:
            # recursive descent: search further in the lower part
            lower_half = sorted_values[0: mid_pos]
            return binary_search(lower_half, search_for)

        if search_for > sorted_values[mid_pos]:
            # recursive descent: continue search in the upper part
            upper_half = sorted_values[mid_pos + 1: len(sorted_values)]
            return binary_search(upper_half, search_for)

    return False
```

To try it out, execute the following code:

```python
def main():
    sorted_values = [1, 2, 3, 4, 5, 7, 8, 9]
    print("Given: ", sorted_values)
    print("search for 5:", binary_search(sorted_values, 5))
    print("search for 6:", binary_search(sorted_values, 6))
```

The expected result is as follows:

```
Given:  [1, 2, 3, 4, 5, 7, 8, 9]
search for 5: True
search for 6: False
```

Optimized algorithm The solution shown is not really optimal because parts of the original data are permanently copied to perform further searches. The entire process can be done completely without potentially time-consuming copying with the help of two index variables. The following solution is certainly preferable:

```python
def binary_search_optimized(values, search_value):
    return binary_search_in_range(values, search_value, 0, len(values) - 1)

def binary_search_in_range(values, search_for, left, right):
    if right >= left:
        mid_idx = (left + right) // 2

        if search_for == values[mid_idx]:
            return True

        # recursive descent: search in the lower / upper part further
        if search_for < values[mid_idx]:
            return binary_search_in_range(values, search_for,
                                          left, mid_idx - 1)
        else:
            return binary_search_in_range(values, search_for,
                                          mid_idx + 1, right)

    return False
```

Solution 3b: Binary Search Iterative (★★☆☆☆)

Your task is to convert the recursive function into an iterative one. As a modification it should return the position of the search value or -1 for not found instead of True or False. Additionally, it should be named binary_search_iterative(values, search_value).

Examples

Input	Search values	Result
[1, 2, 3, 4, 5, 7, 8, 9]	5	4
[1, 2, 3, 4, 5, 7, 8, 9]	6	-1

Algorithm Based on the recursive version just shown, the iterative implementation may be derived quite easily. Use two position markers left and right for left and right, which initially start at the beginning and end (position 0 and len(values) – 1). These two markers determine the respective index boundaries in which further searching is performed. At first, you compare the value in the middle with the one you are searching for. If the values are equal, you return the index. Otherwise, you divide the search area into two parts and continue until either the search is successful or the left and right position markers cross each other.

```python
def binary_search_iterative(values, search_for):
    left = 0
    right = len(values) - 1

    while right >= left:

        mid_idx = (left + right) // 2

        if search_for == values[mid_idx]:
            return mid_idx

        if search_for < values[mid_idx]:
            right = mid_idx - 1
        else:
            left = mid_idx + 1

    return -1
```

Verification

For testing, you use the following inputs, which show the correct operation:

```python
@pytest.mark.parametrize("sorted_values, search_for, expected",
                         [([1, 2, 3, 4, 5, 7, 8, 9], 5, True),
                          ([1, 2, 3, 4, 5, 7, 8, 9],6, False)])
def test_binary_search(sorted_values, search_for, expected):
    assert binary_search(sorted_values, search_for) == expected

@pytest.mark.parametrize("sorted_values, search_for, expected",
                         [([1, 2, 3, 4, 5, 7, 8, 9], 5, True),
                          ([1, 2, 3, 4, 5, 7, 8, 9], 6, False)])
def test_binary_search_optimized(sorted_values, search_for, expected):
    assert binary_search_optimized(sorted_values, search_for) == expected

@pytest.mark.parametrize("sorted_values, search_for, expected",
                         [([1, 2, 3, 4, 5, 7, 8, 9], 5, 4),
                          ([1, 2, 3, 4, 5, 7, 8, 9], 6, -1)])
def test_binary_search_iterative(sorted_values, search_for, expected):
    assert binary_search_iterative(sorted_values, search_for) == expected
```

9.4.4 Solution 4: Insertion Sort (★★☆☆☆)

Section 9.2.1 showed a simplified, easy-to-follow realization of Insertion Sort. In this exercise, the goal is to optimize the whole thing by now finding the insertion position and performing the necessary swapping and insertion in one go. Write an optimized version of insertion_sort(values).

Example

Input	Result
[7, 2, 5, 1, 6, 8, 9, 4, 3]	[1, 2, 3, 4, 5, 6, 7, 8, 9]

Algorithm For all elements, you perform the following procedure, which is described exemplarily for the value sequence 24317. Let's consider 3 as a value to be sorted in. You must swap with the left neighbor starting from its position as long as the neighbor's value is greater than the current one. You have not yet reached the very front in the list. In this case, you swap the 3 only with the 4. Next, you need to swap the 1 all the way to the front. Finally, the 7 is already in the right position.

```python
def insertion_sort(values):
    for i in range(1, len(values)):
        # check if current element is larger than predecessor
        current_idx = i
        while current_idx > 0 and values[current_idx - 1] >
        values[current_idx]:
            swap_positions(values, current_idx - 1, current_idx)
            current_idx -= 1

def swap_positions(values, pos1, pos2):
    values[pos1], values[pos2] = values[pos2], values[pos1]
```

The function to swap the values of two positions can be written very compactly in Python using the tuple notation and also still without parentheses.

Verification

Verify that the implementation produces the desired result for the given sequence of numbers using a unit test:

```python
def test_insertion_sort():
    values = [7, 2, 5, 1, 6, 8, 9, 4, 3]
    insertion_sort(values)

    assert values == [1, 2, 3, 4, 5, 6, 7, 8, 9]
```

9.4.5 Solution 5: Selection Sort (★★☆☆☆)

Write a variation of Selection Sort that uses the maximum instead of the minimum and has the following signature: selection_sort_max_inplace(values).

What needs to be modified so that the sort algorithm leaves the original data unchanged and returns a new sorted list? Implement this requirement in function selection_sort_max_copy(values).

Example

Input	Result
[7, 2, 5, 1, 6, 8, 9, 4, 3]	[1, 2, 3, 4, 5, 6, 7, 8, 9]

Algorithm The list to be sorted is traversed from back to front while the largest element in each case is moved back to the current position. By calling the function find_max_pos(), you determine the position of the maximum from the remaining unsorted subrange. This function was created as a solution to Exercise 11 in Section 6.3.11 for arrays; it can also be used for lists without modification. Subsequently, the element is moved to the back accordingly by swapping it with the current element. This reduces the size of the remaining, not-yet-sorted part until it consists only of the foremost element.

```python
def selection_sort_max_inplace(values):
    for i in range(len(values) - 1, 0, -1):
        max_pos = find_max_pos(values, 0, i + 1)

        swap_positions(values, max_pos, i)
```

The function with the copy functionality is trivial to implement if you have created the previous function:

```python
def selection_sort_max_copy(values):
    copy = list(values)
    selection_sort_max_inplace(copy)
    return copy
```

Verification

Verify that the implementation produces the desired result for the given sequence of numbers using a unit test:

```python
def test_selection_sort_max_inplace():
    values = [7, 2, 5, 1, 6, 8, 9, 4, 3]
    selection_sort_max_inplace(values)

    assert values == [1, 2, 3, 4, 5, 6, 7, 8, 9]
```

9.4.6 Solution 6: Quick Sort (★★★☆☆)

I described Quick Sort in the introductory Section 9.2.4. Whereas the splitting into two ranges with values less than or equal to the pivot elements can be implemented very easily when creating new lists, this is more challenging for a list when performing inplace. Now the partitioning is to be implemented with the function partition(values, left, right). The already existing source code is shown once again:

```
def quick_sort_inplace(values):
    quick_sort_in_range(values, 0, len(values) - 1)

def quick_sort_in_range(values, left, right):
    # recursive termination
    if left >= right:
        return

    partition_index = partition(values, left, right)

    # recursive descent
    quick_sort_in_range(values, left, partition_index - 1)
    quick_sort_in_range(values, partition_index + 1, right)
```

Examples

Input	Result
[5, 2, 7, 1, 4, 3, 6, 8]	[1, 2, 3, 4, 5, 6, 7, 8]
[5, 2, 7, 9, 6, 3, 1, 4, 8]	[1, 2, 3, 4, 5, 6, 7, 8, 9]
[5, 2, 7, 9, 6, 3, 1, 4, 2, 3, 8]	[1, 2, 2, 3, 3, 4, 5, 6, 7, 8, 9]

Algorithm Your goal is to subdivide an array or a list (or a range of them) into two parts by passing the lower start and upper end index and choosing a value at a special position (e. g., foremost element) as the pivot element. Now the two parts are rearranged. All elements with values smaller than or equal to the pivot element should reside in the lower part. Furthermore, all elements with a value larger than the pivot element should reside in the upper part. Here, the two indices left_index and right_index each move inward as long as the conditions values[left_index] <= pivot hold for left and pivot

< values[right_index] for right. If an inappropriately ordered element is found on the left side, the examination starts on the right side. If an inappropriately ordered element is found here as well, the two are swapped. This process is repeated as long as the position markers do not cross each other. Finally, the element from the right_index position is swapped with the pivot element. There is also the special case that the array or list has only two elements. In this case, you also have to make sure that the right value is actually larger than that of the pivot.

```python
def partition(values, left, right):
    pivot = values[left]

    left_index = left + 1
    right_index = right

    while left_index < right_index:
        # move the position left_index to the right, as long as value
        # less than or equal to pivot and left limit less than right limit
        while values[left_index] <= pivot and left_index < right_index:
            left_index += 1

        # move the position right_index to the left, as long as
        value greater
        # than pivot and right limit greater than or equal to left limit
        while pivot < values[right_index] and right_index >= left_index:
            right_index -= 1

        if left_index < right_index:
            swap_positions(values, left_index, right_index)

    # special case 2-element list with wrong sorting, but no
    # pass (left_index ==  right_index) as well as normal case at the
    very end
    if values[right_index] < pivot:
        swap_positions(values, left, right_index)

    return right_index
```

Verification

Let's define the three lists from the introductory examples and use them to check the implementation of Quick Sort:

```
@pytest.mark.parametrize("values, expected",
                         [([5, 2, 7, 1, 4, 3, 6, 8],
                           [1, 2, 3, 4, 5, 6, 7, 8]),
                          ([5, 2, 7, 9, 6, 3, 1, 4, 8],
                           [1, 2, 3, 4, 5, 6, 7, 8, 9]),
                          [[5, 2, 7, 9, 6, 3, 1, 4, 2, 3, 8],
                           [1, 2, 2, 3, 3, 4, 5, 6, 7, 8, 9]]])
def test_quick_sort_inplace(values, expected):
    quick_sort_inplace(values)

    assert values == expected
```

9.4.7 Solution 7: Bucket Sort (★★☆☆☆)

In the introductory Section 9.2.5, a Bucket Sort algorithm was described. In this exercise, you want to create function bucket_sort(values, expected_max) that implements this sorting algorithm for a list of values and an expected maximum value.

Example

Input	Maximum value	Result
[10, 50, 22, 7, 42, 111, 50, 7]	150	[7, 7, 10, 22, 42, 50, 50, 111]

Algorithm Bucket Sort is one of the most straightforward sorting algorithms to implement and also one of the fastest with linear running time—but with the prerequisite of a limited range of values.

First, you create buckets that store the counts of values. Afterwards, Bucket Sort is implemented in two steps:

1. Traverse all input values and assign them to the corresponding buckets. If there are several same elements, you have to increment the counter.

2. The final step is to reconstruct the values based on the counter values.

The described procedure is implemented in Python as follows:

```python
def bucket_sort(values, expected_max):
    buckets = [0] * (expected_max + 1)

    collect_into_buckets(values, buckets)

    results = [0] * len(values)

    fill_result_from_buckets(buckets, results)

    return results
```

The algorithm is thereby described in its basic characteristics. Only the implementation of the two helper functions remains, which is also done straightforwardly. To calculate the count of the respective numbers, you have to iterate through the original values and increment the counter in the bucket corresponding to the current value.

```python
def collect_into_buckets(values, buckets):
    for current in values:
        buckets[current] += 1
```

Based on the quantities in the buckets, the generation of the result is just a little bit more complex. For this purpose, you traverse all buckets. If index *i* contains a quantity greater than 0, this index value has to be copied to the target as often as specified there—in this case, solved by the while loop. You only have to carry the position in the target list separately.

```
def fill_result_from_buckets(buckets, results):
    result_pos = 0

    for i, count in enumerate(buckets):
        while count > 0:
            results[result_pos] = i

            count -= 1
            result_pos += 1
```

Verification

Write a short test function to check your implementation of Bucket Sort with
some values:

```
@pytest.mark.parametrize("values, max, expected",
                         [([10, 50, 22, 7, 42, 111, 50, 7], 150,
                           [7, 7, 10, 22, 42, 50, 50, 111]),
                          ([10, 50, 22, 7, 42, 111, 50, 7], 120,
                           [7, 7, 10, 22, 42, 50, 50, 111]),
                          [[5, 2, 7, 9, 6, 3, 1, 4, 2, 3, 8], 10,
                           [1, 2, 2, 3, 3, 4, 5, 6, 7, 8, 9]]])
def test_bucket_sort(values, max, expected):
    result = bucket_sort(values, max)

    assert result == expected
```

9.4.8 Solution 8: Search in Rotated Data (★★★★☆)

In this exercise, your task is to implement an efficient binary search in a sorted sequence
of integer values. The challenge is that the values are ordered but rotated within
themselves. According to that, the smallest element may not be at the front of the data.
Additionally, the largest element does often not reside at the end of the data (except in
the special case of a rotation by 0 positions).

Tip   Be careful also to check the special case of a rotation of 0 or a multiple of
the length of the data set that would again correspond to a rotation for the value 0.

Solution 8a: Flank Change Efficient (★★★★☆)

Write function find_flank_pos(values) that efficiently finds the position of a flank change in a given sorted sequence of n integer values, say 25, 33, 47, 1, 2, 3, 5, 11, in logarithmic time, which is $O(log(n))$. Write two functions min_value(values) and max_value(values) based on find_flank_pos(values) that, according to their names, determine the minimum and maximum, respectively, from the given sorted but rotated sequence of values.

Examples

Input	Flank position	Minimum	Maximum
[25, 33, 47, 1, 2, 3, 5, 11]	3	1	47
[5, 11, 17, 25, 1, 2]	4	1	25
[6, 1, 2, 3, 4, 5]	1	1	6
[1, 2, 3, 4, 5, 6]	0 (special case)	1	6

Preliminary considerations for the algorithm Let's start with the brute-force version of linear search to check your optimized version against it later on. For the search, you only need to check each element from front to back to determine if the successor of a value is smaller than the current element:

```
def find_flank_pos_simple(values):
    for i, value in enumerate(values):
        next_idx = (i + 1) % len(values)
        if value > values[next_idx]:
            return next_idx

    raise Exception("should never reach here!")
```

Of course, when traversing, you also have to consider the special case that the flank change takes place at the very end of the list. Then you have a non-rotated list as a base.

Algorithm So, how can you proceed to achieve logarithmic running time? In this case, you take advantage of the fact that the value sequence is sorted. The search ranges can always be divided in half, following the idea of binary search. Because there is a rotation, however, you must be careful concerning the indices.

There are three comparisons to be made:

- **Case A: With the predecessor**: If it is larger, you have found the flank change.

- **Case B: With the leftmost element**: If it is larger than the current element, then the flank change must happen somewhere in between. So, you can exclude the right half.

- **Case C: With the rightmost element**: If this is smaller, the flank change must happen on the right side. You can exclude the left half.

At the very beginning, it is crucial to check for the special case of the non-rotated initial dataset. This can be determined by the fact that the far left value is smaller than that on the far right.

With these preliminary considerations, the following implementation emerges:

```python
def find_flank_pos(values):
    return find_flank_pos_in_range(values, 0, len(values) - 1)

def find_flank_pos_in_range(values, left, right):
    mid_pos = left + (right - left) // 2
    mid_value = values[mid_pos]

    # special case no rotation
    if values[left] < values[right]:
        return 0

    prev_index = mid_pos - 1
    if prev_index < 0:
        prev_index = len(values) - 1

    # case A: value to the left of this is larger, then you got a
    # flank change
    if values[prev_index] > mid_value:
        return mid_pos

    if values[left] > mid_value:
        # case B: flank change must be on the left, since first value
        # larger than in the middle
        return find_flank_pos_in_range(values, left, mid_pos + 1)
```

```
if values[right] < mid_value:
    # case C: flank change must be on the right, as last value
    # smaller than in the middle
    return find_flank_pos_in_range(values, mid_pos + 1, right)

raise Exception("should not reach here")
```

Based on this method, it is possible to write the functions for determining minimum and maximum quite simply as follows with the knowledge that the position of the flank change contains the minimum and the position of the maximum is a position to the left of it.

Due to the convenient Python characteristic of supporting negative indexes for access from the end of the data structure, no correction needs to be made for a rotation around 0.

```
def min_value(values):
    flank_pos = find_flank_pos(values)
    return values[flank_pos]

def max_value(values):
    flank_pos = find_flank_pos(values)
    return values[(flank_pos - 1) % len(values)]
```

Verification

Test the determination of the flank change using the following parameterized test— in particular, also the special case of non-rotated input values is verified:

```
@pytest.mark.parametrize("values, expected",
                [([25, 33, 47, 1, 2, 3, 5, 11], 3),
                 ([6, 7, 1, 2, 3, 4, 5], 2),
                 ([1, 2, 3, 4, 5, 6, 7], 0)])
def test_find_flank_pos(values, expected):
    flank_pos = find_flank_pos(values)

    assert flank_pos == expected
```

Solution 8b: Binary Search in Rotated Data (★★★★☆)

Write function binary_search_rotated(values, search_for) that efficiently searches in a sorted sequence of integer values, say the number sequence 25, 33, 47, 1, 2, 3, 5, 11, for a given value and returns its position or -1 if not found.

Examples

Input	Flank position	Search value	Result
[25, 33, 47, 1, 2, 3, 5, 11]	3	47	2
[25, 33, 47, 1, 2, 3, 5, 11]	3	3	5
[25, 33, 47, 1, 2, 3, 5, 11]	3	13	-1
[1, 2, 3, 4, 5, 6, 7]	0 (special case)	5	4
[1, 2, 3, 4, 5, 6, 7]	0 (special case)	13	-1

Algorithm After being able to efficiently determine the flank change in $O(log(n))$, one possibility is to enlarge the list. Thereby you cut out the front part of the list and appends it at the end (this is feasible for medium-sized lists). Afterwards, you can invoke a binary search, which was developed in Exercise 3:

```
25 | 27 | 33 | 2 | 3 | 5      =>   | 2 | 3 | 5 | 25 | 27 | 33
```

However, this procedure causes quite a bit of effort. So how can you improve it?

For this purpose, you adapt the binary search to specify a lower and upper bound. You pick up the idea of the list expansion but make it virtual. Let's take a look at the example of the search for the 47 in the number sequence shown in the exercise, shown in Figure 9-4.

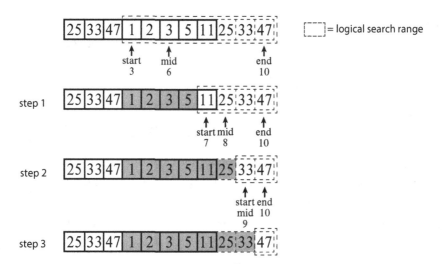

Figure 9-4. *Rotated binary search procedure*

Based on these preliminary ideas, you proceed with the binary search. First, you determine the position of the flank change and use it to specify your search value range. Next, you perform a normal binary search, but you use the modulo operator to bring the extended value range back into the list's boundaries and determine the comparison value based on this.

```python
def binary_search_rotated(values, search_for):
    flank_pos = find_flank_pos(values)

    return binary_search_rotated_in_range(values, search_for, flank_pos,
                                          flank_pos - 1 + len(values))

def binary_search_rotated_in_range(values, search_for, start, end):
    if start > end:
        return -1

    mid_pos = start + (end - start) // 2
    adjusted_mid = mid_pos % len(values)
    mid_value = values[adjusted_mid]

    if mid_value == search_for:
        return adjusted_mid
```

```
if search_for < mid_value:
    return binary_search_rotated_in_range(values, search_for,
                                           start, mid_pos - 1)
if search_for > mid_value:
    return binary_search_rotated_in_range(values, search_for,
                                           mid_pos + 1, end)
```

Python-specific algorithm I have just described a general algorithm. In Python, you can take advantage of the fact that the indices can also be negative and then operate from the end of the list or array.

As before, you take up the idea of performing the binary search with shifted index. Instead of the virtual extension of the output data and the mapping back by modulo to the real value range, you simply use that the value range is shifted by n positions. Thus, instead of searching between 0 and n, you can search in the range between flankpos$-n$ and flankpos -1. Then, to make it work with the termination condition, you need to move it after checking for value equality. Additionally, you need to check for matching start and end. In the actual call, you need to calculate the start and end positions appropriately and cover the special case of no rotation.

```
def binary_search_rotated2(values, search_for):
    flank_pos = find_flank_pos(values)

    start = flank_pos - len(values)
    end = flank_pos - 1
    if flank_pos == 0:
        start = 0
        end = len(values) - 1

    return binary_search_rotated_helper2(values, search_for, start, end)

def binary_search_rotated_helper2(values, search_for, start, end):
    mid_pos = start + (end - start) // 2
    mid_value = values[mid_pos]

    if mid_value == search_for:
        return mid_pos % len(values)

    if start == end:
        return -1
```

```
if search_for < mid_value:
    return binary_search_rotated_helper2(values, search_for,
                                         start, mid_pos - 1)
if search_for > mid_value:
    return binary_search_rotated_helper2(values, search_for,
                                         mid_pos + 1, end)
```

Verification

To check the functionality, you use the value combinations from the introductory example:

```
@pytest.mark.parametrize("values, search_for, expected",
                         [([25, 33, 47, 1, 2, 3, 5, 11], 47, 2),
                          ([25, 33, 47, 1, 2, 3, 5, 11], 3, 5),
                          ([25, 33, 47, 1, 2, 3, 5, 11], 13, -1),
                          ([1, 2, 3, 4, 5, 6, 7], 5, 4),
                          ([1, 2, 3, 4, 5, 6, 7], 13, -1)])
def test_binary_search_rotated(values, search_for, expected):
    pos = binary_search_rotated(values, search_for)

    assert pos == expected
```

9.5 Summary: What You Learned

Even if you will hardly ever program a search or sorting algorithm nowadays yourself, it is still helpful for algorithmic understanding to have done this once.

Simple implementations of (linear) searches tend to have a running time of $O(n)$. You learned how you can benefit from sorted data sets helping you to use binary search as a trickier search and reducing the running time down to $O(log(n))$.

Similar observations apply for sorting: While naive implementations often have a running time of $O(n^2)$, this can usually be reduced to $O(n \times log(n))$ with Merge Sort and Quick Sort. It is fascinating to see how a fixed range of values can have a significant effect. Bucket Sort with a running time of $O(n)$ plays out its strengths with these constraints.

As a nice challenge for the end, you solved a binary search in rotated data sets, where the values are sorted but shifted by some positions.

## CHAPTER 10

Conclusion and Supplementary Literature

Now, having reached the end of this exercise book, let me conclude. Additionally, I will present two logic puzzles before we have a look at the supplementary literature.

10.1 Conclusion

By reading this book, and especially by solving and implementing the exercises, you should have gained good experience. With this knowledge, various tasks from daily practice should now be somewhat easier to complete. Of course, you will profit most if you don't just follow the solutions presented but also experiment and modify them.

10.1.1 Lessons Learned Per Chapter

Let's recap about what was taught in each chapter and what you should have learned.

Mathematical: The chapter on basic mathematical knowledge introduced the modulo operator, which is quite essential, for example, for the extraction of digits and in the calculation of checksums. The exercises on combinatorics showed how small tricks can easily reduce the running time by an order of magnitude. Also, prime numbers offer some interesting facets, for example, variants to their calculation. In retrospect, this turns out to be much easier than perhaps first thought. In general, when trying to find a solution for a problem, the algorithm and the approach should be roughly understood, because then, for example, even decomposition into prime factors loses its possible horror.

© Michael Inden 2022
M. Inden, *Python Challenges*, https://doi.org/10.1007/978-1-4842-7398-2_10

Recursion: The introductory chapter on recursion laid the foundation for a good understanding. The exercises expanded your knowledge. Additionally, you were able to use the acquired basic knowledge profitably in the following chapters. A prime example is various algorithms on trees, which can often be easily expressed recursively—iteratively, for example, a postorder traversal is already challenging, whereas with recursion it is effortless.

However, you recognized that simple recursion does not only possess advantages, but also sometimes requires some patience due to long running times. In the advanced chapter on recursion, you significantly expanded your toolbox with memoization and backtracking. This allowed you to increase performance and to solve entertaining and amusing puzzles, such as Sudoku puzzles or the n-Queens problem. It was also possible to find a way out of a maze. All this required a bit more programming effort but could be implemented without too much complexity.

Strings: Strings are an integral part of almost every program. Besides simple tasks for palindrome checking or string reversing, some tasks could be significantly simplified using suitable auxiliary data structures, such as sets or dictionaries. These helped when checking for well-formed braces, converting a word into Morse code, and other tasks. In general, solving problems is easier the more basic knowledge you have in different areas.

Basic data structures: This chapter deepened your knowledge of basic data structures like lists, sets, and dictionaries. This knowledge is essential in business applications. Not only individually but also in combination, they are useful for solving many tasks, such as the deletion of duplicates from lists. In addition, the exercise of the magic triangle, for example, trains abstract thinking. A small delicacy was to program the auto-completion of Excel itself. It is quite surprising what an elegant implementation this results in. Finally, you developed some functionality for merging lists. This is an elementary component for Merge Sort.

Arrays: Just like strings, arrays are basic building blocks in many programming languages. In Python, lists are often favored, since arrays are not nicely supported in the language. However, there is a valid alternative with NumPy, with which arrays can be easily defined and which can offer significant performance improvements compared to lists.

In particular, it is important to avoid tricky off-by-one errors. In this chapter, you created small helper functions that, when used appropriately, can make algorithms more understandable. For two-dimensional arrays, you learned, among other things, how to model directions and how this helps with filling areas with patterns. More challenging tasks were the spiral traversal as well as the deletion and filling of a Jewels or Minesweeper playfield.

Binary trees: The most complex topic in this book is probably binary trees. Since Python does not provide them, they are presumably not familiar to every Python developer. However, because binary trees are suitable to solve many problems elegantly, this chapter gave an introduction. The exercises helped you get to know binary trees and their possibilities. Besides things like rotation, even mathematical calculations, for example, can be represented and processed very smartly using binary trees. Something to puzzle over was certainly the determination of the least common ancestor. This is especially true for the check for completeness and the graphical output of a binary tree.

Search and sort: Nowadays, you will hardly program a search or sorting algorithm yourself. Still, it is helpful for algorithmic understanding to have dealt with it once. While naive implementations often have a running time of $O(n^2)$, this can usually be reduced to $O(n . log(n))$ with Merge Sort and Quick Sort. It is fascinating to see how a fixed range of values can have a significant effect. Bucket Sort with a running time of $O(n)$ plays out its strengths with these constraints.

10.1.2 Noteworthy

When presenting the solutions, I have sometimes deliberately shown a wrong way or a suboptimal brute force variant to demonstrate the learning effect when working on an improvement. In everyday work, too, it is often preferable to proceed iteratively because the requirements may not be 100 % precise, new requests arise, etc. Therefore, it is a good idea to start with a comprehensible implementation of the task, which allows it to be modified afterward without any problems. It is often even acceptable to take a not-yet-optimal solution that handles the problem in a conceptually correct way.

Thoughts on Maintainability

One also observes the following: Source code is usually read much more often than it is written. Think about your daily work routine. Usually, you do not start on the greenfield but extend an existing system with some functionality or fix a bug. You appreciate it if the original program author has chosen comprehensible solutions and program constructs. Ideally, even unit tests exist as a safety net.

Let's get back to development. Make sure that you think about the problem in advance instead of starting directly with the implementation. The more structured and precisely you have thought through a problem, the clearer your implementation will be. Once the penny has dropped, it is often not too big of a step to create or improve an understandable, well-structured solution. However, if you start too early with an implementation simply as source code, this unfortunately too often ends in a disaster and a failure. As a result, some things remain rather half-baked, and it gets harder to add functionality in a meaningful way.

I like to point out that especially traceability and later simplified maintainability are very important in programming. This is achieved in general by creating small and comprehensible building blocks. With the potentially (and presumably only) minimally poorer performance as well as the lower compactness, they are often easier to live with than with a fairly certain poor maintainability.

Thoughts on Performance

Keep in mind that in today's world of distributed applications, the impact of individual instructions or unoptimized methods on performance is negligible. By contrast, too frequent or too fine-grained REST calls or database accesses may have a much more serious impact on execution time over an algorithm that has not been optimized down to the last detail. Please note that my statements apply primarily to self-written functionalities in business applications. For frameworks and algorithms that experience millions of calls (or more), however, the inner beauty is potentially less important than the performance. There will probably always be a certain trade-off between the two poles: either compact and performance-optimized or understandable, but sometimes a bit slower.

Advantages of Unit Tests

Even when creating only simple programs, you may notice the following fact over and over again: If you test implementations of algorithms purely based on console output, errors often remain unnoticed—mainly for special cases, limits, and so on. Moreover, without supporting unit tests, people tend to think less about the interfaces of classes and methods' signatures. But this is exactly what helps to increase manageability for others. With pytest, writing unit tests is really fun and smooth. This is mainly due to the pleasant and helpful parameterized tests.

By reading this book and reviewing the solutions, you should have gained a good understanding of unit testing in addition to your skills in the topics covered. Even more, when developing solutions, there is a sense of security when the unit tests pass.

10.2 Logic Puzzles

You have dealt with a wide variety of programming puzzles in this book. I present two logic puzzles to you, which have nothing to do with programming. Still, you can learn a lot about problem-solving strategies by answering them. From time to time, something seems impossible at first, and then there is a straightforward solution. If you like, try your hand at the following puzzles:

- Gold Bags–Detect the Fake

- Horse Race–Determine Fastest Three Horses

10.2.1 Gold Bags–Detect the Fake

This puzzle is about 10 gold bags, each filled with 10 coins, each of which weighs 10 g. Thus, each gold bag should weigh 100 g (Figure 10-1).

Figure 10-1. *Gold bags*

An impostor has exchanged the gold coins in a bag for fakes, which, at 9 g instead of 10 g per coin, are somewhat lighter. Find the gold bag containing the fakes with only one weighing. However, you may take different numbers of coins from any bag and weigh them together.

Solution

At first, this task sounds almost impossible since multiple weighing and comparing are not allowed. You might come up with the following trick with a bit of pondering: Line up the bags and number them from 1 to 10. Now work position-based and place as many coins from each corresponding bag as matches its position, and then weigh them all together, as shown in Figure 10-2.

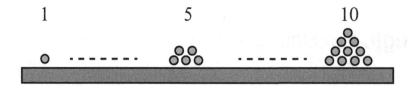

Figure 10-2. *Weighing gold pieces*

Without fakes, the result would be as follows:

$$1\times10+2\times10+3\times10+4\times10+5\times10+6\times10+7\times10+8\times10+9\times10+10\times10$$
$$=10+20+30+40+50+60+70+80+90+100$$
$$=550$$

Let's assume that bag 5 contains the fakes and look at the result:

$$1\times10+2\times10+3\times10+4\times10+\mathbf{5\times9}+6\times10+7\times10+8\times10+9\times10+10\times10$$
$$=10+20+30+40+\mathbf{45}+60+70+80+90+100$$
$$=545$$

Let's now assume that bag 2 contains the fakes and determine the result:

$$1\times10+\mathbf{2\times9}+3\times10+4\times10+5\times10+6\times10+7\times10+8\times10+9\times10+10\times10$$
$$=10+\mathbf{18}+30+40+50+60+70+80+90+100$$
$$=548$$

According to this, you can identify the corresponding bag based on the difference to 550:

$$550 - weighed\ weight = position$$

10.2.2 Horse Race–Determine Fastest Three Horses

This puzzle is about solving the following: 25 racehorses are offered for sale, and you want to buy the three fastest. There is a racetrack with space for a maximum of five horses. Still, you have neither a stopwatch nor any other way of measuring time. However, the horses can compete against each other in races, and you may note the order. Under these restrictions, how do you determine the fastest three, and how do you proceed? How many races with which horses do you have to organize at best?

As a simplification, let's assume here that the horses are not exhausted by the races, run exactly the same speed in each race, and also that no two horses are the same speed (just like in a photo finish, there is always an order and a winner).

Solution

Again, you have to think quite a bit at first to arrange the right races by a clever exclusion procedure and additionally perform as few of them as possible. In fact, only seven races are necessary to determine the fastest three horses. How do you go about it?

Step 1: You let five horses compete against each other in any five races and thus determine the winners of these races. For better traceability, all horses get a number between 1 and 25, which normally says nothing about the placement. In the following, the number is used for better distinguishability. It is possible to label the horses just as well with A, B, C, ... but then you need further distinctions for the races' winners.

You thus determine the winners from all five races and can directly remove all horses in the respective fourth and fifth places from your selection for the next races by the exclusion procedure shown in Figure 10-3.

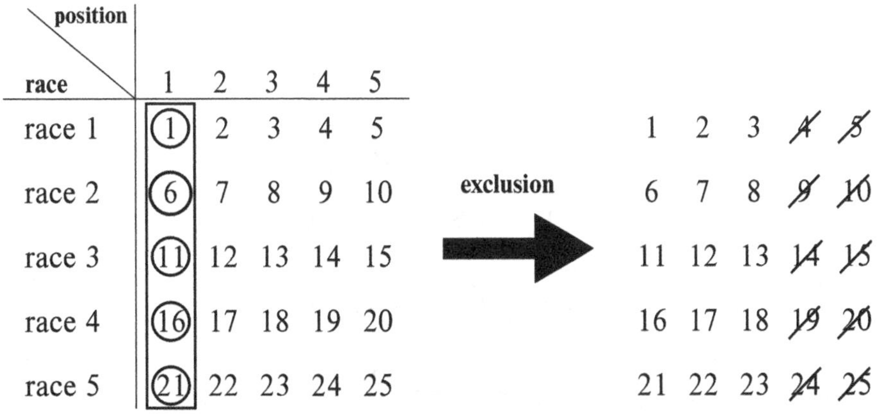

Figure 10-3. *Races 1 to 5*

As a result, 15 horses remain, and if you would like to compare them with each other, at least three races would yet be necessary after these five races. According to my statement, however, a total of seven races is enough, so only two races are still allowed. Consequently, you nevertheless have to reduce the number of horses to be compared to suitably.

Step 2: To have significantly less than 15 horses left for further selection, you need to run another race, one with all the winners. Why? So far, you only know something about the horses within the groups themselves, but not between the groups. To get some information about the relative speeds of the winners, you let them race against each other. Again, the last two cannot be among the fastest three horses. See Figure 10-4.

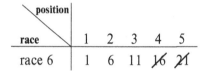

Figure 10-4. *Race of winners*

However, this will automatically eliminate the horses with numbers 17 and 18 (slower than the horse with number 16) and the horses with numbers 22 and 23 (slower than the horse with number 21) as candidates.

Step 3: You mark the exclusions in a matrix, and then you combine the gained knowledge to proceed with the next exclusion. To do this, you insert a > notation for *faster than* into the matrix of horses. Because horse 1 also won in the winner's race, you are sure that horse 1 is definitely the fastest. See Figure 10-5.

$$\boxed{1} > 2 > 3 \quad \cancel{4} \quad \cancel{5}$$
$$\vee$$
$$6 > 7 > 8 \quad \cancel{9} \quad \cancel{10}$$
$$\vee$$
$$11 > 12 > 13 \quad \cancel{14} \quad \cancel{15}$$

$$\cancel{16} \quad \cancel{17} \quad \cancel{18} \quad \cancel{19} \quad \cancel{20}$$

$$\cancel{21} \quad \cancel{22} \quad \cancel{23} \quad \cancel{24} \quad \cancel{25}$$

Figure 10-5. *Best nine at horse racing*

However, there are still nine horses left—actually only eight candidates, since horse 1 is the fastest. That would indicate at least two more races. Let's now consider a bit.

You know the orders by the previous races. Since you want to determine only the fastest three, the horses numbered 8, 12, and 13 are eliminated, and five horses now remain, namely those numbered 2, 3, 6, 7, and 11. See Figure 10-6.

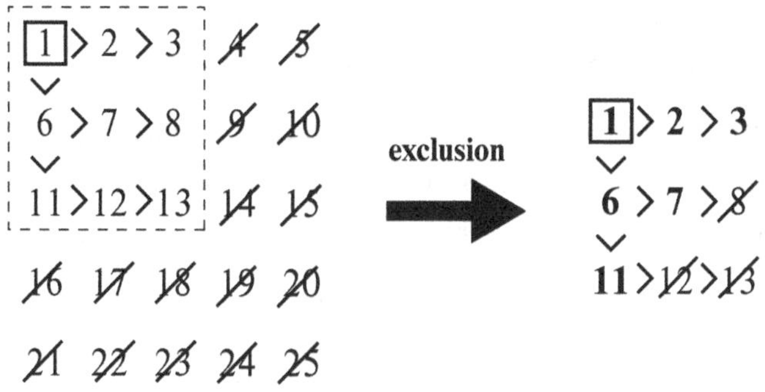

Figure 10-6. *Final exclusion at horse racing*

Thus, you only have to let the other horses (i.e., 2, 3, 6, 7, and 11) compete against each other. The winner and runner-up of this race are the overall second and third horse. This results in the following possible combinations as the final result:

- 1, 2, 3
- 1, 2, 6
- 1, 6, 2
- 1, 6, 7
- 1, 6, 11

10.3 Supplementary Literature

In this book, my main intention was to provide a couple of programming and brainteaser exercises and an entertaining time in solving them. If the exercises are easily solvable for you most of the time, you will find various books below as supplementary reading.

Interestingly, when dealing with a topic, one always comes across previously unknown literature. Some books inspired me, and so I recommend them to you. I group the books thematically, and this should serve as a good starting point for further steps.

10.3.1 Introduction to Algorithms and Data Structures

There are various books for getting started with algorithms and data structures. Let me recommend the following for completion or a different point of view:

- *Grokking Algorithms* [Bha16] by Aditya Y. Bhargava

  A small but fine book, which offers a readable, comprehensible, and entertaining introduction, which is enriched by many illustrations. The examples are in Python.

- *A Common-Sense Guide to Data Structures and Algorithms* [Wen17] by Jay Wengrow

  A wonderful, easy-to-follow book to get started with algorithms and data structures. The extensive illustrations make it easy to understand the steps of the algorithms. Again, the examples are in Python.

- *Problem Solving in Data Structures and Algorithms Using Python* [Jai19] by Hemant Jain

  Of the three books listed here, this is the most comprehensive. It goes far beyond the previous ones in terms of the topics presented. However, it offers fewer explanatory illustrations and is not written as intuitively as the others.

10.3.2 Basic Books

If you want to take a deep dive scientifically into the subject of algorithms and data structures, and you like to learn things from scratch, and you like it a bit more formal, then take a look at one of the following books:

- *Algorithms* [Sed11] by Robert Sedgewick

  This book provides you with an easy-to-read and comprehensible introduction to the subject. An older edition accompanied me in my university studies back in the 1990s. However, this book uses Java as the explanatory language.

- *Data Structures and Algorithms with Object-Oriented Design Patterns in Java* [Pre00] by Bruno R. Preiss

This book provides a solid overview of common data structures and shows how to implement them with Java. Because it was written in 2000, it does not use generics. Nevertheless, it is my favorite concerning Java and data structures. However, this book uses Java as the explanatory language.

- *Data Structures and Problem Solving Using Java* [Wei10] by Mark Allen Weiss

This book by Mark Allen Weiss offers a slightly more practical approach than the previously mentioned one. Due to the publication year of 2010, it uses more modern concepts like generics for the implementation of the data structures. However, this book uses Java as the explanatory language.

10.3.3 Specializing in Interview Questions

In addition to the basic books mentioned earlier, there are some that focus primarily on interview questions or small programming tasks:

- *Top 30 Java Interview Coding Tasks* [Urb18] by Matthew Urban

If you don't have a lot of time and if you are not that interested in background information, this short booklet is definitely something for you. However, this book uses Java as the explanatory language. This book uses unit tests to check the implementation, but they are based on the somewhat outdated JUnit 4 instead of the newer JUnit 5.

- *Daily Coding Problem* [MW19] by Alex Miller and Lawrence Wu

This is another book that provides a lot of information and also exercises including solutions for algorithms and data structures. It focuses on small programming tasks for every day and is based on Python.

10.3.4 Supplements for Job Interviews at Top Companies

To prepare for a job interview at one of the top companies, namely Amazon, Apple, Facebook, Google, and Microsoft, I recommend the following books as a supplement to my book. Some of them go into more depth and offer even trickier tasks or more background knowledge. In addition, all of them also describe the interview process itself and how to prepare for it.

- *Cracking the Coding Interview* [McD16] by Gayle Laakmann McDowell

  This is a great book by an extremely competent author. However, it is advisable to read a book on algorithms beforehand, so that it is easier for you to follow the explanations. The degree of difficulty of some tasks is challenging in parts.

- *Programming Interviews Exposed* [MKG18] by John Mongan, Noah Kindler, and Eric Giguère

  In addition to algorithms and data structures, this book also covers topics such as concurrency, design patterns, and databases. It contains fewer exercises but very good explanations. The solutions are presented in different programming languages.

- *Elements of Programming Interviews in Python* [ALP16] by Adnan Aziz, Tsung-Hsien Lee, and Amit Prakash

  This book covers many different topics, especially data structures and algorithms. It offers a lot of exercises and programming challenges.

PART III

Appendix

APPENDIX A

Short Introduction to pytest

pytest is a framework written in Python that helps in creating and automating test cases. It is easy to learn and takes a lot of the work out of writing and managing test cases. In particular, only the logic for the test cases itself needs to be implemented. Unlike some other frameworks, there is no need to learn a large number of functions to set up test assertions; one is enough.

The module `unittest`, which is integrated in Python, is less easy to handle than pytest and therefore less common. Details about both can be found at `https://knapsackpro.com/testing_frameworks/difference_between/unittest/vs/pytest`. Conveniently, pytest also allows you to use a possibly existing test base, created with `unittest`, permitting a step-by-step migration from `unittest` to pytest.

A.1 Writing and Executing Tests

A.1.1 Installing pytest

Before you can use pytest, you need to install it. This can be done using the `pip` tool, which is simply called `pip` for Linux and Windows but `pip3` for Mac OS.

Open a console and type the following command (in the following text, and this book in general, I always use $ to indicate input on the console, which is the terminal on MacOS or the Windows command prompt):

```
$ pip install -U pytest
```

In addition, a few plugins are quite useful, such as this one for parameterized tests

```
$ pip install parameterized
```

615

© Michael Inden 2022
M. Inden, *Python Challenges*, https://doi.org/10.1007/978-1-4842-7398-2_11

and this one for formatting an HTML page

```
$ pip install pytest-html
```

For configuring pytest in PyCharm, please read the online documentation:
www.jetbrains.com/help/pycharm/pytest.html#9.

A.1.2 First Unit Test

To test a module, a corresponding test module is usually written. To be recognized by
pytest, it should end with the postfix test or _test, such as ex03_palindrome_test.
Often, to validate important functionality, you start by testing a few key functions. This
should be extended step by step. Test cases are expressed as special test functions, which
must be marked with the prefix test_. Otherwise, pytest does not consider them as test
cases and ignores them during test execution.

Let's have a look at an introductory example:

```
def test_index():
    # ARRANGE
    name = "Peter"

    # ACT
    pos = name.index("t")
    expected = 2

    # ASSERT
    assert pos == expected
```

Interestingly, there's no dependency on pytest. In fact, the whole thing is
automatically linked to pytest, and the execution standard assert is varied in such a way
that pytest hooks in and produces test results.

Also worth mentioning is the three-way split with ARRANGE-ACT-ASSERT for preparing
the actions, executing them, and evaluating the results. This structure helps to write
clean and understandable tests. There is not always an ARRANGE part and the comments
can be omitted if you are more experienced. This is described in much more detail in my
book *Der Weg zum Java-Profi* [Ind20].

A.1.3 Executing Tests

To run the unit test with pytest, you can either use

- the command line or
- the IDE.

Executing Tests on the Console

Running the unit tests with pytest can be done from the console in the root directory of your project. In the following code, use python3 and the module specification with -m. This is the only way the tests always run cleanly for me.

```
$ python3 -m pytest
```

This will start all tests and log the result on the console. For this book, it is shortened as follows:

```
$ python3 -m pytest
================= test session starts ===================
platform darwin -- Python 3.10.1, pytest-7.1.1, pluggy-1.0.0
rootdir: /Users/michaeli/PycharmProjects/PythonChallenge
plugins: metadata-2.0.1, html-3.1.1
collected 645 items

tests/appendix/example_test.py .                               [   0%]
tests/ch02_math/ex01_basiscs_test.py ................           [   2%]
tests/ch02_math/ex02_number_as_text_test.py ..........          [   4%]
tests/ch02_math/ex03_perfectnumber_test.py ...........          [   6%]
tests/ch02_math/ex04_primes_test.py ........................    [  10%]
...
tests/ch08_binary_trees/ex08_reconstruction_test.py ...         [  95%]
tests/ch09_search_and_sort/ex01_contains_test.py ....           [  95%]
tests/ch09_search_and_sort/ex02_partition_test.py ..            [  96%]
tests/ch09_search_and_sort/ex03_binary_search_test.py ......    [  96%]
tests/ch09_search_and_sort/ex04_insertion_sort_test.py .        [  97%]
tests/ch09_search_and_sort/ex05_selection_sort_test.py .        [  97%]
tests/ch09_search_and_sort/ex06_quick_sort_test.py ...          [  97%]
```

```
tests/ch09_search_and_sort/ex07_bucket_sort_test.py ...           [ 98%]
tests/ch09_search_and_sort/ex08_search_rotated_sorted_test.py ...... [100%]

=============== 645 passed in 1.97s =====================
```

When getting started with the following parameters,

```
$ python3 -m pytest --html=pytest-report.html
```

an additional HTML report of the test results gets generated. This can be examined with the browser of your choice. An example is shown in Figure A-1.

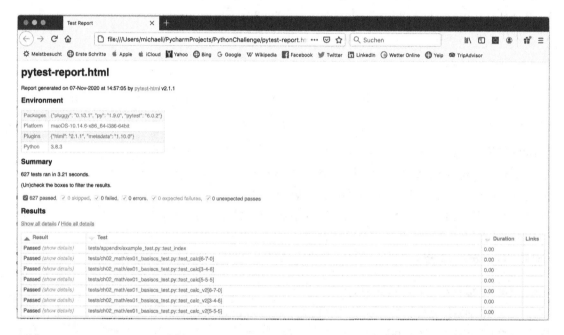

Figure A-1. *HTML representation of a test report*

Executing Tests from the IDE

Alternatively, it is a bit more convenient to start test execution directly in the IDE. Before doing so, however, pytest must be configured correctly. Conveniently, pytest is integrated with the popular IDE PyCharm. Tests can be executed either via a context menu or via buttons in the GUI. This produces output similar to that shown in Figure A-2.

Test Results	1 s 591 ms
✓ ex01_basiscs_test	0 ms
✓ test_calc	0 ms
✓ test_calc_v2	0 ms
✓ test_calc_sum_and_count_all_numbers_div_by_2_or_7	0 ms
✓ test_is_even	0 ms
✓ test_is_odd	0 ms
✓ ex02_number_as_text_test	0 ms
✓ Ex02_NumberAsText_Test	0 ms
✓ test_number_as_text	0 ms
✓ (7-SEVEN)	0 ms
✓ (42-FOUR TWO)	0 ms
✓ (7271-SEVEN TWO SEVEN ONE)	0 ms
✓ (24680-TWO FOUR SIX EIGHT ZERO)	0 ms
✓ (13579-ONE THREE FIVE SEVEN NINE)	0 ms

Figure A-2. *Test run from the GUI of the IDE*

A.1.4 Handling Expected Exceptions

Sometimes test cases are supposed to check for the occurrence of exceptions during processing, and an absence would constitute an error. An example is deliberately accessing a non-existent position of a string. An IndexError should be the result. To handle expected exceptions in the test case in such a way that they represent a test success and not a failure, the executing functionality must be called specifically surrounded by with pytest.raises():

```python
def test_str_to_number_invalid_input():
    with pytest.raises(ValueError):
        str_to_number("ABC")

def test_str_to_number_bonus_invalid_input():
    with pytest.raises(ValueError) as excinfo:
        str_to_number_bonus("Oo128")

    assert str(excinfo.value).find("found digit >= 8") != -1

def test_fib_rec_wrong_input():
    with pytest.raises(ValueError) as excinfo:
        fib_rec(0)

    assert "n must be >= 1" in str(excinfo.value)
```

In the second and third test case, you see how easy it is to access the contents of the thrown exceptions, for example to check the text or other details.

A.1.5 Parameterized Tests with pytest

Sometimes you need to test a large number of value sets. Creating a separate test function for each of them would make the test module quite bloated and confusing. To solve this more elegantly, there are several variants. All of them have their specific strengths and weaknesses.

In the following, assume that calculations are to be checked for fixed ranges of values or a selected set of inputs.[1]

A parameterized test allows you to do just that: write the test function and define a set of inputs and expected results. Based on this, the testing framework automatically executes the test function for all specified combinations of values.

Introduction to Parameterized Tests

With pytest, defining parameterized tests is very simple. All you need to do is apply a suitable import and then specify the desired values as follows:

```python
import pytest

@pytest.mark.parametrize("value1, value2, expected",
                         [("Micha", "Michael", 2),
                          ("rapple", "tables", 4)])
def test_edit_distance(value1, value2, expected):
    result = edit_distance(value1, value2)

    assert result == expected

@pytest.mark.parametrize("sorted_values, search_value, expected",
                         [([1, 2, 3, 4, 5, 7, 8, 9], 5, True),
                          ([1, 2, 3, 4, 5, 7, 8, 9], 6, False)])
def test_binary_search(sorted_values, search_value, expected):
    assert binary_search(sorted_values, search_value) == expected
```

---

[1] If the number of values is huge, it is not a good idea to perform a check for all of them, since this often significantly increases the execution time of the unit tests, without providing any real added value. Especially here, it is recommended to use representatives from equivalence classes, which should drastically reduce the number of test cases. For details, refer to my book *Der Weg zum Java-Profi* [Ind20].

In the code, you see that the parameterized test must be annotated with @ pytest.mark.parametrize. The first parameter specifies the parameter names and the evaluation of the values. These values are passed as a list of tuples. For each parameterization specified as a tuple, a separate test case is created and executed.

Other Possibilities in Parameterized Tests

Ingeniously, all collection literals (i.e., tuples, lists, sets, and dictionaries) can be used when specifying test inputs and results:

```python
@pytest.mark.parametrize("digits, value, expected",
                         [([1, 2, 3, 4, 5, 6, 7, 8, 9], 100,
                          {"1+23-4+5+6+78-9",
                           "12+3+4+5-6-7+89",
                           "123-45-67+89",
                           "123+4-5+67-89",
                           "123-4-5-6-7+8-9",
                           "123+45-67+8-9",
                           "1+2+3-4+5+6+78+9",
                           "12+3-4+5+67+8+9",
                           "1+23-4+56+7+8+9",
                           "1+2+34-5+67-8+9",
                           "12-3-4+5-6+7+89"})])
def test_all_combinations_with_value(digits, value, expected):
    result = all_combinations_with_value(digits, value)

    assert result == expected
```

A.2 Further Reading on pytest

This appendix just provided a first introduction to testing with pytest so you can follow the examples more easily. Of course, there is much more to discover, such as various plugins. More information on how to use pytest appropriately can be found in the following books:

- *Python Testing with pytest: Simple, Rapid, Effective, and Scalable* by Brian Okken [Okk17]

- *pytest Quick Start Guide: Write better Python code with simple and maintainable tests* by Bruno Oliveira [Oli18]

APPENDIX B

Short Introduction to Decorators

In this appendix, I would like to introduce decorators, another topic that allows us to express solutions to cross-cutting functionalities elegantly. Decorators are useful for parameter checks, for example, and are used primarily in this book for advanced recursion topics.

Decorators allow you to add already existing functionality to new functionality transparently, without extensions in the implementation of a function itself. Although writing decorators is pretty straightforward, there are a few specifics to keep in mind. Let's look at this a little more closely when examining parameters for functions.

B.1 Argument Checks by Decorator

Previously, you performed various argument checks, such as to ensure a valid range of values. In Python, these sanity checks can be outsourced to a decorator. Consequently, the actual function code can stay as close as possible to the problem to be solved, without special treatment.

A function to check for positive integers can be implemented as follows where you pass a function as a parameter and use a function as a return:

```python
def check_argument_is_positive_integer(unary_func):
    def helper(n):
        if type(n) == int and n > 0:
            return unary_func(n)
        else:
            raise ValueError("n must be positive and of type int")

    return helper
```

© Michael Inden 2022
M. Inden, *Python Challenges*, https://doi.org/10.1007/978-1-4842-7398-2_12

As a simple example of usage, let's consider the calculation of the factorial where the parameter check is still included:

```
def factorial(n):
    if n <= 0:
        raise ValueError("n must be >= 1")

    if n == 1:
        return 1

    return n * factorial(n - 1)
```

To activate the check, you can wrap the above function with the argument check as follows:

```
factorial = check_argument_is_positive_integer(factorial)
```

It is also possible to define a new function as follows:

```
# wrapping results in new function
checked_factorial = check_argument_is_positive_integer(factorial)
print(checked_factorial(5))
# print(checked_factorial(-5)) # => ValueError
```

NOTE: HIGHER ORDER FUNCTIONS

In this example, the decorator is created using functions or nested functions. There are also higher order functions, which are when a function receives another function as a parameter and returns a function as a result.

B.2 Syntactic Sugar for Decorators

In Python, there is the variant with @. This allows you to place the decorator name directly on top of the function definition:

```
@check_argument_is_positive_integer
def factorial(n):
```

```
if n <= 0:
    raise ValueError("n must be >= 1")

if n == 1:
    return 1

return n * factorial(n - 1)
```

Now you can omit the two lines

```
if n <= 0:
    raise ValueError("n must be >= 1")
```

and write the function in a shorter and clearer way, as follows:

```
@check_argument_is_positive_integer
def factorial(n):
    if n == 1:
        return 1

    return n * factorial(n - 1)
```

NOTE: DIFFERENCE BETWEEN TYPES OF DECORATION

For @<decorator>, the decoration is always done. If you call <decorator>(function) you can also call the function regularly and later switch on the decorator explicitly. For this example, you call the check as follows, where the second call produces a ValueError:

```
# invocation with "factorial" as parameter
print(check_argument_is_positive_integer(factorial)(5))
print(check_argument_is_positive_integer(factorial)(-5))
```

B.3 Checking Multiple Parameters

The check for positive integers can also be extended to multiple parameters (two, in the following code). For example, this may be used for simple arithmetic operations like + and − for natural numbers:

```python
def check_arguments_are_positive_integers(binary_func):
    def helper(param1, param2):
        if type(param1) == int and param1 > 0 and \
            type(param2) == int and param2 > 0:
            return binary_func(param1, param2)
        else:
            raise ValueError("both params must be positive and of type int")

    return helper

@check_arguments_are_positive_integers
def add(value1, value2):
    return value1 + value2

@check_arguments_are_positive_integers
def subtract(value1, value2):
    return value1 - value2
```

NOTE: EXPLICIT CHECKS OR DECORATOR?

Consider the following: As the number of parameters increases, the complexity of the checks also increases, and the comprehensibility potentially decreases. Thus, from about three parameters to be checked, an explicit examination within the respective functions or methods is probably more appropriate. This helps to maintain or even increase traceability and maintainability.

B.4 Logging Function Calls and Parameter Passing

Previously, you considered the somewhat simplified cases of one or two parameters. However, for various decorators, it is important to be able to be called for an arbitrary number of parameters, such as for logging calls or for measuring execution times. For this purpose, the decorator can be defined more generally as follows:

```python
def audit_decorator(func):
    def wrapper(*args, **kwargs):
        print("Before calling " + func.__name__)
```

```
    result = func(*args, **kwargs)
    print("After calling " + func.__name__)
    return result

  return wrapper
```

Let's use this decorator once for logging. You write the following as a combination of two decorators:

```
@audit_decorator
@check_arguments_are_positive_integers
def add(value1, value2):
    return value1 + value2
```

When executing

```
>>> print("add", add(2, 7))
```

You get, however, the name of the inner decorator, here helper, instead of the original function add, which was probably of interest:

```
Before calling helper
After calling helper
add 9
```

Based on these issues, I would like to address one more point explicitly: Decorating has worked quite smoothly so far, but you should consider that in this way, the following attributes of the function are lost:

- __name__ (the name of the function),
- __doc__ (the documentation, the docstring) and
- __module__ (the module where the function was defined).

B.5 Improvement with wraps from the functools Module

Previously, you saw the somewhat irritating output of the wrapping instead of the wrapped function. A workaround is to use wraps from the module functools as follows:

```python
def check_arguments_are_positive_integers(binary_func):
    @wraps(binary_func)
    def helper(param1, param2):
        if type(param1) == int and param1 > 0 and \
            type(param2) == int and param2 > 0:
            return binary_func(param1, param2)
        else:
            raise ValueError("both params must be positive and of type int")

    return helper
```

As a result, the output is as expected:

```
Before calling add
After calling add
add 9
```

In addition, you should add @wraps in audit_decorator.

Let's finish the short introduction with profiling and the measurement of the execution time of functions. For this purpose, you define the following decorator on yourself:

```python
def timed_execution(func):
    @wraps(func)
    def timed_execute(*args, **kwargs):
        start_time = time.process_time()
        result = func(*args, **kwargs)
        end_time = time.process_time()
        run_time = end_time - start_time
        print(f"'{func.__name__}' took {run_time * 1000:.2f} ms")
        return result

    return timed_execute
```

APPENDIX C

Quick Start O-Notation

In this book, the so-called O-notation is used to classify the running time of algorithms. This allows a more formal classification of the complexity of algorithms.

C.1 Estimations with O-Notation

To estimate and describe the complexity of algorithms and classify their running time behavior, it would be impractical to always take measurements. In addition, measurements only reflect the running time behavior under certain restrictions of the hardware (processor clock, memory, etc.). To be able to classify the consequences of design decisions independently of such details and on a more abstract level, computer science uses the so-called *O-notation*, which indicates the upper bound for the complexity of an algorithm. To do so, you are able to answer the following question: how does a program perform when instead of 1,000 input values, for example, 10,000 or 100,000 input values are processed? To answer this question, the individual steps of an algorithm must be considered and classified. The aim is to formalize the calculation of complexity to estimate the effects of changes in the number of input data on the program running time.

Consider the following while loop as an introductory example:

```
i = 0                         // O(1)
while i < n:                  // O(n)
    create_person_in_db(i)    // O(1)
    i += 1                    // O(1)
```

© Michael Inden 2022
M. Inden, *Python Challenges*, https://doi.org/10.1007/978-1-4842-7398-2_13

Any single instruction is assigned a complexity of $O(1)$. The loop itself is assigned the complexity $O(n)$ due to the n executions of the loop body.[1] Adding these values together, the cost of running the program is thus $O(1) + O(n) * (O(1) + O(1)) = O(1) + O(n) * 2$. For an estimation of complexity, constant summands and factors do not matter. Only the highest power of n is of interest. Thus, we get a complexity of $O(n)$ for the program's illustrated piece. This simplification is permissible since, for larger values of n, the influence of factors and smaller complexity classes is insignificant. For the understanding of the considerations in the following sections, this informal definition should be sufficient.

I would like to quote two sentences by Robert Sedgewick that characterize the O-notation, from his standard work *Algorithms* [Sed92]: "[...] the O-notation is a useful tool for specifying upper bounds on the running time, which are independent of the input data's details and the implementation. [...] The O-notation proves extremely useful in helping analysts to classify algorithms according to their performance, and by helping algorithms in their search for the 'best' algorithms." (translated from the German book).

C.1.1 Complexity Classes

To be able to compare the running time behavior of different algorithms with each other, seven different complexity classes are usually sufficient. The following bullet points names the respective complexity class and some examples:

- **$O(1)$**: The constant complexity results in a complexity that is independent of the number of input data n. This complexity often represents **an instruction** or a simple computation that consists of a few computational steps.

- **$O(log(n))$**: With logarithmic complexity, the running time doubles when the input data set n is squared. A well-known example of this complexity is **binary search**.

- **$O(n)$**: In the case of linear complexity, the running time grows proportionally to the number of elements n. This is the case for simple loops and iterations, such as a **search in an array** or a list.

---

[1] The meaning of the notation becomes more understandable on the next page with the presentation of examples for other complexity classes.

- $O(n \times log(n))$: This complexity is a combination of linear and logarithmic growth. Some of the fastest **sorting algorithms** (e. g. Merge Sort) show this complexity.

- $O(n^2)$: When doubling the amount of input data n, the quadratic complexity leads to a quadrupling of the running time. A tenfold increase in the input data already leads to a hundredfold increase in running time. In practice, this complexity is found with **two nested for or while loops**. Simple sorting algorithms usually have this complexity.

- $O(n^3)$: With cubic complexity, a doubling of n already leads to an eightfold increase of the running time. The naive **multiplication of matrices** is an example of this complexity class.

- $O(2^n)$: The exponential complexity results for a doubling of n in a squaring of the running time. At first, this does not sound like much. But with a tenfold increase, the running time increases by a factor of 20 billion! The exponential complexity occurs frequently with **optimization problems** such as the **Traveling Salesman Problem**, where the goal is to find the shortest path between different cities while visiting all cities.

  To cope with the problem of exorbitant running time, the program uses heuristics, which may not find the optimal solution, just an approximation of it, but have much lower complexity and a significantly shorter running time.

Table 13-1 shows impressively which effects the mentioned complexity classes have for different sets of input data n.[2]

---

[2] The time complexity $O(2^n)$ is not shown because its growth is too strong to be expressed meaningfully without the use of powers of 10.

Table 13-1. *Effects of Different Time Complexities*

n	O(log(n))	O(n)	O(n x log(n))	O(n²)	O(n³)
10	1	10	10	100	1.000
100	2	100	200	10.000	1.000.000
1.000	3	1.000	3.000	1.000.000	1.000.000.000
10.000	4	10.000	40.000	100.000.000	1.000.000.000.000
100.000	5	100.000	500.000	10.000.000.000	1.000.000.000.000.000
1.000.000	6	1.000.000	6.000.000	1.000.000.000.000	1.000.000.000.000.000.000

Based on the values shown, you get a feeling for the effects of different complexities. Up to about $O(n \times log(n))$ the complexity classes are favorable. Optimal and desirable, although not achievable for many algorithms, are the complexities $O(1)$ and $O(log(n))$. Already $O(n^2)$ is usually not favorable for larger input sets, but it can be used for simple computations and smaller values for *n* without any problems.

NOTE: INFLUENCE OF INPUT DATA

Some algorithms behave differently depending on the input data. For Quick Sort, the average case results in a complexity of $n \times log(n)$, but this can increase to n^2 in the extreme case. Since the O-notation describes the "worst case," Quick Sort is assigned a complexity of $O(n^2)$.

C.1.2 Complexity and Program Running Time

The numbers calculated by a special O-complexity for a set of input values *n* may sometimes be daunting. Still, they say nothing about the actual execution time, only about its growth when the input set increases. Based on the introductory example, the O-notation makes no statement about the duration of individual calculation steps: The increment i += 1 and the database access `create_person_in_db(i)` were both rated $O(1)$, even though the database access is several orders of magnitude more expensive than the increment concerning execution time.

For "normal" instructions without accesses to external systems, such as file systems, networks or databases (i.e., additions, assignments, etc.), the impact of n is in many cases not decisive for today's computers for typical business applications with user interactions. The impact on actual runtime hardly really matters for small n (< 1000) at complexities $O(n)$ or $O(n^2)$ and even sometimes at $O(n^3)$ nowadays—but this does not mean that you should not use algorithms that are as optimal as possible. Rather, the reverse is true: You can also start with a functionally correct implementation and put it into production. The optimized version may be rolled out sometime later.

All in all, I would like to emphasize once again that even multiple nested loops with the complexity $O(n^2)$ or $O(n^3)$ are often executed much faster in absolute terms than some database queries over a network with complexity $O(n)$. Similar is true for a search in an array ($O(n)$) and access to an element of a hash-based data structure ($O(1)$). For small n, the computation of the hash values can take longer than a linear search. However, the larger n gets, the more the impact of the worse complexity class affects the actual running time.

Short Introduction to Python 3.10

This appendix presents some of the enhancements implemented in Python 3.10, which was released in October 2021. Therein are features that may be relevant to you. I start with improvements to error messages. Then I briefly look at `match` for convenient design and formulation of case distinctions. Finally, I briefly touch on performance improvements as well as type checks and other details.

D.1 Error Messages

Sometimes errors occur in a Python program. Various types of errors can be observed. When creating programs, `SyntaxError` or `IndentationError` arise from time to time. These errors can be fixed easily with the context information and accurate line numbers provided by Python. Let's take a look at two short examples.

D.1.1 Assignment Error Messages

For the sake of demonstrating the improvements in error messages, let's assume you accidentally specified an assignment (=) instead of a comparison (==) in an `if`.

Python 3.9.x

With Python 3.9.x, the error is detected, of course, but gets reported rather unspecifically as `invalid syntax`, as follows:

```
>>> if x = 6:
  File "<stdin>", line 1
```

© Michael Inden 2022
M. Inden, *Python Challenges*, https://doi.org/10.1007/978-1-4842-7398-2_14

```
if x = 6:
     ^
```

```
SyntaxError: invalid syntax
```

Unfortunately, there is no hint of what is wrong with the syntax. Depending on your programming experience, the underlying problem is either quickly found or you are left guessing.

Improvement with Python 3.10

Let's look at how the error message for the same lines changes with Python version 3.10, in particular becoming much more understandable:

```
>>> if x = 6:
  File "<stdin>", line 1
    if x = 6:
        ^^^^^
```

```
SyntaxError: invalid syntax. Maybe you meant '==' or ':=' instead of '='?
```

As you can see, not only is the problem's cause mentioned directly, but two possibilities for remedial action are suggested at once.

D.1.2 Error Messages for Incomplete Strings

Sometimes you might overlook delimiting a string at the beginning or the end with quotation marks. Let's take a look at the error messages generated by different Python versions.

Python 3.9.x

You define a set with some names, but the last one does not end correctly with a quotation mark.

```
>>> data = { "Tim", "Tom", "Mike}
  File "<stdin>", line 1
    data = { "Tim", "Tom", "Mike}
                             ^
```

```
SyntaxError: EOL while scanning string literal
```

Improvement with Python 3.10

With Python 3.10, the problem is directly apparent from the error message, namely the missing quotation mark at the end of the string:

```
>>> data = { "Tim", "Tom", "Mike}
  File "<stdin>", line 1
    data = { "Tim", "Tom", "Mike}
                               ^
SyntaxError: unterminated string literal (detected at line 1)
```

D.2 Case Distinctions with match

In many languages, case distinctions may be expressed using the if statement as well as the switch statement. The latter was missing in Python for a long time. With Python 3.10 comes match, an even more powerful variant for case discrimination with which we can now finally also realize the switch statement. In addition, match enables pattern matching, a method that is used in functional languages such as Erlang/Elixir or Scala, but also makes its way into the current Java 17 (in a trimmed-down form).

Let's look at some possibilities of match again a few examples.

D.2.1 Python 3.9.x

Suppose you want to map HTTP status codes to their meaning. This can be solved with an if cascade as follows (shown here only in excerpts):

```
http_code = 201

if http_code == 200:
    print("OK")
elif http_code == 201:
    print("CREATED")
elif http_code == 404:
    print("NOT FOUND")
elif http_code == 418:
    print("I AM A TEAPOT")
else:
    print("UNMATCHED CODE")
```

However, it is noticeable that this is not easy to read.

Improvement with Python 3.10

Let's look at how much clearer the above construct becomes with the use of match. In particular, with _ you can also include a wildcard case that is jumped to whenever the other cases don't match.

```python
match http_code:
    case 200:
        print("OK")
    case 201:
        print("CREATED")
    case 404:
        print("NOT FOUND")
    case 418:
        print("I AM A TEAPOT")
    case _:
        print("UNMATCHED CODE")
```

Combination of Values

By using the pipe operator (|), it is possible to specify multiple values for which the following action should be executed. This is shown here for Thursday and Friday in combination and Saturday and Sunday:

```python
def get_info(day):
    match day:
        case 'Monday':
            return "I don't like..."
        case 'Thursday' | 'Friday':
            return 'Nearly there!'
        case 'Saturday' | 'Sunday':
            return 'Weekend!!!'
        case _:
            return 'In Between...'
```

More Complex Matching I

You have just seen that you can specify values with the pipe operator as alternatives. However, it is also possible to check iterables for a match:

```python
values = (2,3,4)

match values:
    case [1,2,3,4]:
        print("4 in a row")
    case [1,2,3] | [2,3,4]:
        print("3 in a row")
    case [1,2,4] | [1,3,4]:
        print("3 but not connected")
    case _:
        print("SINGLE OR DOUBLE")
```

More Complex Matching II

The capabilities of match are even more powerful, however, which I'll just hint at here. Please note that you can specify matching patterns and additional conditions after the values in case.

```python
class Gender(Enum):
    MALE = auto()
    FEMALE = auto()

def classify(person):
    match person:
        case (name, age, "male" | Gender.MALE):
            print(f"{name} is a man and {age} years old")
        case (name, age, "female" | Gender.FEMALE):
            print(f"{name} is a woman and {age} years old")
        case (name, _, gender) if gender is not None:
            print(f"no age specified: {name} is {gender}")
        case (name, age, _) if age is not None:
            print(f"no gender specified: {name} is {age} years old.")
```

Here the already mentioned pattern matching takes place. In `case`, it is checked whether there is a match with the pattern, but additionally the specified variables are assigned corresponding values. Details can be found in PEP 622 at www.python.org/dev/peps/pep-0622/. Again, _ serves as a wildcard operator and matches with everything.

Let's call this classification once as follows:

```
classify(("Micha", 50, "male"))
classify(("Lili", 42, Gender.FEMALE))
classify(("NO GENDER", 42, None))
classify(("NO AGE", None, "ALL"))
```

This results in the following outputs:

```
Micha is a man and 50 years old
Lili is a woman and 42 years old
no gender specified: NO GENDER is 42 years old.
no age specified: NO AGE is ALL
```

D.3 Miscellaneous

D.3.1 Improvements in Context Managers

Context managers are helpful for resource management when opening or closing files. But they are also useful for managing database connections and many other resources.

Improvement with Python 3.10

With Python 3.10, their syntax becomes a tiny bit more pleasant when using multiple context managers within one `with` statement:

```
with (
    open("input1.txt") as input_file1,
    open("input2.txt") as input_file2,
):
```

D.3.2 Performance Improvements

Python has been improved internally concerning performance in several places. This mainly applies for constructors like `str()`, `bytes()`, and `bytearray()`. They have become faster by about 30 %. Please consult `https://bugs.python.org/issue41334` for details.

D.3.3 Extension at zip()

Python 3.9.x

Python provides a built-in function called `zip()` that allows you to combine two (or . more precisely, multiple) iterables into a single unit. This may be used to combine, for example, two lists, one of programming languages and another of version numbers:

```
>>> languages = ['Java', 'Python']
>>> versions = [17.0, 3.10]
>>>
>>> print(list(zip(languages, versions)))
[('Java', 17.0), ('Python', 3.10)]
```

If one dataset contains more elements than the other, the merge will be aborted as soon as all elements of the shorter dataset have been processed:

```
>>> number_list = [1, 2, 3, 4, 5, 6]
>>> str_list = ['one', 'two', 'three']
>>>
>>> print(list(zip(number_list, str_list)))
[(1, 'one'), (2, 'two'), (3, 'three')]
```

This is often really a very good default setting to be able to work fault-tolerantly. However, sometimes you want to merge the two datasets only if both can provide the same amount of elements. With Python 3.9.x this was only achievable by the help of additional programming efforts.

Improvement with Python 3.10

Since Python 3.10, zip() supports the parameter strict. Use the value True to specify that an exception should be thrown if one of the iterables is exhausted before the others:

```
>>> number_list = [1, 2, 3, 4, 5, 6]
>>> str_list = ['one', 'two', 'three']
>>>
>>> print(list(zip(number_list, str_list, strict=True)))
Traceback (most recent call last):
  File "<stdin>", line 1, in <module>
ValueError: zip() argument 2 is shorter than argument 1
```

D.3.4 Typechecking Improvements

I have not shown type checks in this book so far, as this is a rather advanced feature of Python. Furthermore, these specifications are optional and only help while coding but are not evaluated at runtime. For clarification, let's assume the following function initially:

```
def identity(value):
    return value
```

Python 3.9.x

To specify for a function that it expects parameters of either type int or float as input and also returns them, you can add the following specifications:

```
def identity(value: Union[int, float]) -> Union[int, float]:
    return value
```

Improvement with Python 3.10

The union of types just shown does get a bit clumsy by explicitly specifying Union. With Python 3.10, the notation looks quite natural and is also shorter and more readable:

```
def identity(value: int | float) -> int | float:
    return value
```

This is described as PEP 604 at `www.python.org/dev/peps/pep-0604/`.

HINT: INTERESTING VIDEO ABOUT WHAT'S NEW IN PYTHON 3.10

To see the new features live in action, I recommend an instructive video available on YouTube at `www.youtube.com/watch?v=5-A435hIYio`).

Bibliography

[ALP16] Adnan Aziz, Tsung-Hsien Lee, and Amit Prakash, *Elements Of Programming Interviews in Python* (CreateSpace Independent Publishing Platform, 2016).

[Bad17] Dan Bader, *Python Tricks: A Buffet of Awesome Python Features* (Dan Bader, 2017).

[Bha16] Aditya Y. Bhargava, *Grokking Algorithms* (Manning, 2016).

[Ind20] Michael Inden, *Der Weg zum Java-Profi* 5th edition (dpunkt.verlag, 2020).

[Jai19] Hemant Jain, *Problem Solving in Data Structures and Algorithms Using Python* 2nd edition (2019).

[McD16] Gayle Laakmann McDowell, *Cracking the Coding Interview* 6th edition (CareerCup, 2016).

[MKG18] John Mongan, Noah Kindler, and Eric Giguère, *Programming Interviews Exposed* 4th edition (Wrox, 2018).

[MW19] Alex Miller and Lawrence Wu, *Daily Coding Problem* (2019).

[Okk17] Brian Okken, *Python Testing with pytest: Simple, Rapid, Effective, and Scalable* (O'Reilly, 2017).

[Oli18] Bruno Oliveira, *pytest Quick Start Guide: Write better Python code with simple and maintainable tests* (Packt Publishing, 2018).

[Pre00] Bruno R. Preiss, *Data Structures and Algorithms with Object-Oriented Design Patterns in Java* (Wiley, 2000).

[Sed92] Robert Sedgewick, *Algorithmen* (Addison-Wesley, 1992).

[Sed11] Robert Sedgewick, *Algorithms* 4th edition (Addison Wesley, 2011).

© Michael Inden 2022
M. Inden, *Python Challenges*, https://doi.org/10.1007/978-1-4842-7398-2

[Urb18] Matthew Urban, *Top 30 Java Interview Coding Tasks* (net-boss, 2018).

[vH16] Rick van Hattern, *Mastering Python.* (Packt Publishing, 2016).

[Wei10] Mark Allen Weiss, *Data Structures and Problem Solving Using Java* 4th edition (Pearson, 2010).

[Wen17] Jay Wengrow, *A Common-Sense Guide to Data Structures and Algorithms* (The Pragmatic Programmers, 2017).

Index

A

© Michael Inden 2022
M. Inden, *Python Challenges*, https://doi.org/10.1007/978-1-4842-7398-2

Printed in the United States
by Baker & Taylor Publisher Services